Thread Time

The Multithreaded Programming Guide

Hewlett-Packard Professional Books

Thread Time
The Multithreaded Programming Guide

Scott J. Norton

and

Mark D. DiPasquale

Hewlett-Packard Company

To join a Prentice Hall PTR internet mailing list, point to
http://www.prenhall.com/register

*Prentice Hall PTR
Upper Saddle River, New Jersey 07458
http://www.prenhall.com*

Library of Congress Cataloging in Publication Data

Norton, Scott J.
    Thread Time: multithreaded programming guide / Scott J. Norton
  Mark D. Dipasquale.
    p. cm.
  Includes bibliographical references and index.
  ISBN 0-13-190067-6
    1. Parallel programming (Computer science) I. DiPasquale, Mark
  D. II. Title.
  QA76.642.N67 1996
  005.2--dc20   96-27686
                             CIP

Editorial/production supervision: *Nicholas Radhuber*
Cover design: *Rod Hernandez*
Manufacturing manager: *Alexis Heydt*
Acquisitions editor: *Karen Gettman*
Editorial Assistant: *Barbara Alfieri*
Manager, Hewlett-Packard Press: *Patricia Pekary*

© 1997 by Hewlett-Packard Company
Published by Prentice Hall PTR
Prentice-Hall, Inc.
A Simon & Schuster Company
Upper Saddle River, New Jersey 07458

The Publisher offers discounts on this book when ordered in bulk quantities.
For more information, contact:

    Corporate Sales Department
    Prentice Hall PTR
    1 Lake St.
    Upper Saddle River, NJ 07458
    Phone: 800-382-3419 Fax: 201-236-7141
    E-mail: dan_rush@prenhall.com

Printed in the United States of America
10 9 8 7 6 5 4 3

ISBN 0-13-190067-6

Prentice-Hall International (UK) Limited, *London*
Prentice-Hall of Australia Pty. Limited, *Sydney*
Prentice-Hall Canada Inc., *Toronto*
Prentice-Hall Hispanoamericana, S.A., *Mexico*
Prentice-Hall of India Private Limited, *New Delhi*
Prentice-Hall of Japan, Inc., *Tokyo*
Simon & Schuster Asia Pte. Ltd., *Singapore*
Editora Prentice-Hall do Brasil, Ltda., *Rio de Janeiro*

To Ann, for her patience, love, and understanding.
— Scott

To my wife, Ann, and daughter, Amy, for their love, patience, and encouragement.
In memory of my father, Dominic T. DiPasquale.
— Mark

Table of Contents

CHAPTER   13

Programming Guidelines   **317**

CHAPTER   14

Debugging Threaded Applications   **345**

CHAPTER   15

Parallel Programming Models and Issues   **375**

Preface

Although threads have been around for decades, the use of threads on UNIX® systems only started to become popular in the early 1990s. During this time, multiprocessor systems, client/server applications, and graphical user interfaces (GUIs) were making their way into the UNIX mainstream. Into this new era for UNIX, threads brought many benefits, but the most important was (and still is) *performance*. A multithreaded program can achieve significant performance gains through concurrent and/or parallel thread execution.

Concurrent thread execution means that two or more threads are *in progress* at the same time. If one thread blocks for some reason, another thread from the same program can execute in its place. This feature is especially relevant for client/server, GUI-based, and general I/O-bound applications. Parallelism occurs when two or more threads *execute simultaneously* across multiple processors. Parallelism exploits the processing power of multiprocessor systems and is especially useful for compute-bound applications. Yet, threads are not a panacea. For example, thread management carries with it a certain amount of overhead. Thus, in order for a program to achieve a net performance gain, the concurrency or parallelism benefit must outweigh the thread management overhead liability. Fortunately, many applications can use threads to achieve significant performance gains.

This book teaches the application of multithreaded programming with the instruction, examples, and reference material needed to exploit this important software technology. *Thread Time* is primarily designed to be a practical guide for programming with POSIX.1c[1] threads (also known as *Pthreads*). The

---

[1] Institute of Electrical and Electronic Engineers (IEEE) Portable Operating System Interface (POSIX) 1003.1; formerly POSIX 1003.4a. Also known as ISO/IEC 9945-1:1990c.

Pthreads interfaces are presented and explained in detail. Code examples are provided, both in this book and on CD-ROM, that show how the interfaces are used. Guidelines teach you when to use threads, how to use them, how to avoid problems, and how to solve problems when they arise.

Thread Time may be suitable as a textbook in an advanced undergraduate or first-year graduate computer science curriculum. Clear objectives are provided at the beginning of each chapter, and exercises that help reinforce your knowledge of the technology are provided at the end of each chapter. The code examples in this book are written in the C programming language.

Chapter Organization and Descriptions

Although this has not been done explicitly, this book can be divided into five parts: *Foundational Information, Pthreads Interfaces and Their Use, Programming with Threads, Advanced Topics,* and *Reference Material.* Depending on your needs, you may wish to skip to a particular part or chapter.

   1. Foundational Information

Chapter 1: The Process Model chapter provides a foundation for understanding the benefits of threads. Herein, we present an overview of two areas: (1) the [single-threaded] process and (2) the process management portion of the UNIX operating system. At the end of this chapter, we draw a few conclusions about the limitations of single-threaded programming. Definitions for the *Process Model,* a *process,* and a *thread* are found in this chapter.

Chapter 2: The Thread Model chapter builds a foundation for programming with threads. Presented are several attributes of programs suitable for threads, several benefits of threads, and a high-level overview of three *Thread Model* operating systems. A number of essential definitions and concepts are provided in this chapter.

Chapter 3: The **Introduction to POSIX** chapter provides a brief introduction to the structure of POSIX and teaches you how to verify which POSIX thread functionality is supported on your system.

   2. Pthreads Interfaces and Their Use

Chapter 4: This chapter presents the **Basic Thread Management** interfaces and explains how they are used. These interfaces allow you to create, terminate, and synchronize threads. Specialized attributes are also available for creating threads with unique characteristics.

Chapter 5: The programmer assumes more responsibility when programming with threads. Thread operations must occur in the correct order, access to shared objects must be coordinated, and all threads must work together to achieve the desired result. Several mechanisms are available to coordinate, or synchronize, threads within a program. The **Thread Synchronization** chapter explains how to use these mechanisms.

Chapter 6: To accommodate varying needs, the scheduling policy and priority of POSIX.1c threads can be programmatically controlled. This chapter presents the **Thread Scheduling** interfaces, explains how they are used, and describes how threads compete for processor time.

Chapter 7: When a single-threaded process receives a signal, the default action is to terminate the process unless a signal handler has been installed. If a signal handler is invoked, program execution is interrupted. In a multithreaded program, signal handling is more flexible. A signal can be handled by a single thread within the program, allowing other threads to continue execution. The **Threads and Signals** chapter presents the Pthreads signal interfaces and explains how they are used.

Chapter 8: When programming with threads, it is often necessary to terminate a thread within the application. Signals appear to provide the most logical means to accomplish thread termination. However, signals have two major drawbacks: (1) if a signal causes a thread to terminate, the entire process terminates and (2) if POSIX allowed a signal to cause thread termination (and not process termination), mutexes and other resources acquired by terminated threads would never be released. The latter case could lead to deadlock. This chapter presents the **Thread Cancellation** interfaces, explains the concept of thread cancellation, and explains how resources are released when a thread is canceled.

Chapter 9: When a multithreaded program is written, a determination must be made as to how global data will be shared among the threads in the process. There are two choices: (1) a global data variable can be *process shared* and protected with synchronization primitives; or (2) a global data variable can be *specific* to each thread. In the second case, **Thread-Specific Data** is employed and synchronization is not required. This chapter presents the thread-specific data interfaces and explains how they are used.

Chapter 10: The HP-UX system includes several **Thread Extensions**, such as read-write locks, enhanced MxN Model scheduling control, processor affinity, and additional mutex types. Many of these features are thread extensions provided by the *X/Open Portability Guide*. Some of these features are provided only by Hewlett-Packard and may not be portable. Nevertheless, all of these are powerful features that can enhance multithreaded programs.

Chapter 11: The **Thread F/X (Effects)** chapter discusses the behavior of common library functions when they are used in multithreaded programs. For example, what happens when a thread calls `fork()`? If a thread locks a file, will other threads in the same program still have access? Are there performance or portability considerations when common library functions are used in multithreaded programs? Questions such as these are answered in this chapter.

3. Programming with Threads

Chapter 12: The **Writing Thread-Safe Code** chapter defines thread-safing terminology and then describes several important facets of writing thread-safe code. At the end of this chapter, we provide a preflight checklist for designing thread-safe libraries.

Chapter 13: The **Programming Guidelines** chapter provides specific guidelines for programming with threads based upon the information presented in the previous chapters. These guidelines include best practices, performance and portability tips, and constructs to avoid.

Chapter 14: You have written your multithreaded application. It compiles. However, when running the application, you notice some unexpected behavior. Perhaps a value from a calculation is incorrect, I/O is interleaved, or performance is poor. Alternatively, you may notice that certain tasks are incomplete or maybe the entire program hangs. The **Debugging Threaded Applications** chapter presents *symptoms*, *probable causes*, and *possible solutions* for you to consider during your systematic debugging process.

4. Advanced Topics

Chapter 15: The **Parallel Programming Models and Issues** chapter discusses several software models suitable for multithreaded programs. Some models are suitable for I/O-bound applications; others are suitable for compute-bound applications. The former exploit the concurrency benefit whereas the latter uses parallelism to exploit the power of multiprocessor systems. A discussion of parallel programming issues follows. Several important issues relating to thread creation, thread synchronization, and multiprocessor cache thrashing are identified. Specific techniques, guidelines, and solutions are also presented.

5. Reference Material

Appendix A: The *Pthread Manual Pages* in this appendix come directly from Hewlett-Packard's HP-UX Release 10.30. They appear in this book exactly as they appear on-line. Many thanks to Hewlett-Packard for allowing us to publish these manual pages.

Appendix B: Glossary

Appendix C: Bibliography

Conventions Used in this Book

1. Chapters

To assist in rapid learning and to provide ease of use, information in this book is presented in modular form. Chapters are divided into sections; each section covers a particular topic. A section is composed of a *title, descriptive picture, synoptic caption, full text explanation,* and *guidelines* or *code examples* as appropriate. Here is a simplified example of a section:

Protecting Shared Objects

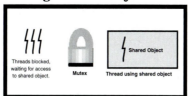

Fig. 3-7 Use a mutex to serialize access to a shared object. If a piece of shared data will never be modified, a mutex is not needed.

A mutex is a *mutual exclusion* object that is used to serialize access to shared objects. Once a thread locks a mutex, other threads wishing to gain access to the shared object block until the mutex is unlocked.

Not all shared objects require protection. For example, if a piece of shared data will never be modified, there is no need to protect that data with a mutex.

Guidelines
* decide which shared objects require serial access
* use one mutex for each shared object requiring serial access

Example
```
/* somewhere in the definitions */
pthread_mutex_t m;
...
/* somewhere in the code */
pthread_mutex_lock(&m);
/* access shared resource here */
pthread_mutex_unlock(&m);
/* continue execution */
...
```

The title of each section is given in the **"Topics Covered"** portion of each chapter introduction. Sections are presented in the same order listed. The last section in each chapter is followed by a chapter summary and exercises.

2. Use of Fonts

- **Bold** is used to indicate great importance.

- *Italics* is used for definition of terms, emphasis, function arguments, or references to chapters (e.g., see Chapter 5, *Thread Synchronization*).

- `Courier` is used for function names [e.g., `pthread_create()`] and for code examples.

- **`Bold courier`** is used for macros and definitions referenced in the text.

CD-ROM and Code Examples

This book contains numerous code examples. To provide focus, many examples omit included files, declarations, and error checking. The CD-ROM packaged with Thread Time contains full, working versions of all code examples presented herein. In addition, templates are provided for several parallel programming models.

The CD-ROM has been formatted in the ISO 9660 and Rock Ridge file system formats. These formats are suitable for use on most operating system platforms. To access the code examples, mount the CD-ROM as a file system. The examples should then be copied to your local file system so that they may be compiled and/or manipulated.

Acknowledgments

We're indebted to the following individuals who performed a full review of the technical material contained herein: Greg Astfalk, Bruce Blinn, Wayne A. Booth, Tom Doeppner, Edith Epstein, Duncan Missimer, Ann Schneider, Richard Marlon Stein, Tom Watson, and Joel Williamson. Their valuable feedback has gone a long way to improve the quality of this book. Special thanks to Ann Schneider for reviewing and editing the manuscript many times and answering countless editing questions at all hours of the night. We would also like to thank Tony Coon, Marti Jones, Doug McKenzie, and Anil Rao for their constructive technical and editorial comments.

We would especially like to thank our families, Ann, Amy, and Ann, for their support, patience, and encouragement throughout the writing of this book.

The Process Model

This chapter provides a foundation for understanding the benefits of threads. Herein, we present an overview of two areas: (1) the [single-threaded] process and (2) the process management portion of the UNIX operating system. At the end of this chapter, we draw a few conclusions about the limitations of single-threaded programming. Definitions for the *Process Model*, a *process*, and a *thread* are found in this chapter.

Topics Covered...

- The [Single-Threaded] Process
- The Context of a Process
- The Process Model Operating System
- Process Scheduling
- Process Context Switches
- Process Life Cycle, Modes, States, and Transitions
- An Illustration of a Process
- The Limitations of Single-Threaded Programs

The [Single-Threaded] Process

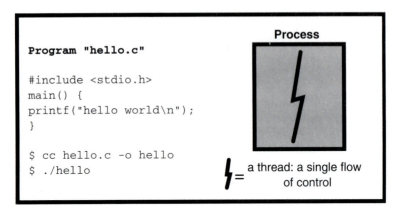

Fig. 1–1 *A process is "an instance of [a] program in execution."[1]*

An application is made up of one or more programs. A program is made up of instructions that the computer executes. A program resides in a file system on disk as an executable file. When a user invokes a program, the computer's operating system creates an entity by which it can manage the program's execution. This entity is called a *process*.

Definition of a Process

A ***process*** is *"an entity composed of resources managed by the operating system and at least one thread."* The resources managed by the operating system include various data structures, open file descriptors, and a memory image. A thread is defined below.

Definition of a Thread

A ***thread*** is *"an independent flow of control within a process, composed of a context (which includes a register set[2] and a program counter) and a sequence of instructions to execute."* An *independent flow of control* is essentially an execution path through the program code in a process. The *register set* and *program counter* contain values that indicate the current state of program execution. Finally, the *sequence of instructions to execute* is the actual program code.

Thus, a single-threaded process has one flow of control through the program code. Put another way, a single-threaded process executes one program instruction at a time.

---

[1] Definition by Maurice Bach in *The Design of the UNIX Operating System.*
[2] Also known as *register context.*

The Context of a Process

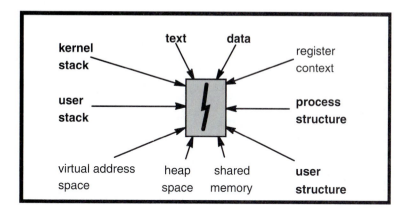

Fig. 1–2 The context of a process includes text, data, a user stack, a kernel stack, a process structure, and a user structure.

This section provides more detail about the context of a process. The context of a process includes the program to be executed and several kernel resources:[3]

- The **text** portion of a process contains the program code.
- The **data** portion of a process contains the global variables to be used by the program.
- Each process has two stacks, a **user stack** and a **kernel stack**. The user stack is used for function calls in the user program. The kernel stack is used for function calls in the kernel on behalf of the process when it makes a system call.
- Each process has a **process structure** assigned to it from the operating system kernel. The kernel maintains access to process structures. whether or not the associated process is running. This is done so that important information can be checked and updated as necessary. A sampling of process structure information includes the process ID, scheduling priority, run state, a signal mask, and much more. The process structure and the values contained therein are part of the context of a process.
- Each process has a **user structure** (also known as *u-area*). U-area information is needed only when the process is actually running. The u-area generally contains or points to items such as the process register state, open file descriptors, open devices, system call arguments, and system call return values. The u-area and the values contained therein are also part of the context of a process.

---

[3] The specific information contained in various kernel data structures may vary among systems.

The Context of a Process (Continued)

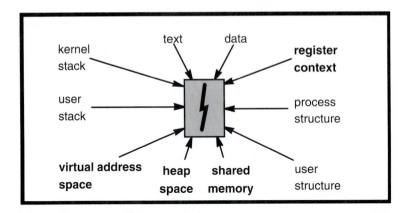

Fig. 1–3 The context of a process also includes its register context, virtual address space, heap space, and shared memory.

- Each process has a **register context**. The register context of a process includes register values and a program counter. The program counter contains the address of the current instruction to be executed by the process. When a process runs, its register context is loaded into the CPU registers. When a process is not running, its register context is stored in a per-process data structure called the *Process Control Block* (PCB). The u-area typically maintains the pointer to the PCB for the process (see Figure 1-6).

- Each process is assigned a **virtual address space**, typically 4 gigabytes in size or greater. Process virtual address space is a range of addresses into which the context of a process is logically mapped. A program's instructions are mapped into process virtual address space at process creation time. When the process runs, the virtual addresses are translated to physical addresses, as necessary, by the kernel's memory management subsystem. The physical addresses represent the locations in physical memory where the program's instructions and data are loaded. Once a program's instructions have been loaded into memory, they are available to be executed by the processor.

- **Heap space** is an available range of addresses within a process' virtual address space. Heap space can be allocated for private data storage using the `malloc()` function.

- Like heap space, **shared memory** is an available range of addresses within a process' virtual memory address space. This address space is allocated using the shared memory interfaces [i.e., `shmget(2)`, `shmdt(2)`, and `shmctl(2)`]. A process can allocate one or more chunks of shared memory, populate them with useful data, and share that data with other processes.

The Process Model Operating System

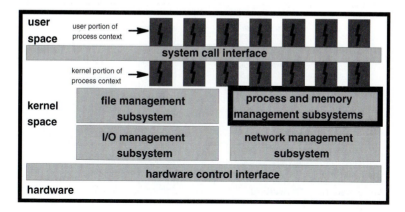

Fig. 1–4 A Process Model operating system kernel manages single-threaded processes as executable entities that can be scheduled to run on a processor. (This figure shows the primary OS components only.)

As we proceed, it is useful to have an understanding of certain process scheduling terminology and mechanics. This section, along with the next three sections in this chapter, provide a scheduling knowledge baseline. In later chapters, we discuss thread scheduling in detail.

A UNIX operating system kernel typically has some form of the following subsystems and interfaces:

1. a system call interface
2. a file subsystem
3. a process and memory management subsystems
4. a I/O subsystem
5. a network management subsystem
6. a hardware control interface

Process scheduling takes place in the process management subsystem of the kernel.

Process Model Definition

Throughout this text, we use the term **_Process Model_** to describe "*an operating system kernel that manages single-threaded processes as executable entities which can be scheduled to run on a processor.*" We use this term to differentiate this type of operating system from one that supports multithreaded processes (programs). Names for operating systems that support multithreaded processes are given in the next chapter.

Process Scheduling

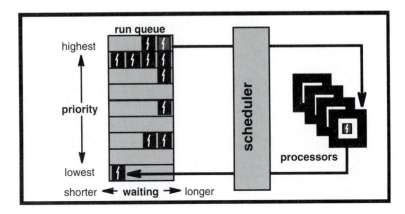

Fig. 1–5 The scheduler mediates between the runnable processes and the available processors. The highest priority, runnable process is always scheduled to run first.

In UNIX, there are two scheduling classes: *timeshare* and *realtime*. Both classes are implemented with a *scheduler* process, a run queue,[4] and a number of kernel routines that assist in process scheduling.

The Timeshare Scheduling Class

The timeshare class uses a priority-based scheduler with a round-robin scheduling policy. The round-robin scheduler selects the highest priority process from the head of the run queue and allows it to execute for a *time-slice*.[5] A process may block, voluntarily give up the CPU, be preempted by a higher priority process, or exit without using its full time-slice. When a process runs, its priority is automatically lowered by the kernel. When the *scheduler* process runs, it raises the priority of any timeshare processes that are not currently running. Hence, this system is designed to provide CPU time to all timeshare processes.

The Realtime Scheduling Class

Realtime processes generally use one of two scheduling policies: round-robin or first-in, first-out (FIFO). The FIFO policy differs from the round-robin policy in one area; there is no concept of a time-slice. A realtime process using the FIFO policy continues to execute until it blocks, voluntarily gives up the CPU, is preempted by a higher priority process, or exits. Also, the priority of a realtime process is *not* adjusted by the kernel. Instead, it is fixed by the user. Finally, realtime processes have higher priority than do timeshare processes. The lowest priority, runnable realtime process executes ahead of any timeshare process.

---

[4] Many systems have one run queue per processor.
[5] A time-slice is a small quantum of time, typically a fraction of a second.

Process Context Switches

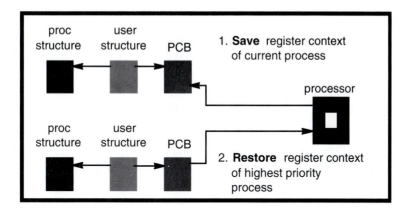

Fig. 1–6 The act of switching from one process to another is called a *context switch*. This figure shows the relationship of the process structure, user structure, and process control block. It also illustrates how the register context of a process is switched at context switch time.

The Mechanics of a Process Context Switch

When a context switch takes place, the current process' process structure is linked back into the run queue[6] in priority order (see Figure 1-5). Then the register context of the current process is copied from the physical processor registers into the PCB of the current process. Next, the process structure of the highest priority process is removed from the run queue. Finally, that process' register context is loaded from its PCB into the physical processor registers.

Recall that the program counter, which is part of the register context of a process, holds the address of the current instruction to be executed. Thus, when the register context is restored, the process can resume execution.

Figures 1-5, 1-6, and 1-7 show the mechanics of a process context switch from different perspectives.

---

[6] This, of course, assumes that the process is still in the *runnable state* (not waiting for some event such as the availability of data). If the process blocks for some reason, it is linked into the *sleep queue* (a place to wait until a particular event occurs).

Process Life Cycle, Modes, States, and Transitions

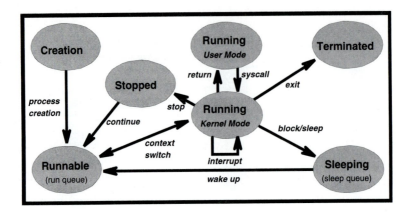

Fig. 1–7 A process can be in only one state at a given point in time. An event, such as a context switch or system call, causes a process to move from one state to another.

The Process Life Cycle

Processes have a life cycle of sorts. They are created, they run, they sleep, and at some point, they are terminated. A process can be in only one state at a given point in time. Processes are created or terminated once, but they can move between other states any number of times during their life.

User Mode and Kernel Mode

A process has two modes of operation: *user* and *kernel*. When a process is in user mode, it is executing user code (e.g., an application). A process enters kernel mode when it makes a system call. While in kernel mode, kernel code executes on behalf of the process to service some request, such as I/O.

A process also enters the kernel during a context switch (see Figure 1-6) or when the hosting processor must service an interrupt. In the former case, the process structure is attached to the run queue or sleep queue, depending on the reason for the context switch. In the latter case, the process is suspended while the kernel launches the appropriate interrupt service routine(s).

Process States

A process can be in any one of six states during its life cycle:

1. **Creation (a.k.a SIDL):** This is the process creation state where the kernel creates the context for the new, child process. During process creation, the *parent* process is in the Running state while the *child* process is in the Creation state.

2. **Runnable (a.k.a. SRUN):** A process that is ready to run is in this state. A runnable process is on the run queue (see also Figure 1-5).

3. **Running (a.k.a. SRUN):** This is the process execution state. A process can execute in either user mode or kernel mode. (Whether a process is running or runnable, the same state name, *SRUN*, is used.)

4. **Sleeping (a.k.a. SSLEEP):** The process is sleeping or blocked in this state. A process can call `sleep()` or become blocked on a system call to enter this state.

5. **Stopped (a.k.a. SSTOP):** A process in the Stopped state is waiting for a **SIGCONT** signal so that it may continue to execute.

6. **Terminated (a.k.a. SZOMB):** When a process calls `exit()`, it enters this state. Upon entering the zombie state, the process surrenders all of its context except for its process structure. The process structure is surrendered at a later time (after the parent process synchronizes with the child).

Process State Transitions

Figure 1-7 summarizes the rules for state transition. Each node represents a particular state. The arrows show the allowable movement between states. Some of the events that cause a process to move between states include:

- process creation, using `fork()`
- context switches (see Figure 1-6)
- execution of user code in user mode
- a system call, which causes the process to switch to kernel mode
- an interrupt
- a call to `sleep()`
- a wakeup from a sleep or block
- a call to `exit()`

An Illustration of a Process

modifier's execution			
Time	read_data()	modify_data()	write_data()
Time 1	read record 1		
Time 2		modify record 1	
Time 3			write record 1
Time 4	read record 2		
Time 5		modify record 2	
Time 6			write record 2
Time 7	read record 3		
Time 8		modify record 3	
Time N	Continue	Until	Done...

Fig. 1–8 The modifier process shows the nature of single-threaded process execution. There is one flow of control—instructions are executed one at a time. When a single-threaded process becomes blocked for any reason, it surrenders the processor.

In this section, we illustrate a single-threaded program "in motion." We use this illustration to show some limitations of single-threaded programs. In the next chapter, we illustrate a multithreaded version of the same program 'in motion' for comparison.

The Program...

A program called modifier reads data from a file, modifies the data, and writes the modified data to another file. Three primary functions are used: read_data(), modify_data(), and write_data(). Assuming that this program runs on a quiet[7] system, the best performance we can hope for is shown in Figure 1-8. However, this is a "best case" execution scenario. In a more realistic case, modifier's execution would be interrupted numerous times while the program blocked (waiting for I/O), was preempted, or when its time-slice ran out. Because this program is single-threaded, if it blocks for any reason, an immediate context switch takes place. This is unfortunate because it may be possible that, for example, while read_data() made a read() system call, modify_data() and/or write_data() could continue to execute. Hence, for the modifier program, performance is less than it could be.

---

[7] A "quiet" system has no other user processes running; the CPUs are readily available.

The Limitations of Single-Threaded Programs

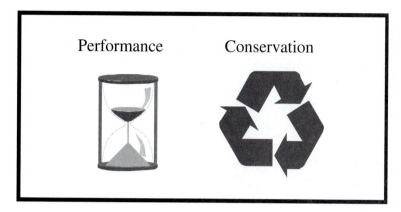

Fig. 1–9 Some programs are not negatively affected by having a single flow of control. Programs like modifier are performance-limited when they are single-threaded. Use of multiple processes might address the performance requirement in some cases, but then resource conservation becomes an issue.

Some programs are ideally suited to run as single-threaded entities. Typically, they have one primary function or any number of small functions that perform very small tasks. The Process Model operating system works fine for such programs. But what happens when we attempt to optimize[8] a program like modifier on a Process Model system?

Modifier is an example of a program that can benefit from multiple flows of control: if one flow blocks, another can execute, or perhaps multiple flows can execute in parallel. One strategy to make this happen is to break out modifier's three main functions into three separate processes. The read_data(), modify_data(), and write_data() processes can communicate with each other using shared memory or pipes. With this strategy, if one process blocks for some reason, other parts of the modifier program may be able to continue. Also, if modifier runs on a multiprocessor system with at least three processors, it is possible that all three modifier processes could run at the same time. In either case, we boost performance. But at what cost? This strategy is not without liability. Creating three processes, plus setting up the resources to move data between the processes, takes at least three times as long as does setting up a single process. In addition, three times the system resources are consumed: three process structures, three user structures, three memory images, etc. In the end, it must be determined whether the net performance gain is outweighed by the overhead liability. Herein lies the limitations of single-threaded program execution. Various strategies to increase performance may not be efficient or practical.

---

[8] Referring to algorithmic, not compiler optimization.

Summary

This chapter is designed to provide a foundation for understanding the benefits of threads. To build this foundation, we presented an overview of two areas: the [single-threaded] process, and the process management portion of the UNIX operating system. Specifically, we examined the makeup of a process and some of the primary functions of the process management subsystem:

- A single-threaded process is a logical, executable entity containing unique resources managed by the operating system and a set of instructions that the computer executes sequentially.

- A single-threaded program (or process) has one flow of control. Thus, only one instruction can be executed at a time.

- The context of a process consists of its data structures (i.e., process structure, user structure, etc.), the values in those data structures, virtual address space, program text, and a register context.

- The Process Model operating system manages processes as single-threaded, executable entities that can be scheduled to run on a processor.

- The round-robin scheduler selects the highest-priority, runnable process from the head of the run queue to execute on an available processor. This action takes place when it is time for a process context switch.

- A context switch removes the currently running process from a processor and restores a new process in its place. At context switch time, the register values in the processor are stored in the PCB of the current process. The process structure of the current process is linked into either the run queue or the sleep queue, depending on the reason for the context switch. The newly scheduled process has its process structure removed from the run queue and its register context loaded into the processor registers.

- A process can be in any one of six states during its life: Creation, Runnable, Running, Sleeping, Stopped, or Terminated. A process can be in only one state at a time. There are specific rules for state transition (e.g., a process cannot jump from the Creation state directly to the Sleeping state).

- A single-threaded program may have performance limitations because there is only one flow of control. Whenever that flow becomes blocked, application performance suffers. Some programs might be good candidates for concurrent or parallel code execution. Trying to fix the problem by using a multi-process strategy introduces resource conservation problems and may cause different performance problems to arise.

Exercises

1. What is a process?
2. What is a thread?
3. What does *single-threaded* mean?
4. What are the major components in the context of a process?
5. Draw the Process Model operating system kernel and label each component.
6. Compare and contrast the timeshare and realtime scheduling classes.
7. Explain the mechanics of a context switch.
8. Describe the mode of process operation (user mode and kernel mode).
9. Draw the state transition diagram for a process. Label each process state, describe each state, and use arrows to show the rules for state transition.
10. Describe the limitations of single-threaded programs.
11. Write a single-threaded program that copies one file to another file.

The Thread Model

This chapter builds a foundation for programming with threads. Presented are several attributes of programs suitable for threads, several benefits of threads, and a high-level overview of three Thread Model operating systems. A number of essential definitions and concepts are provided in this chapter.

Topics Covered...

- Analogy of Single-Threaded Execution
- Analogy of Multithreaded Execution
- The Benefits of Threads
- Thread Context, Modes, States, and Transitions
- User Threads and Kernel Threads
- Bound and Unbound Threads
- The Thread Model Operating System
- Many-to-One Model
- One-to-One Model
- Many-to-Many Model
- An Illustration of a Multithreaded Program

Analogy of Single-Threaded Execution

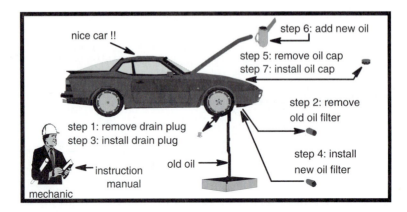

Fig. 2-1 There is one flow of control (one thread) with single-threaded program execution.

We begin this chapter by sharing an analogy that illustrates single-threaded versus multithreaded program execution. Also, we formally introduce the concepts of concurrency and parallelism, and discuss some of the pros and cons of using threads.

The Analogy...

The act of reading an instruction manual and performing the instructions therein is similar to a computer executing program instructions. In this analogy, a mechanic must perform an oil change, so he opens the manual and reads the seven instructions shown in Figure 2-1. By performing these instructions, in order, the task is accomplished.

Recall that single-threaded execution means that there is one flow of control (one thread) through the program instructions. To simulate a single flow of control in this analogy, we must pretend that the mechanic can see and execute only one instruction at a time. Thus, step 2 cannot be executed until step 1 is completed, and so on. This is not unlike a processor executing the instructions of a single-threaded program. Program instructions pass through the program counter one at a time, and the processor executes them. But can this be improved?

As it turns out, the oil change task contains several steps that can be executed independently of one another. For example, while step 1 is in progress (the oil is draining), the mechanic can move on to step 2 or step 5. In addition, steps 1, 2, and 5 can be performed at the same time if more mechanics are available. In effect, our oil change performance can be improved through the use of concurrent and/or parallel execution of these steps.

Analogy of Multithreaded Execution

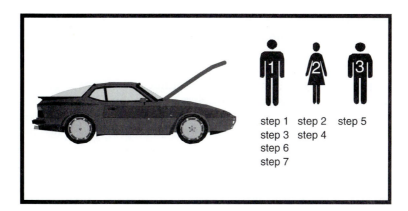

Fig. 2-2 Threads can increase performance through concurrent and/or parallel instruction execution.

A **multithreaded** program has *two or more flows of control (threads)*. When a task contains two or more independent subtasks, the use of multiple threads of control is possible.

A multithreaded program can achieve significant performance gains through the use of concurrent and/or parallel thread execution. Concurrent thread execution (or **concurrency**) means that two or more threads are *in progress* at the same time. Relating this concept to the analogy, once step 1 is in progress (old oil is draining), the mechanic can immediately begin work on step 2 or step 5. This keeps the mechanic busy on our car where he might otherwise begin working on another car. **Parallelism** occurs when two or more threads *execute simultaneously* across multiple processors. Relating this to our analogy, if two or more execution resources (mechanics) are available, multiple steps can be executed in parallel, as illustrated in Figure 2-2.

Whereas concurrency and parallelism offer increased performance, it should be noted that threads are not a panacea. For example, thread management carries with it a certain amount of overhead. Threads must be created, terminated, scheduled, and synchronized. Relating this to the analogy, the oil change task must be divided into subtasks, and each subtask must have its work scheduled with a mechanic. This incremental setup and scheduling takes time. Consequently, it must be determined whether the performance benefit exceeds the additional overhead. One factor to consider is the duration of each subtask that may be assigned its own thread of execution. If the duration is too small, the thread management overhead may cost too much.

Thread synchronization presents another form of overhead. Threads have access to global data, open files, and other shared objects within the process. In most cases, access to shared objects must be synchronized to achieve predictable program output. Similarly, the order of thread execution is important. Referring to the analogy, the new oil should not be added (step 6) until steps 1 through 5 are completed.

Concerning parallelism, the multithreaded analogy illustrates one more interesting point. Even with multiple execution resources available, portions of the oil change task cannot be executed in parallel. Instead, they must be executed *serially*. This situation also holds true for multithreaded programs; portions may run serially for various reasons. For example, when starting a multithreaded program, the initial thread runs by itself as it begins the process of creating other threads. Or, if one or more threads must wait while another thread has a resource locked, thread execution is serialized, at least for a time.

Using Amdahl's Law to Compute Speedup

Amdahl's Law can be used to compute the maximum theoretical "speedup" of a multithreaded application. If threads in a multithreaded application run $M\%$ of the total execution time in parallel on a system with N processors, Amdahl's Law predicts the speedup over single-threaded program execution as follows:

$$\text{speedup} = 1 / (1 - M) + M / N$$

In the multithreaded analogy, 5 of the 7 steps can be executed in parallel and there are three "execution resources" (i.e., processors). Thus, M is approximately 0.7, N is 3, and "speedup" is computed as follows:

$$1 / (1 - 0.7) + 0.7 / 3 = \text{speedup} = 1.88$$

Bear in mind that this speedup of nearly 2x does not account for going from three-way to two-way parallel execution (see Figure 2-2). It also does not account for various real-life performance inhibitors which include:

- threads blocking, waiting for access to shared resources
- threads from other processes competing for CPU time
- thread management overhead
- cache coherency issues (see Chapter 15, *Parallel Programming Models and Issues*)

Still, for many programs, threads provide a performance increase that *far outweighs* the overhead liability. Multithreaded programs can exploit the power of multiprocessor systems and can often make the most efficient use of uniprocessor systems.

The Benefits of Threads

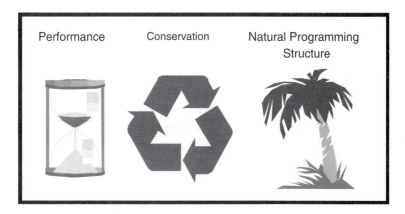

Fig. 2-3 The primary benefit of multithreaded programming is increased performance. Other benefits include resource conservation and a more natural programming structure.

The benefits of threads include:

Increased throughput: Throughput is a measure of the amount of work accomplished over time. A multithreaded application can do more work per unit of time when its threads are execute concurrently or in parallel. The performance benefit from concurrent thread execution is achieved on uniprocessor and multiprocessor systems. However, the performance benefit of parallel thread execution requires a multiprocessor system.

Better response time: Response time is a measure of how quickly an application reacts to an event. Multiple threads of control can improve response time. Each thread can be given the appropriate scheduling policy and priority for the task at hand. For example, in an email application, a low priority thread can save a message while a high priority thread updates the user interface.

Conservation of system resources: By default, threads share access to global data, open files, and a number of other shared objects within a process. Sharing such objects among multiple processes is much more expensive in terms of the memory and kernel resources used, not to mention the setup time.

Faster operations: The context of a thread[1] does not include shared objects or the process memory image. As a benefit of this lightweightness, thread management operations are generally faster than are process management operations.

Natural programming structure: Threads provide a clean, simple manner in which programmers may express logical parallelism in applications.

[1] See the next page for more details.

Thread Context, Modes, States, and Transitions

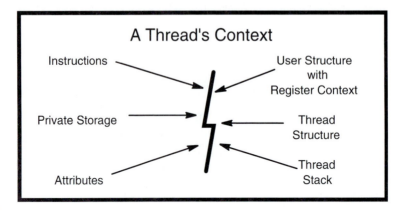

Fig. 2-4 A thread exists within the context of a process and is composed of data structures, a register context, a stack, private storage, attributes, and a set of instructions.

The Context of a Thread

A thread exists within the context of a process and is composed of a thread structure, a user structure with register context, a stack, a private storage area, attributes, and a set of instructions to execute. A thread structure is similar to a process structure but is much smaller. The thread structure typically contains a thread ID, scheduling policy and priority, and a signal mask. The user structure primarily contains a thread's register context that includes a program counter. Each thread has its own stack space for function calling and its own private storage area for data (similar to process heap space). Thread attributes can be defined to give a thread specific characteristics. Finally, each thread has a set of instructions to execute; usually a function within a program.

Modes, States, and Transitions

Threads are similar to processes with respect to life cycle, modes of operation, states, and transitions. A thread can execute in user mode or kernel mode and can be in one of the following six states: Creation, Runnable, Running, Sleeping, Stopped, or Terminated. The rules for state transitions are the same for threads as they are for processes. (If you would like a refresher, please turn back to Chapter 1, *The Process Model*, and review Figure 1-7.)

User Threads and Kernel Threads

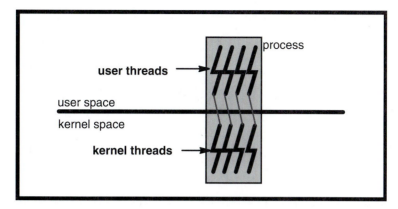

Fig. 2-5 User threads can be created by programmers using thread APIs provided in the threads library. They exist in user space and execute user code. Kernel threads are created using thread functions. Kernel threads exist in kernel space and execute kernel code.

In your experience, you may have heard the terms *user threads* and *kernel threads* applied correctly, incorrectly, or ambiguously. For clarification, we provide a definition for user and kernel threads below:

- **User Threads** can be created, terminated, and synchronized by application programmers using the threads APIs provided in the threads library. User threads are not visible to the kernel. Instead, they exist in user space and execute user code. For a user thread to have access to a processor, it must be associated with a kernel-scheduled entity. One example of a kernel-scheduled entity is a traditional, single-threaded process. Another is a *kernel thread*.

- **Kernel Threads**[2] are created by the thread functions in the threads library. Kernel threads are *kernel-scheduled entities* that are visible to the operating system kernel. A kernel thread may support one or more user threads. Kernel threads execute kernel code or system calls on behalf of user threads.

---

[2] UNIX International (UI) refers to kernel threads as lightweight processes. However, the term *kernel-scheduled entities* works in either world. We use *kernel-scheduled entities* or *kernel threads* in this book.

Bound and Unbound Threads

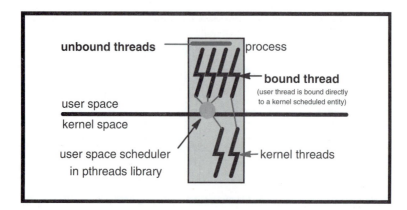

Fig. 2-6 Programmers may bind user threads to kernel threads. An unbound thread competes for processor time with other unbound threads in the process. Bound threads compete with all threads, system wide.

A **bound thread** is a user thread that is bound directly to a kernel thread. An **unbound thread** is a user thread that can execute on top of any kernel thread available in the process.

In Figure 2-6, three user threads are multiplexed on top of one kernel thread. The fourth user thread is bound to one of the two available kernel threads. Recall that thread attributes are part of the context of a thread. One of the thread attributes allows a user thread to be bound to a kernel thread. We discuss thread attributes in general in Chapter 4, *Basic Thread Management*. Binding a user thread to a kernel thread is discussed in Chapter 10, *Thread Extensions*.

Recall that kernel threads are *kernel-scheduled* entities. As such, they are like virtual processors within a process. Unbound threads are multiplexed on top of one or more kernel threads, and they compete with each other on a process-wide scope for CPU execution time. On the other hand, a bound thread is scheduled by the kernel. Bound threads compete with all threads, system-wide, for CPU execution time.

The number of kernel threads allocated to a multithreaded process by default is implementation-dependent. Many implementations allow you to use system calls to adjust the number of kernel threads available within a process.

Note: Not all processes (programs) bind threads in the manner shown in Figure 2-6. This is only an example.

The Thread Model Operating System

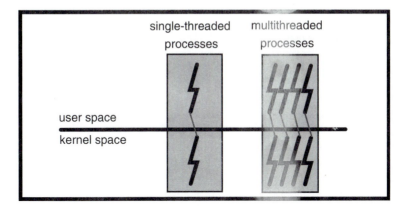

Fig. 2-7 The Thread Model operating system is capable of managing single-threaded as well as multithreaded processes.

Up to this point, we've covered the benefits of threads and some of their technical makeup. Now let's turn our attention to the operating system on which multi-threaded applications run. To do this, we would like to introduce the **Thread Model** operating system.

A ***Thread Model*** operating system *"is capable of managing single-threaded and multithreaded processes."* Over the next few pages, we describe three different Thread Models. The names of the these are:

1. Many-to-One (Mx1)
2. One-to-One (1x1)
3. Many-to-Many (MxN)

As you will soon see, the Thread Model names provide a very good description of how each model supports multithreaded applications.

Many-to-One (Mx1)

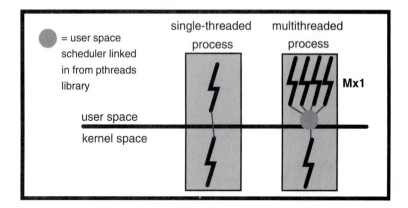

Fig. 2-8 An Mx1 Model supports single-threaded and multithreaded processes. Mx1 means that there can be many user threads, but only one kernel thread per process. Therefore, this model can support concurrent but not parallel thread execution.

Overview

The Mx1 Model is often referred to as a *user threads* implementation. Mx1 is implemented in user space and requires no kernel modifications to support single-threaded as well as multithreaded processes. Put another way, the fact that a process may be multithreaded is completely hidden from the kernel in the Mx1 Model. In the kernel's view, an Mx1 process is single-threaded.

Mx1 means that there can be *M*any user threads, but only *1* kernel-scheduled entity (the process). When the kernel scheduler selects a multithreaded process to run, the user scheduler in the threads library plugs in the context of the highest priority, runnable user thread. The process then executes on behalf of that thread. During the process' time-slice, the library scheduler can switch between runnable threads in the process. However, because the kernel views an Mx1 Model process as single-threaded, if the currently executing thread makes a blocking system call, the whole process becomes blocked.

Advantages of Mx1

- Concurrency

- Fast thread management operations

- Conservation of system resources

- Natural programming structure

- Parallel-Ready: Multithreaded programs on an Mx1 Model system can be placed on a 1x1 or MxN model system, where parallel execution is supported, without changing the source code.

Disadvantages of Mx1

- Physical parallelism is not supported: As stated, the kernel views an Mx1 Model process as single-threaded; therefore, parallelism is not supported.

- Blocking: When a thread is blocked in kernel mode, the kernel sees the whole process as blocked and performs a context switch. Even though there may be runnable threads in the process, they must wait on the blocked thread. However, there are instances where an Mx1 multithreaded process can continue to run: (1) If the executing thread goes to sleep, the user space library scheduler selects another ready-to-run thread from the same process to run; and (2) If the executing thread makes a read() system call to a *nonblocking* device, the threads library can intercede with a *wrapper* routine. A wrapper routine converts the read() call into a nonblocking read, then uses a select() call to poll for data. If the requested data is ready, the thread continues to execute. If the data is not ready, the user space library scheduler attempts to switch to another runnable thread in the process. Wrappers help to support concurrency, but it should be noted that they carry a certain amount of overhead. Not all Mx1 systems support wrapper routines.

- Profiling: Recall that threads are lightweight entities. Whereas this has certain benefits, there are drawbacks for thread-granular application profiling. Context kept with the process, such as CPU usage and other statistics, is not available on a per-thread basis. This makes it difficult to measure the activity of each individual user thread.

- Restrictions: The implementation of the user space scheduler relies on the system's virtual timer. Applications are not allowed to catch **SIGVTALRM** (the virtual timer signal). Other signals may be similarly restricted.

One-to-One (1x1)

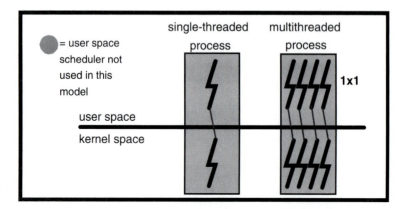

Fig. 2-9 In the 1x1 Model, processes are essentially logical containers for threads. Threads are the kernel scheduled entity. There is no user space library scheduler in the 1x1 Model. Instead, each user thread is bound directly to a kernel thread. The 1x1 Model supports physical parallelism.

Overview

The 1x1 Model supports single-threaded as well as multithreaded processes. 1x1 is implemented in kernel space rather than in user space. Therefore, this model is often referred to as a *kernel threads* implementation.

1x1 means that there is *1* kernel thread for every user thread; each user thread is permanently bound to a kernel-scheduled entity. In a sense, the distinction between a "user" thread and a "kernel" thread goes away in this model. Because each process has multiple kernel threads, parallel thread execution across multiple processors is supported.

This model implements the kernel scheduler only. Although the threads library provides the threads application programming interfaces (as it does in each model: Mx1, 1x1, and MxN), the user space scheduler from that library is not implemented in the 1x1 Model.

In the 1x1 Model, processes are logical containers for threads, and threads are the only scheduled entity. The kernel scheduler no longer selects processes to run; instead, it selects *kernel threads*. Threads selected to run may be from single-threaded or multithreaded processes. Naturally, the highest priority, runnable thread is scheduled to run first.

Advantages of 1x1

- Parallel execution: Multiple threads from the same process can execute in parallel across multiple processors.

- Profiling information: Enough context is available to provide resource usage information for individual threads.

- The same advantages as Mx1.

Disadvantages of 1x1

- More management overhead: Because each user thread is permanently bound to a kernel thread, there is more context to manipulate during operations such as thread creation, termination, scheduling, and synchronization (much less than a process, but more than an unbound thread). Because there is no user space scheduler, the kernel must be involved in all thread management operations. There are two disadvantages with using the kernel's scheduler: (1) Using only one scheduler creates a potential bottleneck; and (2) because the user/kernel boundary is crossed, the kernel scheduler is more expensive to use than is the user space scheduler.

- More kernel resources required: In the Mx1 Model, many user threads are multiplexed on top of a single kernel thread. In the 1x1 Model, one kernel thread is required for each user thread. Thus, more kernel resources are used.

Many-to-Many (MxN)

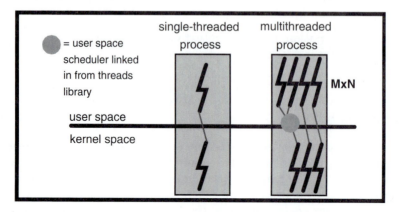

Fig. 2-10 The MxN Model is a superset of the Mx1 and 1x1 Models. It allows you to multiplex user threads on top of kernel threads or to bind user threads to kernel threads. The MxN Model supports physical parallelism.

Overview

The MxN Model supports single-threaded as well as multithreaded processes. MxN is implemented in both user and kernel space. Because kernel modifications are required, the MxN Model is often referred to as a *kernel threads* implementation.

MxN means that there can be *M*any user threads and any *N*umber of kernel threads. The MxN Model allows you to multiplex user threads on top of kernel threads or to bind user threads to kernel threads as necessary to suit program needs. Because each process may have multiple kernel threads, parallel thread execution across multiple processors is supported.

MxN is similar to 1x1 in that processes are no longer the scheduled entity. Here again, processes are logical containers for threads. Kernel threads are the only scheduled entities. However, in addition to the kernel scheduler, the MxN Model implements the user space scheduler in the threads library. The user space scheduler schedules user threads to run on kernel threads available in the process. The kernel scheduler schedules kernel threads to run on processors available in the system. If a user thread is bound to a kernel thread, it is scheduled to run by the kernel's scheduler with no user scheduler involvement.

Advantages of MxN

- Flexibility: Because the MxN Model is basically composed of the Mx1 and 1x1 models, the MxN Model has all of the advantages of Mx1 and 1x1. This provides the flexibility to optimize a program to meet specific needs. The POSIX.1c specification[3] discusses two examples of using processes with bound and unbound threads:

  The first example is a windows server program. The window screen contains thousands of widgets. Each widget has two threads: one to manage the widget user interface, the other to take the appropriate action based on user input. In this example, it would be wasteful to have all of the user threads bound to kernel threads because few widgets will ever be active at the same time. However, with the MxN Model, a combination of bound and unbound threads can be used to manage the application's resources more effectively. For example, the thread that tracks the mouse can be bound to a high-priority kernel thread so that the mouse tracks smoothly. Other user threads within the windows server application can be multiplexed on top of the available kernel threads. As only a few of these threads run at a time, kernel thread resources are likely to be available. In addition, because multiplexed threads are unbound, their scheduling overhead is less than the scheduling overhead required for any bound threads.

  The second example is of a database server that has thousands of clients, where each client is supported by a single thread. Similar to the windows server example, only a fraction of these clients will be active at the same time. In this case, a few bound threads can be dedicated to performing data retrieval for the unbound client threads.

  Both of these examples demonstrate the flexibility of the MxN Model. This model provides the flexibility to choose the best strategy for a given application.

Disadvantages of MxN

- Large scope of potential problems: Incurring any Mx1 or 1x1 model disadvantage is possible.

- Increased complexity: In the MxN Model, the interaction of two schedulers (user and kernel) must be taken into account.

---

[3] POSIX 1003.1c Draft 10, September 1994, section 13.5.1.6.1.1

An Illustration of a Multithreaded Program

multithreaded modifier's execution			
Time	read_data()	modify_data()	write_data()
Time 1	read record 1		
Time 2		modify record 1	
Time 3	read record 2		write record 1
Time 4	read record 3	modify record 2	
Time 5	read record 4	modify record 3	write record 2
Time 6	read record 5	modify record 4	write record 3
Time 7	read record 6	modify record 5	write record 4
Time 8	read record 7	modify record 6	write record 5
Time N	*Continue*	*Until*	*Done...*

Fig. 2-11 The multithreaded version of `modifier` runs in the Mx1, 1x1, and MxN models. However, `modifier` can achieve parallel thread execution only in the 1x1 or MxN models.

In this section, we reexamine the `modifier` program introduced in Chapter 1. Recall that this program's job is to read data, modify it, then write the modified data to another file. The `modifier` program uses three functions to perform these tasks: `read_data()`, `modify_data()`, and `write_data()`.

In this illustration, multiple threads of control are given to the `modifier` program. One thread is assigned to each major function: `read_data()`, `modify_data()`, and `write_data()`. Assuming that `modifier` runs on a 1x1 or MxN model system with at least three processors, program execution could look like that shown in Figure 2-11.[4] Notice how the program starts out in a fashion similar to the single-threaded `modifier` program from Chapter 1, *The Process Model*. However, once the data is flowing, and if modifier has continued access to three processors, the throughput of the multithreaded `modifier` program far exceeds that of the single-threaded version. For example, if `modifier` executes multiple threads in parallel 80% of the time on a system with 12 processors, Amdahl's Law indicates a maximum potential speedup of 3.84x:

$$1 / (1 - 0.8) + 0.8 / 12 = speedup = 3.84$$

In addition to better performance, the multithreaded version of `modifier` has a distinct resource conservation benefit over the multiprocess version described in Chapter 1, *The Process Model*. The multithreaded version requires approximately a third of the resources required by the multiprocess version.

---

[4] Among other things, we do not account for program start-up in this illustration; where the initial thread creates the read, modify, and write threads.

Summary

In this chapter, we explored the use of multiple threads of control in a program. We discussed several benefits of threads and the mechanics of the Mx1, 1x1, and MxN models. Here is a summary:

- *Single-threaded execution* means that there is one flow of control (one thread) through a program. *Multithreaded execution* means that there are two or more flows of control (threads) through a program.
- A program may be a good candidate for threads when it contains two or more independent subtasks of sufficient duration.
- *Concurrency* means that multiple threads are *in progress* at once. Parallelism occurs when two or more threads are *execute simultaneously* across multiple processors.
- The benefits of multithreaded programming include increased throughput, better response time, fast [thread] management operations, conservation of system resources, and a natural programming structure. Performance benefits are realized through concurrent and/or parallel thread execution.
- The context of a thread includes a thread structure, a thread user structure, a register context, stack space, private storage, thread attributes, and a sequence of instructions to execute.
- User threads are created by APIs provided in the user threads library. They run user code in user space and are not directly visible to the kernel. Kernel threads are created using thread system calls. Kernel threads, also known as kernel scheduled entities, execute kernel code and system calls on behalf of user threads.
- A bound thread is a user thread that is bound directly to a kernel thread. An unbound thread is a user thread that is multiplexed on top of kernel threads available in the process.
- The Thread Model operating system is capable of supporting multithreaded as well as single-threaded processes. There are three Thread Models: Mx1, 1x1, and MxN.
- The Many-to-One (Mx1) Model supports multithreaded and single-threaded applications. In general, this model can take advantage of all of the benefits threads have to offer except physical parallelism.
- The One-to-One (1x1) Model supports multithreaded and single-threaded applications. In general, this model can take advantage of all of the benefits threads have to offer.
- The Many-to-Many (MxN) Model supports multithreaded and single-threaded applications. This model can take full advantage of all of the benefits threads have to offer.

Exercises

1. Write your own analogy that describes single-threaded versus multithreaded processes. The analogy should deal with the restrictions of single-threaded processes and the advantages of multithreaded processes.

2. Describe an application that would not benefit from being multithreaded.

3. Describe an application that would benefit from being multithreaded.

4. What are the advantages of the MxN Model over the 1x1 or Mx1 models?

5. Why might you want to bind user threads to kernel threads? Describe a multithreaded application that would benefit from having one or more bound threads.

6. Define concurrency. How does a logically parallel application automatically exploit a multiprocessor system?

Introduction to POSIX

This chapter provides a brief introduction to the structure of POSIX and teaches you how to verify which POSIX functionality is supported on your system.

Topics Covered...

- The POSIX Standard
- POSIX Components
- POSIX Options
- Compile-Time Checking
- Run-Time Checking
- Namespace Reservation

The POSIX Standard

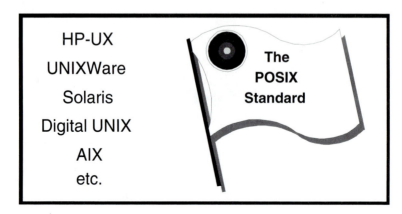

Fig. 3–1 The end-result of standards, such as the POSIX Pthreads standard, is that savings in money and time are realized. POSIX helps application developers create applications that are source-code portable. Ultimately, this brings down costs for end-users and application developers.

Standards are an effective means to save time and reduce costs. An end-user benefits from a standard look-and-feel across applications because less training is required. A developer benefits when applications are *source-code portable* across vendor platforms because porting time is reduced or eliminated. The IEEE Portable Operating System Interface (POSIX) standard helps developers create source-code portable applications.

The POSIX standard is actually a collection of several standards covering languages, commands, methods for testing, and operating system interfaces to functions. This chapter focuses on the latter.

A *POSIX compliant* system is one that conforms to the appropriate POSIX standard. On such a system, you should be able to compile and run an application that makes use of POSIX functions, even if the application was created on a different POSIX compliant system. However, there is a catch. Many applications require more functionality than POSIX covers. Such functionality may be vendor-dependent. Nevertheless, by using POSIX-compliant interfaces, porting efforts can be reduced or eliminated.

POSIX 1003.1c[1] is the portion of the overall POSIX standard covering threads. Included are the functions and application programming interfaces (APIs) that support multiple flows of control (threads) within a process. In the following pages, we discuss the structure of POSIX in general and several methods for verifying POSIX.1c functionality in particular.

---

[1] Formerly POSIX 1003.4a. Also known as ISO/IEC 9945-1:1990c.

POSIX Components

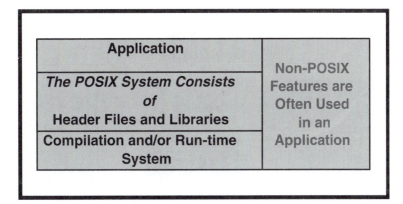

Fig. 3–2 The components of a POSIX System consists of header files and library functions. A compilation system provides the necessary development environment. The run-time system provides the necessary run-time environment. The compilation and run-time systems may be different.

At the top of Figure 3-2 is a POSIX compliant application. Under the application, a POSIX-compliant system has two components that support POSIX applications: *header files* and *libraries*:

- **Header files:** The header files define the supported POSIX APIs on a particular system. Typically, these files reside in /usr/include, but this is not guaranteed. See your vendor's documentation.

- **Libraries:** The libraries contain vendor-supplied functions that provide POSIX functionality for use in application development.

Under the POSIX components is either a **development system** or a **run-time system**:

- **Compilation (or development) system:** The compilation system provides a compiler. The compiler provides a way to link the POSIX environment into the application. Specifically, when invoking the appropriate compile-time flag, the compiler recognizes, or allows, the use of POSIX header files and libraries in your application.

- **Run-time system:** This is the system on which the application is executed. In many cases, the run-time system is the same as the compilation system. However, if the application is run on a different system, care must be taken to ensure that the necessary environment is available. If the run-time system is stripped down and the application uses shared libraries, you will need to ensure that those shared libraries are available on the run-time system.

POSIX Options

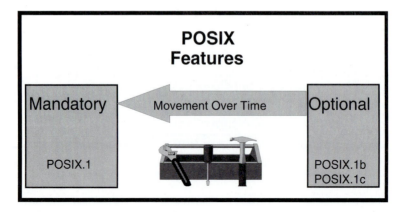

Fig. 3–3 POSIX is a collection of several separate standards that correspond to different parts of a computer system. Feature test macros can be used to determine which POSIX features are supported on your system.

POSIX is not one standard but a collection of several separate standards that correspond to different parts of the computer system. There are POSIX standards for the operating system, commands, languages, and testing methods. For our purposes, we need discuss only the APIs for the operating system.

Mandatory Versus Optional Standards

In general, the functionality specified in POSIX 1003.1 (POSIX.1) are *mandatory* standards for a POSIX-compliant system. Optional POSIX standards include POSIX 1003.1b for real-time applications and POSIX 1003.1c for threaded applications. Over time, some standards move from optional to mandatory (mandatory for POSIX compliance).

Feature Test Macros

All POSIX functions are provided under a feature test macro. Feature test macros are preprocessor constants (`#defines`) that can be used with `#ifdef` conditional statements to determine which POSIX functionality is supported on your system. Before a feature is used, you can verify that it is supported through the appropriate macro. For example, an application requiring the `chown` command can verify `chown`'s availability through the **`_PTHREAD_CHOWN_RESTRICTED`** macro.

We will examine feature test macros in the next section.

Compile-Time Checking

Fig. 3–4 Compile-time checking refers to methods that verify the POSIX features supported by a system. In addition to determining existence, we can also determine the limits of these features where appropriate.

Because POSIX support varies from vendor to vendor, it is important to know which POSIX features are supported on your compilation system. Compile-time checking allows you to verify which POSIX features are supported. There are several ways you can perform compile-time checking: You can read the header files in advance of compilation, use a generic conformance-checking application, or try to compile your own application and see what happens. You can also code an application to use POSIX features, if they are supported, or use alternative features if they are not supported.

Checking Options and Limits

The optional members of POSIX have constants that define their existence. These constants are defined in the header file <unistd.h>. Once you know of the existence of a constant, it is important to know its attributes (lower/upper bounds, size, shape, etc.). The attributes associated with each existing constant are maintained in the header file <limits.h>.

_POSIX_SOURCE and _POSIX_C_SOURCE

_POSIX_SOURCE and **_POSIX_C_SOURCE** allow you to inform the compilation system that you are compiling POSIX source code. The **_POSIX_SOURCE** macro tells the system that your application conforms to the 1990 version of POSIX.1. The more powerful **_POSIX_C_SOURCE** macro allows you to specify a value that indicates the revision of POSIX to which your application conforms. For example, do this to inform the system that your application will use the definitions from the POSIX.1b specification, approved in June of 1995:

```
#define _POSIX_C_SOURCE 199506L
```

An application that uses the **_POSIX_C_SOURCE** to define a particular POSIX revision is allowed to use the previous POSIX definitions, along with the ones in the named revision. For example, revision 199506L is the superset of revision 199309L.

Note: If you use **_POSIX_SOURCE** or **_POSIX_C_SOURCE**, your application is restricted to POSIX and ANSI C functionality. This may be too restrictive for many applications. Code modules requiring access to functionality outside of POSIX and ANSI C should *not* define **_POSIX_SOURCE** or **_POSIX_C_SOURCE**.

To find out which version of POSIX is supported on your system, you can use the **_POSIX_VERSION** feature test macro. This macro returns a POSIX revision value such as 199009L, 199506L. You can use this information to see which options are available on your system (see the example on the next page).

The table below shows the current POSIX revisions and provides a definition for each one:

Table 3–1 _POSIX_VERSION Current Values

Value	Definition
(not defined)	System does not support POSIX
(long)198808L	POSIX.1 is supported (FIPS 151-1[1] compliance)
(long)199009L	POSIX.1 is supported (FIPS 151-2 compliance)
(long)199309L	POSIX.1 and POSIX.1b are both supported
(long)199506L	POSIX.1, POSIX.1b, and POSIX.1c are supported

[1]The U.S. government places standardization requirements on certain software products it purchases. The Federal Information Process Standard (FIPS) outlines some of these. 151-1 covers the 1988 POSIX.1 standard. 151-2 covers the 1990 POSIX.1 standard.

This information can provide a coarse-grained look at what your system supports. Remember that POSIX has many options, and vendors support them to varying degrees. You may have to dig a little deeper before you can determine whether the required POSIX functionality is on your system. Conformance-checking programs can help.

Conformance-Checking Programs

A conformance-checking program is used to check for the availability and size of a variety of POSIX functions. Such a program can simply be a sequence of feature test macros in conditional statements with printf() messages. For example, a generic conformance-checking program could be written to check for the POSIX revision as follows:

Checking Functionality

```
#include <unistd.h>
#include <stdio.h>

#define _POSOX_SOURCE
#define _POSIX_C_SOURCE 199506L

main() {
#ifndef _POSIX_VERSION
    printf("This system does not support POSIX.\n");
#elif _POSIX_VERSION == 198808L /* Find POSIX version */
    printf ("August, 1988 revision of POSIX.1 supported.\n");
#elif _POSIX_VERSION == 199009L
    printf("September, 1990 revision of POSIX.1 supported.\n");
#elif _POSIX_VERSION == 199309L
    printf("September 1993 revision of POSIX.1 supported.\n");
#elif _POSIX_VERSION == 199506L
    printf("June, 1995 revision of POSIX.1 supported.\n");
#endif
}
```

Compile-Time Symbolic Constants

The following table describes the optional Pthread feature test macros. Not all systems support all of these options:

Table 3–2 Compile-Time Symbolic Constants

Name	Description
_POSIX_THREADS	When defined, this system supports POSIX threads.
_POSIX_THREAD_ATTR_STACKADDR	When defined, the system supports the Thread Stack Address Attribute option. If available, this feature allows the application to allocate and manage its own thread stack.

Table 3–2 Compile-Time Symbolic Constants

Name	Description
_POSIX_THREAD_ATTR_STACKSIZE	When defined, the system supports the Thread Stack Size Attribute option. If available, this feature allows the application to control thread stack size. (See the *Creating Specialized Thread Attributes* section in Chapter 4.)
_POSIX_THREAD_PRIORITY_SCHEDULING	When defined, the system supports the Thread Execution Scheduling option. This option, along with the use of a priority-based scheduling policy, allows an application to specify scheduling policies and priorities for threads. (See the *Thread Scheduling Priority Values* section in Chapter 6.)
_POSIX_THREAD_PRIO_INHERIT	When defined, the system supports the Priority Inheritance option. This feature allows an application to use the priority inheritance features with specified mutexes. When a *mutual exclusion object* (mutex) is using the priority inheritance feature, a thread holding the mutex executes at the highest priority of all threads blocked on the mutex. When the mutex is unlocked, the thread continues execution at its original priority.
_POSIX_THREAD_PRIO_PROTECT	When defined, the system supports the Priority Protection option. This feature allows an application to use the priority protection features with specified mutexes. When a thread locks a mutex using the priority protection feature, the thread executes at the priority assigned to the mutex. When the mutex is unlocked, the thread continues execution at its original priority.

Table 3–2 Compile-Time Symbolic Constants

Name	Description
`_POSIX_THREAD_PROCESS_SHARED`	When defined, the system supports the Process-Shared Synchronization option. This feature allows an application to specify whether a specific synchronization variable (i.e., mutex, condition variable, etc.) is to be shared by multiple processes. (See the *Mutex Attributes* and *Condition Variable Attributes* section in Chapter 5.)
`_POSIX_THREAD_SAFE_FUNCTIONS`	When defined, the system supports the Thread-Safe Functions option. Functions allowing access by multiple threads concurrently are generally thread-safe functions. (See the *Reentrant, Thread-Safe, and Unsafe Functions* section in Chapter 12.

Checking Features

Here is an example of a feature-checking program that determines whether
optional Pthread features are supported on your system.

```
#include <unistd.h>
#include <stdio.h>
#define _POSIX_SOURCE
#define _POSIX_C_SOURCE 199506L

main() {
#ifndef _POSIX_THREADS
    printf("This system does not support POSIX threads.\n");
#else
    printf("POSIX threads are supported on this system.\n");
#endif

#ifndef _POSIX_THREAD_ATTR_STACKADDR
    printf("Pthread stack addr attribute is NOT supported.\n");
#else
    printf("Pthread stack addr attribute is supported\n");
#endif

#ifndef _POSIX_THREAD_ATTR_STACKSIZE
    printf("Pthread stack size attribute is NOT supported.\n");
#else
    printf("Pthread stack size attribute is supported\n");
#endif

#ifndef _POSIX_THREAD_PRIORITY_SCHEDULING
    printf("Pthread priority scheduling is NOT supported.\n");
#else
    printf("Pthread priority scheduling is supported\n");
#endif

#ifndef _POSIX_THREAD_PRIO_INHERIT
    printf("Pthread priority inheritance is NOT supported.\n");
#else
    printf("Pthread priority inheritance is supported\n");
#endif

#ifndef _POSIX_THREAD_PRIO_PROTECT
    printf("Pthread priority protection is NOT supported.\n");
#else
    printf("Pthread priority protection is supported\n");
#endif

/* and so on... */

}
```

Checking Limits

Many of the supported features contained in <unistd.h> have numeric parameters associated with them that describe their limits. If you need to know the minimum stack size of a thread or how many threads can be created per process, use the <limits.h> definitions in a conformance-checking program:

```
#include <unistd.h>
#include <stdio.h>
#include <limits.h>

#define _POSIX_SOURCE
#define _POSIX_C_SOURCE 199506L

main() {
#ifndef _POSIX_THREADS
    printf("This system does not support POSIX THREADS.\n");
#else
printf("This system supports POSIX threads.\n");
#ifdef PTHREAD_STACK_MIN
    printf("Minimum stack size per thread: %d\n",
            PTHREAD_STACK_MIN);
#else
    printf("Use sysconf() to get PTHREAD_STACK_MIN\n");
#endif
#ifdef PTHREAD_THREADS_MAX
    printf("Maximum threads per process: %d\n",
            PTHREAD_THREADS_MAX);
#else
    printf("Use sysconf() to get PTHREAD_THREADS_MAX\n");
#endif
#endif
}
```

Table 3-3 provides a list of symbols defined in <limits.h>. All POSIX-compliant implementations define these symbols. The value of these symbols is the minimum value that a POSIX-compliant system may define.

Table 3–3 Minimum Requirements for `<limits.h>` Symbols I

Limit for All Systems	Description	Value
_POSIX_THREAD_DESTRUCTOR_ **ITERATIONS**	This is the maximum number of times the system will try to destroy a thread's thread-specific data values upon thread termination.	4
_POSIX_THREAD_KEYS_MAX	Each process may create this maximum number of data keys.	128
_POSIX_THREAD_THREADS_MAX	Each process may create a maximum of this many threads.	64

The symbols in Table 3-4 are defined in `<limits.h>` if their value is determinate. However, if their value is indeterminate (and is equal to or greater than the stated minimum value), the implementation will not define those symbols. In the latter case, the `sysconf()` function (described the next section) can be used to determine the value of each symbol.

Table 3-4 defines the names of the symbols and their minimum required values. The value of these symbols must be equal to or greater than the minimum values.

Table 3–4 Minimum Requirements for `<limits.h>` Symbols II

Name	Minimum Required Value
PTHREAD_DESTRUCTOR_ITERATIONS	**_POSIX_THREAD_DESTRUCTOR_** **ITERATIONS**
PTHREAD_KEYS_MAX	**_POSIX_THREAD_KEYS_MAX**
PTHREAD_STACK_MIN	0
PTHREAD_THREADS_MAX	**_POSIX_THREAD_THREADS_MAX**

Except for **PTHREAD_STACK_MIN**, the description of the symbols above can be traced to Table 3-3. Each thread has a stack that is a minimum of **PTHREAD_STACK_MIN** bytes in size.

Note: Even if the symbols in Table 3-4 are defined in `<limits.h>`, it is possible that the system may actually support a larger value. For example, the values for **PTHREAD_STACK_MIN** and **PTHREAD_THREADS_MAX** are most likely system-configurable values.

Run-Time Checking

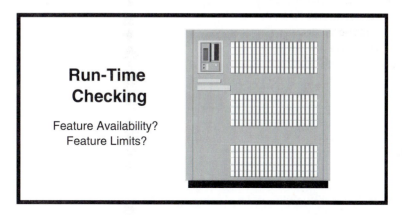

Fig. 3–5 Similar to compile-time checking, run-time checking allows you to check the availability and the limits of POSIX options on your run-time system. The run-time system may support fewer features than does the compilation system.

It is important to remember that the compilation system may support POSIX features that the run-time system does not support. In some situations, the run-time system may be very minimal to save memory, other resources, or cost. In other situations, the version of POSIX supported may differ.

To determine the POSIX functionality supported at run-time (on the run-time system), POSIX provides three functions: pathconf(), fpathconf(), and sysconf(). The first two functions are used to determine whether or not a POSIX feature is supported for a particular file or file descriptor, respectively. The latter function is used to determine configurable system variable values. As pathconf() and fpathconf() are not required to determine support for POSIX.1c features, we will confine our discussion to sysconf().

sysconf()

```
long val = sysconf(int name)
```

The sysconf() function can be used to determine the existence of a POSIX feature. If a feature is not supported, sysconf() returns -1. If there is no such POSIX feature, -1 is returned and errno is set to **EINVAL**. If the feature is supported, a value other than -1 is returned and errno is not changed. The sysconf() function can also be used to return a numeric value that represents a limit for the parameter passed.

The following program uses `sysconf()` to see whether POSIX threads are supported. If POSIX threads are supported, `sysconf()` is used again to determine the maximum number of threads per process.

```
#include <unistd.h>
#include <limits.h>
#include <errno.h>

#define _POSIX_SOURCE
#define _POSIX_C_SOURCE 199506L

main() {

    int rtn;

    /* Startup code goes here */
    rtn = check_required_features();
    if (rtn == -1)
        exit(-1);

    /* Start up threads here. */

    /* The rest of main goes here. */
}

check_required_features() {

    errno = 0;

    switch (sysconf(_SC_THREADS)) {
    case -1: /* Invalid option or threads are not supported. */
        if (errno == EINVAL)
            printf("Invalid option for _SC_THREADS.\n");
        else
            printf("POSIX threads are NOT supported.\n");
        return(-1);
    default: /* Indicate POSIX threads are supported. */
        printf("POSIX threads are supported.\n");

        /* Find out how many threads are supported per process. */
        printf("Number of threads per process supported: %d\n",
                        sysconf(_SC_THREAD_THREADS_MAX));
        return(0);
    }
}
```

Note: A POSIX-compliant system may support values greater than the POSIX defined minimums. Applications can be designed to assess these values and make appropriate accommodations.

The following table maps the `sysconf()` option names for Pthreads with their respective system values:

Table 3–5 Sysconf Options and Return Values

Sysconf Option Name	System Value Returned
`_SC_THREAD_DESTRUCTOR_` `ITERATIONS`	`PTHREAD_DESTRUCTOR_ITERATIONS`
`_SC_THREAD_KEYS_MAX`	`PTHREAD_KEYS_MAX`
`_SC_THREAD_STACK_MIN`	`PTHREAD_STACK_MIN`
`_SC_THREAD_THREADS_MAX`	`PTHREAD_THREADS_MAX`
`_SC_THREADS`	`_POSIX_THREADS`
`_SC_THREAD_ATTR_STACKADDR`	`_POSIX_THREAD_ATTR_STACKADDR`
`_SC_THREAD_ATTR_STACKSIZE`	`_POSIX_THREAD_ATTR_STACKSIZE`
`_SC_THREAD_PRIORITY_` `SCHEDULING`	`_POSIX_THREAD_PRIORITY_` `SCHEDULING`
`_SC_THREAD_PRIO_INHERIT`	`_POSIX_THREAD_PRIO_INHERIT`
`_SC_THREAD_PRIO_PROTECT`	`_POSIX_THREAD_PRIO_PROTECT`
`_SC_THREAD_PROCESS_SHARED`	`_POSIX_THREAD_PROCESS_SHARED`
`_SC_THREAD_SAFE_FUNCTIONS`	`_POSIX_THREAD_SAFE_FUNCTIONS`

Namespace Reservation

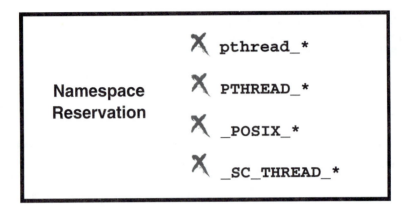

Fig. 3–6 POSIX has namespaces reserved for its use. Namespace reservations are posted by POSIX in advisories called *reserved namespaces*. As a POSIX programmer, you should not use any names or prefixes that POSIX has reserved.

Defining Namespace Pollution and Reservation

Namespace pollution is the result of vendors giving their functions, constants, and macros, *any names they choose*. As a consequence of namespace pollution, collisions may occur among names. In a program, such collisions can cause compile/link failure or some type of unpredictable behavior. **Namespace Reservation** *attempts to avoid namespace collisions by reserving various names or prefixes*.

POSIX Namespace Reservation

POSIX function names, constants, and macros are declared in certain header files and libraries. Many functions or declarations are given standard prefixes in an attempt to make them unique. For example, all of the Pthread functions begin with the prefix **pthread_**. In addition, all of the Pthread constants begin with the prefix **PTHREAD_**.

POSIX posts advisories called *reserved namespaces* to inform the POSIX programming public of those names or prefixes it is likely to define. Once POSIX confirms its decision, these names or prefixes should be considered off-limits. In other words, *do not name your own functions in the same manner*.

Note: If you want to use a **pthread_** or **PTHREAD_** prefix, you may do so, as long as you add a **_np** or **_NP** suffix, respectively.[2] The *np* suffix, in either upper or lower case, stands for *non-portable."*

[2] This advice is given in P1003.1c Draft 10, September 1994, section 2.1.2.1.

Summary

This chapter provided a brief introduction to the structure of POSIX. We discussed the primary goal of POSIX and described why this is important. We also provided several examples to show you how to determine which POSIX.1c functionality is supported on your system.

The following is a summary of what we have covered in this chapter:

- Many vendors have their own implementation of UNIX. Even so, the POSIX standard is designed to allow application developers to create applications that are *source-code portable*. An application that is source-code portable requires little or no change to the program source code to run correctly on a different operating system.

- There are two components in the POSIX system: the header files and the libraries.

- Compile-time checking can be used on your compilation system to check for the availability and limits of POSIX functionality. Compile-time checking uses *feature test macros* (preprocessor #defines) for this purpose.

- Run-time checking can be used on the run-time system to check for the availability and limits of POSIX functionality. Three routines are available: sysconf(), pathconf(), and fpathconf(). Only the sysconf() function is required for POSIX.1c run-time checking.

- Namespace pollution occurs as vendors choose any names they like for their functions, constants, macros. A potential result of namespace collision is compile/link failure or some type of undefined behavior. Namespace reservation attempts to prevent collisions by reserving names for functions, constants, or macros.

Exercises

1. What might be considered the heart of the POSIX standard?
2. What is the primary benefit of the POSIX standard?
3. What are the two major components of the POSIX system?
4. Write a program that performs compile-time checking. This program should check to see whether Pthreads are supported and, if so, how many thread-specific data keys are allowed.
5. Write a program that performs the same test at run-time using the sysconf() function.
6. Provide an example of namespace pollution and describe how this would cause problems in some hypothetical program.

Basic Thread Management

This chapter presents the basic thread management interfaces and explains how they are used. These interfaces allow you to create, terminate, and synchronize threads. Specialized attributes are available for creating threads with unique characteristics.

Topics Covered...

- Relating Process and Thread Model Functions
- Creating a Thread
- Waiting for a Thread
- Detaching a Thread
- Terminating a Thread
- Finding and Comparing Thread IDs
- Performing One-Time Initialization
- Establishing Fork Handlers
- Setting Specialized Thread Attributes
- Handling Thread Management Errors

Relating Process and Thread Model Functions

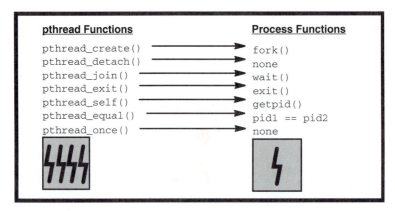

Fig. 4-1 This sampling of Process and Thread Model functions shows that many functions from the Process Model have a Thread Model analog.

In the Process Model, a process is created, has a life cycle, and terminates. When a process is created, it is associated with a piece of code (a program) to execute. During the life cycle of a process, the process will run, sleep, and block many times. When a process terminates, it releases all of its resources in two stages. The first stage is when the process exits. The process' memory and most of its system resources are given back to the system. The kernel stack and process structure (to store the exit status) are retained. The second stage occurs when the parent of the terminated process performs a wait() on the child. The run-time statistics of the child process are saved, and the child's exit status is returned to the parent. The child process' kernel stack and process structure are then released back to the system.

Similarly, in the Thread Model, a thread is created, has a life cycle, and terminates. When a thread is created, it is associated with a piece of code. If the host process (and thus, the program) is single-threaded, the thread is associated with the entire program (see Process Model above). If the host process is multi-threaded, each thread within the process is associated with a function to execute. Threads run, sleep, and block just like processes. When a thread terminates, it performs a thread-level exit. After a thread exits, *the programmer must take steps to ensure that a thread's resources are returned to the system.* This is accomplished by performing a thread level wait operation. Performance and resource availability problems occur if proper attention is not paid to this area.

This is only one of several similarities between threads and processes that will be discussed in this chapter. As we proceed with this chapter, we will discuss the specific functions used to manage thread creation, termination, resource conservation, and other thread operations.

Creating a Thread

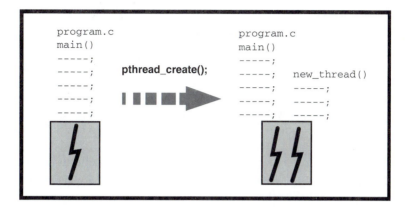

Fig. 4–2 The pthread_create() routine creates a uniquely identifiable thread within the context of a process. The created thread is associated with a function to execute.

Overview

All processes contain at least one thread, which is called the *main* or *initial* thread. For simplicity in our discussion, we'll refer to it as the *initial* thread. The initial thread is created automatically at process creation time. To create additional threads of control within a process, an application must use:

```
int pthread_create(
      pthread_t            *thread_id,
      pthread_attr_t       *attr,
      void                 *(*start_routine)(void *),
      void                 *arg
);
```

This function is similar to the fork() function used to create a new process; however, there are a few differences. For example, the granularity of the code space to be executed differs. fork() creates a process in which the entire code space is scheduled to execute. The pthread_create() function establishes a thread within a process and associates the thread with a function from the code space. Therefore, in a multithreaded process, only a portion of the code space, a function, is scheduled to execute with a thread. That function is allowed to make function calls to any other function within the process code space.

When the call to pthread_create() returns, the thread ID of the new thread is returned in the parameter *thread_id.* The thread ID can be used later to synchronize with the new thread.

The *attr* parameter is a thread attributes object. This object provides a way to configure the new thread. Included among the thread attributes are the thread's stack size, stack address, scheduling policy and priority, and detach state. If the *attr* parameter is **NULL**, the system's default attributes are used to create the thread. We'll discuss thread attributes in greater detail later in this chapter.

The created thread will have the first instruction of the function *start_routine()* loaded into its program counter. *start_routine()* takes only one parameter, *arg*. If more than one parameter is required, an application can have *arg* point to a data structure that contains several fields, each representing a parameter. If *start_routine()* does not require any parameters, *arg* may be set to **NULL**.

By default, a thread inherits its parent's signal mask, scheduling policy, and scheduling priority when it is created. The new thread will not inherit any pending signals from the parent thread.

Guidelines

- The Pthread functions do **not** set the `errno` variable if an error occurs. All Pthread functions have a return value of 0 on successful completion, or an error number indicating the error on failure.

- Do **not** assume that a thread is running (or going to run) after a call to `pthread_create()`. It is possible that the new thread will execute and terminate before the call to `pthread_create()` returns.

- If *arg* is a pointer, it should **not** point to one of the creating thread's local variables. When the creating thread leaves the current function, this local variable is no longer valid.

Example

This is a multithreaded version of the traditional "Hello World!" program. While this is a poor use of threads in real life, the program demonstrates the use of three of the Pthread functions we will discuss in this chapter. Let's start by looking at `pthread_create()` in particular:

```c
#include <pthread.h>
#include <string.h>
#include <stdio.h>
#include <errno.h>

void    fatal_error(int err_num, char *function);
void    thread1_func();

/* Print "Hello World!", then "Good-bye World!" */
main()
{
    pthread_t    tid;
    int          return_val;

    /*
     * Create a new thread to execute thread1_func().
     */
    return_val = pthread_create(&tid, (pthread_attr_t *)NULL,
                        (void *(*)())thread1_func,
                        (void *)NULL);
    if (return_val != 0)
            fatal_error(return_val, "pthread_create()");

    /*
     * Wait for the thread to finish executing, then...
     */
    return_val = pthread_join(tid, (void **)NULL);
    if (return_val != 0)
            fatal_error(return_val, "pthread_join()");

    /* Say Good-bye */
    printf("Good-bye World!\n");
    exit(0);
}


/* Print error information, exit with -1 status. */
void
fatal_error(int err_num, char *function)
{
    char         *err_string;

    err_string = strerror(err_num);
    fprintf(stderr, "%s error: %s\n", function, err_string);
    exit(-1);
}


/* Function to print "Hello World!". */
void
thread1_func()
{
    printf("Hello World!\n");
    pthread_exit((void *)NULL);
}
```

Waiting for a Thread

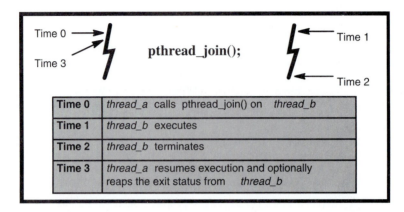

Time 0	*thread_a* calls pthread_join() on *thread_b*
Time 1	*thread_b* executes
Time 2	*thread_b* terminates
Time 3	*thread_a* resumes execution and optionally reaps the exit status from *thread_b*

Fig. 4–3 A thread calling `pthread_join()` on another thread will suspend execution until the target thread has terminated. This function also allows your process to reclaim unused resources, resulting in better performance and resource conservation.

Overview

In the Process Model, a process can suspend its execution and wait for the termination of a child process by calling `wait()` or `waitpid()`. The calling process reaps the exit status and the run-time statistics of the child process. Waiting on child processes should always be done, even if the parent does not care about the exit status of the child process. If this step is omitted, system resources are not released until the parent process terminates.

In the Thread Model, a terminated thread's resources can be reclaimed by using the `pthread_join()` function:

```
int pthread_join(
     pthread_t           thread_id,
     void                **return_val
);
```

A call to `pthread_join()` will suspend the calling thread until the target thread, specified by *thread_id*, terminates. A successful return from this function indicates that *thread_id* has terminated and its resources have been reclaimed. If *thread_id* has already terminated, `pthread_join()` returns immediately with a successful value.

In the Process Model, there is a parent/child relationship between processes. Only a parent process can wait for a child process. The parent/child relationship does not exist between threads in a process. A thread is a sibling of all other threads in the process, regardless of which thread created it. Consequently, a thread can wait for any joinable thread in its process.

Use of this function will provide performance and resource conservation benefits to multithreaded programs. An application should use this function when it needs a return status from a terminating thread or needs to synchronize with the termination of the target thread.

If the *return_val* parameter is not **NULL**, *thread_id*'s exit status is stored in the *return_val* parameter. As you will see later, pthread_exit() is passed a pointer as the terminating thread's exit status. Consequently, the *return_val* parameter of pthread_join() is a pointer to a pointer. In the Process Model, exit() is passed an int for the process exit status, and wait() is passed a pointer to an int in order to retrieve this value.

The return status of a canceled thread (more on this in Chapter 8, *Thread Cancellation*) is **PTHREAD_CANCELED**. If a thread exits with an integer rather than a pointer, the exist status may conflict with the value of **PTHREAD_CANCELED**.

Why is a thread's exit status a pointer instead of an integer? To allow more flexibility for the programmer. This strategy allows a terminating thread to return a pointer to an allocated structure or resource to the joining thread. The structure or resource should be released when the joining thread is finished with it. With this flexibility, a thread has the ability to terminate with significantly more exit status than a process. If you use this feature, it's a good idea to use a dynamically allocated structure (i.e., via malloc()). Remember, the context of the "joined-to" (target) thread will not be around after the call to pthread_join(). The context is reclaimed by the system.

Guidelines

- If multiple threads call pthread_join() specifying the same thread in *thread_id*, the resulting behavior is undefined by POSIX.1c. Some systems may allow each call to return successfully. Other systems may return success to one caller, and return an error to all other callers after *thread_id* terminates. Other systems may return an error immediately when a second call to pthread_join() is made with the same *thread_id*. For maximum portability, pthread_join() should be called only once for any target thread.

- Each process has a limit on the number of threads that may be created in a process. POSIX.1c does not specify if a thread which has terminated, but not yet been joined, counts against this limit. For maximum portability (and because it's the right thing to do!), pthread_join() should be called for all threads that an application creates.

Example

In order to further explore pthread_join(), let's make a few modifications to our multithreaded "Hello World!" program. This program now passes a data structure pointer to the thread1_func() function. thread1_func() modifies the data structure and returns a pointer to it. The main thread retrieves this pointer through pthread_join() and validates its contents.

```c
#include <pthread.h>
#include <stdio.h>
#include <string.h>
#include <errno.h>

#define    MAX_THR_MSG             100
#define    HELLO_MSG               "Hello World!"

struct thr_rtn {
    int         completed;
    char        in_msg[MAX_THR_MSG + 1];
    char        out_msg[MAX_THR_MSG + 1];
};

void       fatal_error(int err_num, char *function);
void       thread1_func(struct thr_rtn *msg);

#define    check_error(return_val, emsg) {                \
               if (return_val != 0)                       \
                       fatal_error(return_val, emsg); \
           }

main()
{
    pthread_t           tid;
    int                 return_val;
    struct thr_rtn      *ptr;
    struct thr_rtn      msg;


    /*
     * Initialize parameter to thread1_func()
     */
    strcpy(msg.in_msg, HELLO_MSG);
    msg.out_msg[0] = NULL;
    msg.completed = 0;

    /*
     * Create a new thread to execute thread1_func()
     */
    return_val = pthread_create(&tid,(pthread_attr_t *)NULL,
                        (void *(*)())thread1_func,
                        (void *)&msg);
    check_error(return_val, "pthread_create()");
```

```c
    /*
     * Wait for the thread to finish executing
     */
    return_val = pthread_join(tid, (void **)&ptr);
    check_error(return_val, "pthread_join()");

    /*
     * Check return parameter for validity
     */
    if (ptr != &msg) {
        fprintf(stderr, "ptr != &msg\n");
        exit(-1);
    } else if (ptr->completed != 1) {
        fprintf(stderr, "ptr->completed != 1\n");
        exit(-1);
    } else if (strcmp(ptr->in_msg, HELLO_MSG) != 0) {
        fprintf(stderr, "ptr->in_msg != %s\n", HELLO_MSG);
        exit(-1);
    } else if (strcmp(ptr->out_msg, HELLO_MSG) != 0) {
        fprintf(stderr, "ptr->out_msg != %s\n", HELLO_MSG);
        exit(-1);
    }

    /* Good-bye */
    printf("Good-bye World!\n");
    exit(0);
}


void
fatal_error(int err_num, char *function)
{
    char      *err_string;

    err_string = strerror(err_num);
    fprintf(stderr, "%s error: %s\n", function, err_string);
    exit(-1);
}


void
thread1_func(struct thr_rtn *msg)
{
    printf("%s\n", msg->in_msg);
    strcpy(msg->out_msg, msg->in_msg);
    msg->completed = 1;
    pthread_exit((void *)msg);
}
```

Detaching a Thread

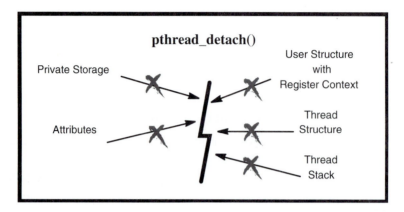

Fig. 4–4 Detaching a thread allows the system (i.e., your process) to reclaim resources immediately upon thread exit. This can be helpful with both performance and resource conservation.

Overview

The Thread Model has a concept called *detaching a thread* which is not readily available in the process model. When a thread is detached, any system resources that it is consuming (thread structure, stack, thread ID, etc.) are reclaimed by the system when the thread terminates. An application does not need to call the `pthread_join()` function for a detached thread (an error will be returned if it does). A thread which is not detached is called a *joinable thread*.

To detach a thread, use the function:

```
int pthread_detach(
    pthread_t           thread_id
);
```

If a thread is detached, its return status is not available to a joining thread. If a thread calls `pthread_join()` with the ID of a detached thread, an error of **EINVAL** is returned. Calling `pthread_detach()` does not cause the target thread to terminate or the calling thread to be suspended until the target thread terminates.

In the Process Model, there is a way to mimic the behavior of "detaching a process." Instead of calling `fork()` to create a child process, call `fork()` to create an intermediate process and `wait()` on the intermediate process. This new intermediate process calls `fork()` to create the real child process. The intermediate process then exits, causing the parent's `wait()` call to return. The real child process has been disassociated from the parent process. The child process will release all of its system resources when it terminates since it no longer has a parent that can `wait()` for it. The `pthread_detach()` function in the Thread Model is a much simpler method.

Guidelines

At some point, either `pthread_detach()` or `pthread_join()` should be called for every thread in an application; otherwise, system resources are wasted until the process terminates. Do not call `pthread_detach()` for the same thread more than once. The resulting behavior is unspecified; however, most systems will either ignore the repeated request or return the error **EINVAL**.

Be cautious when using the thread ID of a detached thread because the thread ID can be reused after the detached thread terminates. An application should verify that detached threads have not terminated before trying to communicate or synchronize with them. This can easily be done by having the detached threads set some global state when they terminate (i.e., an array of status variables, one for each thread).

Why would you want to use detached threads? Performance. Calling the `pthread_join()` function for each thread in an application takes time and may cause the calling thread to be suspended. If an application is not concerned with the return status of a terminated thread or does not need to synchronize with a terminated thread, a detached thread works well. The application should not exit normally until all of its threads have terminated. Since `pthread_join()` cannot be called for detached threads, an application must develop a method to verify that each detached thread exits before the application exits.

X/Open and the XPG 4.2 Standard

While the various POSIX.1 standards do not readily have a concept of *detaching* processes, X/Open's XPG 4.2 standard does. When using `sigaction()` for the signal **SIGCHLD**, you can specify **SIG_IGN** in `sa_handler` and **SA_NOCLDWAIT** in `sa_flags` to change all child processes to be *detached* processes. The child processes of the caller will not be turned into zombies when they terminate. The system automatically reaps their resources when they terminate.

Example

In the following example, the initial thread waits for a request from the user, then creates a thread to perform the requested work. The initial thread is not concerned about when the threads exit or what value they return. Consequently, each thread that is created is also detached. The initial thread does not keep track of the threads it has created. If the user terminates the application, the initial thread calls `exit()`. Calling `exit()` causes all threads, joinable or detached, to terminate, whether or not they have finished executing.

```
#include <pthread.h>

extern void     fatal_error(int err_num, char *function);
extern int      get_user_cmd();
void            thread_func(int cmd);

#define    QUIT         0

#define    check_error(return_val, msg) {                    \
                if (return_val != 0)                         \
                    fatal_error(return_val, msg);  \
            }

main()
{
    pthread_t    tid;
    int          return_val;
    int          cmd;

    while (1) {

        /* Get the user's command */
        cmd = get_user_cmd();
        if (cmd == QUIT)
            break;

        /* Create a new thread */
        return_val = pthread_create(&tid, (pthread_attr_t *)NULL,
                                (void *(*)())thread_func,
                                (void *)cmd);
        check_error(return_val, "pthread_create()");

        /* Now detach the thread */
        return_val = pthread_detach(tid);
        check_error(return_val, "pthread_detach()");
    }

    /* Say Good-bye */
    printf("Program Terminating...\n");
    exit(0);
}


/* Function to process user's command */
void
thread_func(int cmd)
{
    /* Real application processing code goes here... */
    ...

    pthread_exit((void *)NULL);
}
```

Terminating a Thread

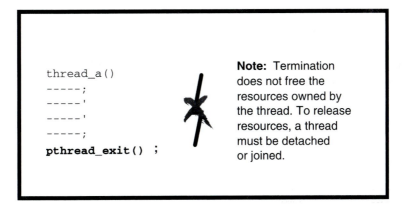

Fig. 4–5 When a thread terminates, it no longer needs to be scheduled. A terminated thread retains its resources unless it has been detached or another thread has joined with the terminated thread.

Overview

A process terminates by calling exit() or by returning from main(). A thread terminates by calling pthread_exit() or by returning from its *start_routine()*. An implicit call to pthread_exit() is made if a thread terminates by returning from its *start_routine()*. The return value of the thread's *start_routine()* is used as the thread's exit status.

The initial thread is allowed to terminate by calling pthread_exit(). However, if the initial thread returns from main() without calling pthread_exit(), an implicit call to exit() is performed. When the last thread terminates, exit(0) is called for the process.

To terminate the calling thread, use the function:

```
int pthread_exit(
     void        *value_ptr
);
```

value_ptr is the thread's exit status. This value is returned to a thread that calls pthread_join() for the terminating thread. However, if the terminating thread is detached, the exit status is lost and cannot be returned to a joining thread.

Because *value_ptr* is a pointer rather than an integer, a thread can exit with significantly more information than a process. A thread can exit with a *value_ptr,* which is a pointer to a data structure containing detailed exit status information. Conversely, a thread can exit with a simple integer indicating success or failure (0 or -1), provided that the proper type casting is performed. Keep in mind that type casting a `void *` to an `int` is system-dependent. Many systems may allow this type casting, but portable applications should not rely on this behavior.

A detached thread should not exit with a status other than **NULL**. The exit status of a detached thread cannot be retrieved via `pthread_join()`. A non-**NULL** exit status for detached threads will be lost and may result in memory leaks in the application.

At some point after a thread terminates, its stack will be reclaimed by the system. Trying to access local variables of a terminated thread results in undefined behavior (potentially a **SIGSEGV** signal). Consequently, a thread's exit status should not be a pointer to one of the thread's local variables.

The previous two examples of the multithreaded "Hello World!" program show two different examples of using *value_ptr* with `pthread_exit()`. The first example passes an integer to `pthread_exit()`. The second example passes a pointer to a data structure.

Resource Reclamation

When a thread terminates, resources available to the process are not released. Process resources such as file descriptors, shared memory, mutexes, and semaphores are all process resources and will not be closed, unlocked, or released when a thread terminates, even if this is the only thread using the resource. Process cleanup actions, such as calling `atexit()` functions, are not performed when a thread terminates.

At some point after a thread terminates, its stack and thread ID are reclaimed by the system. When this happens depends on the detached state of the thread.

Thread Cancellation

A thread may be terminated by another thread by using the thread cancellation interfaces. We'll discuss thread cancellation later in this book, but a brief overview is provided here, as it has an impact on `pthread_exit()`.

A thread can request the termination of another thread by calling the function `pthread_cancel()`. If the target thread has acquired a resource or is terminated in the middle of a critical operation, the application may experience unwanted behavior or may eventually deadlock. POSIX.1c provides two functions that allow a canceled thread to release any acquired resources before it terminates: `pthread_cleanup_push()` and `pthread_cleanup_pop()`. These functions install and remove cancellation cleanup handlers from the calling thread's cancellation stack. When a thread is canceled, any functions pushed but not yet popped are popped and then executed. These functions are responsible for restoring the state of whatever operation the thread was performing (e.g., releasing a locked mutex).

What does thread cancellation have to do with `pthread_exit()`? When a thread terminates, any installed cancellation cleanup handlers are popped and executed. The handlers are called in the reverse order from which they were installed. A benefit of this action is that a thread can call `pthread_exit()` while in the middle of a critical section of code. The cancellation cleanup handlers will restore the state of the critical data (assuming that your cleanup handlers are coded to do the proper things!).

Thread-Specific Data

Another feature, *thread-specific data*, has an impact on `pthread_exit()`. We will explore thread-specific data and the associated Pthread interfaces later in this book. At this point, you need to be aware of only the following:

- A program can have a global variable that each thread accesses through the same variable name, but the contents of the variable is different for each thread. This is known as *thread-specific data*.

- Thread-specific data variables may contain data or dynamically allocated memory that must be released before the thread terminates.

- When creating a thread-specific data variable, a *destructor* function can be associated with the data. This destructor function is called when the thread terminates. It is responsible for releasing any dynamically allocated memory associated with the thread-specific data variable for the terminating thread.

When a thread terminates, the thread-specific data *destructor* functions are called for all non-**NULL** thread-specific data variables of the terminating thread.

Process Termination

If any thread calls `exit()` or `_exit()`, all threads within the process are first terminated, then the process is terminated. Threads terminated as a result of a call to `exit()` or `_exit()` will not execute any cancellation cleanup handlers or thread-specific data destructor functions.

Example

The following example creates three threads and has each thread exit in a different manner. The first thread will exit with an integer status, the second thread with a pointer, and the third thread returns from its start routine with a pointer.

```c
#include <pthread.h>
#include <string.h>
#include <stdio.h>
#include <errno.h>

void    thread1_func(), thread2_func();
void    fatal_error(int err_num, char *function);
int     *thread3_func();

#define    check_error(return_val, msg) {                        \
                if (return_val != 0)                             \
                        fatal_error(return_val, msg); \
            }

int     second_thread = 2;
int     third_thread = 3;

main()
{
    pthread_t    tid[3];
    int          i, return_val;
    long         val;

    /*
     * Create thread #1
     */
    return_val = pthread_create(&tid[0], (pthread_attr_t *)NULL,
                        (void *(*)())thread1_func,
                        (void *)NULL);
    check_error(return_val, "pthread_create() - 1");

    /*
     * Create thread #2
     */
    return_val = pthread_create(&tid[1], (pthread_attr_t *)NULL,
                        (void *(*)())thread2_func,
                        (void *)NULL);
    check_error(return_val, "pthread_create() - 2");

    /*
     * Create thread #3
     */
    return_val = pthread_create(&tid[2], (pthread_attr_t *)NULL,
                        (void *(*)())thread3_func,
                        (void *)NULL);
    check_error(return_val, "pthread_create() - 3");
```

```
    /*
     * Wait for the threads to finish executing.
     * Print out each thread's return status.
     */
    for (i = 0; i < 3; i++) {
        return_val = pthread_join(tid[i], (void *)&val);
        check_error(return_val, "pthread_join()");
        printf("Thread %d returned 0x%x\n", tid[i], val);
    }

    /* Say Good-bye */
    printf("Good-bye World!\n");
    exit(0);
}


/* Print error information, exit with -1 status. */
void
fatal_error(int err_num, char *function)
{
    char        *err_string;

    err_string = strerror(err_num);
    fprintf(stderr, "%s error: %s\n", function, err_string);
    exit(-1);
}


/* Thread functions */

void
thread1_func()
{
    printf("Hello World! I'm the first thread\n");
    pthread_exit((void *) 1);
}



void
thread2_func()
{
    printf("Hello World! I'm the second thread\n");
    pthread_exit((void *)&second_thread);
}



int *
thread3_func()
{
    printf("Hello World! I'm the third thread\n");
    return((void *)&third_thread);
}
```

Finding and Comparing Thread IDs

Fig. 4–6 Similar to `getpid()` in the Process Model, in the Thread Model, `pthread_self()` provides the thread ID of the current thread.

Overview

Each process in a system is identified by a unique process ID of type `pid_t`. The process ID of the current process can be obtained by calling the `getpid()` function. Similarly, each thread in a process can be identified by a unique thread ID of type `pthread_t`. The thread ID of the current thread can be obtained by calling the function:

```
pthread_t pthread_self(void);
```

`pthread_self()` takes no arguments and returns the thread ID of the calling thread.

Thread IDs are guaranteed to be unique only within a process. In general, you should consider that threads are private to a process and will not be known outside of the process. Some implementations may provide system-wide unique thread IDs, but a portable application should not rely on it.

In the Process Model, it is commonly known that the type `pid_t` is a `long` or a `short` (older systems use a `short`). Consequently, it is acceptable to use a simple comparison operator like "`==`" to compare process IDs. In the Thread Model, the thread ID data type `pthread_t` is an opaque data type. `pthread_t` may not be a `long` or `short`. In fact, there are thread packages available today in which the thread ID is actually a data structure. Because `pthread_t` is an opaque data type, comparison operators like "`==`" cannot be used to compare thread IDs.

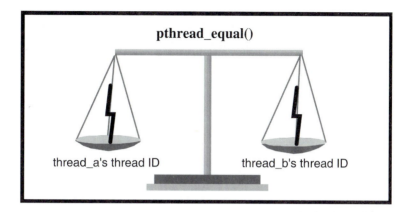

Fig. 4–7 `pthread_equal()` can be used to compare the thread IDs of two threads.

To compare thread IDs, use the function:

```
int pthread_equal(
    pthread_t    thread_1,
    pthread_t    thread_2
);
```

Here are the characteristics of `pthread_equal()`:

- It compares two thread IDs, returning a nonzero value if they are equal, zero if they are not equal.
- It does not verify that the two thread IDs refer to currently valid threads.
- For maximum portability, always use `pthread_equal()` to compare thread IDs. On some systems, this function may be implemented as a macro expression minimize overhead.

Example

The following example is a simple program that shows how to find and compare thread IDs. In this example, one thread is created to execute the function `thread_func()`. The main thread will also call `thread_func()`. This function will obtain the thread ID of the calling thread and compare this ID to the ID of the main thread (saved in a global variable).

This example doesn't call `pthread_join()` for each of the terminated threads. All thread resources will be reclaimed when the process terminates. Since each thread terminates at the same time and then the process terminates, there is no need to join with the threads.

```
#include <pthread.h>
#include <stdio.h>
#include <errno.h>

extern void    fatal_error(int err_num, char *function);
void           thread_func();
pthread_t      main_thread, child_thread;

#define        check_error(return_val, msg) {                    \
                    if (return_val != 0)                         \
                         fatal_error(return_val, msg);       \
                }

main()
{
    int            return_val;

    /*
     * Who are we?
     */
    main_thread = pthread_self();

    /*
     * Create a new thread to execute thread1_func().
     */
    return_val = pthread_create(&child_thread,
                           (pthread_attr_t *)NULL,
                           (void *(*)())thread_func,
                           (void *)NULL);
    check_error(return_val, "pthread_create()");

    /*
     * Call the same function as the child thread. This function
     * will call pthread_exit() for us (we never return).
     */
    thread_func();
}

void
thread_func()
{
    pthread_t            calling_thread;

    calling_thread = pthread_self();

    if (pthread_equal(calling_thread, main_thread) == 0) {
       printf("Main  thread in thread_func()\n");
    } else {
       printf("Child thread in thread_func()\n");
    }

    pthread_exit((void *)NULL);
}
```

Performing One-Time Initialization

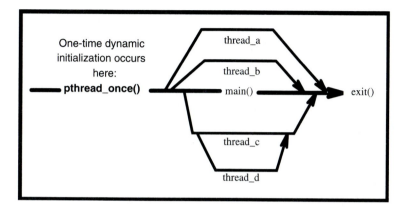

Fig. 4–8 Use `pthread_once()` to guarantee that some initialization code will be called only once.

Overview

Many library routines and large applications are dynamically initialized. Rather than initializing a module at process start-up time, initialization is done the first time that the module or function is invoked. Dynamic initialization is typically performed for modules that may not always be used by an application. If the module is never called, there is no performance penalty at process start-up time. Dynamic initialization is usually accomplished with code similar to the following:

```
static int          func_x_initialized = 0;

void func_x_init()
{
      /* Initialization code for func_x() here */
      ...
}

void func_x()
{
      if (func_x_initialized == 0) {
            func_x_init();
            func_x_initialized = 1;
      }

      /* Code for func_x() here */
      ...
}
```

This strategy works well in the Process Model. However, in the Thread Model, this approach causes a race condition. If two threads call func_x() simultaneously, they both see that func_x_initialized is zero and execute the initialization function. Even if func_x_initialized is set to one before calling the initialization function, a race condition would still exist:

- On a multiprocessor system, both threads could see that the value is set to zero at the same time.
- On a single processor system, the first thread could be context switched out between the check of func_x_initialized and the setting of it to one, allowing another thread to also execute func_x_init().

To prevent this type of dynamic initialization race condition, the following function has been provided:

```
pthread_once_t       once_control = PTHREAD_ONCE_INIT;

int pthread_once(
      pthread_once_t       *once_control,
      void                 (*init_func)(void)
);
```

Thepthread_once() function provides a way to guarantee that an initialization function is called once, and only once, in a multithreaded application. The once_control parameter is used to determine whether init_func() has previously been called. If not, init_func() will be called. Init_func() does not have a parameter. When pthread_once() returns, you are guaranteed that init_func() has completed.

If the thread executing init_func() is canceled, the once_control parameter will reflect that init_func() has not been called. Since the canceled thread was not able to completely finish executing init_func(), initialization is not complete. If init_func() can be canceled and it contains initialization components that can be performed only once, init_func() needs to be able to detect which components have already been initialized and skip them.

The behavior of pthread_once() is undefined if once_control is not a global variable, a static variable, or is not initialized with the PTHREAD_ONCE_INIT macro. Each initialization function should have its own once_control variable. The once_control variable should be passed only to pthread_once() with its associated initialization function.

Example

Here is what our previous example of dynamic initialization looks like when we use the pthread_once() function:

```c
#include <pthread.h>

static pthread_once_t    func_x_initialized = PTHREAD_ONCE_INIT;

extern void    fatal_error();
#define        check_error(return_val, msg) {                      \
                    if (return_val != 0)                           \
                            fatal_error(return_val, msg);          \
               }
void
func_x_init()
{
    /* Initialization code for func_x() here */
    ...
}

void
func_x()
{
    (void) pthread_once(&func_x_initialized, func_x_init);

    /* Code for func_x() here */
    ...
}

main()
{
    pthread_t        tid1, tid2;
    int              return_val;

    /* Thread 1 calls func_x() */
    return_val = pthread_create(&tid1, (pthread_attr_t *)NULL,
                                (void *(*)())func_x,
                                (void *)NULL);
    check_error(return_val, "pthread_create() - 1");

    /* Thread 2 calls func_x() */
    return_val = pthread_create(&tid1, (pthread_attr_t *)NULL,
                                (void *(*)())func_x,
                                (void *)NULL);
    check_error(return_val, "pthread_create() - 2");

    /* We call func_x() also */
    func_x();
}
```

Establishing Fork Handlers

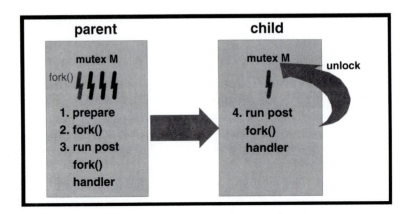

Fig. 4–9 When a thread calls `fork()`, a single-threaded process will be created. The thread in the child process will be a copy of the calling thread. If the state of the calling process contains a mutex, use `pthread_atfork()` to clean up the new process and prevent potential deadlock.

Overview

In a single-threaded process, a call to the `fork()` function creates a child process which is a duplicate of the calling process. This is not exactly what happens when a multithreaded process calls `fork()`. The new child process will contain a copy of the caller's address space as before, but the child process will contain only one thread. This thread is a duplicate of the thread calling `fork()`.

At first glance, this doesn't seem like much of a problem. However, the child process contains an address space duplicated from the parent process. This includes the state of resources such as mutexes (see Chapter 5, *Thread Synchronization*, for more information on mutexes). If these mutexes were locked in the parent when `fork()` was called, they will be locked in the child. Some of these mutexes may have been locked by threads that do not exist in the child process. These mutexes will never be unlocked in the child process. This situation can lead to deadlock in the child process if the one and only thread tries to acquire one of the locked mutexes (the owning thread does not exist to unlock the mutex).

This problem with `fork()` occurs with any resource that a thread has acquired. For example, memory that has been allocated by a thread will also exist in the child process. The thread allocating this memory does not exist in the child to release the memory. As a result, the child process will immediately have a memory leak.

Fork Handlers

How does an application get around this problem so that `fork()` can be called safely? Fork handlers can be installed with:

```
int pthread_atfork(
     void                    (*prepare)(void),
     void                    (*parent)(void),
     void                    (*child)(void)
);
```

This function will install fork handlers that will be called before and after the `fork()` operation. The fork handlers are automatically called by the system in the context of the thread that called `fork()`. The *prepare* fork handler will be called before the `fork()` operation is started. The *parent* fork handler will be called in the parent process after the `fork()` operation has completed. The *child* fork handler will be called in the child process after the `fork()` operation has completed. Any of the *prepare*, *parent*, or *child* fork handlers may be **NULL** if fork handling is not desired in the respective area.

When a `fork()` occurs, the *prepare* fork handlers are called in the opposite order from which they were established, Last-In, First-Out (LIFO). The *parent* and *child* fork handlers are called in the order in which they were established, First-In, First-Out (FIFO).

How does the `pthread_atfork()` function help our problem with `fork()`? The intent of `pthread_atfork()` is to allow the application to install prepare handlers that will acquire all of the application's mutex locks. When fork processing is complete, all mutex locks in the parent will be owned by the thread calling `fork()`. All locks in the child process will be owned by the only thread in the child process. The *parent* and *child* fork handlers are called in the parent and child processes and should release all of the mutex locks acquired by the *prepare* handler. The mutex state in the child process will now be consistent so that deadlock is avoided when the child process needs to lock a mutex. The fork handlers are written and supplied by the application.

The installation order of fork handlers must be ordered in a way that will not cause deadlock when mutexes are locked by the fork handlers (we'll talk about creating a mutex lock order in Chapter 12, *Writing Thread-Safe Code*). An application should be careful about when it calls `fork()`. The fork handlers should not try to lock a mutex already owned by the thread calling `fork()`.

Thread-specific data destructor functions are not called when a `fork()` occurs. The space for any dynamically allocated thread-specific data is lost in the child process for all but the thread calling `fork()`.

Example

The following code fragment shows how a library installs fork handlers. The function lib_init() installs fork handlers to make the library fork-safe. Assume that lib_init() is called sometime during the application's lifetime to initialize the library [possibly by the library itself via pthread_once()].

```
#include <pthread.h>
pthread_mutex_t    mutex_A, mutex_B;

#define  check_error(return_val, msg) {                      \
             extern void     fatal_error(int, char *);        \
             if (return_val != 0)                             \
                    fatal_error(return_val, msg);             \
         }

void lib_init()
{
        int     ret_val;

        /* Library initialization goes here */

        /* Install fork handlers for the library */
        ret_val = pthread_atfork(lib_prepare, lib_post, lib_post);
        check_error(ret_val, "pthread_atfork()");
}

void lib_prepare()
{
        int     ret_val;

        /* Acquire both mutex_A and mutex_B.*/
        ret_val = pthread_mutex_lock(&mutex_A);
        check_error(ret_val, "lib_prepare() mutex_A");

        ret_val = pthread_mutex_lock(&mutex_B);
        check_error(ret_val, "lib_prepare() mutex_B");
}

void lib_post()
{
        int     ret_val;

        /* Release both mutex_A and mutex_B */
        ret_val = pthread_mutex_unlock(&mutex_B);
        check_error(ret_val, "lib_post() mutex_B");

        ret_val = pthread_mutex_unlock(&mutex_A);
        check_error(ret_val, "lib_post() mutex_A");
}
```

Creating Specialized Thread Attributes

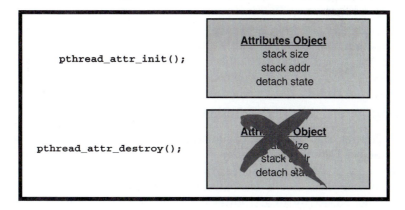

Fig. 4–10 An attributes object is associated with every thread. It is created prior to creating a thread and should be destroyed after the thread has been created.

Overview

One of the parameters to `pthread_create()` is a thread attributes object. The new thread is created according to the attributes specified in the thread attributes object. If this parameter is **NULL**, the new thread is created with the system's default attributes.

Thread attributes objects allow an application to create specialized threads. For example, one group of threads may need extremely large stacks, while another group may need high priority realtime scheduling behavior. These attributes can be set and passed to `pthread_create()` to create specialized threads.

Initializing Thread Attributes Objects

An attributes object must be initialized before its attributes can be accessed. To initialize a thread attributes object, use the function:

```
int pthread_attr_init(
    pthread_attr_t     *attr
);
```

This function initializes the thread attributes object *attr*. After initialization is complete, all attributes in *attr* have the system's default values. If POSIX does not specify a default value for an attribute, portable applications should not rely on a particular system's default attribute value.

Once the attributes object has been initialized, the thread attributes may be changed to contain nondefault values. A single thread attributes object can be used to create multiple threads. If all threads in an application will posses the same attributes, only one thread attributes object is needed for all calls to `pthread_create()`.

After a thread has been created with a thread attributes object, the thread will not be affected if the attributes object changes. The thread attributes are, in effect, copied from the attributes object to the thread when the thread is created.

Destroying Thread Attributes Objects

After all threads needing the attributes object *attr* have been created, the attributes object is no longer needed. Therefore, from a resource conservation viewpoint, it is a good idea to destroy the attributes object. Destroying the attributes object does not affect threads that have been created with the attributes object. Destroy an attributes object by using the following function:

```
int pthread_attr_destroy(
        pthread_attr_t      *attr
);
```

Naturally, an application should not rely on the value of *attr* after *attr* has been destroyed; in fact, `pthread_attr_destroy()` may set *attr* to an invalid value. After an attributes object has been destroyed, it can later be reinitialized with `pthread_attr_init()`.

Note: `pthread_attr_t` is an opaque object; it is not guaranteed to be the same on all systems. It may be a data structure, a pointer, a descriptor similar to a file descriptor, or some other data type. Do not try to copy *attr* into another variable. Referring to copies of *attr* results in undefined behavior.

Thread Attributes

The following attributes are available for creating customized threads:

- `stacksize`: This attribute allows an application to specify a nondefault stack size for the new thread. POSIX.1c does not define a default value for this attribute. Each system will define its default thread stack size. This value may not be the same on all systems. The default stack size may not be large enough for all threads. Unlike single-threaded processes, thread stack sizes are fixed. Thread stacks do not grow dynamically.

- `stackaddr`: This attribute allows an application to allocate and manage its own thread stacks. Full responsibility of the stack allocation, management, and deallocation for the thread is placed on the application. POSIX.1c does not specify a default value for this attribute, although most implementations will treat **NULL** as the default value. If an application allocates a stack for the new thread, this attribute should be set to contain the base address of the stack. This stack must have a size of at least **PTHREAD_STACK_MIN** bytes. **Note:** if this attribute is used, the attributes object should be used to create only one thread. If multiple threads are created from this attributes object, the threads all share one stack and will make a mess out of the application!

- detachstate: This attribute allows an application to specify whether the created thread is detached or joinable. If the value of this attribute is set to **PTHREAD_CREATE_DETACHED**, any threads created with this attributes object will be detached and cannot be specified in calls to pthread_join() or pthread_detach(). If the value is **PTHREAD_CREATE_JOINABLE**, any threads created with this attributes object will be joinable. The default value of this attribute is **PTHREAD_CREATE_JOINABLE**.

The contentionscope, inheritsched, schedpolicy, and schedparam scheduling attributes are also available. These attributes and their associated interfaces will be discussed further in Chapter 6, *Thread Scheduling*.

Thread Stack Sizes

Each system defines a default value for thread stack sizes. The default value should be adequate for most multithreaded applications. On HP-UX, the default stack size is 64K. There are situations where a thread allocates large arrays as local (automatic) variables on the stack, calls recursive functions or make several levels of nested procedure calls. Any of these conditions may require the thread to have a stack size larger than the system default stack size. If a large number of threads that require small stacks are needed, the default stack size may consume too much memory in the process.

If the default stack size is not adequate for your needs, you must estimate your stack needs, add this to the value **PTHREAD_STACK_MIN**, and set the stacksize attribute accordingly for new threads. **PTHREAD_STACK_MIN** bytes is the amount of stack space needed by the system. Estimating required stack sizes can be a bit of a problem for programmers. To estimate the stack size, you need to include space for a stack frame, parameters, and the local variables for each nested function call. This can be tricky when a thread calls functions in a different module or functions in an external library. You will need to experiment until you find the proper stack size. Fortunately, most systems provide a red-zone guard page at the end of a stack to help detect stack overflow. If stack overflow occurs, the chosen stack size is too small. It's usually wise to allocate a stack that is a little larger than what you think the thread needs.

Most applications do not need to allocate their own thread stacks. By default, the system allocates a stack for each thread. However, some applications want complete control over the memory allocation in the process. In this situation, the application can allocate and manage its own thread stacks. Be aware, the system will not allocate red-zone guard pages when the application allocates thread

stacks. The responsibility for creating red-zone guard pages for application created stacks is placed on the application. On some hardware architectures, stacks
grow from high to low addresses, requiring red-zone guard pages at the bottom of
the stack. Others grow from low to high addresses, requiring red-zones at the top
of the stack. Consult your system's documentation to determine where to place
the red-zone page. Threads created with application-allocated stacks should be
created with a detachstate of **PTHREAD_CREATE_JOINABLE** so that the stack
can be properly reclaimed by the application on thread termination.

Setting/Getting Thread Attributes

The stacksize, stackaddr and detachstate attributes can be retrieved from
or set in the thread attributes object with the functions described below. The *attr*
parameter represents a thread attributes object that must have been previously
initialized with pthread_attr_init(). The second parameter contains either
the attribute value being set or a pointer to where the retrieved attribute value
is returned (depending on whether it is a set or a get function).

```
int pthread_attr_getstacksize(
      pthread_attr_t      *attr,
      size_t              *stacksize
);

int pthread_attr_setstacksize(
      pthread_attr_t      *attr,
      size_t              stacksize
);

int pthread_attr_getstackaddr(
      pthread_attr_t      *attr,
      void                **stackaddr
);

int pthread_attr_setstackaddr(
      pthread_attr_t      *attr,
      void                *stackaddr
);

int pthread_attr_getdetachstate(
      pthread_attr_t      *attr,
      int                 *detachstate
);

int pthread_attr_setdetachstate(
      pthread_attr_t      *attr,
      int                 detachstate
);
```

Example

The following code initializes a thread attributes object, retrieves the default stack size, and, if less than four pages, increases the stack size. The thread to execute the function `thread1_func()` is created, and the thread attributes object is destroyed. Remember, once a thread has been created, it's safe to destroy the thread attributes object. A thread attributes object is needed only to create a thread, not while the thread is running.

```
#include <pthread.h>
#include <unistd.h>

extern void fatal_error(int err_num, char *function);
extern void thread1_func();

#define      check_error(return_val, msg) {                    \
                 if (return_val != 0)                          \
                       fatal_error(return_val, msg); \
             }
main()
{
    pthread_t       tid;
    pthread_attr_t  attr;
    size_t          stacksize;
    int             ret_val, pagesize;

    /* Create the attr object */
    ret_val = pthread_attr_init(&attr);
    check_error(ret_val, "pthread_attr_init()");

    /* Set the stacksize to (default stacksize * 4) */
    ret_val = pthread_attr_getstacksize(&attr, &stacksize);
    check_error(ret_val, "pthread_attr_getstacksize()");

    pagesize = (int) sysconf(_SC_PAGESIZE);
    if (stacksize < (pagesize * 4)) {
          stacksize = pagesize * 4;
          ret_val = pthread_attr_setstacksize(&attr, stacksize);
          check_error(ret_val, "pthread_attr_setstacksize()");
    }

    /* Create a new thread to execute thread1_func() */
    ret_val = pthread_create(&tid, &attr,
                            (void *(*)())thread1_func,
                            (void *)NULL);
    check_error(ret_val, "pthread_create()");

    /* It's safe to destroy the attr object now */
    ret_val = pthread_attr_destroy(&attr);
    check_error(ret_val, "pthread_attr_dest()");

    /* Rest of the program goes here */
    ...
}
```

Handling Thread Management Errors

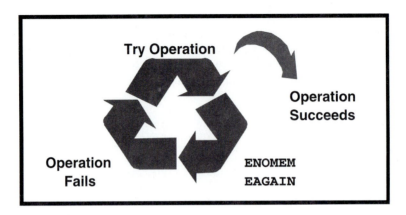

Fig. 4–11 For robustness, some operations should *try again* if certain errors are returned. For example, when creating a thread, the system may be out of memory only temporarily.

All examples presented so far check for errors from all thread management functions. If an error occurred, it was treated as a fatal error, and the application terminates. This behavior may not be appropriate for all possible error return values. Many applications need to attempt to recover from errors, rather than giving up immediately.

As an example, the pthread_create() function can return the error **EAGAIN** because the system lacks the resources to create a new thread or because the application has already created the maximum number of threads. If this error occurs, the application may want to pass the work onto an existing thread or to try again until the thread create function succeeds. Treating this error (and possibly other errors) as fatal does not provide for a very robust application, especially if the application executes on a busy system.

If the error **ESRCH** is returned by pthread_join(), the application may not want to terminate. This error is returned for any of three conditions; (1) the target thread has already been joined; (2) the target thread is a detached thread; or (3) the target thread does not exist. Most applications should be able to recover from this error, especially if they are not interested in the target thread's exit status.

These are just two cases where errors returned by thread management functions need not be treated as fatal. Examine all possible error returns for the functions your application uses and make your application resilient when they occur. If your application runs on more than one vendor's system, check each system's documentation for additional error return values. Some systems may provide additional error return values beyond what POSIX.1c specifies.

Summary

This chapter has explained the basic thread management functions. These functions allow an application programmer to create, terminate, and synchronize threads. We also explored specialized attributes that are available for creating threads with specific characteristics.

Here is a summary of what we have discussed:

- Many Thread Model functions have Process Model analogs. For example, pthread_create() creates a new thread, whereas fork() creates a new process. pthread_join() is similar to wait(). pthread_exit() is similar to exit(). Some Pthread functions have no Process Model analog, such as pthread_detach() and pthread_once().

- The pthread_create() function is used to create a new thread. In a multithreaded process, all threads except for the initial thread are created using this function. pthread_create() has four parameters: a *thread ID*, thread *attr*ibutes, *start_routine()*, and an *arg*ument.

- The pthread_join() function allows the calling thread to wait on the termination of a target thread. The calling thread is suspended until the target thread exits. After the target thread exits, the calling thread will resume execution and may optionally obtain the exit status of the target thread. In addition, the resources consumed by the target thread are released back to the system.

- The pthread_detach() function allows the resources of a thread to be released upon its termination. A thread that is detached cannot be joined. The caller does not wait for the target thread to terminate.

- The pthread_exit() function terminates the execution of the calling thread. This routine may be called explicitly by the thread or implicitly when *start_routine()* terminates. However, when the last thread (usually the main thread) in a process terminates, an implicit call to exit() is made if it is not explicitly called. This allows the system to clean up the host process.

- The pthread_self() function in the Thread Model is similar to the getpid() function in the Process Model. It allows a thread to find its own thread ID.

- Thread IDs are not necessarily kept in a simple variable type such as short or long. Therefore, where needed in application programming, it is necessary to have a function that can reliably compare the thread IDs of two threads. The pthread_equal() function compares the IDs of two threads. It returns a nonzero value for equal thread IDs and a zero value for unequal thread IDs.

- The `pthread_once()` function guarantees that an initialization function will be called only one time.

- Each thread has an attributes object associated with it that describes such characteristics such as stack size, detach state, scheduling policy, and scheduling priority. These attributes are given to the thread at thread creation time. Thread creation attributes "live" in an attributes object. In general, the attributes from one attributes object may be shared among any number of threads. When all of the threads using a particular attributes object have been created, it is a good idea to destroy the attributes object to conserve process resources. To initialize an attributes object, use the function `pthread_attr_init()`. If you do not explicitly create an attributes object for a thread, a default attributes object will be assigned by the system. Use the `pthread_attr_destroy()` function to destroy an attributes object.

- The function `pthread_atfork()` allows an application to ensure that process resources such as mutexes are not locked in the child process (which would cause deadlock for the child).

- When a function returns an error, depending on the error, it may be appropriate for the function to be called again. For example, when using the function `pthread_create()`, there may not be enough memory to create a new thread. For robustness, rather than allowing the application to fail, this function could be called again after releasing some system resources that are consuming memory.

Exercises

1. Describe the parameters to the `pthread_create()` function by naming them and by providing at least one characteristic for each. If you are going to create multithreaded applications with maximum portability in mind, what idea(s) might you have with respect to thread creation?

2. Describe a program where you could make use of the `pthread_join()` function (how or why is this function used?). What kind of thread is not joinable?

3. Describe how we might simulate the functionality of the `pthread_detach()` function in the Process Model (using processes). Describe two attributes of a detached thread.

4. Describe what happens when a thread in a multithreaded application calls `exit()`. How can the initial thread terminate without terminating the entire process?

5. Describe a program where the `pthread_self()` function could be used.

6. Describe a program where the `pthread_equal()` function could be used. Why do we need the `pthread_equal()` function?

7. Describe a program where the `pthread_once()` function could be used. Why do we need this function?

8. When is a fork handler necessary? Why?

9. What is the purpose of thread attributes? How long is a thread attributes object needed? Why are thread attributes destroyed? Under what circumstance(s) should a thread attributes object not be used in the creation of multiple threads?

10. When is it appropriate to try again after an error has been returned from a function call?

11. In Chapter 1, Exercise #11, you wrote a single-threaded copy program. Convert this program into a multithreaded program. Use two threads.

CHAPTER 5

Thread Synchronization

The programmer assumes more responsibility when programming with threads. Thread operations must occur in the correct order, access to shared objects must be coordinated, and all threads must work together to achieve the desired result. Several mechanisms are available to coordinate, or synchronize, threads within a program. This chapter explains how to use these mechanisms.

Topics Covered...

- Thread Synchronization
- Mutexes
- Mutex Attributes
- Initializing and Destroying Mutexes
- Locking and Unlocking Mutexes
- Example: Mutexes and Spinlocks
- Condition Variables
- Condition Variable Attributes
- Initializing and Destroying Condition Variables
- Waiting on a Condition
- Signaling a Condition
- Example: Condition Variables and Barriers
- Semaphores
- Initializing and Destroying Semaphores
- Locking and Unlocking Semaphores
- Handling Synchronization Errors
- Memory Models and Synchronization

Thread Synchronization

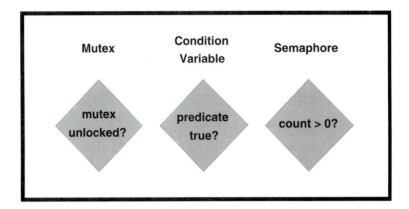

Fig. 5–1 The following primitives are tools for thread synchronization: mutexes, condition variables, and semaphores.

In the previous chapter we explored one type of thread synchronization: waiting for a thread to terminate. This was accomplished with the `pthread_join()` function. If a thread's return value is not needed and synchronizing with the thread upon termination is not needed, the `pthread_detach()` function should be called instead of `pthread_join()`.

This limited synchronization support is not sufficient for multithreaded applications. Threads need to synchronize access to shared resources and data structures. Threads may also need to rendezvous with other threads at a specific point.

Two primitives are available for synchronization between threads: mutexes and condition variables. These primitives can be used for both data protection and communication between threads within a process. They can also be used for synchronizing threads in multiple processes. Most other synchronization facilities can be built using these primitives.

Additionally, the POSIX.1b semaphores have been modified for use by threads within multithreaded processes. Like mutexes, semaphores may also be used to synchronize threads in multiple processes.

Mutexes, condition variables, and semaphores are not the only synchronization methods in existence. Other facilities include spinlocks, read-write locks and barriers. This chapter concentrates on the primitives provided by the POSIX.1c standard. Examples are provided that show how to build spinlocks and barriers using the POSIX.1c synchronization primitives. Read-write locks are described in Chapter 10, *Thread Extensions*.

Mutexes

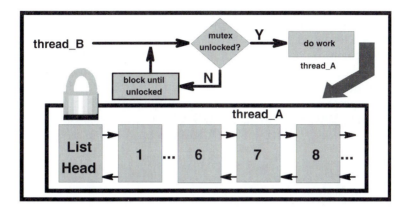

Fig. 5–2 A *mutex* is a *mutual exclusion* object that is used to synchronize access to a shared object. An example of a shared object is global data. When a thread acquires a mutex for a particular shared object, other threads that wish to access that object will block until the mutex is freed.

Why do we need to synchronize threads? As an example, consider a module that maintains a linked list of data structures. To maintain this list, several functions are provided: `list_add()`, `list_delete()`, and `list_lookup()`. A global variable, `list_head`, contains a pointer to the head of the list. Each data structure on the list contains forward and backward pointers to the next and previous entries on the list. The list is sorted numerically by an ID in each data structure.

This appears to be a pretty simple module. Let's explore what can happen in a multithreaded application. Suppose thread *A* is in the middle of a list delete operation for structure ID number 7. To do this, thread *A* must walk the list starting with `list_head`. When thread A finds the desired structure, it removes the structure from the list. Removing a structure from the list involves disconnecting the forward and backward pointers and connecting the previous list structure to the next list structure.

This is pretty simple and straightforward. Now let's have thread *B* perform a lookup operation on structure ID number 13. Thread *B* walks the list, starting with `list_head`, looking for a structure with an ID of 13. When it finds the desired structure, a pointer to the structure is returned. Simple, right?

What happens if thread *B* is doing the lookup at the same time that thread *A* is performing the delete operations? Maybe nothing, maybe disaster. When both operations are occurring simultaneously, we have what is called a *race condition*.

What's the race condition in the example? Thread *A* is in the middle of disconnecting the list pointers for structure ID number 7. Thread *B* is walking the list looking for ID number 13. Thread *B* could be looking at structure ID number 7 while the list manipulation is occurring. Thread B will decide that this structure isn't the requested structure and go to the next structure on the list via the forward pointer. However, thread A just disconnected this structure from the list. What does the forward pointer really point to? This field could be valid, it could be garbage, or it could have been set to **NULL**. In any case, we have an operation that has been compromised by the race condition.

Every shared data variable or shared resource (e.g., the linked list in the example) should be protected by some form of synchronization. A mutex is commonly used for synchronization between threads within a process. As we've just seen, without synchronization, extremely bad things can happen in a multithreaded application.

Definition of a Mutex

What is a mutex? A mutex (*mutual exclusion*) is an object that allows multiple threads to synchronize access to shared resources. A mutex has two states: locked and unlocked. Once a mutex has been locked by a thread, other threads attempting to lock the mutex will block until they can lock the mutex. When the locking thread unlocks (releases) the mutex, one of the threads blocked on the mutex will acquire it.

Using Mutexes

How can a mutex be used to remove the race condition in the previous example? The list module would have one mutex allocated to it. This mutex will protect the forward and backward pointers of all structures in the list. Before walking the list, a thread must acquire the mutex. Once an operation (i.e., add, delete, or lookup) has completed, the mutex is unlocked, allowing another thread to acquire the mutex and perform an operation.

In the example, thread A would have acquired the mutex first. This mutex would be held until the pointer manipulation for structure ID number 7 was completed. Once complete, the list is in a consistent state, and the mutex is released. Thread B will now acquire the mutex and can safely traverse the list of structures. No one will be adding or deleting structures during this time as thread B "owns" the mutex.

You, as the programmer, must decide how to properly and effectively make use of mutexes to provide synchronization within an application. This can be the hardest and most frustrating part of parallel programming. A poor synchronization strategy can lead to performance problems and obscure race conditions. These race conditions can be extremely hard to debug. Later in this book we'll discuss some different synchronization strategies to help get you started. In the meantime, let's take a look at the mutex interfaces provided by POSIX.1c.

Mutex Attributes

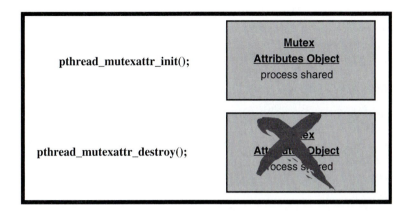

pthread_mutexattr_init();

Mutex Attributes Object
process shared

pthread_mutexattr_destroy();

Mutex Attributes Object
process shared

Fig. 5–3 Attributes objects are used to define the specific characteristics of threads, mutexes, and condition variables. For example, by default, a mutex can be used only by threads within the calling process. However, you can configure a mutex attributes object to allow threads from other processes to use the associated mutex or mutexes. To conserve process and system memory resources, destroy unneeded attributes objects immediately.

Overview

As with thread creation, mutexes also have an attributes object that can be used to specify certain characteristics for a mutex. The mutex attributes object is passed to the mutex initialization function to specify a desired type of mutex. Mutex attributes are optional. A default mutex will be created if specialized attributes are not specified.

Initializing Mutex Attributes Objects

An attributes object must be initialized before its attributes can be accessed. To initialize a mutex attributes object, use the function:

```
int pthread_mutexattr_init(
    pthread_mutexattr_t      *attr
);
```

This function initializes the mutex attributes object *attr*. After initialization is complete, all attributes in *attr* have the system's default values. If POSIX does not specify a default value for an attribute, portable applications should not rely on a particular system's default attribute value.

Once the attributes object has been initialized, the mutex attributes may be changed to contain nondefault values. A single mutex attributes object can be used to initialize multiple mutexes. If all the mutexes in an application are going to possess the same attributes, only one mutex attributes object is needed for all mutexes.

After a mutex has been initialized with an attributes object, the attributes for the mutex cannot be changed.

Destroying Mutex Attributes Objects

After all mutexes needing the attributes object *attr* have been initialized, the attributes object is no longer needed. Therefore, from a resource conservation viewpoint, it is a good idea to destroy the attributes object. Destroying the attributes object does not affect mutexes that have been initialized with the attributes object. Destroy an attributes object by using the following function:

```
int pthread_mutexattr_destroy(
    pthread_mutexattr_t                 *attr
);
```

Naturally, an application should not rely on the value of *attr* after *attr* has been destroyed. In fact, `pthread_mutexattr_destroy()` may set *attr* to an invalid value. After an attributes object has been destroyed, it can later be reinitialized with `pthread_mutexattr_init()`.

Note: `pthread_mutexattr_t` is an opaque object; it is not guaranteed to be the same on all systems. It may be a data structure, a pointer, a descriptor similar to a file descriptor, or some other data type. Do not copy *attr* into another variable. Referring to copies of *attr* results in undefined behavior.

Mutex Attributes

Only one attribute has been defined by POSIX.1c for creating customized mutexes:

- `process-shared`: This attribute allows an application to specify whether a mutex is to be used by threads only within the process or shared by threads in multiple processes. If the value **PTHREAD_PROCESS_PRIVATE** is specified for this attribute, the mutex will be used only by threads within the calling process (this is the default value). If the value of this attribute is set to **PTHREAD_PROCESS_SHARED**, the mutex is intended to be used by threads in multiple processes. It is the application's responsibility to allocate the mutex in memory that is shared between these multiple processes.

Note: If an application's mutexes are not going to be shared by multiple processes, do not use the **PTHREAD_PROCESS_SHARED** option. The performance of mutexes created with the **PTHREAD_PROCESS_PRIVATE** option will generally be faster on most systems.

If a process terminates while one of its threads has a process shared mutex acquired, the mutex is never released. This will cause deadlock in other processes using the mutex. If process shared mutexes are used, always release any locked mutexes before calling exit().

As you will see later in this book (Chapter 10, *Thread Extensions*), there are additional non-POSIX attributes that may also be used for creating customized mutexes. These attributes allow an application to specify fast, recursive, and debug mutexes. In this chapter, only the "strict" POSIX.1c mutexes are discussed.

Setting/Getting Mutex Attributes

The process-shared attribute can be retrieved from or set in the mutex attributes object with the functions described below. The *attr* parameter represents the mutex attributes object that must have been previously initialized with pthread_mutexattr_init(). The second parameter contains either the attribute value being set or a pointer to where the retrieved attribute value is returned (depending on whether it is a set or a get function).

```
int pthread_mutexattr_getpshared(
    pthread_mutexattr_t      *attr,
    int                      *pshared
);

int pthread_mutexattr_setpshared(
    pthread_mutexattr_t      *attr,
    int                      pshared
);
```

Example

The following code fragment shows how to allocate and initialize a mutex that is shared with other processes. A mutex attributes object is initialized with the process-shared attribute set to *shared*. The mutex must be allocated in shared memory that all processes needing the mutex can access. Once allocated, the mutex is initialized and the attributes object destroyed. Remember, only one thread should initialize the mutex. All other threads can use the mutex once it has been initialized.

```
pthread_mutex_t      *mtx;    /* global process shared mutex */

#define MTX_SIZE     sizeof(pthread_mutex_t)
#define KEY          8254

extern void fatal_error(int err_num, char *func);

#define     check_error(return_val, msg) {                 \
                if (return_val != 0)                       \
                        fatal_error(return_val, msg);  \
            }

main()
{
        pthread_mutexattr_t      mtx_attr;
        int                      ret_val;
        key_t                    shmid;

        /* Initialize the mutex attributes */
        ret_val = pthread_mutexattr_init(&mtx_attr);
        check_error(ret_val, "mutexattr_init failed");

        /* Set pshared to process shared */
        ret_val = pthread_mutexattr_setpshared(&mtx_attr,
                                        PTHREAD_PROCESS_SHARED);
        check_error(ret_val, "mutexattr_setpshared failed");

        /* Allocate the mutex in shared memory */
        shmid = shmget(KEY, MTX_SIZE, 0666|IPC_CREAT);
        if (shmid == -1) {
                perror("shmget():");
                exit(-1);
        }

        mtx = (pthread_mutex_t *) shmat(shmid, (char *)0, 0);
        if ((int)mtx == -1) {
                perror("shmat():");
                exit(-1);
        }

        /* Initialize the mutex and destroy the attributes */
        ret_val = pthread_mutex_init(mtx, &mtx_attr);
        check_error(ret_val, "mutex_init failed");

        ret_val = pthread_mutexattr_destroy(&mtx_attr);
        check_error(ret_val, "mutexattr_destroy failed");

        /* Rest of application code here */
        ...
}
```

Initializing and Destroying Mutexes

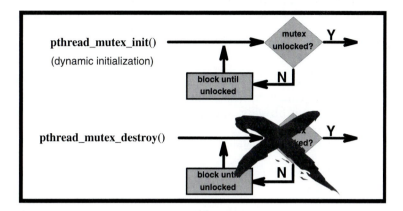

Fig. 5–4 Mutexes may be created statically or dynamically. If nondefault attributes are required, use dynamic initialization. To conserve process and system memory resources, destroy mutexes when they are no longer needed.

Overview

Each mutex in an application must be initialized before it can be used. An application has two choices for mutex initialization: static initialization or dynamic initialization. If a mutex is statically allocated [e.g., it was not allocated via `malloc()`], either method can be used. If the mutex is dynamically allocated, the dynamic initialization method must be used.

Initializing Mutexes

To statically initialize a mutex with default mutex attributes, use the macro:

```
pthread_mutex_t mutex = PTHREAD_MUTEX_INITIALIZER;
```

To dynamically initialize a mutex (possibly with nondefault mutex attributes), use the function:

```
int pthread_mutex_init(
    pthread_mutex_t        *mutex,
    pthread_mutexattr_t    *attr
);
```

The `pthread_mutex_init()` function will initialize *mutex* with the mutex attributes specified in *attr*. If *attr* is **NULL**, the mutex is initialized with the default mutex attributes. After a mutex has been initialized, the mutex is in the unlocked state and ready for use.

A default mutex may be statically allocated and initialized with the macro **PTHREAD_MUTEX_INITIALIZER**. The mutex is initialized with the system default mutex attribute values. If the default mutex attributes are not acceptable, the application should dynamically initialize the mutex with the appropriate attributes.

A mutex should be initialized only once. Initializing a mutex multiple times may result in incorrect program behavior. Some systems return an error if an application tries to initialize an already initialized mutex; others may not. Some systems may not return an error if a locked mutex is reinitialized (this can have disastrous results on an application).

Destroying Mutexes

Once an application is finished with a mutex, the mutex should be destroyed as the system may have allocated resources for the mutex. These resources should be released when the mutex is no longer needed.

To destroy a mutex, use the function:

```
int pthread_mutex_destroy(
     pthread_mutex_t          *mutex
);
```

Naturally, an application should not rely on the value of *mutex* after *mutex* has been destroyed; in fact, `pthread_mutex_destroy()` may set *mutex* to an invalid value. However, after this mutex has been destroyed, it can later be reinitialized with `pthread_mutex_init()`.

A locked mutex should never be destroyed. Some systems detect this and return an error. Others may allow the destruction to proceed and the application to eventually "fall on its face."

Mutexes and Undefined Behavior

Why is there so much "undefined" behavior with mutexes? POSIX.1c wanted to leave as much room as possible for implementations to optimize mutex performance at the expense of reduced error checking. Mutexes reduce the amount of parallelism and increase overhead within an application. Consequently, mutex operations need to be as fast as possible so that the reduction in parallelism is for the shortest time possible. Many systems optimize for performance by having fewer error checks. For maximum portability, initialize a mutex only once and destroy a mutex only when it is in the unlocked state.

Example

The following code fragment shows how to initialize and destroy mutexes. Three different mutexes are allocated. The first mutex has an attributes object and is dynamically initialized. The second mutex is dynamically initialized with default attributes. The third mutex is statically initialized with default attributes.

```
pthread_mutex_t      *mtx1;    /* global process shared mutex */
pthread_mutex_t      mtx2;
pthread_mutex_t      mtx3 = PTHREAD_MUTEX_INITIALIZER;

extern void          fatal_error(int err_num, char *func);

#define    check_error(return_val, msg) {                    \
              if (return_val != 0)                           \
                    fatal_error(return_val, msg); \
           }

main()
{
       pthread_mutexattr_t      mtx_attr1;
       pthread_t                tid1;
       pthread_t                tid2;
       int                      ret_val;
       extern void              start_routine();

       /*
        * Initialize the attributes for mtx1
        */
       ret_val = pthread_mutexattr_init(&mtx_attr1);
       check_error(ret_val, "mutexattr_init failed");

       /*
        * mtx1 is shared between multiple processes
        */
       ret_val = pthread_mutexattr_setpshared(&mtx_attr1,
                                 PTHREAD_PROCESS_SHARED);
       check_error(ret_val, "mutexattr_setpshared failed");

       /*
        * Allocate mtx1 in shared memory
        */
       ...

       /*
        * Initialize mtx1, then destroy the attributes
        */
       ret_val = pthread_mutex_init(mtx1, &mtx_attr1);
       check_error(ret_val, "mutex_init 1 failed");
```

```
ret_val = pthread_mutexattr_destroy(&mtx_attr1);
check_error(ret_val, "mutexattr_destroy failed");

/*
 * Initialize mtx2 with default attributes.
 * mtx3 has already been statically initialized.
 */
ret_val = pthread_mutex_init(&mtx2,
                             (pthread_mutexattr_t *)NULL);
check_error(ret_val, "mutex_init 2 failed");

/*
 * Create two threads to do the work
 */
ret_val = pthread_create(&tid1, (pthread_attr_t *)NULL,
                         (void *(*)())start_routine, NULL);
check_error(ret_val, "pthread_create 1 failed");

ret_val = pthread_create(&tid2, (pthread_attr_t *)NULL,
                         (void *(*)())start_routine, NULL);
check_error(ret_val, "pthread_create 2 failed");

/*
 * Wait for the threads to finish
 */
ret_val = pthread_join(tid1, (void **)NULL);
check_error(ret_val, "pthread_join: tid1");

ret_val = pthread_join(tid2, (void **)NULL);
check_error(ret_val, "pthread_join: tid2");

/*
 * Destroy the mutexes
 */
ret_val = pthread_mutex_destroy(mtx1);
check_error(ret_val, "mutex_destroy mtx1");

ret_val = pthread_mutex_destroy(&mtx2);
check_error(ret_val, "mutex_destroy mtx2");

ret_val = pthread_mutex_destroy(&mtx3);
check_error(ret_val, "mutex_destroy mtx3");

/* Release shared memory from mtx1 and exit */
...

exit(0);
}
```

Locking and Unlocking Mutexes

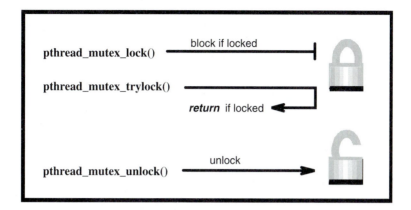

Fig. 5–5 To lock a mutex, blocking if it is not available, use `pthread_mutex_lock()`. Use `pthread_mutex_trylock()` to attempt to lock a mutex and return an error if it is not available. To unlock a mutex, use `pthread_mutex_unlock()`. Always check the return value to determine success or failure.

Overview

There are three functions for locking and unlocking mutexes. Each function takes one parameter, a pointer to the mutex to be locked or unlocked. Since mutex operations can fail, make sure to check for error return values.

The functions used to lock and unlock mutexes are not async-signal safe (see Chapter 7, *Threads and Signals*). They should not be called from a signal handler.

As stated earlier, several extensions have been made to mutexes. These extensions will be discussed later in Chapter 10, *Thread Extensions*. This section discusses only the POSIX.1c locking and unlocking interfaces.

Locking a Mutex

To lock a mutex, use the function:

```
int pthread_mutex_lock(
      pthread_mutex_t              *mutex
);
```

This function will not return until *mutex* has been locked by the calling thread. The mutex remains locked until it is unlocked by the calling thread. If *mutex* is currently locked, the calling thread blocks until the mutex becomes available.

Note: Do not attempt to relock a mutex that is currently locked by the calling thread. This action results in undefined behavior. Some systems return an error of **EDEADLK**, but others may allow the application to deadlock. POSIX.1c does not require systems to support the concept of mutex ownership.

If a signal is delivered to a thread waiting for a mutex, the signal is handled by the waiting thread. After the signal has been handled, the thread will continue waiting for the mutex. An error of **EINTR** is not returned.

Conditionally Locking a Mutex

To lock a mutex conditionally, use the function:

```
int pthread_mutex_trylock(
    pthread_mutex_t          *mutex
);
```

This function attempts to lock *mutex*. If *mutex* cannot be locked, the function returns immediately with an error of **EBUSY**. The calling thread does not block and wait for the mutex. Otherwise, the mutex is locked by the calling thread. Conditional locking is useful when implementing a spinning lock or when attempting to acquire locks out of order (see Chapter 12, *Writing Thread-Safe Code*).

Unlocking a Mutex

To unlock a mutex, use the function:

```
int pthread_mutex_unlock(
    pthread_mutex_t          *mutex
);
```

This function unlocks *mutex*. If threads are currently blocked waiting for *mutex*, the scheduling policies of the waiting threads determine which thread acquires *mutex* next. For threads with realtime scheduling policies, the highest priority, longest waiting thread acquires the lock next.

Do not attempt to unlock a mutex that is locked by a different thread. Some systems return an error, others may simply unlock the mutex. In either case, this action can lead to incorrect application behavior as another thread assumes it has the mutex locked. Do not attempt to unlock an unlocked mutex.

Performance

The mutex locking strategy a programmer chooses can make or break the application when it comes to performance. A poor synchronization strategy can lead to excessive serialization of a parallel application. Later in this book we'll discuss some different synchronization strategies to help you maximize the performance of your application.

Example

```
pthread_mutex_t          mtx = PTHREAD_MUTEX_INITIALIZER;
struct list              *list_head;

void
list_add(struct list *add)
{
      struct list  *curr, *prev;
      int          ret_val;
      extern void  fatal_error(int err_num, char *func);

      if ((ret_val = pthread_mutex_lock(&mtx)) != 0)
            fatal_error(ret_val, "thr1 mutex lock failed");

      if (list_head == (struct list *)NULL) {
          add->next = (struct list *)NULL;
          add->prev = (struct list *)NULL;
          list_head = add;
      } else {
          /* Find insertion point for add */
          for (curr=list_head; curr!=NULL; curr=curr->next) {
                  if (curr->list_id > add->list_id)
                          break;
                  prev = curr;
          }

          if (curr == list_head) {
                  /* new head of list */
                  add->prev = (struct list *)NULL;
                  add->next = list_head;
                  list_head->prev = add;
                  list_head = add;
          } else if (curr == (struct list *)NULL) {
                  /* new tail of the list */
                  add->next = (struct list *)NULL;
                  add->prev = prev;
                  prev->next = add;
          } else {
                  /* somewhere in between */
                  add->next = curr;
                  add->prev = prev;
                  prev->next = add;
                  curr->prev = add;
          }
      }

      if ((ret_val = pthread_mutex_unlock(&mtx)) != 0)
            fatal_error(ret_val, "thr1 mutex unlock failed");
}
```

Example: Mutexes and Spinlocks

When a mutex is not immediately acquired by `pthread_mutex_lock()`, the locking thread must block and wait for the mutex to become available. How a thread blocks is undefined by POSIX.1c. A system has three ways to implement mutex blocking: a) block immediately; b) spin in a loop attempting to acquire the mutex and block if it is not acquired after a certain number of iterations; or c) spin in a loop forever until the mutex is locked.

Single-processor systems usually cause the thread to block immediately if the mutex is not available. Because the system has only one processor, spinning on the mutex only wastes CPU cycles as the thread owning the mutex cannot execute to release the mutex. Multiprocessor systems may use any of the three options, although most systems will cause the locking thread to either block immediately or perform a limited spin.

There are situations when you may want to have spin-only or limited spin mutexes. If your locks are held only for short durations, a spin-only mutex may increase performance as threads do not context switch when waiting for a lock. Be careful when using spin-only mutexes; the potential for wasting CPU cycles is extremely high. Before considering spinning mutexes, you need to ensure that the thread that owns the mutex is running on another processor and will release the mutex in a short amount of time. If this cannot be controlled, spinning for the mutex will waste time and hurt application performance. Consider the case where a thread owns a mutex and is blocked in a system call. A spin-only mutex will cause other threads attempting to acquire the mutex to spin until they can acquire the mutex. Since the owning thread is blocked in a system call, potentially for a long time, the other threads waste CPU cycles until the owning thread unblocks and releases the mutex. This scenario is further complicated if the thread owning the mutex is context switched by the scheduler.

Limited-spin mutexes are a better choice if you cannot guarantee that the thread owning the mutex is currently running. The thread attempting to lock the mutex will spin for a short duration, attempting to lock the mutex on each iteration. If the mutex cannot be acquired after this time, the thread blocks, waiting for the mutex. You'll need to tune the amount of time spent spinning, but studies have shown that allowing the thread to spin for 50-100% of the time it takes to block or context switch a thread is most effective. If the mutex is not acquired in a short time (e.g., the owner may be blocked), the thread blocks and doesn't waste many CPU cycles.

The following example shows an implementation of spinlocks based on mutexes. There are two versions of the spinlock function: one for spin-only spinlocks and one for limited-spin spinlocks. You'll need to tune the **MAX_SPIN** define and set the `single_processor` variable accordingly on your system (see Chapter 10, *Thread Extensions*).

```
#define my_spinunlock        pthread_mutex_unlock
#define my_spintrylock       pthread_mutex_trylock
#define MAX_SPIN             ...
int                          single_processor;

my_spinlock_init(pthread_mutex_t *mtx)
{
      int     ret_val;

      ret_val = pthread_mutex_init(mtx, (pthread_mutexattr_t *)NULL);

      /* Set single_processor to 0 or 1 */
      single_processor = ...
      return(ret_val);
}


/* Spin-only spinlock */
int
my_spinlock_spin(pthread_mutex_t *mtx)
{
      int     ret_val;

      if (single_processor)
            return(pthread_mutex_lock(mtx));

      /* Spin forever while the mutex is locked */
      while ((ret_val = pthread_mutex_trylock(mtx)) == EBUSY)
                  ;
      return(ret_val);
}


/* Limited-spin spinlock */
int
my_spinlock_limited(pthread_mutex_t *mtx)
{
      int     ret_val;
      int     count = MAX_SPIN;

      if (single_processor)
            return(pthread_mutex_lock(mtx));

      /* Spin for a limited time or until we acquire the mutex */
      while ((--count) &&
            ((ret_val = pthread_mutex_trylock(mtx)) == EBUSY))
                  ;
      if ((count == 0) && (ret_val == EBUSY))
            return(pthread_mutex_lock(mtx));

      return(ret_val);
}
```

Condition Variables

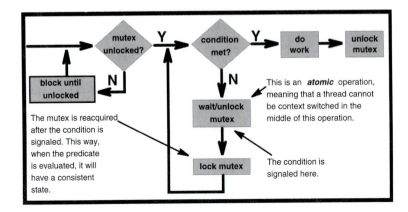

Fig. 5–6 Condition variables allow threads to wait on the occurrence of some event. Another thread in the application will cause this event to take place. When this happens, one or more of the waiting threads will be signaled and subsequently awakened.

Condition variables are a useful synchronization mechanism when a thread needs to wait for an event to happen (e.g., wait until there is more work available). If the event has not occurred (e.g., work is not available), a thread will **wait** on a condition variable. At some time in the future, another thread will cause the event to occur (i.e., create work) and **signal** the condition variable to wake-up one or more threads waiting on the condition variable.

Condition variables contain three components: the condition variable, an associated mutex, and a predicate. You, as the programmer, must define all three components. The predicate is the condition (or value) that a thread will check to determine whether it should wait for an event. The associated mutex is the lock that protects the predicate. A thread using condition variables to wait for an event will do something similar to the following pseudocode:

```
lock associated mutex
while (predicate is not true)
     wait on condition variable
do work
unlock associated mutex
```

The check for the predicate not being true is analogous to asking "is there more work on the queue for me to process?" An important point about condition variables is that the associated mutex is automatically released by the system when a thread waits on a condition. The releasing of the mutex is done atomically with respect to waiting on the condition. When the condition is signaled, the associated mutex is reacquired before the thread returns from the condition wait. This behavior allows other threads to acquire the mutex to either: (a) wait on the condition, or (b) update the predicate and signal the condition.

Notice that the predicate evaluation and condition wait is done in a loop. This is because condition variables are subject to *spurious wakeups*. A spurious wakeup occurs when a thread blocked on a condition variable is awakened when it should actually continue to wait. Looping on the predicate prevents a thread from proceeding when the thread is incorrectly unblocked due to a spurious wakeup. A thread receiving a normal UNIX signal while waiting on a condition may return from the wait due to a spurious wakeup.

The previous pseudocode showed how a thread waits on a condition variable. The following pseudocode shows how a thread signals a condition variable:

```
lock associated mutex
set predicate to true
signal condition variable (wake-up one or all)
unlock associated mutex
```

As noted earlier, the associated mutex protects the predicate of a condition variable. Consequently, the mutex should be held while changing the state of the predicate (or in the previous analogy, while work is added to the work queue).

The mutex is not required to be held when the condition is signaled, however, an application may experience lost wake-ups if the mutex is not held. To see why, consider the case where thread A has acquired the mutex and determined that the predicate is not true. Before thread A waits on the condition variable, thread B issues a signal on the condition. Because thread A has not actually waited on the condition variable yet, the signal from thread B is lost. Because of the potential for lost wake-ups, always hold the associated mutex while signaling a condition variable.

Condition variables provide a mechanism to stop threads from proceeding if an event has not occurred. Another method to accomplish this can severely waste machine time: Have the thread spin and poll until it is allowed to continue. For example:

```
lock associated mutex
while (predicate is not true) {
        unlock associated mutex
        give up the processor or sleep
        lock associated mutex
}
do work
unlock associated mutex
```

Let's take a closer look at how to use condition variables now.

Condition Variable Attributes

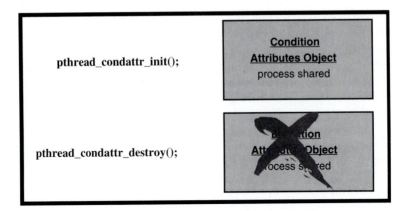

Fig. 5–7 Condition variables (like mutexes and threads) have attributes objects that define their specific characteristics. By default, a condition variable can be used only by a thread within the calling process. The condition variable's attributes object can be configured to allow threads from other processes to use the associated condition variable.

Overview

As with mutexes, condition variables also have an attributes object that can be used to specify certain attributes for a condition variable. The condition variable attributes object is passed to the condition variable initialization function to specify a desired type of condition variable. Condition variable attributes are optional. A default condition variable will be created if specialized attributes are not specified. The condition variable attribute functions are identical to the mutex attribute functions, except that they operate on condition variable attributes.

Initializing Condition Variable Attribute Objects

An attributes object must be initialized before its attributes can be accessed. To initialize a condition variable attributes object, use the function:

```
int pthread_condattr_init(
    pthread_condattr_t      *attr
);
```

This function initializes the condition variable attributes object *attr*. After initialization is complete, all attributes in *attr* have the system default values. If POSIX does not specify a default value for an attribute, portable applications should not rely on a particular system's default attribute value.

Once the attributes object has been initialized, the condition variable attributes may be changed to nondefault values. A single condition variable attributes object can be used to initialize multiple condition variables. If all condition variables in an application are going to have the same attributes, only one condition variable attributes object is needed.

After a condition variable has been initialized with an attributes object [through `pthread_cond_init()`], the attributes for the condition variable cannot be changed.

Destroying Condition Variable Attribute Objects

After all of the condition variables using the attributes object *attr* have been initialized, the attributes object may be destroyed. Destroying the attributes object will not affect condition variables that have been initialized with the attributes object. Destroy an attributes object by using the following function:

```
int pthread_condattr_destroy(
    pthread_condattr_t              *attr
);
```

Naturally, an application should not rely on the value of *attr* after *attr* has been destroyed. In fact, `pthread_condattr_destroy()` may set *attr* to an invalid value. After an attributes object has been destroyed, it can later be reinitialized with `pthread_condattr_init()`.

Note: `pthread_condattr_t` is an opaque object. It is not guaranteed to be the same on all systems. It may be a data structure, a pointer, a descriptor similar to a file descriptor, or some other data type. Do not copy *attr* into another variable. Referring to copies of *attr* results in undefined behavior.

Condition Variable Attributes

Only one attribute has been defined by POSIX.1c for creating customized condition variables. This attribute and its valid values are identical to the POSIX.1c `process-shared` mutex attribute:

- `process-shared`: A value of **PTHREAD_PROCESS_PRIVATE** indicates that the condition variable will be used only by threads within the calling process (the default value). A value of **PTHREAD_PROCESS_SHARED** indicates that the condition variable will be used by threads in multiple processes. If a condition variable is created with the **PTHREAD_PROCESS_SHARED** attribute, the condition variable's associated mutex should also be created with the **PTHREAD_PROCESS_SHARED** attribute.

If an application's condition variables are not going to be shared by multiple processes, do not use the **PTHREAD_PROCESS_SHARED** option. Condition variables created with the **PTHREAD_PROCESS_PRIVATE** option will generally perform faster on most systems.

There are currently no attribute extensions for condition variables. However, this may change in the future.

Setting/Getting Condition Variable Attributes

The `process-shared` attribute can be retrieved from or set in the condition variable attributes object with the functions described below. The *attr* parameter represents the condition variable attributes object that must have been previously initialized with `pthread_condattr_init()`. The second parameter contains either the attribute value being set or a pointer to where the retrieved attribute value is returned (depending on whether it is a set or a get function).

```
int pthread_condattr_getpshared(
    pthread_condattr_t      *attr,
    int                     *pshared
);

int pthread_condattr_setpshared(
    pthread_condattr_t      *attr,
    int                     pshared
);
```

Example

The following code fragment shows how to allocate and initialize a condition variable that is shared with other processes. A condition variable attributes object is initialized with the `process-shared` attribute set to *shared*. The condition variable must be allocated in shared memory that all processes needing the condition variable can access. Once allocated, the condition variable is initialized and the attributes object destroyed. Remember, only one thread should initialize the condition variable. All other threads can use the condition variable once it has been initialized.

```
pthread_mutex_t      *mtx;    /* global process shared mutex */
pthread_cond_t       *cond;   /* global process shared condvar */

extern void fatal_error(int err_num, char *func);

#define     check_error(return_val, msg) {                  \
                if (return_val != 0)                        \
                        fatal_error(return_val, msg);       \
            }

main()
{
        pthread_mutexattr_t     mtx_attr;
        pthread_condattr_t      cond_attr;
        int                     ret_val;

        /* Initialize the attributes */

        ret_val = pthread_mutexattr_init(&mtx_attr);
        check_error(ret_val, "mutexattr_init failed");
        ret_val = pthread_condattr_init(&cond_attr);
        check_error(ret_val, "condattr_init failed");

        /* Set pshared to process shared */

        ret_val = pthread_mutexattr_setpshared(&mtx_attr,
                                    PTHREAD_PROCESS_SHARED);
        check_error(ret_val, "mutexattr_setpshared failed");
        ret_val = pthread_condattr_setpshared(&cond_attr,
                                    PTHREAD_PROCESS_SHARED);
        check_error(ret_val, "condattr_setpshared failed");

        /* Allocate the objects in shared memory */
        ...

        /* Initialize the objects and destroy the attributes */

        ret_val = pthread_mutex_init(mtx, &mtx_attr);
        check_error(ret_val, "mutex_init failed");
        ret_val = pthread_cond_init(cond, &cond_attr);
        check_error(ret_val, "cond_init failed");

        ret_val = pthread_mutexattr_destroy(&mtx_attr);
        check_error(ret_val, "mutexattr_destroy failed");
        ret_val = pthread_condattr_destroy(&cond_attr);
        check_error(ret_val, "condattr_destroy failed");

        /* Rest of application code here */
        ...
}
```

Initializing and Destroying Condition Variables

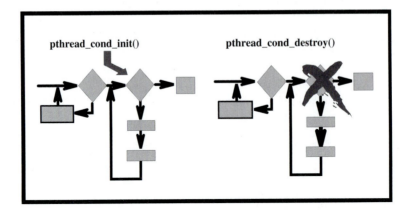

Fig. 5–8 Condition variables may be created statically or dynamically. If nondefault attributes are required, dynamic initialization must be used. To conserve process (and system) memory resources, destroy condition variables that are no longer needed.

Overview

Each condition variable in an application must be initialized before it can be used. As with mutexes, an application has two choices for condition variable initialization: static initialization or dynamic initialization. If a condition variable is statically allocated [e.g., it was not allocated via malloc()], either method can be used. If the condition variable is dynamically allocated, the dynamic initialization method must be used. Condition variable initialization is identical to mutex initialization.

Initializing Condition Variables

To statically initialize a condition variable with default attributes, use:

```
pthread_cond_t cond = PTHREAD_COND_INITIALIZER;
```

To dynamically initialize a condition variable, use the function:

```
int pthread_cond_init(
        pthread_cond_t          *cond,
        pthread_condattr_t      *attr
);
```

The pthread_cond_init() function will initialize *cond* with the condition variable attributes specified in *attr*. If *attr* is **NULL**, the condition variable is initialized with the default condition variable attributes.

A condition variable may be statically allocated and initialized with the macro **PTHREAD_COND_INITIALIZER**. The condition variable will be initialized with the system default condition variable attribute values. If the default condition variable attributes are not acceptable, the application should dynamically initialize the condition variable with the appropriate attributes.

Like mutexes, a condition variable should be initialized only once. Initializing a condition variable multiple times may result in incorrect program behavior. Some systems return an error if an application tries to initialize an already initialized condition variable; others may not. Some systems may not return an error if a busy condition variable is reinitialized (this can have disastrous results on an application).

Destroying Condition Variables

A condition variable should be destroyed once an application is finished using it as the system may have allocated resources for the condition variable. These resources should be released when the condition variable is no longer needed.

To destroy a condition variable, use the function:

```
int pthread_cond_destroy(
     pthread_cond_t          *cond
);
```

Do not rely upon the value of *cond* after *cond* has been destroyed. As with other Pthread destroy functions, pthread_cond_destroy() may set *cond* to an invalid value. After a condition variable has been destroyed, it can later be reinitialized with pthread_cond_init().

A busy condition variable (one that threads are currently waiting on) should never be destroyed. Some systems detect this and return an error. Others may allow the destruction to proceed and the application to eventually "fall on its face." How does an application know that a condition variable is not being used? If the application doesn't know, it shouldn't destroy the condition variable. An application that destroys a condition variable (or mutex) without knowing whether threads are still using it will experience random failures.

Waiting on a Condition

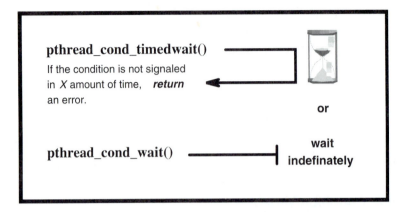

Fig. 5–9 A thread can wait on a condition variable for a specified amount of time or indefinitely. Use `pthread_cond_timedwait()` to wait for a specific amount of time. To to wait indefinitely, use `pthread_cond_wait()`. These functions release the associated mutex before blocking, then require the mutex before returning. This allows access to the mutex by other threads.

Overview

Condition variables have a predicate and an associated mutex. A thread should lock the associated mutex and check the predicate. If the predicate is not true, the thread waits on the condition variable. If the predicate is true, the thread continues its execution.

Condition variables are useful in the boss/worker thread model. In this model, one thread is the *boss*. The boss thread is responsible for distributing work to all the *worker* threads. When a worker thread finishes a task, it checks the work queue for more work to process. If work is not available, the thread must wait for work. To accomplish this, the thread locks the work queue mutex and tries to remove a task from the work queue. If the thread removes a task, it releases the mutex and processes the requested work. If there is no work available, the thread waits on the work queue condition variable. When waiting on the condition variable, the mutex is automatically released by the system. This allows the boss thread to lock the mutex and place tasks on the work queue. The mutex will automatically be reacquired for the worker thread before returning from the condition wait. When the thread is signaled, it rechecks the work queue.

Condition Wait

Two functions are available for a thread to wait on a condition variable. One performs a normal wait operation; the other performs a timed wait operation:

```
int pthread_cond_wait(
    pthread_cond_t          *cond,
    pthread_mutex_t         *mutex
);

int pthread_cond_timedwait(
    pthread_cond_t          *cond,
    pthread_mutex_t         *mutex,
    struct timespec         *abstime
);
```

These functions cause the caller to wait until the condition variable *cond* is signaled. The condition variable's associated *mutex* should be locked before either of these functions are called. Don't rely on an error being returned if you forget to lock the mutex before calling these functions. Many systems allow the condition wait to continue, leaving a race condition between the condition wait and condition signal. This may cause a wake-up signal to be lost.

Both functions atomically release *mutex* and block the caller on the condition variable *cond*. Because this is an atomic operation, it is not possible for another thread to acquire *mutex* and issue a condition signal (e.g., a wake-up) before the caller has blocked on *cond*.

Before returning from either of these functions, *mutex* is automatically reacquired by the calling thread. The mutex is reacquired regardless of whether the function returns success or an error. The order in which unblocked threads acquire *mutex* is dependent upon each thread's scheduling policy and priority.

The programmer must ensure that only one mutex is associated with a condition variable. These functions will not return an error if multiple threads wait on the same condition variable with different mutexes. Unpredictable behavior results in this situation (usually lost wake-ups).

The pthread_cond_timedwait() function is identical to the function pthread_cond_wait(), except that the calling thread specifies a time at which to terminate the condition wait. If a condition signal has not occurred before the specified time, *abstime*, has passed, this function returns to the caller with an error of **ETIMEDOUT**. Keep in mind that *abstime* is the absolute time at which the thread quits waiting, not the time interval that the thread will wait.

Absolute Timeouts

Most programmers think about timeouts in terms of how long to wait, rather than what time the wait should expire. The following code fragment shows how to construct an absolute time value for pthread_cond_timedwait() when a timeout interval is desired. The secs and nano_secs variables represent the desired timeout interval:

```
#define NANO_SECS_PER_SECOND        1000000000
clock_gettime(CLOCK_REALTIME, &abstime);
abstime.tv_sec  += secs;
abstime.tv_nsec += nano_secs;
if (abstime.tv_nsec >= NANO_SECS_PER_SECOND) {
        abstime.tv_nsec -= NANO_SECS_PER_SECOND;
        abstime.tv_sec += 1;
}
```

Spurious Wakeups and Condition Wait

Condition waits are subject to spurious wakeups. When returning from a condition wait, do not assume the predicate is true. A spurious wakeup may occur, causing these functions to return a successful value. An example of a spurious wakeup occurs when a signal (like **SIGUSR1** or **SIGALRM**) is delivered to a thread blocked in pthread_cond_wait(). After handling the signal, the thread may return a successful value from pthread_cond_wait(), even though the condition signal has not yet occurred.

On multiprocessor systems, waking up exactly one thread when a condition is signaled can be an expensive operation. To allow systems to provide fast condition variable operations, POSIX.1c allows more than one thread to return from a condition wait when the condition is signaled. This relaxed specification may occasionally cause a spurious wakeup to occur on multiprocessor systems (on most systems this should be a rare occurrence). Because of the potential for spurious wakeups, the condition predicate should **always** be re-evaluated after returning from pthread_cond_wait() or pthread_cond_timedwait(), regardless of the return value.

Condition Wait and Thread Cancellation

We talked briefly about thread cancellation in Chapter 4, *Basic Thread Management*. We'll get into the details about thread cancellation later in this book. However, you need to be aware that thread cancellation has some impact on condition variable operations.

Both pthread_cond_wait() and pthread_cond_timedwait() are cancellation points. If a thread is canceled while blocked in one of these functions, the condition variable's associated *mutex* is reacquired by the canceled thread before the cancellation cleanup handlers are called. This behavior has been implemented so that the cancellation cleanup handlers execute in the same state as the critical code that was canceled (i.e., the canceled thread held the associated mutex lock).

Because of this behavior, an application using condition variables and the cancellation facilities should always install cancellation cleanup handlers to unlock the condition variable's associated mutex (see Chapter 8, *Thread Cancellation*).

Example

The following code fragment shows how a consumer thread waits on a condition variable:

```
extern pthread_mutex_t    job_lock;
extern pthread_cond_t     job_cv;
extern int                job_count;

extern struct job_req     *job_dequeue();
extern void               process_job(struct job_req *ptr);
extern void               fatal_error(int err, char *f);

void consumer_thread()
{
        struct job_req        *curr_job;
        int                   ret_val;

        for ( ; ; ) {
            /* Acquire the condvar's associated mutex lock */
            if ((ret_val = pthread_mutex_lock(&job_lock)) != 0)
                    fatal_error(ret_val, "mtx_lock failed");

            /*
             * Wait for a job request. This test is the condition
             * variable predicate. If no jobs are available,
             * wait for one. The condition wait releases the
             * mutex so that another thread can place jobs on the
             * queue. The mutex is reacquired before returning
             * from the condition wait.
             */
            while (job_count == 0)
                    pthread_cond_wait(&job_cv, &job_lock);

            /*
             * Get the job_request
             */
            curr_job = job_dequeue();
            if (curr_job != (struct job_req *)NULL)
                    job_count--;

            /*
             * Release the associated mutex
             */
            if ((ret_val = pthread_mutex_unlock(&job_lock)) != 0)
                    fatal_error(ret_val, "mtx_unlock failed");

            /*
             * Process the job request
             */
            if (curr_job != (struct job_req *)NULL)
                    process_job(curr_job);
        }
}
```

Signaling a Condition

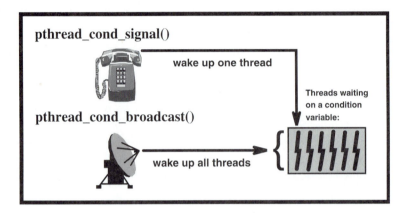

Fig. 5–10 When a condition occurs, you may wake-up at least one thread that is waiting on the event by using `pthread_cond_signal()`. To wake-up all threads waiting on the event, use `pthread_cond_broadcast()`.

Overview

We've seen how a thread waits on a condition variable. Now let's explore how to signal a condition variable to wake-up any waiting threads.

In the boss/worker model that we discussed in the previous section, we left the example with one thread waiting on a condition variable. When the worker thread waited on the condition variable, the associated mutex was automatically released. Before returning from the condition wait, the mutex is automatically reacquired by the waiting thread. This behavior allows the boss thread to lock the mutex and place work on the queue while the worker thread is waiting. After returning from the condition wait, the worker thread rechecks the work queue (the condition predicate) for work to be processed. If work is available, the thread dequeues a task from the queue and processes the work. Otherwise, the thread waits on the condition variable for the work queue again.

At some point, the boss thread will have work for the worker thread(s). When work is available, the boss first acquires the mutex that protects the work queue. Remember, in this example, the state of the work queue (empty or not empty) is the condition predicate. The mutex protecting the predicate is also the same mutex that is associated with the condition variable. Once the mutex has been acquired, the boss thread places the work on the work queue. The boss then sends a condition signal to the condition variable for the work queue. This condition signal will wake-up one of the threads waiting on the work queue's condition variable. After the condition signal completes, the boss thread releases the mutex.

It is important to note that the boss thread holds the associated mutex during the condition signal. This is not required. However, for predictable scheduling behavior, it is highly advisable. The boss thread should lock the associated mutex before updating the predicate; otherwise, condition signals may be lost and several race conditions introduced.

Signaling Condition Variables

Two functions are available for a thread to signal a condition variable. One performs a normal signal operation (signal one thread); the other performs a broadcast operation (signal all threads).

```
int pthread_cond_signal(
     pthread_cond_t          *cond
);

int pthread_cond_broadcast(
     pthread_cond_t          *cond
);
```

The `pthread_cond_signal()` function signals at least one thread waiting on *cond*. In general, only one thread will return from its condition wait. It's possible for more than one thread to return due to a spurious wakeup. This function should be used when only one thread needs to be signaled.

The `pthread_cond_broadcast()` function signals all threads waiting on *cond*. The scheduling policies and priorities of the unblocked threads determine the order in which these threads return from their condition wait. This function is used when the caller needs all threads to wake-up and continue executing. The unblocked threads do not simultaneously return from their condition wait as each thread must acquire the condition variable's associated mutex before returning. When an unblocked thread acquires the mutex in order to return from the condition wait depends on when the previous unblocked thread releases the mutex.

If no threads are blocked on the condition variable *cond*, these functions have no effect. Condition signals do not *pend* if there are no waiters. Because of the potential for spurious wakeups, all threads waiting on a condition variable should **always** re-evaluate the condition predicate in a loop around the condition wait.

Condition Signals and Performance

To issue a condition wake-up, applications generally use code similar to the following code fragment:

```
pthread_mutex_lock(&mtx);
predicate = TRUE;
pthread_cond_signal(&cond);
pthread_mutex_unlock(&mtx);
```

When a waiting thread is awakened, it reacquires the condition variable's associated mutex. In the above example, the awakened thread may immediately block on the mutex as the thread issuing the signal has the mutex acquired. A waiting thread could context switch two times before it completes a condition wait. Whether the waiting thread blocks on the mutex depends on how quickly it is scheduled to run after being signaled.

The condition predicate *must* be protected by the condition variable's associated mutex. However, the condition signal does not require the mutex to be held. Consider the following code:

```
pthread_mutex_lock(&mtx);
predicate = TRUE;
pthread_mutex_unlock(&mtx);
pthread_cond_signal(&cond);
```

This code also provides correct behavior with respect to condition variables. It does not cause lost wake-ups or race conditions as the condition predicate is protected by the mutex. When a waiting thread has been awakened, it will be able to immediately reacquire the mutex without blocking. This behavior provides for faster application performance as only one context switch is required to perform a condition wait. If a condition variable is signaled when the mutex is not held, the condition signal must be sent *after* the condition predicate has been updated. Failure to follow this rule results in lost wake-ups.

Multiple Condition Variables

When using static data structures, it is sometimes necessary to use two condition variables. Consider the producer/consumer situation where work is stored in a fixed size queue. The maximum outstanding number of jobs that can be in the queue at any time is 50. When the boss thread places work on the queue, it signals the workers. Occasionally the boss cannot place work on the queue because the queue is full. In this situation, another condition variable is required.

With static data structures, two condition variables are needed. You are now familiar with the first one: worker threads wait on a condition variable when the queue is empty. The second condition variable is waited on by the boss thread. When the queue is full, the boss thread waits on the new condition variable. As threads remove work from the queue, they signal the new condition variable. The boss thread is then allowed to place more work on the queue.

When designing an application, evaluate the costs associated with static (fixed-size) data structures and dynamic (linked list) data structures. Static structures require the overhead of two condition variables but ensure that the producer doesn't overrun the consumers. Dynamic data structures require only a single condition variable, but allows the producer to overrun the consumers. The dynamic method makes for a more robust application as the load on the application increases and decreases. Sometimes a dynamic method with producer limits provides the best approach, requiring two condition variables.

Example

The following code fragment shows how a producer thread signals a condition variable. In the example, the producer thread first creates a new job request. The associated mutex lock is acquired, and the job_cv condition variable is signaled. The mutex lock is released, and the process starts over again until there are no more job requests to produce.

```
extern pthread_mutex_t    job_lock;
extern pthread_cond_t     job_cv;
extern struct job_req     *create_job();
extern void               job_enqueue(struct job_req *ptr);
extern void               fatal_error(int err, char *f);
extern int                job_count;

void producer_thread()
{
        struct job_req    *curr_job;
        int               ret_val;

        for ( ; ; ) {
            /* Create the next job request */
            if ((curr_job = create_job()) == NULL)
                    pthread_exit((void *)NULL);

            /* Acquire the associated mutex lock */
            if ((ret_val = pthread_mutex_lock(&job_lock)) != 0)
                    fatal_error(ret_val, "mtx_lock failed");

            /* Put the job_request on the queue */
            job_enqueue(curr_job);
            job_count++;

            /* Signal the condvar to wake-up one thread */
            if ((ret_val = pthread_cond_signal(&job_cv)) != 0)
                    fatal_error(ret_val, "cond_signal failed");

            /* Release the associated mutex */
            if ((ret_val = pthread_mutex_unlock(&job_lock)) != 0)
                    fatal_error(ret_val, "mtx_unlock failed");
        }
}
```

Example: Condition Variables and Barriers

In the previous sections, we have shown how condition variables can be useful in producer-consumer problems. In this section, we show how these synchronization primitives can be used to implement thread barriers.

Some applications need to synchronize the execution of several threads. At some point, a thread may need to halt and wait until other threads have reached the same point. Once all threads have reached that point, they should all proceed simultaneously. This behavior can be achieved through the use of a barrier synchronization primitive.

A barrier consists of two basic functions: (a) an initialization function to establish the number of threads that synchronize at the barrier and (b) a wait function that blocks the caller until the specified number of threads have blocked at the barrier.

The example in this section shows how a barrier can be implemented using condition variables. The functions needed to provide barrier synchronization primitives are `barrier_init()` and `barrier_wait()`.

The `barrier_init()` function is called to initialize a barrier with the number of threads needing to synchronize at the barrier. A barrier should not be used until it is initialized. The function in the example is dynamic in that it allows the application to change the number of threads needing to synchronize on the barrier.

This function returns zero if it successfully initializes a barrier, **EBUSY** if the barrier cannot be reinitialized because it is being used, or a positive error number if a failure occurs using the barrier's mutex or condition variable.

The `barrier_wait()` function is called when a thread must wait for other threads to reach the same barrier. It causes the caller to block on the barrier's condition variable until the specified number of threads reach the barrier. This function returns zero when a thread is allowed to continue execution, and an error number if an error occurs while waiting on the barrier. Once the specified number of threads reach the barrier, the threads return, and the barrier resets for subsequent use.

When a thread enters the `barrier_wait()` function, it saves away the value of the barrier predicate. The thread is not allowed to return from this function until the barrier predicate value changes (performed by the last thread entering the barrier). This behavior allows the barrier to be used immediately after releasing threads, even if all threads have not yet returned from their barrier wait.

```
#include <pthread.h>
#include <errno.h>

/*
 * Barrier data structure.
 */
typedef struct barrier_struct {
        int             valid;          /* initialized barrier? */
        pthread_mutex_t mutex;          /* mutex variable */
        pthread_cond_t  cv;             /* condition variable */
        int             barrier_val;    /* # of threads to wait */
        int             blocked_threads; /* # of threads waiting */
        int             predicate;      /* condition predicate */
} barrier_t;

/* Mutex to protect barrier initialization */
pthread_mutex_t  barrier_init_mutex = PTHREAD_MUTEX_INITIALIZER;

#define BARRIER_VALID    546731



/* Barrier initialization */
int
barrier_init(barrier_t *b, int val)
{
     int    ret_val;

     /* Only allow one barrier init at a time to remove races. */
     ret_val = pthread_mutex_lock(&barrier_init_mutex);
     if (ret_val != 0)
            return(ret_val);

     /* Reinitializing the barrier count value? */
     if (b->valid == BARRIER_VALID) {
            /* Acquire the mutex for the barrier */

            ret_val = pthread_mutex_lock(&b->mutex);
            if (ret_val != 0) {
                   (void) pthread_mutex_unlock(&barrier_init_mutex);
                   return(ret_val);
            }

            /* If the barrier is currently busy, return an error. */
            if (b->blocked_threads != 0) {
                   (void) pthread_mutex_unlock(&b->mutex);
                   (void) pthread_mutex_unlock(&barrier_init_mutex);
                   return(EBUSY);
            }
```

```
                /* Reset the barrier count value and return. */
                b->barrier_val = val;
                ret_val = pthread_mutex_unlock(&b->mutex);
                if (ret_val != 0) {
                        (void) pthread_mutex_unlock(&barrier_init_mutex);
                        return(ret_val);
                }

        } else {
                /* Initializing a barrier from scratch. */
                ret_val = pthread_mutex_init(&b->mutex, NULL);
                if (ret_val != 0) {
                        (void) pthread_mutex_unlock(&barrier_init_mutex);
                        return(ret_val);
                }

                ret_val = pthread_cond_init(&b->cv, NULL);
                if (ret_val != 0) {
                        (void) pthread_mutex_unlock(&barrier_init_mutex);
                        return(ret_val);
                }

                b->barrier_val = val;
                b->blocked_threads = 0;
                b->predicate = 0;
                b->valid = BARRIER_VALID;
        }

        /* Release the lock and return. */
        ret_val = pthread_mutex_unlock(&barrier_init_mutex);
        if (ret_val != 0)
                return(ret_val);
        return(0);
}
```

```
/* Wait on a barrier */
int
barrier_wait(barrier_t *b)
{
     int    ret_val, predicate;

     /* Is this a valid barrier? */
     if (b->valid != BARRIER_VALID)
            return(EINVAL);

     /* Acquire the mutex for the barrier and condition variable. */
     ret_val = pthread_mutex_lock(&b->mutex);
     if (ret_val != 0)
            return(ret_val);

     /* Save away our predicate value for this wait operation */
     predicate = b->predicate;

     /* Increment blocked counter and perform barrier operation.*/
     b->blocked_threads++;
     if (b->blocked_threads == b->barrier_val) {
            /* Reset the barrier for its next use */
            b->predicate += 1;
            b->blocked_threads = 0;

            /* Last thread: wake-up all blocked threads. */
            ret_val = pthread_cond_broadcast(&b->cv);
            if (ret_val != 0) {
                    (void) pthread_mutex_unlock(&b->mutex);
                    return(ret_val);
            }
     } else {
            /* Wait until all threads have reached this point */
            while (b->predicate == predicate) {
                    ret_val = pthread_cond_wait(&b->cv, &b->mutex);
                    if ((ret_val != 0) && (ret_val != EINTR)) {
                            (void) pthread_mutex_unlock(&b->mutex);
                            return(ret_val);
                    }
            }
     }

     /* Release the mutex for the barrier and condition variable. */
     ret_val = pthread_mutex_unlock(&b->mutex);
     if (ret_val != 0)
            return(ret_val);

     return(0);
}
```

Semaphores

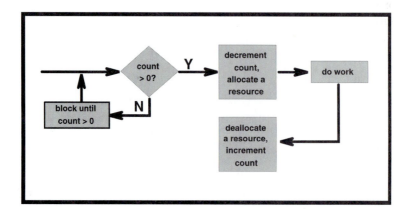

Fig. 5–11 A semaphore is similar to a mutex in that it can be used to synchronize access to an object. However, semaphores are more expensive. A *binary* semaphore is like a mutex. A *counting* semaphore can protect multiple objects. In addition, *named* and *unnamed* semaphores have unique characteristics. There is no *ownership* concept with semaphores.

Semaphores are not part of the POSIX.1c threads specification. They were introduced in POSIX.1b as a mechanism for synchronizing processes. Semaphores can also be used to synchronize threads within a process. Consequently, semaphores have value in multithreaded applications.

Semaphores are similar to mutexes. They provide synchronization between entities (processes or threads) that share resources. The difference is that one semaphore can regulate access to multiple resources. A semaphore is initialized with an integer count value equal to the number of resources available. When a thread needs access to one of the resources, it acquires the semaphore (by decrementing the count). If no resources are available (the count is zero), the thread blocks until the resource becomes available (the count is greater than zero). When a thread is finished with a resource, it releases the semaphore (by incrementing the count). If threads are blocked on the semaphore, one of the blocked threads is chosen to acquire the resource next.

Traditionally, semaphore operations have been known as *P* and *V* operations. For many people, this has been a source of confusion and complexity, making semaphores hard to use. The P and V operation names come from E. W. Dijkstra, the developer of semaphores as a programming synchronization model. The *P* stands for *prolagen*, which in Dutch translates to *"try to decrease."* The *V* stands for *verhogen*, which translates to *"increase."* Based on what you've seen about semaphores so far, you can see that a *P* operation is equivalent to acquiring the semaphore. The *V* operation is the same as releasing the semaphore.

The simplest form of a semaphore is a *binary* semaphore. A binary semaphore has a count value of one. A mutex is essentially a binary semaphore. A binary semaphore has two states, locked and unlocked (acquired or not acquired). All other semaphores are *counting* semaphores. These semaphores have a count value greater than one. Each time the semaphore is acquired, its value is decremented by one. Each time the semaphore is released, its value is incremented by one. There is no concept of a semaphore *owner*. In other words, thread A may acquire the semaphore, but thread B can release the semaphore.

How would an application make use of semaphores? Let's assume we have an application that contains ten threads. These threads need to download several files to different computers via modems. However, the computer has only four modems available for use by the application.

A semaphore is initialized with the number of available modems (four). Each thread that wishes to download a file must first acquire the semaphore (a P operation). If no modems are available, the thread blocks until the semaphore is available. Once the semaphore has been acquired, the thread can use one of the modems to download the file. When the thread is finished using the modem, it releases the semaphore (a V operation). Releasing the semaphore allows another thread to obtain the semaphore and thus gain access to one of the four modems.

Counting semaphores can be a very powerful synchronization method when an application needs to regulate access to several shared resources. However, a semaphore operation is usually much more expensive than a mutex operation. On most systems, a semaphore operation is performed by the kernel (i.e., a system call), whereas mutex operations are performed in user-space.

POSIX.1b has introduced two types of semaphores, *named* semaphores and *unnamed* semaphores.

A named semaphore is a semaphore that has a name associated with it (similar to a file name). Named semaphores support open, close, and unlink operations, similar to files. Named semaphores are most useful when synchronizing multiple processes. A process using named semaphores is not required to allocate the semaphore in memory shared with other processes using the semaphore.

Unnamed semaphores resemble mutexes. These semaphores possess initialize and destroy functions. If multiple processes wish to use unnamed semaphores, the semaphore must be allocated in shared memory. Multithreaded applications using semaphores to synchronize threads within the application should use unnamed semaphores.

In this section, our discussion is limited to the unnamed semaphores specified in POSIX.1b. If you are interested in named semaphores, we urge you to look at the POSIX.1b specification for complete details.

Initializing and Destroying Unnamed Semaphores

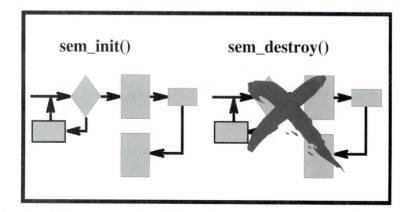

Fig. 5–12 To initialize an unnamed semaphore, use `sem_init()`. This routine allows you to specify who has access to the semaphore, as well as the number of resources requiring synchronized access. When a semaphore is no longer needed, destroy it with `sem_destroy()`.

Initializing an Unnamed Semaphore

Each semaphore in an application must be initialized before it can be used. A semaphore is initialized with a count value that is equal to the number of resources requiring regulated access.

To initialize an unnamed semaphore, use the function:

```
int sem_init(
        sem_t                          *sem,
        int                            pshared,
        unsigned int                   value
);
```

The `sem_init()` function initializes *sem* with *value*. *value* is the counting value that represents the number of resources requiring synchronized access via *sem*.

The *pshared* argument specifies who has access to this semaphore. A value of zero indicates the semaphore is used only by threads within the calling process. A nonzero value indicates that the semaphore is shared by threads in multiple processes. If the semaphore is shared by multiple processes, it is the application programmer's responsibility to allocate the semaphore in shared memory.

If a process terminates while one of its threads has a process shared semaphore acquired, the semaphore is never released. This will cause deadlock in other processes using the semaphore. If process shared semaphores are used, always release any locked semaphores before calling `exit()`.

Note: Do not copy *sem* into another variable. Referring to copies of *sem* results in undefined behavior in the semaphore operations.

Destroying an Unnamed Semaphore

When an application is finished using an unnamed semaphore, it should destroy the semaphore with the following function:

```
int sem_destroy(
        sem_t                           *sem
);
```

The `sem_destroy()` function will destroy the unnamed semaphore *sem*. Do not destroy a semaphore until all threads have finished using it. If threads are currently using or blocked on *sem* when it is destroyed, undefined behavior results. Some systems detect this and return an error of **EBUSY**. Others may allow the destruction to proceed and the application to eventually "fall on its face." How does an application know that a semaphore is not being used? If the application doesn't know, it shouldn't destroy the semaphore. An application that destroys a semaphore without knowing whether threads are still using it will experience random failures.

The semaphore *sem* can be reused later if it is properly reinitialized with the `sem_init()` function.

Error Return Values

All semaphore functions introduced by POSIX.1b use the old error reporting mechanism. These functions return 0 on success and -1 on error, with `errno` set to the appropriate error.

Example

The following code fragment shows how to initialize and destroy semaphores. In this example, one semaphore is initialized. An additional thread is created to execute `start_routine()`. When the application is ready to terminate, the semaphore is destroyed.

The semaphore is used only by threads within the process. If this semaphore were shared between multiple processes, the example would allocate *sem* in shared memory. Remember, only one thread should initialize *sem*.

```
sem_t       sem;

#define SEM_RESOURCES       2

main()
{
        pthread_t           tid1;
        int                 ret_val;
        extern void         start_routine();
        extern void         fatal_error(int err, char *f);

        /*
         * Initialize the semaphore. Note: errno can be set.
         * The semaphore should be initialized before any threads
         * are created so that we don't have threads accessing an
         * uninitialized semaphore.
         */
        if (sem_init(&sem, 0, SEM_RESOURCES) != 0) {
            perror("sem_init() failed");
            exit(-1);
        }

        /*
         * Create an additional thread to do work
         */
        ret_val = pthread_create(&tid1, (pthread_attr_t *)NULL,
                                (void *(*)())start_routine,
                                (void *)NULL);
        if (ret_val != 0)
             fatal_error(ret_val, "pthread_create 1 failed");

        /* We're a thread too... */
        start_routine();

        /* wait for thread to finish */
        if ((ret_val = pthread_join(tid1, (void **)NULL)) != 0)
             fatal_error(ret_val, "pthread_join: tid1");

        /*
         * Destroy the semaphore. Wait until all threads have
         * terminated before destroying the semaphore. We don't
         * want threads accessing a destroyed semaphore.
         */
        if (sem_destroy(&sem) != 0) {
            perror("sem_destroy() failed");
            exit(-1);
        }

        exit(0);
}
```

Locking and Unlocking Semaphores

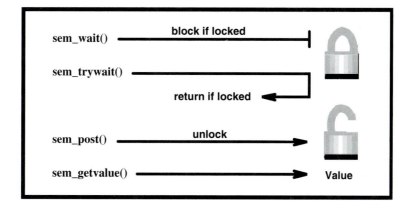

Fig. 5–13 To wait on a semaphore indefinitely, use sem_wait(). To attempt to lock a semaphore but continue executing if it is unavailable, use sem_trylock(). To unlock a semaphore, use sem_post(). To check the current value of a semaphore, use sem_getvalue().

Locking a Semaphore

To lock a semaphore, use the function:

```
int sem_wait(
      sem_t        *sem
);
```

The sem_wait() function does not return successfully until *sem* has been locked by the calling thread. If the current value of *sem* is greater than zero, the semaphore value is decremented by one, and the function returns immediately with the lock held. Otherwise, the calling thread blocks until it acquires the semaphore. The semaphore remains locked until sem_post() is called for *sem*. If this function is interrupted by a signal, it returns with an error and without having acquired the semaphore.

Unlike mutexes, this function returns **EINTR** if interrupted by a signal. The caller does not continue waiting for the semaphore after handling the signal.

Conditionally Locking a Semaphore

To conditionally lock a semaphore, use the function:

```
int sem_trywait(
      sem_t        *sem
);
```

This function attempts to lock *sem*. If the current value of *sem* is greater than zero, the semaphore value is decremented by one, and the function returns immediately with the lock held. If the semaphore value is not greater than zero, the calling thread will not block. Instead, the function returns -1 and sets `errno` to **EBUSY**.

Unlocking a Semaphore

To unlock a semaphore, use the function:

```
int sem_post(
    sem_t                    *sem
);
```

The `sem_post()` function unlocks *sem*. To perform an unlock operation, the semaphore value for *sem* is incremented by one. If threads are currently blocked waiting for *sem*, the scheduling policies of the waiting threads determine which thread acquires *sem* next. For threads with realtime scheduling policies, the highest priority, longest waiting thread acquires the semaphore next.

The `sem_post()` function is the only semaphore synchronization function that may be called from a signal handler.

Getting the Semaphore Value

To examine or read the current value of a semaphore, use the function:

```
int sem_getvalue(
    sem_t                    *sem,
    int                      *sem_value
);
```

This function returns the current value for *sem* in *sem_value*. Be careful, as this is the value of the semaphore at the time of the function call. This value may change [via the `sem_wait()` or `sem_post()` functions] any moment after the value is obtained.

If the semaphore is currently not available, either zero or a negative number is returned. If a negative number is returned, its absolute value is the number of threads blocked on *sem*.

Example

In the previous section's example, a semaphore was initialized and two threads called `start_routine()`. In this example, those threads obtain a file for downloading, acquire a semaphore for modem access, and download the file. After the file has been downloaded, the semaphore is released, allowing other threads access to the modems.

```
extern sem_t sem;
extern char  *get_download_file();
extern void  prepare_file(), download_file();

void
start_routine()
{
      char   *file;
      int    value;

      for ( ; ; ) {
            /*
             * Get the next file to download, return if no
             * more. Otherwise, prepare the file for
             * downloading.
             */
            file = get_download_file();
            if (file == (char *)NULL)
                  return;
            prepare_file(file);

            /*
             * Acquire a semaphore for modem access
             */
            (void) sem_getvalue(&sem, &value);
            printf("current sem value = %d\n", value);
            while (sem_wait(&sem) != 0) {
                  if (errno != EINTR) {
                        perror("sem_wait() failed\n");
                        exit(-1);
                  }
            }

            /*
             * Chose a modem and download the file
             */
            download_file(file);

            /*
             * Release the semaphore for modem access
             */
            if (sem_post(&sem) != 0) {
                  perror("sem_post() failed");
                  exit(-1);
            }
      }
}
```

Handling Synchronization Errors

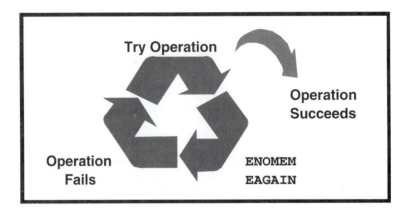

Fig. 5–14 Robust applications will allow some operations to *try again* if they fail initially.

All examples presented so far check for errors from all synchronization primitives. If an error occurred, it was treated as a fatal error, and the application terminates. This behavior may not be appropriate for all applications. Many applications need to attempt to recover from errors rather than giving up immediately.

As an example, the `pthread_mutex_init()` and `pthread_cond_init()` functions can return the errors **EAGAIN** and **ENOMEM** because the system lacks the resources or memory to initialize the mutex or condition variable. If these errors occur, the application may want to call the function in a loop until it succeeds or attempt to release memory or other system resources, so that it eventually succeeds. Treating all errors as fatal does not provide for a very robust application, especially if the application executes on a busy system.

Error checking of synchronization operations takes time and further reduces application parallelism. Do you really need to check for error returns when using mutex, condition variable, and semaphore objects? We can't recommend that you don't; however, there are a few things we can point out. Most of the POSIX.1c specified errors occur when an application uses an invalid object (e.g., it isn't initialized or it's been destroyed) or when the proper locking sequence hasn't been followed (e.g., trying to lock a mutex that the thread already owns or unlocking a mutex owned by another thread). If you can guarantee that your application behaves properly, it should never experience errors when using synchronization objects.

Should you choose to ignore errors, we urge you to at least check for errors when developing and debugging your application. These error checks can be performed under `#ifdef` **DEBUG** and turned off for the real application. Trying to debug a problem because a mutex lock operation failed, but the thread still executed the critical section of code, can be extremely difficult.

Memory Models and Synchronization

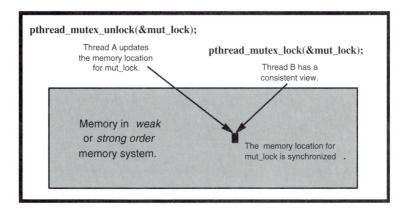

Fig. 5–15 For machines with *weakly ordered* memory operations, POSIX has identified several functions that synchronize memory with respect to threads. Synchronization primitives should be used when simultaneous reading and writing of the same memory location is possible.

Strong Memory Order

In older multiprocessor systems, memory is strictly multiplexed. A processor reads and writes memory in the order specified by the application code. This memory access is interleaved with the memory access by multiple processors. The memory appears to be accessed in a global order as it would be accessed on a single-processor system. The memory operations of these machines are *sequentially consistent* or *strongly ordered*.

Threads on a sequentially consistent multiprocessor can synchronize with ordinary memory instructions. Consider a thread that performs some work, then sets a global variable to indicate that the work has been completed:

```
Thread 1                    Thread 2
data_avail = 0;             if (data_avail) {
ptr = NULL;                     assert(ptr != NULL);
ptr = get_data();              ...
data_avail = 1;             }
```

Because memory accesses are sequentially consistent, thread 2 can assume that if `data_avail` is nonzero, `ptr` contains valid data.

Weak Memory Order

Modern multiprocessor systems do not guarantee that memory access is strongly ordered. The memory ordering requirements are relaxed to obtain greater performance. On these systems, when a processor stores values in location A and then location B, other processors reading from location B and then location A may see the new value in location B but the old value in location A. The memory operations of these machines are *weakly ordered*.

The previous example code does not work properly on a weakly ordered multiprocessor. It's possible for a thread to read `data_avail` and see a nonzero value while `ptr` is **NULL**, triggering the assertion. Proper synchronization can be achieved only by using special instructions that force an order on memory operations. Applications must use synchronization primitives to ensure that changes to a memory location are ordered with respect to reads or writes of the same memory location by other threads.

Synchronizing Memory

POSIX has identified several functions that synchronize memory with respect to other threads. When these functions are called, memory is synchronized so that future access to a memory location obtains the correct value. On weakly ordered multiprocessor systems, these functions use special instructions to force an order on memory operations. The following list contains the POSIX functions that synchronize memory with respect to other threads:

- `fork()`
- `pthread_create()`
- `pthread_join()`
- `pthread_mutex_lock()`
- `pthread_mutex_trylock()`
- `pthread_mutex_unlock()`
- `pthread_cond_broadcast()`
- `pthread_cond_signal()`
- `pthread_cond_timedwait()`
- `pthread_cond_wait()`
- `sem_post()`
- `sem_trywait()`
- `sem_wait()`
- `wait()`
- `waitpid()`

The following functions (described in Chapter 10, *Thread Extensions*) also synchronize memory with respect to other threads:

- `pthread_rwlock_rdlock()`
- `pthread_rwlock_tryrdlock()`
- `pthread_rwlock_trywrlock()`
- `pthread_rwlock_unlock()`
- `pthread_rwlock_wrlock()`

By using the above functions, an application can ensure that a memory location cannot be written by one thread while another thread is reading or writing to the same memory location. Because memory is synchronized by these functions, an application does not need to be concerned about whether it is running on a system with strong or weak memory ordering. The example shown earlier in this section behaves properly if the threads acquire a mutex before accessing the two global variables and release the mutex afterward.

Synchronizing Simple Data Types

Synchronization is required whenever a thread writes to a memory location that other threads could be simultaneously reading or writing. This requirement applies even if the thread is accessing a simple data type, such as an integer. On some machines, integers may not be aligned to the data bus width or be larger than the data bus width, requiring multiple memory cycles to read or write one memory location. If the application allows simultaneous access to memory locations, it's possible for a thread to access a memory location where some bits of the integer have the old value while other bits have the new value.

Some systems guarantee that a read or write of an integer completes as one atomic instruction in one memory cycle. Portable applications should not rely on this feature, but should rather use synchronization primitives to prevent simultaneous read and write access to a memory location.

The following example shows how simple data types, such as integers, should be protected by a mutex to prevent simultaneous access. The mutex will ensure that thread 1 atomically increments `num_threads` and that thread 2 does not obtain a value from `num_threads` that is a mix of the old value and new value:

Thread 1	Thread 2
`pthread_mutex_lock(&mtx);`	`pthread_mutex_lock(&mtx);`
`num_threads += 1;`	`curr_val = num_threads;`
`pthread_mutex_unlock(&mtx);`	`pthread_mutex_unlock(&mtx);`

Unless the system supports an atomic fetch and increment instruction, the statement `num_threads += 1;` is actually several instructions: (1) the contents of `num_threads` is fetched from memory, (2) `num_threads` is incremented by one, and 3) `num_threads` is written back to memory. The mutex will ensure that `num_threads` is incremented atomically with respect to access by other threads.

Cheating

There is one situation when an application does not need to use synchronization primitives when accessing global data: the data is read-only. If read-only data is statically initialized, synchronization is not needed by multiple threads. If data is dynamically initialized, synchronization is not needed if the data is initialized before the threads are created [the `pthread_create()` function synchronizes memory]. Remember, to prevent a race condition, one thread cannot write a memory location while another thread is reading or writing that memory location. Allowing multiple threads to simultaneously read a memory location is allowed and doesn't create a race condition.

Summary

This chapter has explained that, in a multithreaded application, the *programmer* has the responsibility to ensure that thread operations occur in the correct order, that access to shared data is coordinated, and that all threads work together to achieve the desired result. We focused primarily on three synchronization objects in our discussion: mutexes, condition variables, and semaphores.

- A *mutex* is a *mutual exclusion* object that is used to synchronize access to a shared object. An example of a shared object is global data. When a thread acquires a mutex for a particular shared object, other threads that wish to access that object block until they can lock the mutex.

- Attributes objects are used to define the specific characteristics of threads, mutexes, and condition variables. By default, a mutex can be used only by threads within the calling process. However, a mutex attributes object can be configured to allow threads from other processes to use the mutex. To conserve process and system resources, destroy unneeded attributes objects immediately.

- Mutexes may be initialized statically or dynamically. If nondefault attributes are required, use dynamic initialization. To conserve process and system resources, destroy mutexes when they are no longer needed.

- To lock a mutex, use `pthread_mutex_lock()`. To attempt to lock a mutex but return an error if it is not available, use `pthread_mutex_trylock()`. To unlock a mutex, use `pthread_mutex_unlock()`. Always check the return value to determine success or failure.

- Condition variables are used by threads to wait on the occurrence of an event. Another thread in the application causes the event to occur. When the event occurs, one or more of the waiting threads are signaled and allowed to continue.

- As mentioned earlier, condition variables (like mutexes and threads) have attributes objects that define their specific characteristics. By default, a condition variable can be used only by a thread within the calling process. However, the condition variable's attributes object can be configured to allow threads from other processes to use the condition variable.

- Condition variables may be statically or dynamically initialized. If nondefault attributes are required, dynamic initialization must be used. To conserve process and system resources, destroy condition variables that are no longer needed.

- A thread can wait on a condition variable indefinitely or until a specified time passes. Use `pthread_cond_timedwait()` to wait until a specific time. To wait indefinitely, use `pthread_cond_wait()`. These functions automatically release the associated mutex before blocking and automatically reacquire the mutex before returning. Releasing the mutex allows access to the predicate by other threads, including the one that will eventually change the predicate.

- When an event occurs, one thread that is waiting on the event is signaled by using `pthread_cond_signal()`. To signal all threads waiting on the event, use `pthread_cond_broadcast()`.

- A semaphore is similar to a mutex in that it can be used to synchronize access to an object. However, semaphore operations can be more expensive than mutex operations. A *binary* semaphore is similar to a mutex. A *counting* semaphore regulates access to multiple objects. *Named* and *unnamed* semaphores have unique characteristics. There is no *ownership* concept with semaphores.

- Use `sem_init()` to initialize a semaphore. The *pshared* argument specifies whether other processes access the semaphore. When a semaphore is no longer needed, destroy it with `sem_destroy()`.

- To wait on a semaphore indefinitely, use `sem_wait()`. To attempt to lock a semaphore but return an error if it is unavailable, use `sem_trywait()`. To unlock a semaphore, use `sem_post()`. To check the current value of a semaphore, use `sem_getvalue()`.

- Some operations may fail due to insufficient system resources. Perhaps memory is low or there are not enough processes. To provide a more robust application, some operations should *try again* or try for a limited number of times before failing.

- Older multiprocessor systems use a sequentially consistent or strongly ordered memory model. This model causes all memory operations to be ordered in the order they were executed in the application code. Newer multiprocessor systems use a weakly ordered memory model. This model does not ensure that memory operations are ordered in the same way they were ordered in the application. A multithreaded application should use functions that synchronize access to memory to ensure that threads obtain the correct values from memory locations. The synchronization primitives and thread/process creation/wait functions synchronize memory with respect to threads.

Exercises

1. Write a code segment that prevents the following race condition: The integer variable `val` is initialized to zero. Thread *A* increments int `val`. Thread *A* is context switched out, and thread *B* starts executing and increments `val`. Later, thread *A* executes and prints `val`; which is 2 instead of 1. Your code segment should guarantee that the expected `value` will always be printed.

2. Write a program that allows threads to wait until "event *X*" occurs. The signaled thread should print a message saying "Condition met. Processing...".

3. Write a program that starts processing a task when the seventh thread waits. All seven threads should be signaled to work on the task at once.

4. Write a code segment in which a semaphore manages two resources: `input_1` and `input_2`. Write a second code segment where a thread waits to acquire an input resource. However, before waiting, the thread should determine whether an input resource is available. What problem(s), if any, may arise from this strategy?

5. Write a code module that initializes a mutex. Make it robust. If there is not enough memory for the call to complete successfully, it should try again some reasonable number of times.

6. In a multithreaded program, when can you get away with not synchronizing global data?

Thread Scheduling

To accommodate varying needs, the scheduling policies and priorities of POSIX.1c threads can be programmatically controlled. This chapter presents the thread scheduling interfaces, explains how they are used, and describes how threads compete for processor time.

Topics Covered...

- Thread Scheduling Contention Scope
- Thread Scheduling Policies
- Thread Scheduling Priority Values
- Thread Scheduling Allocation Domains
- Thread Creation Scheduling Attributes
- Dynamic Thread Scheduling
- Yielding the Processor
- Priority Inversion and Mutexes

Thread Scheduling Contention Scopes

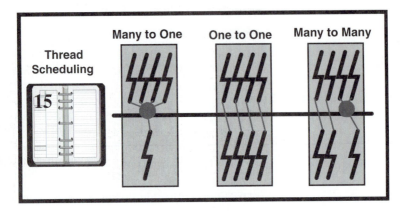

Fig. 6–1 Threads are scheduled entities that compete with each other for processor time. The *contention scope* describes how the threads will compete. An *unbound* thread competes with other unbound threads in its process. However, a *bound* thread competes with all other bound threads in the system.

Before getting into scheduling, let's back up and revisit the three thread models. This reference will serve as the basis for the discussion in this section. When we refer to a kernel entity, we are referring to the kernel-scheduled entity on which a system implements threads. This entity could be a process, a kernel thread, a lightweight process, or some other kernel-scheduled entity. What each system uses to implement threads may be different. Figure 6-1 shows how threads in the different models map to kernel entities.

In the Mx1 threads model, each user thread is multiplexed on top of one kernel entity. These threads are known as *unbound* user threads. An unbound thread is not directly bound to a kernel entity. In this model, the threads library contains a user space scheduler responsible for scheduling the user threads on the single kernel entity. The kernel is responsible for scheduling the kernel entity on a processor.

In the 1x1 threads model, each user thread is bound directly to a kernel entity. These threads are known as *bound* user threads. The threads library does not contain a scheduler. The kernel is completely responsible for the scheduling of all threads on processors.

In the MxN model, user threads can be *bound* to a kernel entity, as in the 1x1 model; or *unbound*, as in the Mx1 model. The application determines which threads are bound and which threads are unbound. The threads library contains a user space scheduler responsible for scheduling the unbound user threads on kernel entities. The kernel is responsible for scheduling the bound user threads.

POSIX.1c defines two different models for scheduling threads, the Process Scheduling model and System Scheduling model. These thread scheduling models are known as the Thread Scheduling Contention Scope. A thread's scheduling contention scope must be chosen at thread creation time. This scope cannot be changed after a thread is created. Selecting a contention scope is how an application specifies a bound or an unbound thread.

In the System Scheduling Scope, each thread competes for system resources (like the CPU) with all other system scope threads in the system. Threads that have the System Scheduling Scope are bound threads. The kernel is responsible for scheduling all threads of this type. In the Process Model, all processes are scheduled under the System Scheduling model.

In the Process Scheduling Scope, each thread competes for the system resources with all other process scope threads within the process. Threads in the Process Scheduling Scope are unbound threads. The threads library is completely responsible for scheduling all threads of this type onto kernel entities. How Process Scheduling Scope threads are scheduled with respect to System Scheduling Scope threads is system-dependent.

Each system supports at least one of the scheduling contention scopes. A system is not required to support both. If both scopes are supported, the default scheduling contention scope for a new thread is the Process Scheduling Scope.

The scheduling contention scope is used to indicate whether a bound or unbound thread should be created. Why would an application want to use one instead of the other?

The Process Scheduling Scope allows for extremely lightweight thread creation, termination, and synchronization of threads. The kernel is not involved in the creation, termination or synchronizing of a Process Scheduling Scope thread. However, these threads do not have true system-wide realtime behavior. Because the kernel does not know the scheduling requirements of the unbound user threads, these requirements cannot be factored into the kernel's decisions on resource allocation.

The System Scheduling Scope allows a user thread to have true realtime behavior as the kernel knows the scheduling requirements of the thread. The kernel takes these scheduling requirements into account when making resource allocation decisions (like who should execute next). System Scheduling Scope threads take longer to create, terminate, and synchronize because the kernel must be involved in all operations.

Later in this book we'll talk more about when it's best to use bound or unbound threads.

Thread Scheduling Policies

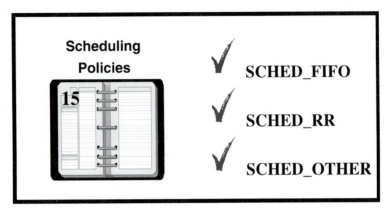

Fig. 6–2 POSIX.1c defines three scheduling policies for threads. Each policy has its own characteristics that affect how and when a thread will receive the processor resources with respect to other threads. Each scheduling policy has a priority range.

POSIX.1c has not added new scheduling policies for threads. Instead the scheduling policies from POSIX.1b were changed to provide for the scheduling of threads instead of processes. We will only briefly review the POSIX scheduling policies in this book. Detailed analysis of the POSIX scheduling policies can be found in other books devoted to POSIX.1b.

Each thread in a process will be scheduled according to a scheduling policy and its associated attribute. POSIX has defined three scheduling policies: **SCHED_FIFO**, **SCHED_RR**, and **SCHED_OTHER**. Systems may define additional scheduling policies and should thoroughly document the effects of those additional policies.

SCHED_FIFO

The **SCHED_FIFO** (First In, First Out) policy is a realtime priority based scheduling policy. For each priority value, the system keeps a list of threads containing that priority value. Threads on these priority lists are ordered by how long they have been on the list. When a thread is ready to execute, it is placed on the tail of its priority list.

When the system is ready to execute a new thread, it chooses the thread from the head of the highest priority **SCHED_FIFO** list (i.e., the highest priority, longest waiting thread). The chosen thread executes until (a) the thread terminates, (b) the thread blocks [e.g., waiting for a mutex, blocked in `read()`] or relinquishes the processor, or (c) the thread is preempted by a higher priority thread. There is no time-slice associated with the **SCHED_FIFO** policy. Be careful when using this scheduling policy, a high-priority compute-bound application can completely monopolize the system.

The **SCHED_FIFO** policy is not a true FIFO scheduling policy. Threads are scheduled according to their priority value. Threads of the same priority are then scheduled in FIFO order.

The **SCHED_FIFO** scheduling policy contains at least 32 different priority values. Systems may support more values, but a minimum of 32 is guaranteed. These priority values may or may not overlap the priority values from other policies. Consult your system's documentation for details on how the **SCHED_FIFO** policy and priorities interact with other scheduling policies. For maximum portability, do not rely on the interactions between different scheduling policies.

SCHED_RR

The **SCHED_RR** (Round Robin) policy is identical to the **SCHED_FIFO** policy except that each thread is given a time-slice when executing. When a thread has executed for a duration equal to its time-slice, the system context switches the thread and places the thread at the end of its priority list. The highest priority, longest waiting thread is then chosen to execute next. If a thread is preempted by a higher priority thread, the preempted thread will use the rest of its unused time-slice when it resumes execution. This scheduling policy ensures that if multiple threads with the same priority exist, one thread will not monopolize the system.

The **SCHED_RR** policy contains at least 32 different priority values. Systems may support more values, but a minimum of 32 is guaranteed. These priority values may or may not overlap the priority values from other policies. Consult your system's documentation for details on how the **SCHED_RR** policy and priorities interact with other scheduling policies. For maximum portability, do not rely on the interactions between different scheduling policies.

Be careful when using the **SCHED_FIFO** and **SCHED_RR** scheduling policies. It is possible for an application to monopolize the system with these policies. As a result, many systems allow only privileged applications to use these policies (at least for bound System Scheduling Scope threads). Consult your system's documentation to determine whether special privileges are required.

SCHED_OTHER

The **SCHED_OTHER** policy is a scheduling policy whose behavior is defined by each implementation. POSIX.1b does not specify the behavior of this policy, only that the policy must be provided. A system may choose to map **SCHED_OTHER** to **SCHED_FIFO**, **SCHED_RR**, or some other system-defined scheduling policy. Most UNIX systems map **SCHED_OTHER** to a timeshare scheduling policy. The timeshare scheduling policy will be discussed in Chapter 10, *Thread Extensions*.

Why does POSIX.1b define an undefined scheduling policy? **SCHED_OTHER** is intended to permit an application to notify the system that the application no longer needs realtime scheduling. This works great if **SCHED_OTHER** is defined to be a nonrealtime scheduling policy (such as a timeshare policy). An application can switch between realtime priority-based scheduling when realtime behavior is required and a general timeshare policy when realtime behavior isn't required. However, if a system maps **SCHED_OTHER** to **SCHED_FIFO** or **SCHED_RR**, applications using this policy may not behave as expected. When an application changes its policy to **SCHED_OTHER** to signify that it doesn't need realtime scheduling, it will continue to use realtime scheduling.

The priority values for the **SCHED_OTHER** scheduling policy are undefined. These priority values may or may not overlap the priority values from other policies. Consult your system's documentation for details on how the **SCHED_OTHER** policy and priorities interact with other policies. For maximum portability, do not rely on the interactions of different scheduling policies.

If you want your application to be portable, do not rely on the behavior of the **SCHED_OTHER** policy. The behavior of applications using the **SCHED_OTHER** policy may change when the application is run on different systems.

A Thread's Scheduling Policy and Priority

A thread is given its initial scheduling policy and priority when it is created. A thread may either inherit its policy and priority from the creating thread or have one specified by the creating thread. A thread's policy and priority may also be changed dynamically while the thread is executing.

This discussion is only an overview of the POSIX.1b scheduling policies. For more detailed information, consult your system documentation or the POSIX.1b and POSIX.1c standards.

Scheduling Policies and Synchronization Primitives

The scheduling policies and priorities of threads blocked on synchronization objects determine the order in which threads are unblocked. For threads using the **SCHED_FIFO** and **SCHED_RR** scheduling policies, the highest priority, longest waiting thread is unblocked when the object is released (or signaled, in the case of condition variables). Threads using the **SCHED_OTHER** scheduling policy are not required to be unblocked in any specified order. Some systems unblock the longest waiting thread, others may unblock a random thread. The unblocked thread is guaranteed to acquire the synchronization object next.

Threads using **SCHED_OTHER** should not rely on a system's order of unblocking threads to acquire synchronization objects. If ordered unblocking is required, the threads should use one of the realtime scheduling policies.

Thread Scheduling Priority Values

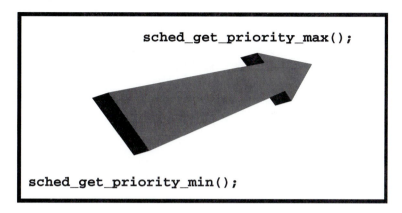

Fig. 6–3 POSIX.1c provides functions that allow you to determine the minimum and maximum priority values for each scheduling policy.

Overview

Now that we know about thread scheduling policies and priorities, how do we determine the valid priority values on a system?

POSIX has defined that a system must have at least 32 priority values for **SCHED_FIFO** and 32 priority values for **SCHED_RR**. A system may support more than 32 priorities for each policy. In fact, most systems will probably support at least 128 realtime priorities. The priority values are not defined. They may start at 0, 64, 256, or any other value a system chooses. **SCHED_FIFO** and **SCHED_RR** may also have different ranges of priority values. For example, **SCHED_FIFO** may use the values 1 through 64, and **SCHED_RR** may use the values 65 through 128. How then does an application assign a priority value in a portable manner?

To obtain the minimum and maximum priorities for a scheduling policy, use the following functions:

```
int    sched_get_priority_min(int  policy);

int    sched_get_priority_max(int  policy);
```

For a given scheduling *policy*, these functions will return the minimum and maximum priority values.

Because the actual policy for **SCHED_OTHER** is implementation-defined, it shouldn't be surprising that the valid priority values for **SCHED_OTHER** are also implementation-defined. However, the above functions will return the minimum and maximum priority values when **SCHED_OTHER** is specified in *policy*.

Zero-Relative Priorities

Unspecified priority values can be difficult to deal with if the minimum value is not zero. For application programmers, it is often easier to deal with priority ranges that are relative to zero. There's an easy way to accomplish this:

Use the sched_get_priority_min() and sched_get_priority_max() functions to initialize the variables fifo_min, fifo_max, rr_min, and rr_max with the minimum and maximum priorities for the **SCHED_FIFO** and **SCHED_RR** policies.

Now create a function similar to:

```
int
convert_relative_prio(int policy, int priority,
                struct sched_param *param)
{
    switch(policy) {
    case SCHED_RR:
        param->sched_priority = priority + rr_min;

        /* Did we overflow the maximum SCHED_RR priority? */

        if (param->sched_priority > rr_max) {
                param->sched_priority = rr_max;
                /* or maybe return an error? */
        }
        break;

    case SCHED_FIFO:
        param->sched_priority = priority + fifo_min;

        /* Did we overflow the maximum SCHED_FIFO priority? */

        if (param->sched_priority > fifo_max) {
                param->sched_priority = fifo_max;
                /* or maybe return an error? */
        }
        break;

    /*
     * Add other system defined scheduling policies here
     */
    case ...:
        break;

    default:
        return(-1);
    }
    return(0);
}
```

The `convert_relative_prio()` function allows the use of priorities relative to zero (low priority) in your application. This function is independent of the system-specific values assigned as the minimum and maximum priorities for a scheduling policy. To obtain a zero-relative scheduling priority value, you can do the following in your application:

```
if (convert_relative_prio(SCHED_FIFO, 24, &param)) {
        fprintf(stderr, "priority conversion error\n");
        exit(-1);
}
```

There is one problem that needs to be addressed in this function. What if the requested priority value is higher than the maximum value? This function, as described above, silently truncates the priority to the maximum value. This action may not produce the desired results for all applications. An application will have two threads that it thinks have different priorities when, in fact, they have the same priority. This problem arises if an application's range of priorities is greater than the system's range of priorities. If an application assumes a range of only 32 priorities, it is will not have this problem, as POSIX mandates a minimum of 32 priorities.

Portability Hints

- Be careful when mixing scheduling policies in an application. There is no guarantee that a high-priority **SCHED_RR** thread will be scheduled to run before a low-priority **SCHED_FIFO** thread. Some systems use the same priority range for these policies, while others may have the **SCHED_FIFO** priority range higher than the **SCHED_RR** priority range.

- How threads with different scheduling policies are scheduled relative to one another is undefined by POSIX. Each system will define and document this behavior. Do not rely on a system's behavior being portable to other systems.

Thread Scheduling Allocation Domains

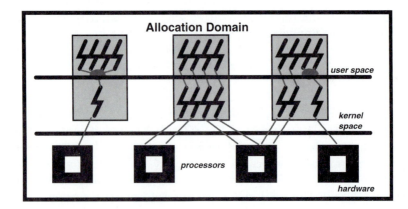

Fig. 6–4 A *scheduling allocation domain* consists of one or more processors. Threads compete for available processors within their scheduling allocation domain based on their scheduling policy and priority.

A thread's scheduling allocation domain is the set of processors on which it is allowed to execute. Threads compete for a processor in their scheduling allocation domain, based on their scheduling policy and priority and their scheduling contention scope.

A scheduling allocation domain contains one or more processors. Unfortunately, scheduling allocation domains are not fully specified by POSIX.1c. For a multiprocessor machine, the operating system may: (1) place all processors in one domain, (2) place each processor in a separate domain, or (3) spread M processors across N domains. A system may also change the number of processors in a domain at any time. Threads may migrate from one domain to another. The scheduling allocation domain may be assigned on a per-thread, per-process, or per-system basis. What your system has chosen in regard to scheduling allocation domains should be documented in your system documentation.

The amount of control an application has over scheduling allocation domains is implementation defined. If a system allows an application control over scheduling allocation domains, the method of control is not portable. POSIX.1c does not specify mechanisms to control scheduling domains on multiprocessor machines. Check your system's documentation to determine whether and how you can control the scheduling allocation domains on your system.

Why is the area of scheduling allocation domains implementation-defined? One reason is that multiprocessor architectures can vary greatly. The way a system with four processors chooses to implement scheduling policies may be significantly different than a system with 2048 or 4096 processors. To obtain maximum performance from these systems, the scheduling policies and domains may be fine-tuned in different ways.

What does all this mean to you as an application developer? The most important thing to keep in mind is that threads compete for processors within their own scheduling allocation domain. This scheduling allocation domain may not include all processors in the system. As an example, consider a four-processor system with one scheduling allocation domain containing all four processors. When any processor is ready to execute a new thread, the highest priority, longest waiting thread in the entire system is chosen. Now, let's take that same four-processor machine and place each processor in a separate scheduling allocation domain. Each thread in the system will be in one of these domains. When processor 2 is ready to execute a new thread, the system will choose the highest priority, longest waiting thread from processor 2's domain. There may be a higher priority thread in processor 1's domain, but it will not be chosen.

Most UNIX systems with a small number of processors (less than 32) place all processors in one scheduling allocation domain. Threads compete for all processors on the system. The highest priority, longest waiting thread executes on the next available processor. At times, this effect may not be desirable. As a result, many systems allow an application to bind a thread directly to a specific processor. When binding a thread to a processor, the application effectively changes the scheduling allocation domain of that thread to contain one processor (the processor to which the thread is bound).

Thread Creation Scheduling Attributes

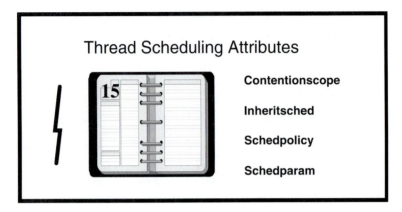

Fig. 6–5 Four thread attributes relate to scheduling. You may define the scheduling contention scope, the scheduling inheritance mechanism, and the scheduling policy and priority.

Scheduling Attributes

The thread attributes object contains several scheduling attributes that can be customized for new threads. By specifying a thread's scheduling parameters at creation time, an application doesn't need to make additional function calls to change the scheduling parameters after the thread is created.

There are four scheduling attributes in the thread attributes object:

- `contentionscope`: This attribute specifies the scheduling contention scope for the new thread. For an unbound thread (the Mx1 or MxN threads models), specify **PTHREAD_SCOPE_PROCESS**. For a bound thread (the 1x1 threads model), specify **PTHREAD_SCOPE_SYSTEM**. Note: A system is required to support one contention scope or the other, but not both. Some systems may support both contention scopes (i.e., the MxN threads model), in which case the default value is **PTHREAD_SCOPE_PROCESS**.

- `inheritsched`: This attribute specifies how the new thread obtains its scheduling policy and associated attributes. If the value of this attribute is **PTHREAD_INHERIT_SCHED**, the scheduling policy and associated attributes will be inherited from the creating thread. The `schedpolicy` and `schedparam` attributes are ignored. A value of **PTHREAD_EXPLICIT_SCHED** causes the scheduling policy and associated attributes of the new thread to be set to the values specified in the `schedpolicy` and `schedparam` attributes. POSIX.1c does not specify a default value for this attribute. Most systems use **PTHREAD_INHERIT_SCHED** as the default value.

- `schedpolicy`: This attribute specifies the scheduling policy for the new thread. If the scheduling policy requires an attribute (e.g., a scheduling priority value), it is stored in the `schedparam` attribute. The valid POSIX.1c values for the `schedpolicy` attribute are **SCHED_FIFO**, **SCHED_RR**, and **SCHED_OTHER**. Your system may have other policies (like a time-share policy) that can also be used. These other policies may not be supported on all systems. A portable application should use only the scheduling policies specified by POSIX.

* `schedparam`: This attribute specifies the scheduling attributes that are required with the policy specified in the `schedpolicy` attribute. The **SCHED_FIFO** and **SCHED_RR** policies require only the `sched_priority` member of this attribute to be set. This attribute contains the priority used to schedule the new thread. If the value of the `schedpolicy` attribute is **SCHED_OTHER** or a system-defined scheduling policy, consult your system's documentation to determine whether and how the `schedparam` attribute should be set.

Setting/Getting Scheduling Attributes

The `contentionscope`, `inheritsched`, `schedpolicy`, and `schedparam` attributes can be set and retrieved with the functions described below. The *attr* parameter represents the thread attributes object that must have been previously initialized with `pthread_attr_init()`. The second parameter contains either the attribute value being set or a pointer to where the retrieved attribute value is returned (depending on whether it is a set or a get function).

```
int pthread_attr_getscope(
      pthread_attr_t        *attr,
      int                   *contentionscope
);

int pthread_attr_setscope(
      pthread_attr_t        *attr,
      int                   contentionscope
);

int pthread_attr_getinheritsched(
      pthread_attr_t        *attr,
      int                   *inheritsched
);

int pthread_attr_setinheritsched(
      pthread_attr_t        *attr,
      int                   inheritsched
);
```

```
int pthread_attr_getschedpolicy(
      pthread_attr_t        *attr,
      int                   *schedpolicy
);


int pthread_attr_setschedpolicy(
      pthread_attr_t        *attr,
      int                   schedpolicy
);


int pthread_attr_getschedparam(
      pthread_attr_t             *attr,
      struct sched_param         *schedparam
);

int pthread_attr_setschedparam(
      pthread_attr_t             *attr,
      struct sched_param         *schedparam
);
```

Example

The following example shows how the thread scheduling attributes can be used
together in an application. This example creates three threads. Thread 1 is a
high-priority thread scheduled in the **SCHED_FIFO** policy. Thread 2 is a low-priority thread scheduled in the **SCHED_RR** policy. Thread 3 is a low-priority thread.
The scheduling policy for thread 3 is not important.

```
extern void        *thread1_func(), *thread2_func(), *thread3_func();
extern void        fatal_error(int err_num, char *func);
#define            check_error(return_val, msg) {                 \
                        if (return_val != 0)                      \
                              fatal_error(return_val, msg);       \
                   }

main()
{
      pthread_t    pth_id[3];
      int          ret_val, scope;
      pthread_attr_t        attr;
      struct sched_param    param;

      /* Initialize the threads attributes object */
      (void)pthread_attr_init(&attr);

      ret_val = pthread_attr_setinheritsched(&attr,
                                    PTHREAD_EXPLICIT_SCHED);
```

```
        check_error(ret_val, "attr_setinheritched()");

        /* We want bound threads if they are available. */
        ret_val = pthread_attr_getscope(&attr, &scope);
        check_error(ret_val, "attr_getscope()");
        if (scope != PTHREAD_SCOPE_SYSTEM) {
                scope = PTHREAD_SCOPE_SYSTEM;
                ret_val = pthread_attr_setscope(&attr, scope);
                if ((ret_val != 0) && (ret_val != ENOTSUP))
                        fatal_error(ret_val, "attr_setscope()");
        }

        /* Thread 1 is a high priority SCHED_FIFO thread.*/
        ret_val = pthread_attr_setschedpolicy(&attr, SCHED_FIFO);
        check_error(ret_val, "attr_setschedpolicy() 1");

        param.sched_priority = sched_get_priority_max(SCHED_FIFO);
        ret_val = pthread_attr_setschedparam(&attr, &param);
        check_error(ret_val, "attr_setschedparam() 1");

        ret_val = pthread_create(&pth_id[0], &attr, thread1_func,NULL);
        check_error(ret_val, "pthread_create() 1");

        /* Thread 2 is a low priority SCHED_RR thread. */
        ret_val = pthread_attr_setschedpolicy(&attr, SCHED_RR);
        check_error(ret_val, "attr_setschedpolicy() 2");

        param.sched_priority = sched_get_priority_min(SCHED_RR);
        ret_val = pthread_attr_setschedparam(&attr, &param);
        check_error(ret_val, "attr_setschedparam() 2");

        ret_val = pthread_create(&pth_id[1], &attr, thread2_func, NULL);
        check_error(ret_val, "pthread_create() 2");

        /* Thread 3 is a low priority "execute whenever" thread. */
        ret_val = pthread_attr_setschedpolicy(&attr, SCHED_OTHER);
        check_error(ret_val, "attr_setschedpolicy() 3");

        param.sched_priority = sched_get_priority_min(SCHED_OTHER);
        ret_val = pthread_attr_setschedparam(&attr, &param);
        check_error(ret_val, "attr_setschedparam() 3");

        ret_val = pthread_create(&pth_id[2], &attr, thread3_func, NULL);
        check_error(ret_val, "pthread_create() 3");

        /* Destroy the thread attributes object */
        (void) pthread_attr_destroy(&attr);
        /* Rest of application code goes here */
        ...
}
```

Dynamic Thread Scheduling

Fig. 6–6 A thread's scheduling policy and priority can be changed *on the fly*!!

Overview

Setting a thread's scheduling policy and priority at creation time is generally sufficient for most applications. The scheduling policy and priority usually does not need to change during a thread's lifetime. However, there are situations when a thread's scheduling policy or priority must change.

Imagine a multithreaded control program that monitors and maintains the nuclear reactor in a power plant. Several of the threads in the application monitor various gauges whose readings should rarely, if ever, reach a dangerous level. Since it is expected that these levels would never rise, these threads are given a low priority within the **SCHED_RR** scheduling policy. The rest of the program's threads are monitoring critical gauges that have a higher chance of reaching a critical level. These threads are given medium priority in the **SCHED_FIFO** scheduling policy. All threads in the program will obtain a reading from their respective gauges. If the readings are acceptable, the threads suspend themselves for a small time period [using nanosleep()]. This process is repeated in a loop forever.

Now, suppose one of the gauges monitored by a low-priority **SCHED_RR** thread suddenly started to go critical (never say something won't happen!). While the thread is attempting to handle the situation, one (or several) of the medium-priority threads may wake up and preempt the low-priority thread. The low-priority thread may not receive enough execution time to handle the problem. For that matter, the low-priority thread may not receive any execution time, depending on what the medium-priority threads are doing! This fixed-priority implementation could lead to a very dangerous situation (e.g, a nuclear meltdown).

Functions are available that allow an application to set and retrieve the scheduling policy and parameters of executing threads. In the nuclear power plant scenario, when the low priority thread's gauges go critical, the thread should change its scheduling policy and priority so that it is a high-priority thread within the **SCHED_FIFO** policy. If the scheduling priority is changed to the highest priority on the system, the thread is always scheduled before any other thread. By using the **SCHED_FIFO** policy, the thread will be guaranteed to execute until it either completely handles the problem or blocks waiting for an event to occur (wait for a nuclear scientist to decide what to do?).

Differing thread scheduling policies and priorities can be useful in many applications. A server may want threads servicing user requests to have a high priority for user responsiveness while the processing threads have a medium or low priority. A windowing system may want the thread managing the mouse to have a high priority while threads managing other widgets have lower priorities.

Dynamically Setting/Getting Thread Scheduling Attributes

To obtain the scheduling policy and parameters of a specific thread, use the function:

```
int pthread_getschedparam(
      pthread_t                          thread,
      int                                *policy,
      struct sched_param                 *param
);
```

This function will retrieve the scheduling policy and associated parameters for the thread specified in *thread*. The thread's scheduling policy and parameters will be returned in the *policy* and *param* parameters, respectively.

To change the scheduling policy and parameters of a specific thread, use the function:

```
int pthread_setschedparam(
      pthread_t                          thread,
      int                                policy,
      struct sched_param                 *param
);
```

This function will change the scheduling policy and associated parameters for the thread specified in *thread*. The thread's new scheduling policy and parameters are contained in the *policy* and *param* parameters, respectively. For the **SCHED_FIFO** and **SCHED_RR** policies, only the *sched_priority* member of the sched_param structure is required. For **SCHED_OTHER** and other system-defined scheduling policies, consult your system's documentation to see what parameters are required in the `sched_param` structure.

Whenever a thread's scheduling policy or priority is changed, the thread is context switched out and placed at the end of the priority list of its new priority. The scheduling subsystem then determines which thread is allowed to execute next. This could be the same thread if the new priority makes it the highest priority thread on the system.

Certain scheduling policies and priorities are restricted to privileged users on many systems. System administrators don't want random applications to execute as high-priority **SCHED_FIFO** threads unless they really need to! Check your system's documentation for any restrictions before using the realtime scheduling policies.

Example

Let's revisit our example program from the previous section and modify it to use `pthread_getschedparam()` and `pthread_setschedparam()`.

Assume that later in the application the initial thread noticed that the low-priority **SCHED_OTHER** thread was handling an event that was time-critical. The initial thread saves away the **SCHED_OTHER** thread's scheduling attributes and changes its scheduling policy to **SCHED_RR**. Once the event has completed, the initial thread restores the thread's scheduling attributes.

```
extern void        fatal_error(int err_num, char *func);
#define             check_error(return_val, msg) {              \
                        if (return_val != 0)                    \
                                fatal_error(return_val, msg); \
                    }

main()
{
        pthread_t     pth_id[3];
        int           ret_val;
        int           old_policy;
        pthread_attr_t              attr;
        struct sched_param          param, old_param;

        /* Application code here */
        ...

        /*
         * Some event has happened that pth_id[2] is responsible
         * for handling. Save away its current scheduling
         * attributes
         */
        ret_val = pthread_getschedparam(pth_id[2], &old_policy,
                                        &old_param);
        check_error(ret_val, "pthread_getschedparam()");

        /*
         * Set the new scheduling attributes.
         */
        param.sched_priority = sched_get_priority_max(SCHED_RR);

        ret_val = pthread_setschedparam(pth_id[2], SCHED_RR, &param);
        check_error(ret_val, "pthread_setschedparam()");

        /*
         * Wait for pth_id[2] to finish the critical task
         */
        ...

        /*
         * Reset the scheduling attributes
         */
        ret_val = pthread_setschedparam(pth_id[2], old_policy,
                                        &old_param);
        check_error(ret_val, "pthread_setschedparam()");

        /* Rest of application code goes here */
        ...
}
```

Yielding the Processor

Fig. 6–7 The `sched_yield()` function can be called by a thread that might dominate the processor. The calling thread yields the processor so that another thread may execute.

Overview

We've already seen one way of relinquishing the processor to allow another thread to run: call `pthread_setschedparam()` for the current thread specifying its current scheduling policy and priority. This action causes the calling thread to be placed at the tail of its scheduling priority list, allowing another thread of equal or higher priority to run next.

You may find certain situations where it would be useful to give up the processor and let another thread run. A function has been designed specifically for this purpose. To allow another thread to run, use the function:

```
int    sched_yield(void);
```

This function places the calling thread at the end of its scheduling priority list. The scheduling system then chooses the highest priority, longest waiting thread to execute next.

Be careful, this is not a general-purpose yield function in the presence of real-time priority threads. `sched_yield()` yields the processor only to another thread of equal or higher priority. If the calling thread is the highest priority thread on the system and there are no threads of equal priority ready to run, the calling thread is chosen to execute again (i.e., this call was a "no-op").

Priority Inversion and Mutexes

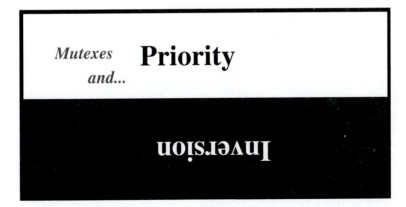

Fig. 6–8 Priority inversion describes a situation in which a high-priority, ready-to-run thread cannot execute because it is waiting on a resource held by a lower priority thread. The lower priority thread must execute first to release the resource.

Overview

Priority inversion occurs any time that a low-priority thread blocks a high-priority thread. Realtime applications always have some amount of priority inversion. When a low-priority thread has a mutex lock that a high-priority thread is trying to acquire, the high-priority thread experiences priority inversion. The trick is to have the priority inversion for the smallest amount of time possible.

Initially you may think that this isn't that much of a problem. As soon as the mutex is released, the high-priority thread will acquire it. What if the low-priority thread is preempted by a medium-priority thread? The low-priority thread holding the mutex may not be allowed to execute for quite some time. During this period, the high-priority thread is ultimately blocked by the medium-priority thread.

This section will explore a few *tricks of realtime trade* that can be applied to mutexes to minimize the amount of time threads experience priority inversion. Mutexes have two methods for minimizing priority inversion: (1) the Priority Inheritance Protocol and (2) the Priority Ceiling Protocol Emulation.

The Priority Inheritance Protocol for mutexes causes a thread to inherit the highest priority of all threads that it blocks while holding a mutex. The intent of this protocol is to remove the scenario that was presented earlier with the low-, medium-, and high-priority threads. If applied to the previous example, when the high-priority thread blocks on the mutex, the low-priority thread temporarily executes at the priority of the high-priority thread. The medium-priority thread is now prevented from preempting this thread. The low-priority thread executes until it releases the mutex; the high-priority thread then acquires the mutex and starts executing. This behavior ensures that the priority inversion is bounded for the smallest amount of time possible.

The Priority Ceiling Protocol Emulation associates a priority with a mutex. This priority must be equal to or greater than the priority of the highest priority thread that can lock the mutex. When a thread locks the mutex, it temporarily executes at the priority assigned to the mutex. This ensures that threads holding a mutex are given priority above all other threads. If a low-priority thread blocks a high-priority thread while holding a mutex, the high-priority thread is blocked only for the duration of one critical section because the low-priority thread cannot be preempted.

Mutex Scheduling Priority Attributes

The following scheduling priority attributes are available for creating mutexes:

- `protocol`: This attribute allows an application to specify which protocol to assign to the mutex. A value of **PTHREAD_PRIO_NONE** indicates that a thread's priority and scheduling are not be affected when the thread locks this mutex. A value of **PTHREAD_PRIO_INHERIT** indicates that the Priority Inheritance Protocol is applied when a thread locks this mutex. A value of **PTHREAD_PRIO_PROTECT** indicates that Priority Ceiling Protocol Emulation is applied when a thread locks this mutex. POSIX.1c does not specify a default value for this attribute; most systems will have a default value of **PTHREAD_PRIO_NONE**.

- `prioceiling`: This attribute allows an application to specify the priority ceiling to assign to a mutex. This is the priority that is assigned to a thread (temporarily) when it locks the mutex. The priority value must be in the priority range for **SCHED_FIFO**. This attribute is ignored if the `protocol` attribute for this mutex is not **PTHREAD_PRIO_PROTECT**.

There is a problem with the way POSIX.1c defines the behavior of Priority Ceiling Protocol Emulation. The `prioceiling` attribute must contain a valid priority within the **SCHED_FIFO** scheduling policy. Only the priority for the locking thread is changed when it locks a **PTHREAD_PRIO_PROTECT** mutex. What happens if the locking thread's scheduling policy is not **SCHED_FIFO**? The priority specified in the `prioceiling` attribute may not be a valid priority in the locking thread's scheduling policy. POSIX.1c does not specify a behavior for this situation. Consult your system's documentation to determine what happens on your system. For maximum portability, only threads having the **SCHED_FIFO** scheduling policy should use **PTHREAD_PRIO_PROTECT** mutexes.

There is also a problem with the definition of the Priority Inheritance Protocol in POSIX.1c. When a thread blocks on a **PTHREAD_PRIO_INHERIT** mutex, the thread owning the mutex will execute at the priority of the blocked thread if the blocked thread has a higher priority. What happens if the blocked thread's scheduling policy is not the same as the policy of the thread owning the mutex? The priority of the blocked thread may not be a valid priority in the scheduling policy of the thread owning the mutex. POSIX.1c does not specify a behavior for this situation. Consult your system's documentation to determine what happens on your system. For maximum portability, only threads with the same scheduling policy should use **PTHREAD_PRIO_INHERIT** mutexes.

Note: While these priority inversion attributes provide some nice realtime features, they can be extremely expensive. Each time a mutex is locked (or each time a thread blocks on a mutex), a thread's scheduling priority may need to change. This action can be extremely expensive compared with the amount of time it takes to lock a mutex. Use these attributes only when you really need to minimize priority inversion.

Since these attributes are optional parts of the POSIX.1c standard, it is possible that not all systems will support these features. Check your system before building an application which uses these features. The feature test macros which indicate if these features are available are **_POSIX_THREAD_PRIO_INHERIT** and **_POSIX_THREAD_PRIO_PROTECT**.

Setting/Getting Mutex Scheduling Priority Attributes

The `protocol` and `prioceiling` attributes can be retrieved from or set in the mutex attributes object with the functions described below. The *attr* parameter represents the mutex attributes object that must have been previously initialized with `pthread_mutexattr_init()`. The second parameter contains either the attribute value being set or a pointer to where the retrieved attribute value is returned (depending on whether it is a set or a get function).

```
int pthread_mutexattr_getprotocol(
    pthread_mutexattr_t      *attr,
    int                      *protocol
);

int pthread_mutexattr_setprotocol(
    pthread_mutexattr_t      *attr,
    int                      protocol
);

int pthread_mutexattr_getprioceiling(
    pthread_mutexattr_t      *attr,
    int                      *prioceiling
);
```

```
int pthread_mutexattr_setprioceiling(
    pthread_mutexattr_t      *attr,
    int                       prioceiling
);
```

Dynamically Changing the Mutex Priority Ceiling

One of the crucial elements of Priority Ceiling Protocol Emulation is that the priority assigned to a mutex is equal to or greater than the priority of the highest priority thread that can lock the mutex. During the course of execution, an application may dynamically raise the priority of a thread. If the new priority is higher than the priority of a mutex, Priority Ceiling Protocol Emulation will not prevent priority inversion.

To prevent this situation from occurring, there are functions that dynamically set and get the prioceiling attribute of a specific mutex. If a thread's priority is never raised above a mutex's prioceiling priority, these functions will not be needed.

To retrieve or change the prioceiling attribute of a specific mutex, use the following functions:

```
int pthread_mutex_getprioceiling(
    pthread_mutex_t          *mutex,
    int                      *prioceiling
);

int pthread_mutex_setprioceiling(
    pthread_mutex_t          *mutex,
    int                       prioceiling,
    int                      *old_ceiling
);
```

The pthread_mutex_getprioceiling() function returns the current value of the prioceiling attribute for *mutex* in *prioceiling*.

The pthread_mutex_setprioceiling() function will first lock *mutex*. If the mutex is currently locked, the calling thread blocks until the mutex is acquired. Once *mutex* has been locked, the priority ceiling of *mutex* is changed to the value specified in *prioceiling*, and *mutex* is unlocked. The old priority ceiling for the mutex will be returned in *old_ceiling*.

Example

The following code fragment shows how to use the mutex priority protocols. Three mutexes are initialized with different priority protocols. When a thread tries to lock a mutex of type **PTHREAD_PRIO_PROTECT**, an error could be returned if the thread's priority is higher than the mutex priority ceiling. If this occurs, the priority ceiling of the mutex is raised to equal the priority of the thread.

```
pthread_mutex_t        m1, m2, m3;
extern void            fatal_error(int err_num, char *func);

#define         check_error(return_val, msg) {              \
                    if (return_val != 0)                    \
                        fatal_error(return_val, msg); \
                }

main()
{
        int    min, max, pri, ret_val;
        pthread_mutexattr_t    attr;

        /* Initialize the mutex attribute structure */
        ret_val = pthread_mutexattr_init(&attr);
        check_error(ret_val, "mutexattr_init()");

        /* Initialize mutex 1 without priority inversion protocols */
        ret_val = pthread_mutexattr_setprotocol(&attr,
                                        PTHREAD_PRIO_NONE);
        check_error(ret_val, "attr_setprotocol() 1");

        ret_val = pthread_mutex_init(&m1, &attr);
        check_error(ret_val, "mutex_init() 1");

        /* Initialize mutex 2 with priority inheritance */
        ret_val = pthread_mutexattr_setprotocol(&attr,
                                        PTHREAD_PRIO_INHERIT);
        check_error(ret_val, "attr_setprotocol() 2");

        ret_val = pthread_mutex_init(&m2, &attr);
        check_error(ret_val, "mutex_init() 2");

        /* Initialize mutex 3 with priority protect */
        ret_val = pthread_mutexattr_setprotocol(&attr,
                                        PTHREAD_PRIO_PROTECT);
        check_error(ret_val, "attr_setprotocol() 3");

        max = sched_get_priority_max(SCHED_FIFO);
        min = sched_get_priority_min(SCHED_FIFO);
        pri = ((min + max) / 2);
```

```
        ret_val = pthread_mutexattr_setprioceiling(&attr, pri);
        check_error(ret_val, "attr_setprotocol() 3");

        ret_val = pthread_mutex_init(&m3, &attr);
        check_error(ret_val, "mutex_init() 3");

        /* Mutex initialization complete, destroy the attributes. */
        ret_val = pthread_mutexattr_destroy(&attr);
        check_error(ret_val, "pthread_mutexattr_destroy()");

        /* Rest of application code goes here */
        ...
}

void
thread_func()
{
        int    policy, ceiling, old_ceiling, ret_val;
        struct sched_paramparam;

        /* Lock mutex 3, raise its priority if we have a higher */
        /* priority than the mutex. */

        ret_val = pthread_mutex_lock(&m3);
        if (ret_val == EINVAL) {
                /* Find out our current scheduling priority */
                ret_val = pthread_getschedparam(pthread_self(),
                                            &policy, &param);
                check_error(ret_val, "getschedparam()");

                /* Reset the mutex priority ceiling */
                ceiling = param.sched_priority;

                ret_val = pthread_mutex_setprioceiling(&m3,
                                                ceiling,
                                                &old_ceiling);
                check_error(ret_val, "setprioceiling()");

                /* Now lock the mutex */
                ret_val = pthread_mutex_lock(&m3);
                check_error(ret_val, "mutex_lock() 2");

        } else if (ret_val != 0) {
                fatal_error(ret_val, "mutex_lock(m3)");
        }

        /* Rest of thread function here */
        ...
}
```

Summary

This chapter discussed how threads are scheduled in relation to other threads within a process and within the entire system. Use of the Pthread interfaces to control thread scheduling was demonstrated. Specifically:

- The thread *scheduling contention scope* defines how a thread will compete with other threads for the system resources. If a thread is *unbound*, it will compete with other unbound threads within the host process. However, if a thread is *bound*, it will compete with all bound threads in the system.

- Three scheduling policies are used to schedule threads: **SCHED_FIFO**, **SCHED_RR**, and **SCHED_OTHER**. Each policy uses a different method for allocating processors to threads. Each policy has its own priority range. When intermixing these policies in an application, care should be given so that all threads will get to execute.

- A *scheduling allocation domain* consists of one or more processors, Threads compete for available processors within their scheduling domain, based on their scheduling policy and priority.

- There are four thread attributes that relate to scheduling: scheduling contention scope, inheritance, policy, and priority.

- A thread may dynamically change the scheduling policy and priority of any thread in its process.

- The `sched_get_priority_min()` and `sched_get_priority_max()` functions can be used to obtain the minimum and maximum priorities for each scheduling policy (respectively).

- The `sched_yield()` function is used by a thread to yield the processor to another thread of equal or higher priority. This function is typically called by threads that might dominate the processor for long time periods.

- Priority inversion arises when a high-priority thread cannot execute because it is waiting on a resource that is held by a low-priority thread. The low-priority thread must run first in order to release the needed resource. However, the low-priority thread may be preempted by a medium-priority thread! The bottom line? The high-priority thread does not get to run. To minimize priority inversion with mutexes, use the priority inheritance or priority ceiling protocols.

Exercises

1. Based on your knowledge of applications in general and thread contention scope in particular, what applications might run better with bound threads? Unbound threads? A mixture of bound and unbound threads? Why?

2. Write a program with three threads where each one uses a different scheduling policy. Have each thread report their minimum and maximum priorities. If you have access to a system from another vendor, run the same program on that system and determine whether the priority ranges are the same.

3. Using the same program created for #2, have the **SCHED_RR** thread convert the other two threads' scheduling policy to **SCHED_RR**. Then assign all threads a priority between the minimum and the maximum. Each thread should report its policy and priority.

4. Use two threads in a program that tests yielding the processor. Give both threads the **SCHED_FIFO** scheduling policy, but give thread 1 higher priority. Thread 1 should print 1s and thread 2 should print 2s to a file. Thread 1 should yield the processor after printing ten 1s. If there are no takers, thread 1 should repeat the operation. Does thread 2 get to run? If so, if not, why?

5. Write a program containing three threads that use the **SCHED_FIFO** scheduling policy. Give thread 1 the highest priority, thread 2 the middle priority, and thread 3 the lowest priority. Thread 3 should run first, acquire a mutex, and sleep with the mutex locked. The sleep should be long enough for thread 2 to begin execution, then it should release the mutex and terminate. Thread 2 should spin in a loop. Next, thread 1 should attempt to acquire the mutex. When thread 1 acquires the mutex, it should print "got it!" and the program should terminate. Does this program experience priority inversion? If so, fix the problem using the inheritance protocol. If not, describe why not and, for prevention sake, implement priority ceiling protocol emulation.

Threads and Signals

When a single-threaded process receives a signal, the default action is to terminate the process unless a signal handler has been installed. If a signal handler is invoked, program execution is interrupted. In a multithreaded program, signal handling is more flexible. A signal can be handled by a single thread, allowing other threads within the program to continue execution. This chapter presents the Pthreads signal interfaces and explains how they are used.

Topics Covered...

- Signals in the Thread Model
- Synchronous and Asynchronous Signals
- Examining/Changing a Thread's Signal Mask
- Sending Signals to Threads
- Waiting for a Signal
- Async-Signal Safe Thread Functions
- A New Signal Delivery Method: **SIGEV_THREAD**

Signals in the Thread Model

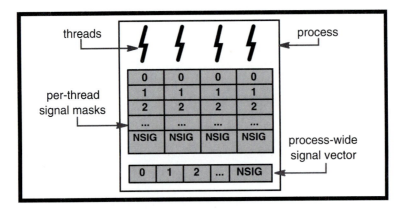

Fig. 7–1 In the POSIX.1c Thread Model, there is a process-wide set of signal actions, and each thread has its own signal mask.

In the Process Model, an application needs to worry only about one thread of control. Each process contains its own set of signal actions (the set of signal handlers and signal actions) and signal mask. Each process can send and receive signals to and from other processes. When a process receives a signal, it has to worry only about applying the action of the signal to one thread of control, the process itself.

In the Thread Model, the traditional signal model is changed slightly. Each process has a set of signal actions that is still established with the sigaction() function. The set of signal actions is shared by all threads within the process. Rather than using a process-wide signal mask, each thread in the process contains a signal mask. A thread's signal mask is inherited from its creating thread.

Individual threads can send signals to other processes or to threads in their own process. Signals cannot be sent to threads in another process as thread IDs are guaranteed to be unique only within the process.

If a signal is sent to a thread, only that thread will handle the signal. If a signal is sent to a process [i.e., via the kill() function], one and only one thread in the process that does not have the signal blocked will handle the signal. Which thread handles the signal is undefined. When a signal is sent to a process, there is no way to guarantee that a particular thread handles the signal (unless all other threads in the process block the signal). If a signal is repeatedly sent to the process, different threads may receive signal each time.

Because there is no way to guarantee that a specific thread receives a signal, a new set of functions have been provided that allow a thread to synchronously wait for an asynchronous signal sent to the process. An application can create additional threads that act as signal-handling threads. These threads asynchronously wait for and process the signals as they are received.

When a thread handles a signal, if the action for the signal causes the thread to be terminated, stopped, or continued, the entire process will be terminated, stopped, or continued. This behavior is the same whether the signal was sent to the thread or the process. Do not use signals to stop or terminate threads in an application as the signal will stop or terminate the entire application.

POSIX chose this method because only terminating the receiving thread has negative side-effects on a process. Consider a thread that obtains a mutex lock, then receives a **SIGKILL** signal before unlocking the mutex. If only the receiving thread were to be terminated, the mutex would never be unlocked. The application ends in deadlock when another thread tries to acquire the mutex. There is a new mechanism that can be used to cleanly terminate threads within a process: thread cancellation. This will be discussed in Chapter 8, *Thread Cancellation*.

Synchronous and Asynchronous Signals

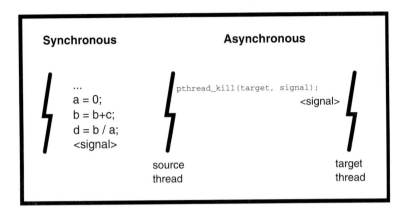

Fig. 7–2 Synchronous signals result from some action the thread has taken, such as divide by zero. On the other hand, asynchronous signals are *delivered* to a target thread asynchronously via operations such as the `pthread_kill()` function.

What are synchronous and asynchronous signals? Whether a signal is synchronous or asynchronous depends on the event that caused the signal to be generated. Signals are not defined such that a specific signal number is synchronous or asynchronous. The signal source must be examined to determine this property of signals.

A synchronously generated signal is a signal that has been generated by the operating system as a result of a thread's action. For example, when a thread causes a floating point exception, performs a divide by zero, or executes an illegal instruction, a signal is generated synchronously. Synchronously generated signals are delivered only to the thread that caused the signal to be generated.

An asynchronously generated signal is a signal that has been generated due to an action not attributable to a specific thread. Signals sent via the `kill()` function, signals sent from the keyboard, and signals generated due to timer expiration are examples of asynchronously generated signals. All signals can be generated asynchronously [i.e., they can be sent via `kill()`]. Asynchronously generated signals are delivered to the process. One thread within the process that does not have the signal blocked will receive the signal.

The difference between synchronous and asynchronous signals is important to remember. Most signals that an application handles are asynchronous. Features such as timers and asynchronous I/O generate asynchronous signals. At first this may not seem important, but what if two threads start asynchronous I/O operations that generate the same signal upon completion? When the first asynchronous I/O completes, a signal is generated for the process. Because the signal is sent to the process, the thread starting the asynchronous I/O may not be the thread that receives the signal. To further complicate matters, both asynchronous I/O operations may generate the same signal, making it hard to know which I/O completed first.

What does all this mean to the programmer? If an application desires one specific thread to handle an asynchronous signal, it must ensure that all other threads block that signal. This arrangement guarantees which thread in the application receives the signal. If more than one thread can handle the signal, the application should provide a signal handler that different threads may execute. Remember, signal handlers are maintained at the process level. Per-thread signal handlers are not supported; however, they can be constructed out of the existing signal and Pthread functions. We'll explore how per-thread signal handlers can be implemented in Chapter 9, *Thread-Specific Data*.

How does an application make a signal handler generic? As an example, consider a multithreaded application that has threads performing asynchronous I/O operations. For each read or write, a table entry is created to denote that an outstanding asynchronous I/O operation is in progress. The process will receive a signal when the I/O operation completes. The signal handler removes the table entry for the I/O operation. The signal handler doesn't need to be called by the thread that started the I/O operation.

Another option is to have all threads in the process block all signals. Create one thread that doesn't block signals. The sole purpose of this thread is to handle all signals sent to the process. Additionally, this thread may even dispatch tasks to other threads in the process depending on the signal received. For example, **SIGUSR1** may indicate that the process should perform event X. When **SIGUSR1** is delivered, the receiving thread may direct another thread to perform event X (through some form of synchronization).

Examining/Changing a Thread's Signal Mask

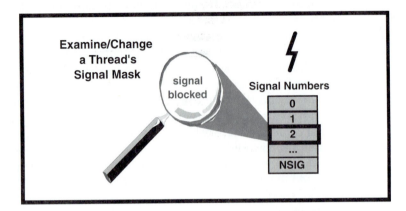

Fig. 7–3 In the Thread Model, the function `pthread_sigmask()` should be used to block or unblock signals for threads.

Overview

In the Process Model, a process blocks or unblocks signals by calling the `sig-procmask()` function. The use of `sigprocmask()` in a multithreaded application results in undefined behavior. Although most UNIX systems will have the `sigprocmask()` function change the signal mask of the calling thread, portable applications should not rely on this behavior. Threads can block or unblock signals by calling the `pthread_sigmask()` function. This function is identical to the `sigprocmask()` function, except that it changes the signal mask of the calling thread:

```
int pthread_sigmask(
    int                 how,
    sigset_t            *set,
    sigset_t            *oset
);
```

The *how* parameter specifies how the calling thread's signal mask should be changed. The legal values for *how* are:

- **SIG_BLOCK**: Add the signals specified in *set* to the calling thread's signal mask.

- **SIG_UNBLOCK**: Remove the signals specified in *set* from the calling thread's signal mask.

- **SIG_SETMASK**: Replace the calling thread's signal mask with the signal mask specified in *set*.

The *set* parameter contains the set of signals to be blocked or unblocked from the calling thread's signal mask, according to the *how* parameter. By specifying a value of **NULL** for *set*, the signal mask of the calling thread can be obtained without changing the signal mask. In this case, the *how* parameter is ignored.

If the *oset* parameter is not **NULL**, the old signal mask of the calling thread is returned in *oset*.

Example

The following code is from an application that blocks **SIGALRM** while executing a critical section of code that cannot be interrupted. First, the signal mask of the thread is obtained. If **SIGALRM** is not currently blocked, it is blocked from the calling thread. After the critical section of code has completed, the thread's signal mask is restored.

```
#define GET_PTHREAD_SIGMASK      0  /* can be any value */

/* Application code here */
...

/*
 * Find out the current signal mask. Notice that the
 * "how" parameter can be anything if we are only
 * inquiring about the current signal mask.
 */
pthread_sigmask(GET_PTHREAD_SIGMASK, (sigset_t *)NULL, &oldset);

sigmask_changed = 0;
if (!sigismember(&oldset, SIGALRM)) {
        sigmask_changed = 1;
        sigemptyset(&newset);
        sigaddset(&newset, SIGALRM);
        pthread_sigmask(SIG_BLOCK, &newset, &oldset);
}

/* Application code here */
...

/* Restore the old signal mask now */

if (sigmask_changed)
        pthread_sigmask(SIG_UNBLOCK, &oldset, (sigset_t *)NULL);
```

Sending Signals to Threads

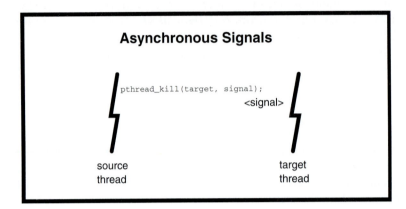

Fig. 7–4 The `pthread_kill()` function can be used to send a signal to a thread (within the same process) in much the same way that the `kill()` function can be used to send a signal to a process.

Overview

In the Process Model, a process can send a signal to another process via the `kill()` function. To send a signal to a thread, use the `pthread_kill()` function. This function allows a thread to asynchronously send a signal to a specific thread in its process.

```
int pthread_kill(
     pthread_t              thread,
     int                    signal
);
```

The signal specified in the *signal* parameter will be sent to *thread*. If *signal* is zero, error checking is performed but a signal is not sent. Since thread IDs are not guaranteed to be known outside of a process, a thread cannot send a signal to a specific thread in another process.

Keep in mind the rules for signals in a multithreaded process when using this function. If a signal results in *thread* being stopped, continued, or terminated, the entire process is stopped, continued, or terminated. Since the default action for most signals is termination, directing signals at a thread can be dangerous. When an application uses this function, it should either have signal handlers installed for the signals sent, or the target threads should be using one of the `sigwait` functions (described in the next section).

Example

The following example program installs a signal handler for **SIGUSR1** and creates a thread to perform application-specific work. After the thread is created, the initial thread sends the signal **SIGUSR1** to the other thread. The signal handler for **SIGUSR1** prints a message upon receipt of the signal.

```
#include <signal.h>
#include <pthread.h>
#include <stdio.h>
#include <errno.h>

extern void     fatal_error(int err_num, char *func);
void            thread_func();
void            sig_handler();

main()
{
    pthread_t           tid;
    int                 ret_val;
    struct sigaction    act, oact;

    sigfillset(&act.sa_mask);
    act.sa_handler = sig_handler;
    act.sa_flags = 0;

    if (sigaction(SIGUSR1, &act, &oact) != 0) {
            perror("sigaction() failed");
            exit(-1);
     }

    /* Create a new thread */
    ret_val = pthread_create(&tid, (pthread_attr_t *)NULL,
                        (void *(*)())thread_func, NULL);
    if (ret_val != 0)
            fatal_error(ret_val, "pthread_create()");

    /* Send SIGUSR1 to the created thread */

    ret_val = pthread_kill(tid, SIGUSR1);
    if (ret_val != 0)
            fatal_error(ret_val, "pthread_kill()");

    /* Now wait for the thread */

    ret_val = pthread_join(tid, (void **)NULL);
    if (ret_val != 0)
            fatal_error(ret_val, "pthread_join()");

    /* Say Good-bye */
    printf("Program Terminating...\n");
    exit(0);
}
```

```
/* Thread start_routine */
void
thread_func()
{
    /*
     * Real application "processing" code goes here...
     * Some application specific code will later cause the
     * while loop to terminate so that the program
     * terminates.
     */

    while (1) {
        ...
    }

    pthread_exit((void *)NULL);
}


/* Signal handling function */
void
sig_handler(sig)
int    sig;
{
    printf("signal number %d received\n", sig);
    return;
}
```

Waiting for a Signal

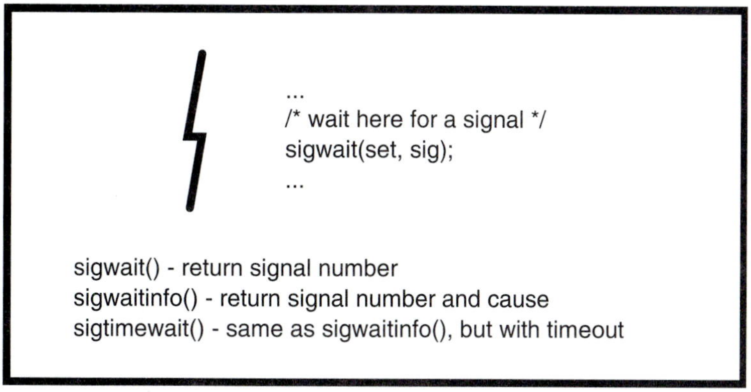

```
       ...
       /* wait here for a signal */
       sigwait(set, sig);
       ...


sigwait() - return signal number
sigwaitinfo() - return signal number and cause
sigtimewait() - same as sigwaitinfo(), but with timeout
```

Fig. 7–5 Threads provide more flexibility in dealing with signals. Threads can wait for signals with the `sigwait` functions, preventing interruption of your code.

Overview

The traditional method for using signals within a process can be clumsy and awkward. For one application to communicate with another using signals, the application installs handlers for the signals that it is interested in catching. Afterward, the application continues about its business. At some point, one of the signals is delivered, interrupting the application. The interruption may arrive at any time. To make matters worse, there is a very limited set of functions that may be safely called from signal handlers.

Fortunately, we are no longer limited to this model.

One of the benefits of programming with threads is that the application programmer has more flexibility in dealing with signals. There are three functions that allow a thread to wait for an asynchronous signal. With these functions, an application can establish specific threads as signal-handling threads. For example, an application has its threads block all signals and then creates one or more threads that call the signal-waiting functions. When the desired signal is delivered to the process, it is directed to one of the threads waiting for that specific signal. When the thread returns from the signal-waiting function, the signal number is returned.

Because signal handlers are not involved, the thread handling the signal is not restricted to a limited set of async-safe functions that may be called. The signal-handling thread can perform operations like locking mutexes or semaphores. These operations cannot be performed in a signal handler. Later, we'll examine an example where this can be beneficial.

Sigwait functions

To wait for an asynchronous signal, use one of the following functions:

```
int sigwait(
        sigset_t           *set,
        int                *sig
);

int sigwaitinfo(
        sigset_t           *set,
        siginfo_t          *info
);

int sigtimedwait(
        sigset_t           *set,
        siginfo_t          *info,
        struct timespec    *timeout
);
```

These functions block the calling thread until one of the signals specified in *set* is delivered to the process or calling thread. If one of the specified signals is currently pending, these functions return immediately. Upon return, the signal is no longer pending. If multiple threads wait for the same signal, when the signal is delivered, only one thread returns from its sigwait function. Which thread returns is not defined.

It's important that the signals specified in *set* be blocked in all threads prior to calling these functions or undefined behavior will result. If the signals are not blocked, one the signals could be delivered to the thread before it calls one of the sigwait functions. If all threads in the application do not block the signals, the signal may be delivered to a thread that is not in a sigwait function. Depending on the current action of the signal, the process could be terminated. It is usually wise to have the initial thread block the signals of interest before creating threads. All threads created then inherit the signal mask of the initial thread.

The sigwait() function returns the delivered signal number in the *sig* parameter. The sigwaitinfo() function is identical to the sigwait() function, except that the siginfo_t structure associated with the signal delivered is returned in the *info* parameter, instead of the signal number. The siginfo_t structure contains the signal number and the cause of the signal. The sigtimedwait() function is identical to the sigwaitinfo() function, except that a timeout value is specified, indicating the maximum amount of time to wait for one of the specified signals in *set*. An error is returned if one of the signals is not delivered before the timeout occurs.

Be careful of the return values when using these functions. The `sigwait()` function comes from POSIX.1c and employs the new return value behavior. It returns zero on success and the error number on failure. The `sigwaitinfo()` and `sigtimedwait()` functions come from POSIX.1b and employ the traditional return value behavior. These functions return the delivered signal number on success and -1 on error, with `errno` indicating the error.

Do not call the `sigwait` functions for a signal whose action is set to **SIG_IGN**. Most systems immediately discard signals that are ignored. If a signal's action is set to **SIG_DFL**, and the default action is to ignore the signal, you may have to install a dummy signal handler in order to wait for the signal with these functions.

Note: POSIX.1c has stated that undefined behavior may result if an application uses `sigaction()` and one of the `sigwait` functions concurrently on the same signal. In short, it is guaranteed that an application can use one or the other, but not both at the same time. The safest approach when both functions are needed is to use `sigaction()` at the beginning of the application. Later, when a `sigwait` function is needed, the application doesn't need to worry about unspecified behavior.

Example

The following example shows how an application can use `sigwait()` to perform signal handling. Rather than have the application interrupted by signals, a dedicated thread is provided to handle all signals.

```
#include <signal.h>
#include <pthread.h>
#include <stdio.h>
#include <errno.h>

extern void    fatal_error(int err_num, char *func);
void           thread_sigwait();

main()
{
    pthread_t    tid;
    int          ret_val;
    sigset_t     set;

    /* Block signals from being delivered to this thread */

    sigfillset(&set);
    pthread_sigmask(SIG_SETMASK, &set, (sigset_t *)NULL);

    /* Create a signal handling thread */
    ret_val = pthread_create(&tid, (pthread_attr_t *)NULL,
                        (void *(*)())thread_sigwait,NULL);
```

```
        if (ret_val != 0)
                fatal_error(ret_val, "pthread_create()");

        /* Application processing code here */
        ...

        /* Wait for the thread to terminate */
        ret_val = pthread_join(tid, (void **)NULL);
        if (ret_val != 0)
                fatal_error(ret_val, "pthread_join()");

        /* Say Good-bye */
        printf("Program Terminating...\n");
        exit(0);
}


/*
 * Signal handling thread start_routine. Note: This is NOT a
 * signal handler
 */
void
thread_sigwait()
{
    sigset_t      set;
    int           sig;
    int           ret_val;

    /*
     * Block all signals from being delivered to this thread.
     */
    sigfillset(&set);
    pthread_sigmask(SIG_SETMASK, &set, (sigset_t *)NULL);

    /*
     * Wait for a signal to arrive and process it.
     */
    while (1) {
            ret_val = sigwait(&set, &sig);

            if (ret_val == 0) {
                printf("signal number %d received\n", sig);

                if (sig == SIGINT)
                    break;

                /* Signal processing code here */

                ...
            } else {
                fatal_error(ret_val, "sigwait()");
            }
    }
    pthread_exit((void *)NULL);
}
```

Async-Signal Safe Thread Functions

```
/* signal handler code */
sig_hdlr() {                       - Calls no pthread_* functions
    ...;                           - Does not use locking
    ...;
    ...;
async_signal_safe_function();
    ...;                           This function should be
    ...;                           documented as
    ...;                           async-signal safe.
}
```

Fig. 7–6 An acync-signal safe function is one that can be invoked from a signal handler. None of the pthread_*() functions are async-signal safe.

What is an async-signal safe function? It is a function that may be invoked from a signal handler. No function should be considered async-signal safe unless it is explicitly stated to be safe.

None of the pthread_*() functions are async-signal safe. Do not call any of these functions from within a signal handler. Initially, this may not seem like a severe restriction. However, a thread may want to terminate upon receipt of a specific signal. A thread cannot safely call pthread_exit() from a signal handler.

Even worse, a thread cannot call pthread_mutex_lock() from within a signal handler. If a thread attempts to lock a mutex inside of a signal handler, the application may become deadlocked. As an example, suppose thread A locks mutex X and starts executing a critical section of code. A signal is delivered to thread A, which causes the thread to execute a signal handler. The signal handler also calls pthread_mutex_lock() to lock mutex X. The thread is now deadlocked because it is trying to acquire a mutex that it has already acquired.

In a multithreaded application, chances are pretty good that the signal handler will access global data. To access this data, synchronization with the other threads must take place or several threads could be modifying the same global data simultaneously. None of the POSIX synchronization functions can be called from within signal handlers [except for sem_post()]. This restriction makes the sigwait functions extremely attractive for signal handling. When a thread handles a signal after returning from the sigwait() function, it can acquire locks without worry of self-deadlock if global data must be modified. The sigwait() functions eliminate the need for signal handlers to be installed in multithreaded applications.

The following table lists the POSIX functions that are async-signal safe. These are the only functions that may safely be called from within a signal handler:

Table 7–1 POSIX Async-Signal Safe Functions

• _exit()	• getgroups()	• sigpending()
• access()	• getpgrp()	• sigprocmask()
• aio_error()	• getpid()	• sigsuspend()
• aio_return()	• getppid()	• sleep()
• aio_suspend()	• getuid()	• stat()
• alarm()	• kill()	• sysconf()
• cfgetispeed()	• link()	• tcdrain()
• cfgetospeed()	• lseek()	• tcflow()
• cfsetispeed()	• mkdir()	• tcflush()
• cfsetospeed()	• mkfifo()	• tcgetattr()
• chdir()	• open()	• tcgetpgrp()
• chmod()	• pathconf()	• tcsendbreak()
• chown()	• pause()	• tcsetattr()
• clock_gettime()	• pipe()	• tcsetpgrp()
• close()	• read()	• time()
• creat()	• rename()	• timer_getoverrun()
• dup2()	• rmdir()	• timer_gettime()
• dup()	• sem_post()	• timer_settime()
• execle()	• setgid()	• times()
• execlv()	• setpgid()	• umask()
• fcntl()	• setsid()	• uname()
• fdatasync()	• setuid()	• unlink()
• fork()	• sigaction()	• utime()
• fstat()	• sigaddset()	• wait()
• fsync()	• sigdelset()	• waitpid()
• getegid()	• sigemptyset()	• write()
• geteuid()	• sigfillset()	
• getgid()	• sigismember()	

The functions in Table 7-1 are also the only functions guaranteed to be fork-safe in a multithreaded application. If a thread calls fork(), only async-signal safe functions should be called in the child process (until one of the exec functions is called).

If this list of functions is too restrictive for your signal-handling needs, one of the sigwait functions should be used instead of signal handlers. On return from a sigwait function, a thread is not limited to calling only async-signal safe functions.

A New Signal Delivery Method: SIGEV_THREAD

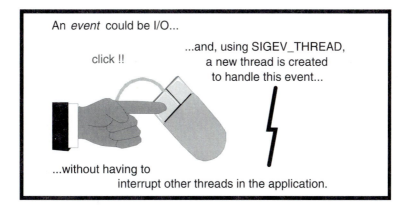

Fig. 7–7 The **SIGEV_THREAD** feature has been provided for event notification. When the event occurs, the system creates a new thread to handle it.

Overview

In the Process Model, only one type of event notification was available: signals. When the system needed to notify the application that an event had occurred, a signal was delivered to the process. Examples of event notification include timer expiration, asynchronous I/O completion, and the arrival of a message.

Event notification with signals has the disadvantage that the application is interrupted to process the event (i.e., a signal handler is called). If the application is performing a time-critical task, this task is put on hold until the signal handler returns.

Since applications can have multiple threads of control, event notification with threads rather than signals is now available.

The sigevent structure defined in POSIX.1b has been extended to support **SIGEV_THREAD**. Rather than delivering a signal when an event occurs, the system creates a new thread to execute an event handler (similar to a signal handler). The event handler is passed one argument. This mechanism allows an application to be notified of the occurrence of an event without interrupting currently running threads.

Thread event notification is useful when it takes a significant amount of time to process an event. Using signals to process long events causes extended interrupts in currently running threads. Do not use thread event notification if it takes less time to process the event than to create the notification thread.

SIGEV_THREAD

To use thread event notification, an application should place the following information in a `sigevent` structure:

a) Specify **SIGEV_THREAD** in the *sigev_notify* member.

b) Specify the name of the handler function (i.e., the thread start routine) in the *sigev_notify_function* member.

c) In the *sigev_value* member, specify the value to be passed as a parameter to the handler function.

d) If the notification thread is to be created with default thread attributes specify **NULL** in the *sigev_notify_attributes* member. Otherwise, store the thread creation attributes object in this member.

The `sigevent` structure is passed as a parameter to the asynchronous I/O functions, message queue functions, and timer functions. Unfortunately, only functions using `sigevent` structures can make use of this feature. **SIGEV_THREAD** cannot be used for signals generated via other methods [e.g., a user sent this process a signal via `kill()`].

There are a few things to note regarding **SIGEV_THREAD**. If a thread creation attributes object is not specified (i.e., *sigev_notify_attributes* is **NULL**), the notification thread is created with a detach state of **PTHREAD_CREATE_DETACHED**. Since there are no threads in the application that know the ID of the notification thread, no thread can join with the notification thread after it terminates. If a thread creation attributes object is specified, do not set the `detachstate` to **PTHREAD_CREATE_JOINABLE**.

The initial state of the signal mask for the notification thread is implementation-defined. For maximum portability, do not rely on the signal mask being initialized to any value.

Be careful when using **SIGEV_THREAD** in conjunction with interval timer operations. POSIX.1b has specified that for values of **SIGEV_SIGNAL**, only one signal from a timer will be pending at a time. If an interval timer expires before the previous interval's signal has been delivered, a timer overrun count is incremented. Unfortunately, POSIX.1c did not specify what happens for values of **SIGEV_THREAD**. If the first notification thread hasn't terminated, will a second thread be created when the timer expires a second time? Will the overrun count be incremented instead? Each system will define its own behavior. Check your system documentation before using **SIGEV_THREAD** with interval timers.

Example

The following code comes from an application that uses POSIX.1b message queues to communicate with other processes. The code initializes a sigevent structure with **SIGEV_THREAD**. The function sigev_thr_func() is the start routine for the new thread. It is passed a parameter with a value of one (from the sigev_value field). Finally, mq_notify() is called to request notification when a message arrives on the message queue.

When a message arrives, a new thread is created by the system that calls the sigev_thr_func() function. The sigev_value member is passed as a parameter to this function. The created thread can call mq_receive() to obtain the new message.

```c
#include <pthread.h>
#include <signal.h>
#include <mqueue.h>

mqd_t       mq_des; /* msg queue descriptor */

main()
{
    struct sigevent     evp;
    void                sigev_thr_func();

    /* Program startup code here */
    ...

    /* Setup event notification for msg queues */
    evp.sigev_notify = SIGEV_THREAD;
    evp.sigev_value.sival_int = 1;
    evp.sigev_notify_function = (void *(*)())sigev_thr_func;
    evp.sigev_attributes = (pthread_attr_t *)NULL;

    /* Request notification when a message arrives */
    mq_notify(mq_des, &evp);

    /* Rest of application code here */
    ...
}

void
sigev_thr_func(union sigval value)
{
        printf("Msg arrived, received %d\n",value.sival_int);

        /* Event handling code. if sival_int == 1, a msg has */
        /* arrived and we should call mq_receive() to get it. */
        ...

        pthread_exit(0);
}
```

Summary

This chapter demonstrated that multithreaded programs are more flexible constructs for using signals. For example, it is not necessary to interrupt the entire application when a signal is received. The signal is directed to a particular thread. You can also avoid using signal handlers altogether. Here are the highlights of this chapter:

- Each process has a set of signal actions. Each thread has a signal mask. A thread may send a signal to another thread within the same process. However, a thread may not send a signal to a thread in another process.

- When a signal is sent to a process, there is no guarantee which thread will handle it; however, you can direct most asynchronous signals to a particular thread through the use of signal masks.

- A signal is deemed *synchronous* or *asynchronous*, depending on how it was generated. A synchronous signal is generated due to the action of a specific thread, such as an illegal instruction, and is always delivered to the thread that generated it. An asynchronous signal is delivered to the process, typically from another source such as `kill()`, timer expiration, or asynchronous I/O completion.

- To examine or change a thread's signal mask, use `pthread_sigmask()`. Do not use the `sigprocmask()` function in a multithreaded program.

- A thread can use the `pthread_kill()` function to send a signal to another thread within its process. However, remember the rules for signals in a multithreaded application. If you send a signal that stops, continues, or terminates a thread, this will affect the entire process, not just the target thread.

- You can set up a multithreaded process in such a way that one or more threads will be available to handle a signal. There are three signal-waiting functions that provide a succession of features: `sigwait()` returns a signal number; `sigwaitinfo()` returns a `siginfo_t` structure; `sigtimedwait()` also returns a `siginfo_t` structure, but waits only for a specified amount of time.

- An async-signal safe function can be called from within a signal handler without adverse ramifications. None of the Pthread functions are async-signal safe.

- The **SIGEV_THREAD** feature allows you to write a signal handler that will not interrupt threads within the application. When the awaited signal arrives, a new thread is created to respond to the event.

Exercises

1. Describe synchronous and asynchronous signals. How are they differentiated? Give examples.

2. Using code segments, describe how an asynchronous signal sent to the process can be handled by a particular thread.

3. Describe an async-signal safe function.

4. Write a code segment consisting of three threads. Thread *A* should send a signal to threads *B* and *C*. Thread *B* should print a message containing the signal number. Thread *C* should print both the signal number and the cause of the signal.

5. Write a code segment that uses **SIGEV_THREAD** to provide notification of an I/O event.

Thread Cancellation

When programming with threads, it is often necessary to terminate a thread within the application. Signals appear to provide the most logical means to accomplish thread termination. However, signals have two major drawbacks: (1) if a signal causes a thread to terminate, the entire process terminates and (2) if POSIX allowed a signal to cause thread termination (and not process termination), mutexes and other resources acquired by terminated threads would never be released. The latter case could lead to deadlock. This chapter presents the thread cancellation interfaces, explains the concept of thread cancellation, and explains how resources are released when a thread is canceled.

Topics Covered...

- Thread Cancellation
- Thread Cancelability States
- Thread Cancellation Points
- Setting Thread Cancelability States
- Creating a Cancellation Point
- Installing Cancellation Cleanup Handlers
- Canceling a Thread
- Async-Cancel Safety

Thread Cancellation

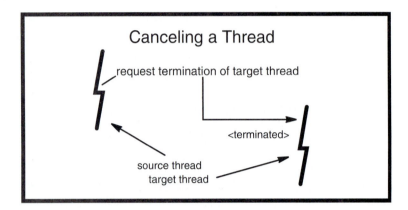

Fig. 8–1 Thread cancellation is a mechanism that allows a thread (the *source thread*) to terminate another thread (the *target thread*) within an application.

Thread cancellation is a mechanism that allows one thread in an application to terminate another thread in a clean and controlled manner. The "to-be-canceled" target thread is allowed to control when it is canceled. A list of functions to execute in the event that the thread is canceled can be specified. These functions, known as *cancellation cleanup handlers*, should release any mutexes (or other resources) that the thread is holding before the thread terminates. In the signal model, an application is allowed to install only one handler for each signal. Multiple cancellation cleanup handlers can be installed by multithreaded applications.

As you can see, thread cancellation is very similar to thread signals. Both models allow the thread to control when the event (signal delivery or cancellation) is allowed to happen. Additionally, both models allow threads to specify handlers (signal handlers or cancellation cleanup handlers) to execute when the event occurs.

When a thread wants to cancel another thread, it sends a cancellation request to the target thread. The requesting thread does not wait for the target thread to be canceled. During the time between sending the cancellation request and the termination of the target thread, the target thread is said to have a *pending cancellation request*. When the target thread notices the pending cancellation request, it will process or act on the cancellation request. The thread's cancellation cleanup handlers are called when it is canceled.

Thread cancellation can be useful for many types of applications, most notably those that perform heuristic searches. When one thread finds an answer, it can cancel the other threads also participating in the search. Cancellation can also be useful when an application accepts input from a user and a previous user request needs to be terminated.

Thread Cancelability States

cancelstate and canceltype	
cancelstate	**canceltype**
PTHREAD_CANCEL_ENABLE	PTHREAD_CANCEL_DEFERRED or PTHREAD_CANCEL_ASYNCHRONOUS
PTHREAD_CANCEL_DISABLE	**canceltype** does not have an effect when **cancelstate** is disabled. Cancellation requests are held pending.

Fig. 8–2 Each thread can have its `cancelstate` enabled or disabled. When enabled, the `canceltype` becomes important. The `canceltype` determines whether a thread can be canceled immediately or at specific places known as *cancellation points*.

A thread is allowed to control how and when it is canceled. Two cancellation attributes are associated with each thread: `cancelstate` and `canceltype`:

- `cancelstate`: Cancellation can be either enabled or disabled. By default, cancellation requests are enabled. If a thread starts an operation that cannot or should not be terminated, cancellation can be disabled. When disabled, any cancellation requests are held pending until cancellation is enabled again. Enabling and disabling cancellation is similar to blocking and unblocking signals. Valid values for a thread's cancelability state are: **PTHREAD_CANCEL_ENABLE** (the default value for all newly created threads) and **PTHREAD_CANCEL_DISABLE**.

- `canceltype`: Unlike signals, cancellation requests are processed only at certain points when a thread is executing. These points are known as *cancellation points* (more on this in the next section). When a thread is delivered a cancellation request, the request is held pending until the thread reaches a cancellation point. This behavior is known as *deferred cancelability*. A thread may change its cancelability type to asynchronous. With *asynchronous cancelability*, cancellation requests are acted upon at any time instead of only at predefined cancellation points. Valid values for the cancelability type are: **PTHREAD_CANCEL_DEFERRED** (the default value for all threads) and **PTHREAD_CANCEL_ASYNCHRONOUS**.

This mechanism offers a thread more control over cancellation than it has over signals. In the signal model, a thread is allowed only a few options: accept the signal, block the signal, or ignore the signal. With thread cancellation, a thread can block and unblock cancellation requests. Additionally, a thread can specify when cancellation requests are processed (immediately or at predefined functions).

Disabling cancellation during critical code sections may not provide an application with the desired cancellation behavior. The purpose of thread cancellation is to provide an application with the ability to cleanly terminate a thread. This operation is most useful when a thread is indefinitely blocked. Disabling a thread's cancellation state removes the ability to terminate the thread when the thread is blocked for indefinite periods. This does not imply that an application should never disable cancellation. There are situations where an application cannot tolerate a thread being canceled or where the back-out path to cleanup the state of a canceled thread is too complicated. In these instances, an application may want to disable cancellation. Applications should use this feature carefully.

A library routine should not explicitly enable cancellation. If an application disables cancellation, the library routine would allow the thread to be canceled. Because the application disabled cancellation, it is probably not prepared to handle the thread being canceled.

When a thread's cancelability type is set to **PTHREAD_CANCEL_ASYNCHRONOUS**, the thread can be canceled at any time, possibly in the middle of a critical code section which does not contain a failure back-out path. When having an asynchronous cancelability type, a thread should not acquire any resources and should call only async-cancel safe functions. If this advice is not followed, the thread needs to install cancellation cleanup handlers for every resource it acquires. If cleanup handlers are not installed, acquired resources are not released when the thread is canceled.

Cancellation Points

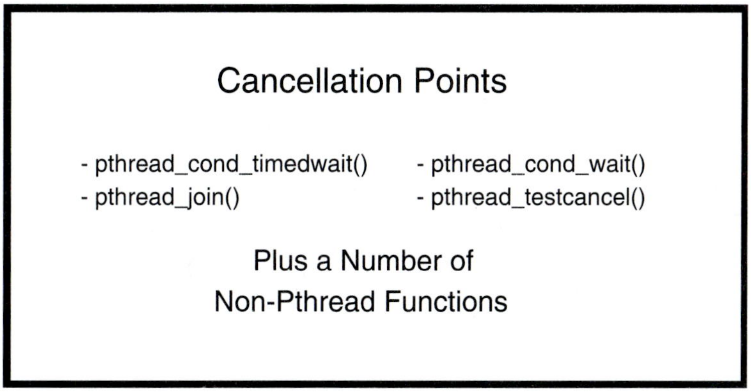

Fig. 8–3 When a thread reaches a cancellation point, it acts upon any pending cancellation requests, provided the thread's cancelstate is enabled.

Cancellation points are places where a thread must act on a pending cancellation request if cancellation is enabled. Cancellation points are the only places a thread may be canceled if its cancelability type is **PTHREAD_CANCEL_DEFERRED**. According to POSIX.1c, a thread needs to process a pending cancellation request only if it is about to block indefinitely. This is the minimum requirement in processing cancellation requests. Most systems cancel the target thread if the thread is blocked indefinitely inside a function that is a cancellation point.

Cancellation requests are acted upon in the following Pthread functions:

- `pthread_cond_timedwait()`   - `pthread_join()`
- `pthread_cond_wait()`   - `pthread_testcancel()`

Note: `pthread_mutex_lock()` is not a cancellation point. Making this function a cancellation point would put undue burden on all applications. Every time a mutex is locked, a cancellation cleanup handler would need to be installed, placing a huge burden on multithreaded applications. Applications should not leave mutexes locked for long periods as threads that are blocked on mutexes cannot be canceled.

The following list contains all the non-Pthread functions that are cancellation points:

- `aio_suspend()`   - `nanosleep()`   - `sigwaitinfo()`
- `close()`   - `open()`   - `sleep()`
- `creat()`   - `pause()`   - `system()`
- `fcntl()`   - `read()`   - `tcdrain()`
- `fsync()`   - `sem_wait()`   - `wait()`

- mq_receive()
- mq_send()
- msync()

- sigsuspend()
- sigtimedwait()
- sigwait()

- waitpid()
- write()

The following list contains additional functions at which a cancellation point may occur, depending on certain conditions or actions taken inside the functions:

- closedir()
- ctermid()
- fclose()
- fflush()
- fgetc()
- fgets()
- fopen()
- fprintf()
- fputc()
- fputs()
- fread()
- freopen()
- fscanf()
- fseek()
- ftell()
- fwrite()
- getc()
- getc_unlocked()

- getchar()
- getchar_unlocked()
- getcwd()
- getgrgid()
- getgrgid_r()
- getgrnam()
- getgrnam_r()
- getlogin()
- getlogin_r()
- getpwnam()
- getpwnam_r()
- getpwuid()
- getpwuid_r()
- gets()
- lseek()
- opendir()
- perror()
- printf()

- putc()
- putc_unlocked()
- putchar()
- puts()
- putchar_unlocked()
- readdir()
- remove()
- rename()
- rewind()
- rewinddir()
- scanf()
- tmpfile()
- tmpnam()
- ttyname()
- ttyname_r()
- ungetc()
- unlink()

Each system contains additional functions not controlled by POSIX that are cancellation points. Examples are system calls such as msgrcv(), msgsnd(), and putmsg(). If a function can return with an **EINTR** error, chances are that it is a cancellation point. Check your system's documentation to determine whether any non-POSIX functions are cancellation points.

If a thread is blocked in one of the above functions, a cancellation request may terminate the thread. What happens if a cancellation request occurs at the same time that the function unblocks (e.g., the waited-for signal has arrived)? POSIX.1c leaves it up to each system to define whether the function returns or the cancellation request is acted upon. Most systems allow the function to return and the cancellation request remains pending. Portable applications should not rely on this behavior.

If an application is a library supplied to other application developers, the library should specify every routine that contains a cancellation point. If a library routine calls any of the above functions, the routine contains a cancellation point. Application programmers need to know this so that cancellation cleanup handlers can be installed before calling the library routine. If this information is not known, thread resources are not released when a thread is canceled while in the library routine.

Setting Thread Cancelability States

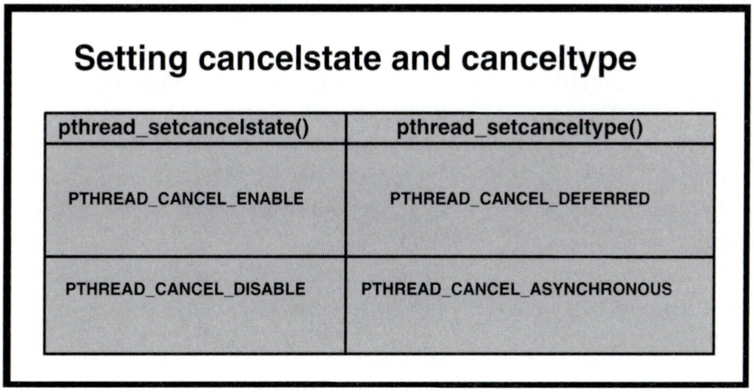

Fig. 8–4 Use the `pthread_setcancelstate()` function to enable or disable the `cancelstate` for a thread. Use the `pthread_setcanceltype()` function to choose a deferred or asynchronous `canceltype`.

Overview

When created, a thread has a cancelability state of **PTHREAD_CANCEL_ENABLE** and a cancelability type of **PTHREAD_CANCEL_DEFERRED**. The following two routines can be used to change the cancelability state and type of the calling thread:

```
int pthread_setcancelstate(
        int                 state,
        int                 *oldstate
);

int pthread_setcanceltype(
        int                 type,
        int                 *oldtype
);
```

The function `pthread_setcancelstate()` changes the cancelability state of the calling thread to the value specified in the *state* parameter. *State* may be either **PTHREAD_CANCEL_ENABLE** or **PTHREAD_CANCEL_DISABLE**. The previous cancelability state is returned in the *oldstate* parameter. If cancelability is disabled, cancellation requests remain pending until the state is enabled.

The function `pthread_setcanceltype()` changes the cancelability type of the calling thread to the value specified in the *type* parameter. *Type* may be either **PTHREAD_CANCEL_DEFERRED** or **PTHREAD_CANCEL_ASYNCHRONOUS**. The previous cancelability type is returned in the *oldtype* parameter.

Changing a thread's cancelability state or type during an operation should be paired with a call to restore the state and type when the operation completes.

Example

The following code fragment shows how to change a thread's cancelability type and state. Assume that the code comes from a simple database-like application.

This example first verifies that the thread does not have asynchronous cancelability to ensure that the data buffer processing is not interrupted asynchronously (it holds a mutex). Verification of the cancelability type must be performed if the function is called by threads with both cancelability types. Once the buffer has been processed, it is ready for writing. When a buffer write has started, it must complete without interruption. Consequently, the thread's cancelability state is disabled. If the thread were canceled while writing the buffer, this record would be lost and never entered into the database.

```
/*
 * Make sure we cannot be canceled asynchronously while holding
 * the mutex. We don't check for errors since the only error for
 * the pthread_setcancel*() functions is EINVAL and we know we
 * are passing a valid type/state.
 */
type = PTHREAD_CANCEL_DEFERRED;
(void) pthread_setcanceltype(type, &oldtype);

/* do data buffer processing here */
(void) pthread_mutex_lock(&write_mtx);

...

(void) pthread_mutex_unlock(&write_mtx);

/*
 * We are going to physically write the database
 * record now. We cannot be canceled here.
 */
state = PTHREAD_CANCEL_DISABLE;
(void) pthread_setcancelstate(state, &oldstate);

write_physical_record(buffer);

/*
 * Restore cancelability state and type
 */
(void) pthread_setcancelstate(oldstate, &state);
(void) pthread_setcanceltype(type, &oldtype);
```

Creating a Cancellation Point

```
my_function() {
    ...;
    ...;
    /* insert cancellation point before
     * long I/O operation
     */
    pthread_testcancel();
    read();
    ...;
    ...;
}
```

Fig. 8–5 Use the `pthread_testcancel()` function to create a cancellation point.

Overview

Sometimes a thread may want to process any pending cancellation requests before executing long or critical code segments. For example, a thread may disable cancelability for an extended period to prevent it from being terminated during an operation. Before disabling cancelability, the thread should act on any pending cancellation requests.

To check for and process a pending cancellation request, use the function:

```
void pthread_testcancel(void);
```

The `pthread_testcancel()` function creates a cancellation point inside of an application. Each time this function is called, it checks for pending cancellation requests against the calling thread. If a cancellation request is pending, the calling thread is terminated. If the calling thread has its cancelability state set to **PTHREAD_CANCEL_DISABLE**, a pending cancellation request will not be processed. In other words, when a thread says *disabled*, it really is disabled!

Example

Let's go back to the code fragment from the previous section. Assume that it takes a long time to execute the function `write_physical_record()`. Disabling cancelability for this amount of time may not be desirable as cancellation requests should not be held pending for too long. The example has been modified to process cancellation requests before calling `write_physical_record()`. Additionally, the example checks for pending cancellation requests after returning from the function so that cancellation requests are blocked for the shortest amount of time possible.

```
...

/*
 * make sure we cannot be canceled asynchronously while holding
 * the mutex. We don't check for errors since the only error for
 * the pthread_setcancel*() functions is EINVAL and we know we
 * are passing a valid type/state.
 */
type = PTHREAD_CANCEL_DEFERRED;
(void) pthread_setcanceltype(type, &oldtype);

/* do some data buffer processing here */
(void) pthread_mutex_lock(&write_mtx);

...

(void) pthread_mutex_unlock(&write_mtx);

/*
 * we are going to physically write the database
 * record now. We cannot be canceled here. Act on any
 * cancellation requests before writing the buffer (i.e.,
 * last chance!).
 */
pthread_testcancel();

state = PTHREAD_CANCEL_DISABLE;
(void) pthread_setcancelstate(state, &oldstate);

write_physical_record(buffer);

/*
 * Restore cancelability state and type. Act on any
 * cancellation requests that may have arrived while
 * we blocked them.
 */
(void) pthread_setcancelstate(oldstate, &state);
(void) pthread_setcanceltype(type, &oldtype);

pthread_testcancel();

...
```

Installing Cancellation Cleanup Handlers

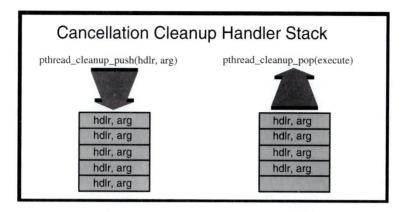

Fig. 8–6 Use the `pthread_cleanup_push()` function to install one cleanup handler onto the calling thread's cancellation cleanup handler stack. These handlers are used to release various resources, such as mutex locks, when the thread acts upon a cancellation request. Use the `pthread_cleanup_pop()` function to remove handlers from the cleanup handler stack.

Overview

Examine this small code fragment:

```
(void) pthread_mutex_lock(&tmp_mtx);
if (global_data_ptr != NULL) {
      write(fd, global_data_ptr, sizeof(global_data_ptr));
      free(global_data_ptr);
      global_data_ptr = NULL;
}
(void) pthread_mutex_unlock(&tmp_mtx);
```

Suppose that another thread in this process issues a `pthread_cancel()` request to the thread executing the above code fragment. The thread executing this code will be canceled while in the `write()` function call. Whether the thread is canceled before or after the write completes is unknown. Two problems arise when this thread is terminated:

- The mutex `tmp_mtx` is not unlocked by the canceled thread. Any other thread that executes this code will block, forever trying to acquire `tmp_mtx`. Because this mutex will never be released, the application is deadlocked.

- If the thread executing this code has its cancelability type set to **PTHREAD_CANCEL_ASYNCHRONOUS**, it could be canceled after the write has completed. At this point, the data has been written out, but the global state in the application indicates that the data has not been written out (`global_data_ptr` is not **NULL**). Asynchronous cancelability can be extremely dangerous.

These problems occur with more than just mutex locks. Any resource that a thread acquires could be left in a locked state if the owning thread is canceled. How does an application avoid these problems? A thread may install cancellation cleanup handlers to release any acquired resources when it is canceled. Multiple cancellation cleanup handlers may be installed by a thread. When a thread is terminated, the cancellation handlers are executed in Last-In, First-Out (LIFO) order. The last handler to be installed will be the first handler to be executed.

When a thread executes `pthread_exit()`, any cancellation cleanup handlers installed for the thread are executed. This behavior is a kind of safety catch-all feature. If an error occurs several levels deep in an application, causing the thread to terminate itself, any resources allocated by the higher levels can be released by the cancellation cleanup handlers.

`pthread_cond_wait()` and `pthread_cond_timedwait()` are cancellation points. If a thread is canceled while in a condition wait, the mutex associated with the condition is reacquired before any of the cancellation activities take place. The mutex is locked when the cancellation cleanup handlers are called. The cleanup handler associated with a condition wait should release the mutex.

Installing/Removing Cancellation Cleanup Handlers

To install (push) and remove (pop) cancellation cleanup handlers, use the following functions:

```
int pthread_cleanup_push(
      void                (*routine)(void *),
      void                *arg
);

int pthread_cleanup_pop(
      int                 execute
);
```

The `pthread_cleanup_push()` function installs the cancellation cleanup handler *routine* for the calling thread. Each handler is pushed onto the calling thread's cancellation cleanup stack. If the handler *routine* is ever invoked, it is passed *arg* as its sole parameter.

The function `pthread_cleanup_pop()` removes the top cancellation cleanup handler from the calling thread's cancellation stack. If the *execute* parameter is nonzero, the handler is also invoked and passed *arg* as a parameter.

Each cancellation cleanup handler on a thread's cancellation stack will be called under the following conditions:

- The thread calls `pthread_exit()`.

- The thread is canceled as a result of a call to `pthread_cancel()`.

The cancellation handlers are popped from the terminating thread's cancellation stack and executed in LIFO order. The handler most recently pushed is executed first.

Additionally, the function at the top of a thread's cancellation stack is invoked when:

- The thread calls `pthread_cleanup_pop()` with the *execute* parameter containing a nonzero value.

Lexical Scope

On most systems, these functions are implemented as macros. Both functions must appear as pairs in the same lexical scope. `pthread_cleanup_push()` can be thought of as the open brace ('{') character and `pthread_cleanup_pop()` as the close brace ('}') character. In fact, many systems have the push macro contain the '{' and the pop macro contain the '}' to force a thread to make these calls within the same lexical scope. Do not `longjmp()` or `return` out of a function between these calls.

Condition Variables and Cancellation

Both `pthread_cond_wait()` and `pthread_cond_timedwait()` are cancellation points. If a thread is canceled while in a condition wait, the condition variable's associated mutex is reacquired by the canceled thread before the cleanup handlers are called. This causes the cleanup handlers to execute in the same state as the critical code that was canceled (i.e., the canceled thread held a mutex lock). An application using condition variables and the cancellation facilities should always install cancellation cleanup handlers to unlock the condition variable's associated mutex.

Joining Threads and Cancellation

The `pthread_join()` function is a cancellation point. If a thread is canceled while joining with a target thread, the target thread is not joined. It's wise to have the cleanup handler for the joining thread call `pthread_detach()` on the target thread. Otherwise, the target thread's resources will never be released back to the system.

Example

The following code fragment shows how to use cancellation cleanup handlers in an application. In this example, a thread calls `malloc()` to allocate memory. After the memory is allocated, a function that contains a cancellation point is called. This function could be something like `read()`, `write()`, or `fscanf()`. If the thread is canceled while this memory is allocated, the memory is lost. Consequently, a cancellation cleanup handler, `cleanup_func()`, is installed to release this memory in the event that the thread is canceled.

```
void cleanup_func(char *ptr)
{
     free(ptr);
}


void start_routine()
{
     char    *ptr;

     /* Allocate memory for our buffer, install a cleanup */
     /* handler in case we are canceled. */
     ptr = (char *) malloc((size_t)1024);
     if (ptr == NULL) {
            fprintf(stderr, "Out of memory\n");
            exit(-1);
     }

     pthread_cleanup_push((void (*)())cleanup_func, (void *)ptr);

     /* Code to do things to ptr goes here */
     ...

     /* Finished with ptr, free() it up and remove the */
     /* cancellation cleanup handlers */
     pthread_cleanup_pop(0);
     free(ptr);

     pthread_exit(0);
}
```

There are two things to note here:

- Resources such as mutexes and semaphores can also be released by the cancellation cleanup handlers.

- The example could have passed `pthread_cleanup_pop()` a nonzero value and could have had `cleanup_func()` release the memory, rather than calling `free()` inside of `start_routine()`.

Canceling a Thread

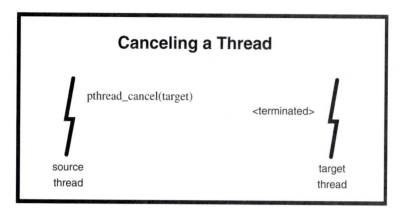

Fig. 8–7 Use the `pthread_cancel()` function to request cancellation of a thread. Although the function will return immediately, the target thread will be canceled according to the thread's `cancelstate` and `canceltype`.

Overview

To cancel a specific thread, use the following function:

```
int pthread_cancel(
        pthread_t               target_thread
);
```

The `pthread_cancel()` function issues a cancellation request to the thread *target_thread*. This function will not wait for the thread to be canceled. It returns immediately after sending the cancellation request.

When the target thread is actually canceled depends on the value of the target thread's cancelability state and type. If the thread's cancelability state is set to **PTHREAD_CANCEL_DISABLE**, the request will remain pending until the thread enables cancelability. Otherwise, if the thread has its cancelability type set to **PTHREAD_CANCEL_DEFERRED**, the request will remain pending until the thread calls a function that contains a cancellation point. If the cancelability type is **PTHREAD_CANCEL_ASYNCHRONOUS**, the request may be acted upon by the target thread at any time.

When a thread is canceled, cancellation cleanup handlers that have been installed are called by the canceled thread. After the cleanup handlers have been called, thread-specific data destructors for the thread are called (more on this in the next chapter). Finally, after all cleanup handlers and thread-specific data destructor functions have been called, the target thread terminates. The return status of a canceled thread is **PTHREAD_CANCELED**. This status is returned to a joining thread.

Example

In the following example, one *boss* thread and several *worker* threads are represented. The *boss* thread receives and places tasks on a task queue for the *worker* threads to process. For certain requests, the *boss* thread performs the task. One of the tasks requires the termination of one random *worker* thread in the application. The target worker thread is canceled while it is in a condition wait.

```c
#include <stdio.h>
#include <stdlib.h>
#include <pthread.h>

struct job_task {
      int               type;
      int               num;
      struct job_task   *next;
      struct job_task   *prev;
      /* Fill in application-specific fields */
};

void                    work_threads()
void                    task_enqueue(struct job_task *);
int                     task_queue_empty()
struct job_task         *task_dequeue();

#define QUIT              1
#define ADD_WORKER        2
#define TERMINATE_WORKER  3
#define PROCESS_WORK      4

#define MAX_THREADS       10

extern pthread_mutex_t   *task_lock;
extern pthread_cond_t    *task_cv;


void boss_thread()
{
      pthread_t          thread;
      struct job_task    *task;
      int                task_size, type, ret;
      int                pthread_id_last = 0;
      pthread_t          pthread_id[MAX_THREADS];

      task_size = sizeof(struct job_task);
      for ( ; ; ) {
            /* Get the next work item to be performed */
            task = (struct job_task *) malloc(task_size);
```

```
    if (task == (struct job_task *)NULL) {
        fprintf(stderr, "boss_thread(): ENOMEM\n");
        exit(-1);
    }
    type = get_next_job(task);

    /* Process the task. It may be a terminate request, */
    /* add an additional work thread request, terminate */
    /* a work thread request, or an actual request.     */
    if (type == QUIT) {
        exit(0);

    /* Add an additional worker thread */
    } else if (type == ADD_WORKER) {
        free((void *)task);
        if (pthread_id_last < MAX_THREADS) {
            pthread_id_last++;
            ret = pthread_create(
                    &pthread_id[pthread_id_last],
                    NULL, (void *(*)())work_threads,
                    NULL);
            if (ret != 0)
                fatal_error(ret,"pthread_create()");
        }

    /* Terminate a worker thread */
    } else if (type == TERMINATE_WORKER) {
        free((void *)task);
        if (pthread_id_last > 0) {
            thread = pthread_id[pthread_id_last];
            ret = pthread_cancel(thread);
            if (ret != 0)
                fatal_error(ret, "pthread_cancel()");
            pthread_id_last--;
            (void) pthread_join(thread, (void **)NULL);
        }

    /* Queue up request for a thread to process. */
    } else {
        (void) pthread_mutex_lock(task_lock);
        task_enqueue(task);

        /* Signal the condition to wakeup worker threads */
        (void) pthread_cond_signal(task_cv);
        (void) pthread_mutex_unlock(task_lock);
    }
  }
 }
}
```

```
void
work_thread_cleanup(pthread_mutex_t *lock)
{
      pthread_mutex_unlock(lock);
}

void
work_threads()
{
      struct job_task      *task;

      for ( ; ; ) {
            /* Get the next task to be processed. */
            (void) pthread_mutex_lock(task_lock);
            pthread_cleanup_push((void (*)())work_thread_cleanup,
                              (void *)task_lock);

            while (task_queue_empty())
                  pthread_cond_wait(task_cv, task_lock);

            pthread_cleanup_pop(0);
            task = task_dequeue();
            (void) pthread_mutex_unlock(task_lock);

            /* Process the task. */
            ...

            /* Release memory from task structure. */
            free((void *)task);
      }
}
```

Async-Cancel Safety

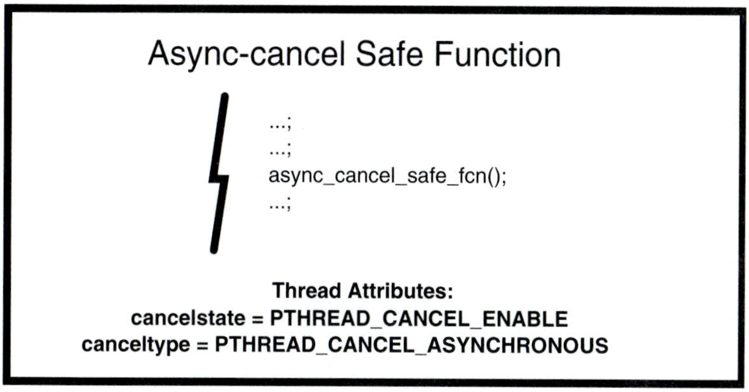

Fig. 8–8 An async-cancel safe function is any function that can safely be called for a thread that has its `cancelstate` enabled and its `canceltype` set to asynchronous.

What is an async-cancel safe function? It is a function that may be called by a thread when the thread's cancelability state is set to **PTHREAD_CANCEL_ENABLE** and the cancelability type is set to **PTHREAD_CANCEL_ASYNCHRONOUS**. If a thread is canceled in an async-cancel safe function, no state will be left by the thread in the function.

Async-cancel safe functions generally do not acquire resources to perform the function's task. If they do and if the calling thread is canceled, the acquired resources are never released. Generally, only functions that access local non-static variables and do not allocate resources can be considered async-cancel safe.

It is possible (but not easy) to construct an async-cancel safe function that acquires resources. A function can install a cancellation cleanup handler for each resource it acquires. In the event of being canceled, the cancellation cleanup handler needs to be passed enough state to undo the partially completed operation. Complex functions may find this extremely difficult and will generally declare that they are not async-cancel safe.

Only the POSIX functions `pthread_cancel()`, `pthread_setcancelstate()`, and `pthread_setcanceltype()` are async-cancel safe. All other functions in the POSIX and C standards are not guaranteed to be async-cancel safe. A library that is supplied to application developers should specify whether or not each routine in the library is async-cancel safe.

Threads with asynchronous cancelability enabled should call only async-cancel safe functions. Otherwise, when they are canceled, resources may be left in an inconsistent state. This situation can lead to deadlock if mutexes are involved.

Summary

In this chapter, the thread cancellation mechanism was described. This mechanism allows a thread to terminate another thread within the same process. Thread cancellation facilities are provided because of the limitations with signals. For example, if a signal causes a thread to terminate, the entire process is terminated. Here is a recap of thread cancellation:

- Thread cancellation is a mechanism that allows a thread within a process to terminate another thread. The target thread is allowed to set cancellation attributes that control when it is canceled.

- Two thread attributes are used to determine when a thread will act upon a cancellation request: `cancelstate` and `canceltype`. When a thread's `cancelstate` is enabled, the thread acts upon a cancellation request, according to its `canceltype`. If a thread's `canceltype` is set to the deferred mode, the thread is canceled only when executing functions known as *cancellation points*. If `canceltype` is set to the asynchronous mode, the target thread acts upon a cancellation request immediately.

- A *cancellation point* is a place where a thread may be canceled if the thread's `cancelstate` is enabled. Certain functions are designated as *cancellation points*. When a thread reaches a cancellation point, it will act upon any pending cancellation requests. If no cancellation requests are pending, the thread continues execution.

- The `pthread_setcancelstate()` function is used to enable or disable cancellation for the calling thread. The `pthread_setcanceltype()` function is used to set the calling thread's cancellation type to deferred or asynchronous mode.

- A cancellation point can be created any place in an application by calling the `pthread_testcancel()` function. A thread calling this function acts upon cancellation requests if cancellation is enabled.

- A thread can cancel another target thread by calling `pthread_cancel()`. The target thread will act upon the cancellation request, according to its `cancelstate` and `canceltype` attributes.

- A thread can install cancellation cleanup handlers to release resources, such as mutex locks, before the thread terminates. Handlers are installed onto a cancellation cleanup handler stack. They are popped and executed in LIFO order when the thread terminates. Remember that the `pthread_cleanup_push()` and `pthread_cleanup_pop()` functions must be used in pairs within the same lexical scope.

- An async-cancel safe function is any function that can safely be called when a thread has its `cancelstate` enabled and its `canceltype` set to asynchronous mode.

Exercises

1. Name two reasons that thread cancellation may be preferable over signals for thread termination.

2. What happens to cancellation requests if the target thread has its `cancelstate` set to disabled and its `canceltype` set to asynchronous? What would be the effect of cancellation points in this situation?

3. Write a program with two threads. Set thread A's `cancelstate` to enabled and its `canceltype` to asynchronous. Thread A should acquire mutex M and spin. Thread B should send a cancellation request to thread A, then attempt to lock mutex M. When thread B acquires mutex M, it should print "got M." What happens when the program executes in this order?

4. In the same program created in #3, thread **A** should install cancellation cleanup handlers for mutex M. Again, thread A should acquire mutex M and spin. Then thread B should send the cancellation request to thread A and attempt to lock the mutex.What happens now?

5. Adjust the program created in #4. Thread A's `canceltype` should be set to deferred. Write the code necessary to make thread B successful in acquiring the mutex.

CHAPTER 9

Thread-Specific Data

When a multithreaded program is written, a determination must be made as to how global data is shared among the threads in the process. There are two choices: (1) a global data variable can be *process-shared* and protected with synchronization primitives, or (2) a global data variable can be *specific* to each thread. In the second case, thread-specific data is employed, and synchronization is not required. This chapter presents the thread-specific data interfaces and explains how they are used.

Topics Covered...

- Thread-Specific Data
- Creating Thread-Specific Data Keys
- Deleting Thread-Specific Data Keys
- Accessing Thread-Specific Data Elements
- The Special Case, `errno`
- Per-Thread Signal Handlers

Thread-Specific Data

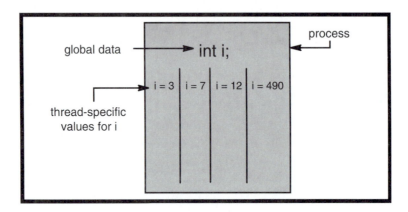

Fig. 9–1 A good example of thread-specific data is `errno`. There is one global variable called `errno` in each process, but each thread within a process has its own private copy.

Thread-specific data is global data that is private or specific to a thread. Each thread has a different value for the same thread-specific data variable. Why would an application need thread-specific data? Consider a function that allocates a resource specific to the calling thread. This resource is allocated in global data because it will be used by multiple functions. Now, suppose a different thread calls one of these functions. This thread will use the global data that was specific to the first thread. If this data is allocated as thread-specific data, each thread calling these functions would access its own copy of the data. The global variable `errno` is a perfect example of thread-specific global data.

Thread-specific data is implemented in a Key/Value model. An application must associate a key with each thread-specific data variable. The key is shared by all threads in the process (i.e., it's a global variable). When a thread references this key, it references its own private copy of the global data. Each thread can associate a `void *` pointer with each key. You, as the programmer, must allocate and maintain what the thread-specific data pointer references [e.g., a per-thread data structure allocated via `malloc()`]. Remember, you get storage for only one pointer with each key.

Thread-specific data within an application can be thought of as a two-dimensional table. The rows represent each of the threads in the process. The columns represent the different keys that have been created. To find the thread-specific data for a specific key, a thread indexes into the table with its thread ID and the key being accessed. The following table shows how this can conceptually be viewed.

Table 9-1 Example of Thread-Specific Data in an Application

	Key1	**Key2**	**Key3**	**Key4**	**Key5**
Thread 1	NULL	NULL	NULL	NULL	NULL
Thread 2	NULL	NULL	256	0x4001cd00	78
Thread 3	0x400031c0	NULL	512	0x400035c8	NULL
Thread 4	0x40004658	NULL	128	NULL	10245
Thread 5	NULL	NULL	64	0x4001cf30	NULL

To find a thread-specific data value in the above table, find the row for the desired thread and the column for the key. The box where the row and column intersect contains the thread-specific data associated with the key for the desired thread. There are a few interesting things to note in the table:

- **Thread 1** has not allocated any thread-specific data.
- **Key2** has not been used by any threads in the application.
- **Key1** and **Key4** store pointers as thread-specific data. These are usually pointers to (per-thread) dynamically allocated memory.
- **Key3** and **Key5** store integers as thread-specific data rather than pointers (use the proper type casting if you do this).

Note that this table represents only a conceptual view of how thread-specific data is implemented by a system. The actual implementation chosen by a system may be quite different from this two-dimensional table.

Thread-specific data is most useful when existing single-threaded code needs to be used in a multithreaded application. Some functions maintain static data across function calls or return pointers to static data. In a multithreaded application, this static data may need to be specific to each thread. If this data is treated as global process shared data, incorrect behavior may result when multiple threads call the functions simultaneously. These functions can be changed to treat the static data as thread-specific data to maintain existing function semantics. Many library routines use thread-specific data so the function interface doesn't need to change to operate correctly in multithreaded applications.

Some systems provide compiler supported thread-specific data, also known as *thread local storage*. This feature is much easier for applications to use. An application declares the thread-specific data the way it would normally declare global data, but prefixing the declaration with something like `__thread` or `thread_specific`. Compiler-supported thread-specific data is currently not supported by POSIX.1c and is beyond the scope of this chapter.

Creating Thread-Specific Data Keys

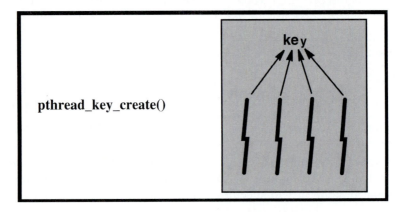

Fig. 9–2 Use the `pthread_key_create()` function to create a thread-specific data key. This key is used by all threads within a process to gain access to a piece of thread-specific data. A *destructor* function can be specified to free a thread's allocated thread-specific data on termination.

Overview

To use thread-specific data, an application must first create a thread-specific data key. This key is used by all threads in the process to access the thread-specific data represented by the key. Only one thread should create a key for any piece of thread-specific data. Once a key has been created, all threads can access their thread-specific data for the key.

Thread-specific data keys should be allocated in global memory that is accessible to all threads. It is generally wise for an application to create all thread-specific data keys in `main()` before any threads have been created. Otherwise, a thread may try to access one of the keys before it has been created.

To allocate a thread-specific data key, use the function:

```
int pthread_key_create(
    pthread_key_t      *key,
    void               (*destructor)(void *)
);
```

This function creates a thread-specific data key and returns the key in *key*. Each thread has one pointer's worth of thread-specific storage for *key*. For each thread, an initial value of **NULL** is assigned to the thread-specific data associated with *key*. After returning from the `pthread_key_create()` function, any thread in the process can access its thread-specific data associated with *key*.

When a thread terminates, the function calling `pthread_exit()` may not know that thread-specific data exists for the terminating thread. Even if the caller knows, it may not know how to free the thread-specific data resources for the thread. This is likely to happen if `pthread_exit()` is called several levels deep in an application when the thread detects an error. When a thread-specific data key is created, the caller is allowed to specify a *destructor* function to be called when a thread terminates. This destructor function is responsible for releasing any resources associated with *key* for the terminating thread.

For example, thread *A* calls `malloc()` to allocate the thread-specific data associated with the key *my_data*. If thread *A* were to terminate before calling `free()` on the allocated data, memory is lost. To resolve this, create a destructor function for the key *my_data*. When thread *A* is terminated, the destructor function for the key should release the allocated thread-specific memory.

A different destructor function should be installed for each key, unless the destroy action is the same for all keys. When the destructor function is called, the key is not passed as a parameter.

When a thread terminates, it examines each of its thread-specific data keys. If any of the keys have non-**NULL** values for the thread and the key contains a destructor function, the destructor function is called for the key. The current value of the key is passed as a parameter to the destructor function.

Destructor functions may call functions that use thread-specific data. It's possible that a function called by a destructor function may allocate additional thread-specific data. Because of this, if there are still non-**NULL** values associated with the keys for the terminating thread, the destructor functions are called again. This sequence repeats until all the keys have **NULL** values for the thread. Some systems terminate this loop after **PTHREAD_DESTRUCTOR_ITERATIONS** iterations, but don't rely on it. POSIX.1c allows a system to loop infinitely.

Example

```
void           key1_destruct(void *value);
pthread_key_t key1;

main()
{
        ...

        /* Create key1 with a destructor function. */
        ret_val = pthread_key_create(&key1, key1_destruct);
        check_error(ret_val, "pthread_key_create() failed");
        ...
}

void key1_destruct(void *value)
{
        free(value);
}
```

Deleting Thread-Specific Data Keys

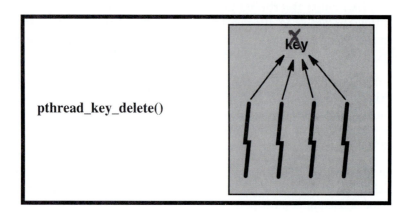

Fig. 9–3 Use the `pthread_key_delete()` function to delete keys that are no longer needed. Once a key is deleted, it is no longer available to any thread within the application.

Overview

There may be times when an application no longer needs to use a thread-specific data key. If this ever occurs, the application should remove the thread-specific data key from the system. Once a key has been removed, threads in the application cannot use the key.

To remove a thread-specific data key, use the function:

```
int pthread_key_delete(
    pthread_key_t      key
);
```

This function removes *key* from the application's set of thread-specific data keys. `pthread_key_delete()` may be called at any time, even if threads have non-**NULL** values associated with *key*. However, when this function is called, the thread-specific data destructor function associated with *key* is not called for any of the threads.

After *key* has been deleted, if any thread has allocated memory associated with *key*, a memory leak occurs. This situation arises because the thread-specific data destructor functions are not called when a key is deleted. Make sure that each and every thread in an application has released all memory associated with a key before deleting the key.

Example

Let's take our previous example and modify it to destroy the thread-specific data key:

```c
#include <pthread.h>
#include <stdlib.h>

void    fatal_error(int err_num, char *function);
void    key1_destruct(void *value);

#define check_error(return_val, msg) {                      \
        if (return_val != 0)                                \
                fatal_error(err_num, function);             \
}

pthread_key_t           key1;

main()
{
        int     ret_val;

        /*
         * Create key1 with a destructor function
         */
        ret_val = pthread_key_create(&key1, key1_destruct);
        check_error(ret_val, "pthread_key_create() failed");

        /* Rest of application code goes here. */
        ...

        /*
         * Be sure to verify that all threads are done with the
         * key before deleting it.
         */
        ret_val = pthread_key_delete(key1);
        check_error(ret_val, "pthread_key_delete() failed");
}

void
key1_destruct(void *value)
{
        free(value);
}
```

Accessing Thread-Specific Data Elements

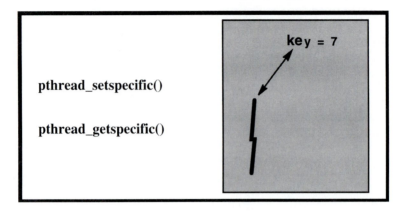

Fig. 9–4 Use the `pthread_setspecific()`/`pthread_getspecific()` functions to set and get thread-specific data.

Overview

With the thread-specific data interfaces, an application cannot just declare a variable to be thread-specific. Threads must use a set of interfaces to access thread-specific data. These interfaces permit the thread to obtain a thread-specific data value. Thread-specific data values are usually pointers to memory dynamically allocated by the thread.

To access thread-specific data, use the following functions:

```
int pthread_setspecific(
    pthread_key_t     key,
    void              *value
);

void *pthread_getspecific(
    pthread_key_t     key
);
```

The *key* parameter in both functions is the thread-specific data key that was created with `pthread_key_create()`. This key is used to store and retrieve the thread-specific data value associated with *key* for the calling thread. *key* should be allocated as global data so that all threads can access their thread-specific data.

The `pthread_setspecific()` function allows an application to assign *value* to the thread-specific data *key* for the calling thread. Each thread may associate a different *value* with *key*. The contents of *value* are decided by the caller. In most cases, *value* will be a pointer to memory or a data structure allocated via `mal-loc()`.

The `pthread_getspecfic()` function retrieves the thread-specific value associated with *key* for the calling thread and returns the value to the caller. If *key* is invalid, undefined behavior results; however most systems will return **NULL**.

Performance

Accessing thread-specific data can be an expensive operation. Each time a thread-specific data value is be stored or retrieved, a function call must be made. If an application has several thread-specific data keys that it must access in the same code segment, it is wise to coalesce these keys into one key. Rather than providing a separate key for each thread-specific data value, create a data structure that contains a field for each of the thread-specific data values. One key is associated with this new data structure. When a thread needs to access the thread-specific data values, it calls `pthread_getspecific()` with the new key. A pointer to the data structure is returned, and the thread-specific data values are accessed through this pointer. This technique will help improve the performance of an application that uses significant amounts of thread-specific data.

Example

The following code shows two different examples of using the functions `pthread_setspecific()` and `pthread_getspecific()`. For key1, only an integer value is stored as thread-specific data. Consequently, no destructor function is needed to release memory in the event that the thread is terminated. For key2 however, the thread-specific data is `malloc()`'ed data, so a destructor function is needed.

```
#include <pthread.h>
#include <stdlib.h>
#define    check_error(return_val, msg) {                     \
                if (return_val != 0)                          \
                      fatal_error(return_val, msg); \
            }

pthread_key_t        key1, key2;
void                 destruct(void *value), start_func(int num);

main()
{
        int          ret_val;
        pthread_t    tid1;

        /* Create key1 and key2 thread-specific data keys */
        ret_val = pthread_key_create(&key1, (void *) NULL);
```

```
        check_error(ret_val, "key_create 1 failed");

        ret_val = pthread_key_create(&key2, destruct);
        check_error(ret_val, "key_create 2 failed");

        /* Create a thread to do the work. */
        ret_val = pthread_create(&tid1, (pthread_attr_t *)NULL,
                            (void *(*)())start_func,
                            (void *) 1);
        check_error(ret_val, "Thread 1 create failed");

        /* We're a thread too */
        start_func(0);

        /* Wait for the thread to finish.*/
        ret_val = pthread_join(tid1, (void **)NULL);
        check_error(ret_val, "Thread 1 wait failed");

        /* Delete the thread-specific data keys. */
        ret_val = pthread_key_delete(key1);
        check_error(ret_val, "key_delete 1 failed");

        ret_val = pthread_key_delete(key2);
        check_error(ret_val, "key_delete 2 failed");
}

void start_func(int thread_num)
{
        char            *buf;

        pthread_setspecific(key1, (void *)thread_num);
        buf = (char *) malloc(100);
        pthread_setspecific(key2, (void *)buf);

        /* The rest of the application code goes here. */
        /* key1 and key2 can be accessed as global TSD now */
        ...

        /* clean up the thread-specific data. */
        pthread_setspecific(key1, (void *)NULL);
        buf = pthread_getspecific(key2);
        free(buf);
        pthread_setspecific(key2, (void *)NULL);
}

void destruct(void *value)
{
        free(value);
}
```

The Special Case, errno

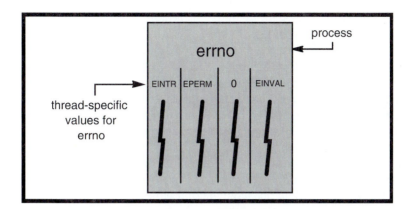

Fig. 9–5 `errno` is a special case of thread-specific data.

The global variable `errno` is a special case of thread-specific data. The `errno` variable is maintained on a per-thread basis. If `errno` were not thread-specific, an application could never rely on its value. Between the time a function sets `errno` to indicate an error and the time a thread reads the contents of `errno`, another thread's function call could fail and reset `errno`. The thread would then get the wrong `errno` value.

Accessing `errno` through the thread-specific data interfaces could be painful for existing code that already accesses `errno` as a global variable. For compatibility reasons, POSIX.1c made `errno` the exception. `errno` is a thread-specific data variable; however, threads do not need to use the thread-specific data interfaces to access `errno`. A thread can continue to access `errno` as it always has - as a global variable. Internally, the system maintains a separate `errno` variable for each thread. Because of this requirement, many systems require multithreaded applications to be compiled with the **-D_REENTRANT** compile flag. Check your system's documentation to see if this is required. As a recommended exercise, take a look at `/usr/include/errno.h` and see how `errno` is defined on your system for multithreaded applications.

Some applications maintain a global variable similar to the `errno` variable. Whenever an error occurs, the error is stored in this variable and accessed later by other functions. If a multithreaded application needs to use an application-defined global error variable, it should use thread-specific data to maintain this variable on a per-thread basis.

Example: Per-Thread Signal Handlers

The following module shows an example of implementing per-thread signal handlers using thread-specific data.

An array of structures is maintained, one for each signal. Each structure contains: (a) a valid member to indicate whether it has been initialized with a key and signal, (b) a thread-specific data key for the signal, and (c) a signal member indicating the signal represented by this structure. The thread-specific data key is used to store and retrieve the actual per-thread signal handler function.

The `install_thread_handler()` function and `sig_handler()` function must both synchronize on `sig_list[]`, the array of signal structures. However, `pthread_mutex_lock()` is not async-signal safe and `sig_handler()` is a signal handler. To get around this problem, signals are blocked from delivery in both of these functions. When signals are blocked, there is no way a signal could be delivered, causing the thread to execute `sig_handler()` and to deadlock on itself.

To install per-thread signal handlers, the `install_thread_handler()` function first looks for an entry in the `sig_list[]` array for the specified signal. If an entry is not found, a new entry is initialized. Initializing an entry entails setting the valid field, the signal field, initializing the thread-specific data key for signal, and calling `sigaction()` for the signal. A process-shared signal handler, `sig_handler()`, is installed for the signal through `sigaction()`. Finally, the per-thread signal handler is saved as thread-specific data using the thread-specific data key associated with the signal's entry in `sig_list[]`.

When one of the desired signals is delivered to a thread, the process-shared signal handler `sig_handler()` is invoked. This function will find the entry for the signal in the `sig_list[]` array. Once found, the thread-specific data key associated with the signal is used to obtain the per-thread signal handler. The per-thread handler is then called.

POSIX doesn't define the values of the signal numbers. Consequently, this example does not rely on the value of a signal number and must search and compare signal numbers in the `sig_list[]` array. If the signal numbers on your system start at a known value and are always incremented by one, you could change this code to use the signal number as an index into the `sig_list[]` array. If you're careful, you may even be able to remove the need for the mutex lock. Be careful if you attempt this, your code may not be portable if it relies on the actual signal numbers.

```
#include <pthread.h>
#include <signal.h>
pthread_mutex_t    handler_lock = PTHREAD_MUTEX_INITIALIZER;
pthread_once_t     sig_list_init = PTHREAD_ONCE_INIT;

struct per_thread_sigs {
    int            valid;
    pthread_key_t  key;
    int            signal;
};

#define MAX_SIGS            40
struct per_thread_sigs      sig_list[MAX_SIGS];

void
initialize_handlers()
{
    bzero((char *)sig_list, sizeof(sig_list));
}

int
install_thread_handler(int sig, void (*handler)())
{
    int    i;
    void   sig_handler();
    struct sigaction    act;
    sigset_t            blocked_sigs, old_sigs;

    /*
     * Block all signals from delivery while in this function.
     * Doing this is the only way we are allowed to try to acquire
     * the handler_lock mutex in the signal handler. If we don't do
     * this, it's possible we could take a signal in the middle of
     * this function while we hold the lock. In the signal handler,
     * the lock will be acquired resulting in deadlock.
     */
    sigfillset(&blocked_sigs);
    pthread_sigmask(SIG_SETMASK, &blocked_sigs, &old_sigs);

    /* Initialize the sig_list[] if it hasn't been done. */
    (void) pthread_once(&sig_list_init, initialize_handlers);

    /* Find the signal or a place for it in sig_list[] */
    (void) pthread_mutex_lock(&handler_lock);
    for (i = 0; i < MAX_SIGS; i++) {
            if (sig_list[i].signal == sig)
                    break;
            if (! sig_list[i].valid)
                    break;
    }
```

```
/* Too many signals handled already? */
if (i >= MAX_SIGS) {
        (void) pthread_mutex_unlock(&handler_lock);
        pthread_sigmask(SIG_SETMASK, &old_sigs, NULL);
        return(-1);
}

/* Have we already installed a handler for this signal? */
if (! sig_list[i].valid) {

        /* Create a TSD key for this signal */
        if (pthread_key_create(&sig_list[i].key, NULL) != 0) {
                (void) pthread_mutex_unlock(&handler_lock);
                pthread_sigmask(SIG_SETMASK, &old_sigs, NULL);
                return(-1);
        }

        /* Mark the entry as valid for this signal. */
        sig_list[i].valid = 1;
        sig_list[i].signal = sig;

        /* Install a process-wide handler for the signal. */
        /* Block signals while the signal handler is executing */

        act.sa_handler = sig_handler;
        act.sa_flags = 0;
        sigfillset(&act.sa_mask);
        if (sigaction(sig, &act, NULL) != 0) {
                (void) pthread_mutex_unlock(&handler_lock);
                pthread_sigmask(SIG_SETMASK, &old_sigs, NULL);
                return(-1);
        }
}

/* Store the per-thread handler in TSD */
(void) pthread_setspecific(sig_list[i].key, (void *)handler);

/* Release the lock, restore the signal handler */
(void) pthread_mutex_unlock(&handler_lock);
(void) pthread_sigmask(SIG_SETMASK, &old_sigs, NULL);

return(0);
}
```

```
void
sig_handler(int sig)
{

        int        i;
        void       (*thr_handler)();
        sigset_t   blocked_sigs, old_sigs;

        /*
         * Block all signals from delivery while in this function.
         * Doing this is the only way we are allowed to try to acquire
         * the handler_lock mutex in the signal handler. If we don't do
         * this, it's possible we could take a signal in the middle of
         * this function while we hold the lock.
         */
        sigfillset(&blocked_sigs);
        pthread_sigmask(SIG_SETMASK, &blocked_sigs, &old_sigs);

        /* Find the signal or a place for it in sig_list[] */
        (void) pthread_mutex_lock(&handler_lock);
        for (i = 0; i < MAX_SIGS; i++) {
                if (sig_list[i].signal == sig)
                        break;
                if (! sig_list[i].valid)
                        break;
        }

        /* We can't have this handler if signal is not in the list */
        if ((i >= MAX_SIGS) || (! sig_list[i].valid)) {
                printf("ERROR: signal %d, not set\n", sig);
                exit(-1);
        }

        /* Get the per-thread signal handler */
        thr_handler = (void (*)())pthread_getspecific(sig_list[i].key);

        /* Release the mutex, restore signal mask */
        (void) pthread_mutex_unlock(&handler_lock);
        pthread_sigmask(SIG_SETMASK, &old_sigs, NULL);

        /* Valid signal handler for this thread? */
        if (thr_handler == NULL) {
                printf("ERROR: signal %d, no thread handler\n", sig);
                exit(-1);
        }

        /* Call the per-thread signal handler */
        (*thr_handler)(sig);
}
```

Summary

When a multithreaded program is written, a determination must be made as to how global data is shared among the threads in the process. In the Threads Model, the programmer has two choices: (1) a global data variable can be process-shared and protected with synchronization primitives, or (2) a global data variable can be specific to each thread. In the second case, synchronization is not required. Here is a summary of the material presented on thread-specific data:

- Thread-specific data is global data that is specific to a thread. Each thread has its own private copy of the data. This obviates the need for synchronization. `errno` is a good example of thread-specific data.

- Use the `pthread_key_create()` function to create a thread-specific data key. A key can be used by all threads to gain access to their own thread-specific data values associated with the key. A destructor function can be specified to free a thread's allocated thread-specific data when the thread terminates.

- Use the `pthread_key_delete()` function to delete thread-specific data keys that are no longer needed in your application. Once a key is deleted, it cannot be used by any thread within the application.

- Thread-specific data must be accessed via the `pthread_setspecific()` and `pthread_getspecific()` functions. These functions store and retrieve the thread-specific data values associated with a key for the calling thread.

- `errno` is a special case of thread-specific data. A thread-specific `errno` is automatically set-up for each thread. Without this, a thread couldn't rely on `errno` values as it executes. A thread does not need to use the thread-specific data interfaces to access its thread-specific `errno`.

- You can implement per-thread signal handlers using thread-specific data.

Exercises

1. When should a thread-specific data destructor routine be used?
2. What is a good application for thread-specific data (besides `errno`)?
3. Write a program with two threads. Create a thread-specific data key along with a destructor routine. The thread *A* should write "good morning" and thread *B* should write "good night" into their respective thread-specific data. Each thread should print its ID and message. Finally, clean-up the thread-specific data and unneeded key before terminating the program.

Thread Extensions

The HP-UX system includes several thread extensions such as read-write locks, enhanced MxN Thread Model scheduling control, processor affinity, and additional mutex types. Many of these features are extensions provided by the *X/Open Portability Guide*. Some of these features are provided by HP and may not be portable. Nevertheless, all of these are powerful features that can enhance multithreaded applications.

Topics Covered...

- HP and X/Open Thread Extensions
- Thread Stack Attributes
- Suspending and Resuming Threads
- Mutex Extensions
- Condition Variable Expiration Time
- Read-Write Locks
- Read-Write Lock Attributes
- Initializing and Destroying Read-Write Locks
- Locking and Unlocking Read-Write Locks
- The Timeshare Scheduling Policy
- Thread to Processor Binding
- Thread Concurrency and MxN Threads
- Scheduling Unbound Kernel Entities

HP and X/Open Thread Extensions

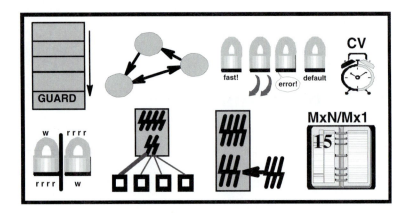

Fig. 10–1 The HP-UX and X/Open Thread Extensions provide several portable and non-portable features to support a more robust programming environment.

Hewlett-Packard and X/Open have implemented several extensions to the POSIX.1c threads programming environment. Many of these extensions were implemented to resolve shortcomings of the POSIX.1c standard. Others provide the programmer with additional control and features to support a more robust programming environment.

The extensions provided on HP-UX include: an additional thread stack attribute, suspending and resuming threads, four types of mutexes, read-write locks, concurrency and scheduling control in the MxN Threads Model, a timeshare scheduling policy, and the ability to bind threads to specific processors on multiprocessor machines.

Most of the extensions discussed in this chapter are extensions that have been provided by X/Open. All major UNIX systems will support these features, and applications can use the features in a portable manner.

All HP-only Pthread extensions provided on HP-UX have _np at the end of function names and **_NP** at the end of macro names. The *np* stands for "non-portable." This naming convention will help distinguish which features are portable and which are non-portable.

Thread Stack Attributes

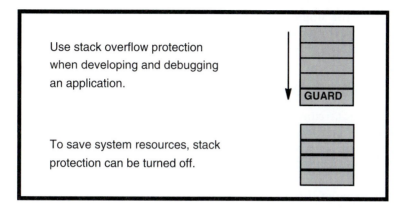

Fig. 10–2 A guard page is used to detect stack overflow. When stack overflow is detected, a signal is delivered to the offending thread. Overflow detection can be turned off, allowing you to save system resources. However, debugging an application that suffers from stack overflow can be extremely difficult.

Overview

Most systems add a guard page to the end of a thread's stack. The guard page is intended to detect stack overflow. If a thread overflows its stack, a signal is delivered to the thread. This feature aids in debugging as thread stacks cannot grow dynamically. If a thread's stack isn't large enough, the programmer will find out quickly.

The guard page can also be a source of problems. By default, one page of memory is dedicated to the guard page. If a system has a 4K page size and an application creates thousands of threads, a large amount of memory is dedicated to guard pages for stack protection. To a certain degree, it's not all that important. It's only virtual memory, right? Not quite. The system may also allocate swap space for this memory.

Some applications may wish to save virtual memory and swap space by not creating a guard page for each thread's stack. A thread attribute has been designed to control the size of the guard area in a thread's stack. Be cautious when using this attribute. Without stack protection, it is difficult to detect and debug stack overflow errors. If you use this feature, we recommend that you develop and debug your application with stack protection enabled. After the application is completely bug free, disable stack protection.

Certain threads may require a guard area that is larger than one page at the end of their stack. Consider a thread that allocates an array whose total size is 30K.

If the thread incorrectly indexes into this array, it's possible that it may index well past the one-page guard area into another thread's stack area. If this occurs, the system will not detect the stack overflow (unless the access is made to an address within the single guard page). Applications that allocate large amounts of data on the stack may wish to increase the size of the guard area to help detect incorrect application behavior.

Thread `guardsize` Attribute

The `guardsize` attribute allows an application to specify the size of the guard area for threads created with an attributes object. The size of the guard area is specified in bytes. Most systems round up the guard size to the nearest page size. If the value zero is specified, a guard area will not be created.

The default value of the `guardsize` attribute is **PAGESIZE** bytes. The value of **PAGESIZE** is hardware-dependent and may vary from system to system (even between systems from the same vendor). This attribute is ignored if the `stack-addr` attribute is not **NULL**. In this case, the application is responsible for creating guard pages for the thread stacks.

Getting/Setting Thread Stack Attribute Extensions

The `guardsize` attribute can be retrieved from or set in the thread attributes object with the functions described below. The *attr* parameter represents the thread attributes object, which must have been previously initialized with the function `pthread_attr_init()`. The second parameter contains either the attribute value being set or a pointer to where the retrieved attribute value is returned (depending on whether it is a set or a get function).

```
int pthread_attr_getguardsize(
    pthread_attr_t         *attr,
    size_t                 *guardsize
);

int pthread_attr_setguardsize(
    pthread_attr_t         *attr,
    size_t                 guardsize
);
```

Setting the Default Stack Size on HP-UX

A thread is created with a default stack size if either (1) the *attr* parameter to pthread_create() is **NULL**, or (2) the stacksize attribute in the *attr* parameter is not changed after the attribute is initialized. On HP-UX, threads with default stack sizes are cached after they terminate. When a thread is created, if a cached thread is available, the cached thread (and its stack) are reused. Caching threads can result in significant performance improvements for applications which create and terminate many threads.

In some applications, the default stack size needed by threads in the application may not be the same value that the system uses for a default stack size. When this occurs, the application cannot take advantage of the performance benefit realized by caching threads.

On HP-UX, an application can use the following function to change the default stack size; thus utilizing the performance benefit of cached threads:

```
int pthread_default_stacksize_np(
        size_t          new_size,
        size_t          *old_size

);
```

The pthread_default_stacksize_np() function causes the threads library to change the default value of the stacksize thread attribute to the value specified in *new_size*. This function must be called before any threads are created or any thread attributes objects are initialized. The value of *new_size* must be greater than or equal to **PTHREAD_STACK_MIN**.

If *old_size* is not **NULL**, the previous default stack size is returned in *old_size*. If *new_size* is set to zero, this function will only query the current default stack size. This function may be called at any time if *new_size* is zero.

After the default stack size has been changed, the threads library will cache threads that have stacks with a size of *new_size*, instead of those with a stack size of *old_size*. An application that has threads using stacks of the same size can obtain a significant performance improvement from the thread cache.

Example

The following code initializes a thread attributes object and specifies that stack protection should be disabled for the to-be-created thread. The new thread is created executing the function thread1_func(), and the thread attributes object is destroyed. Remember, once a thread has been created, it's safe to destroy the thread attributes object.

```
#include <pthread.h>

extern void fatal_error(int err, char *func);
extern void thread1_func();

#define    check_error(return_val, msg) {                     \
                  if (return_val != 0)                        \
                          fatal_error(return_val, msg);  \
              }

main()
{
    pthread_t       tid;
    pthread_attr_t  attr;
    int             return_val;

    /*
     * Create the attr object
     */
    return_val = pthread_attr_init(&attr);
    check_error(return_val, "pthread_attr_init()");

    /*
     * Set the guardsize attribute to have no stack protection
     */
    return_val = pthread_attr_setguardsize(&attr, 0);
    check_error(return_val, "pthread_attr_setguardsize()");

    /*
     * Create a new thread to execute thread1_func()
     */
    return_val = pthread_create(&tid, &attr,
                              (void *(*)())thread1_func,
                              (void *)NULL);
    check_error(return_val, "pthread_create()");

    /*
     * It's safe to destroy the attr object now
     */
    return_val = pthread_attr_destroy(&attr);
    check_error(return_val, "pthread_attr_destroy()");

    /* Rest of the program goes here */
    ...
}
```

Suspending and Resuming Threads

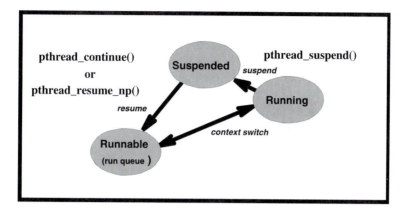

Fig. 10–3   Threads may be suspended and resumed using the `pthread_suspend()`, `pthread_continue()`, and `pthread_resume_np()` functions.

Overview

Some applications may need to suspend some or all of the threads in the application. The most common need for thread suspension comes from a garbage collector facility. In a garbage collector, one thread suspends all threads involved in a particular task. Once the threads have been suspended, the garbage collector thread cleans up any "garbage" created by the other threads. When the garbage collector thread has finished its task, the suspended threads are allowed to resume execution.

Suspending Threads

To suspend a thread, use the function:

```
int pthread_suspend(
    pthread_t          thread

);
```

This function suspends the thread specified by *thread*. The calling thread blocks until the target thread has been suspended. The target thread may not be suspended immediately. If *thread* specifies the calling thread (i.e., self-suspension), the caller is suspended while in this function and does not return until resumed by another thread.

Exactly when the target thread is suspended is implementation-dependent. Most systems suspend the target thread immediately if the thread is currently blocked or waiting on a scheduling run queue. Otherwise, the target thread is suspended when it makes its next system call.

Each time a thread is suspended, the thread's suspension count is incremented. If the target thread is already suspended when this function is called, the suspension count is incremented, and the call returns immediately.

Resuming Threads

To resume a suspended thread, use either of the following functions:

```
int pthread_continue(
    pthread_t            thread
);

int pthread_resume_np(
    pthread_t            thread,
    int                  flags
);
```

These functions resume a suspended thread. If *thread* is not suspended, the functions have no effect and do not return an error. The pthread_continue() function resumes the execution of a thread, regardless of how many times it was suspended. The pthread_resume_np() function is an HP-only function that provides the application with the ability to control how a thread is resumed. A suspended thread can be resumed in one of two methods indicated by the *flags* parameter:

PTHREAD_COUNT_RESUME_NP: This option causes the target thread's suspension count to be decremented by one. If the resulting suspension count is greater than zero, the thread remains suspended. Once the thread's suspension count reaches zero, the thread is allowed to continue execution. When using this option, one call to pthread_resume_np() is required for every call made to pthread_suspend() with the same target thread.

PTHREAD_FORCE_RESUME_NP: This option causes the target thread's suspension count to be set to zero. The thread is immediately resumed and allowed to continue execution. Be careful when intermixing this option with the **PTHREAD_COUNT_RESUME_NP** option on the same target thread. It's easy to get the suspend and resume calls out of order if both options are used.

We strongly encourage you to use the **PTHREAD_COUNT_RESUME_NP** option unless you absolutely require a forced resume. Consider the case where two threads have suspended the same target thread. If the first thread issues a forced resume, the target thread continues execution. However, the second thread expects that the target thread is still suspended. In general, a thread should not resume execution until all threads suspending it are ready for the target thread to resume.

Why is there a forced resume option? There are cases where a forced resume may be necessary. An event may occur that needs to be handled by the suspended thread immediately, regardless of what may happen to other threads in the application. The application doesn't want to wait for the threads that issued a suspend to issue the matching resume. A forced resume is useful in this situation.

Synchronization

Do not use these functions as a synchronization method between threads. An application cannot guarantee that a thread will be suspended before the thread executes a specific section of code. Because the application cannot control exactly when the target thread is suspended, these functions are not useful as synchronization primitives.

It's usually not wise to have one thread suspend a target thread and a different thread resume the target thread. If the two threads issuing the suspend and resume are not synchronized, it's possible that the resume could be issued before the suspend. In this situation, the target thread is left suspended, as resuming a thread that is not suspended has no effect.

In many cases, it's possible to avoid the need for suspending and resuming threads through the proper use of synchronization primitives. Even a garbage collector facility can be implemented without suspending threads. If each thread is required to acquire a mutex before creating garbage, the garbage collector needs only to acquire the proper mutex to ensure that it can safely clean-up the garbage. If you can avoid the need to suspend and resume threads by using alternate mechanisms (such as synchronization primitives), we strongly encourage you to use the alternate mechanism.

Deadlock

The thread suspend and resume capabilities need to be used carefully by an application. It is extremely easy to create a deadlock with these features. Consider the following situation: thread A is performing an operation that acquires mutex X. Thread B calls `pthread_suspend()`, specifying thread A as the target thread. Thread A is now suspended while it owns mutex X. Before resuming thread A, thread B calls a function that needs to acquire mutex X. Thread B is now deadlocked as thread A is suspended and cannot release the mutex.

This situation can be further complicated when libraries provided by the system acquire mutex locks. The application does not know if and when a library routine may acquire a mutex. A call to `malloc()` will require a mutex lock to be acquired so that `malloc()` and `free()` can synchronize access by multiple threads. If the target thread is suspended during one of these function calls, it is not safe to call either of these functions until the target thread is resumed.

After a thread has been suspended, it is safe to call only functions that the target thread does not call. For example, if the target thread never calls `malloc()` or `free()`, it's safe to call `malloc()` and `free()` after suspending the thread.

Example

The following example shows how to suspend and resume a thread. The main thread is suspended and some action is performed. Once the action has completed, the main thread is resumed. A counting resume is used as other threads may have also suspended the main thread.

```
extern pthread_t   main_thr_id;
extern void           fatal_error(int err, char *func);

#definecheck_error(return_val, msg) {                    \
            if (return_val != 0)                         \
                    fatal_error(return_val, msg);    \
}


void
func()
{
     int     ret;

     . . .

     /* Don't suspend ourselves*/
     if (pthread_equal(pthread_self(), main_thr_id))
          return;

     /* Suspend the main thread */
     ret = pthread_suspend(main_thr_id);
     check_error(ret, "pthread_suspend()");

     /* Perform action which requires the thread to be suspended */
     . . .

     /* We're done, resume the main thread */
     ret = pthread_resume_np(main_thr_id, PTHREAD_COUNT_RESUME_NP);
     check_error(ret, "pthread_resume_np()");


     . . .

}
```

Mutex Extensions

Fig. 10–4 Four types of mutexes are supported: fast, recursive, error checking, and default. Fast mutexes provide the best performance. Recursive mutexes may be locked by a thread multiple times and must be unlocked the same number of times before it is actually unlocked. The error-checking mutex will return an error if it is used incorrectly (e.g., locked twice by the same thread). Default mutexes comply with the exact semantics required by POSIX.1c.

Overview

The mutex synchronization primitive has been enhanced to support four different types of mutexes: normal, recursive, error-checking, and default. Operations on normal mutexes do not provide error checking. Error checks take time and hurt application performance. Error-checking mutex operations provide help to detect incorrect application usage and are useful during application development. Recursive mutexes allow a mutex to be locked multiple times by the same thread. The default mutex follows the POSIX.1c guidelines for mutexes: the results of recursively locking the mutex, unlocking an unlocked mutex, or unlocking a mutex locked by another thread are undefined.

Mutex `type` Attribute

The `type` attribute allows an application to specify the type of mutex to be initialized. Four different types of mutexes are available:

PTHREAD_MUTEX_NORMAL: This type of mutex provides the fastest mutex lock and unlock operations. These mutexes do not prevent self-deadlock. If a thread tries to recursively lock a mutex of this type, the thread will deadlock on itself. If a thread tries to unlock a mutex that is unlocked or locked by a different thread, undefined behavior results.

PTHREAD_MUTEX_RECURSIVE: This type of mutex allows the mutex to be locked recursively by the same thread. Since the concept of an owner is maintained, only the locking thread is allowed to unlock the mutex. If the mutex is locked multiple times, it must be unlocked the same number of times before another thread can acquire the mutex. These mutexes are useful when you have recursive functions needing a mutex lock or multiple code paths that enter a function, sometimes with the lock held and sometimes without the lock held.

PTHREAD_MUTEX_ERRORCHECK: If a thread tries to recursively lock a mutex of this type, an error is returned. These mutexes support the concept of an owner; a thread can unlock only a mutex that it has locked. As these mutexes detect incorrect mutex usage, they are extremely useful during an application's development and debugging phases. Once the application is bug free, the mutexes can be changed to normal mutexes to provide better application performance.

PTHREAD_MUTEX_DEFAULT: This type of mutex provides the exact semantics as specified by POSIX.1c. If a thread tries to recursively lock a mutex of this type, undefined behavior results. If a thread tries to unlock a mutex that is unlocked or locked by a different thread, undefined behavior results. Most systems will map this mutex type into one of the other three mutex types, but portable applications should not rely on this behavior.

The default value of the `type` attribute is **PTHREAD_MUTEX_DEFAULT.** If specific mutex behavior with respect to error checking or recursive locking is desired, use one of the other mutex types.

Getting/Setting Mutex Attribute Extensions

The `type` attribute can be retrieved from or set in the mutex attributes object with the functions described below. The *attr* parameter represents the mutex attributes object that must have been previously initialized with the function `pthread_mutexattr_init()`. The second parameter contains either the attribute value being set or a pointer to where the retrieved attribute value is returned (depending on whether it is a set or a get function).

```
int pthread_mutexattr_gettype(
    pthread_mutexattr_t     *attr,
    int                     *type
);

int pthread_mutexattr_settype(
    pthread_mutexattr_t     *attr,
    int                     type
);
```

Example

The following code fragment shows how to allocate and initialize a recursive mutex and a normal mutex. A mutex attributes object is initialized and the `type` attribute set to specify a recursive mutex. The recursive mutex is initialized, then the `type` attribute is set to specify a normal mutex. Once the normal mutex is initialized, the attributes object is destroyed.

```
pthread_mutex_t      r_mtx;    /* recursive mutex */
pthread_mutex_t      n_mtx;    /* normal mutex */
extern void          fatal_error(int err, char *func);

#define      check_error(return_val, msg) {                \
                if (return_val != 0)                       \
                        fatal_error(return_val, msg);  \
             }
main()
{
      pthread_mutexattr_t     mtx_attr;
      int                     ret_val;

      /* Initialize the mutex attributes */
      ret_val = pthread_mutexattr_init(&mtx_attr);
      check_error(ret_val, "mutexattr_init failed");

      /* Set the type attribute to recursive */
      ret_val = pthread_mutexattr_settype(&mtx_attr,
                                    PTHREAD_MUTEX_RECURSIVE);
      check_error(ret_val, "mutexattr_settype failed");

      /* Initialize the recursive mutex */
      ret_val = pthread_mutex_init(&r_mtx, &mtx_attr);
      check_error(ret_val, "mutex_init failed");

      /* Set the type attribute to normal */
      ret_val = pthread_mutexattr_settype(&mtx_attr,
                                    PTHREAD_MUTEX_NORMAL);
      check_error(ret_val, "mutexattr_settype failed");

      /* Initialize the normal mutex */
      ret_val = pthread_mutex_init(&n_mtx, &mtx_attr);
      check_error(ret_val, "mutex_init failed");

      /* Destroy the attributes object */
      ret_val = pthread_mutexattr_destroy(&mtx_attr);
      check_error(ret_val, "mutexattr_destroy failed");

      /* Rest of application code here */
      ...
}
```

Condition Variable Expiration Time

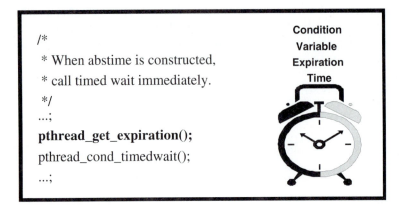

Fig. 10–5 Using `pthread_cond_timedwait()`, a thread can wait for an absolute time. The `get_expiration_time()` function allows a thread to construct a relative timeout value for use in `pthread_cond_timedwait()`.

Overview

When a thread waits on a condition variable, it has the option to wait until a specified time passes. The `pthread_cond_timedwait()` function does not take an interval or relative timeout value. A thread must pass the absolute time at which the condition wait should expire.

When a thread wants to wait for a specified time interval relative to when the wait starts, it must construct an absolute time from the desired time interval. To accomplish this, the thread must obtain the current time (in seconds and nano-seconds) and add to that the desired time interval. The resulting time is then passed to the `pthread_cond_timedwait()` function.

Constructing a Relative Timed Wait

A convenience function has been provided to help construct an absolute time based on a time interval:

```
int get_expiration_time(
    struct timespec     *delta,
    struct timespec     *abstime
);
```

The *delta* parameter is an input parameter and specifies the number of seconds and nanoseconds to add to the current time. The *abstime* parameter is an output parameter. This function adds *delta* to the current time and returns the resulting absolute time in *abstime*.

After calling `get_expiration_time()`, the *abstime* parameter should be used in a call to `pthread_cond_timedwait()` to perform a relative condition wait. The condition timed wait should be performed immediately after constructing *abstime*. The *abstime* parameter represents the time at which the wait expires. If a thread were to construct an *abstime* value and then do other things before the condition timed wait, the time represented by *abstime* may pass before the condition timed wait function is called. In this case, the condition timed wait function will return the error **ETIMEDOUT** immediately, rather than waiting the desired *delta* time interval.

Example

```
pthread_mutex_t         job_lock = PTHREAD_MUTEX_INITIALIZER;
pthread_cond_t          cond = PTHREAD_VOND_INITIALIZER;
int                     no_jobs = 1;

void start_routine()
{
        struct timespec     delta, abstime;
        int                 ret;

        (void) pthread_mutex_lock(&job_lock);

        /* Determine the timeout value for the condition wait */
        delta.tv_sec = 120;
        delta.tv_nsec = 0;

        (void) get_expiration_time(&delta, &abstime);

        /* Wait until the event occurs or until we timeout */
        while (no_jobs) {
                ret = pthread_cond_timedwait(&cond, &job_lock,
                                            &abstime);
                if (ret == ETIMEDOUT){
                        (void) pthread_mutex_unlock(&job_lock);
                        pthread_exit((void *)-1);
                }
        }

        /* Get the next job */
        ...

        /* Release the condition variable's associated mutex */
        (void) pthread_mutex_unlock(&job_lock);

        /* Rest of application code */
        ...
}
```

Read-Write Locks

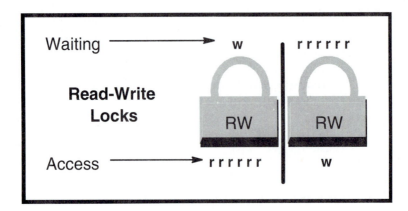

Fig. 10–6 As an alternative to always serializing access to a shared object, read-write locks serialize access only when writing takes place. Multiple threads can read from an object in parallel.

When a mutex is locked, a module's code path is serialized until the mutex is unlocked. Excessive locking can lead to serialization of an application. Consider a database that has search, add, and delete operations. Each of these operations can take a long time and require locking to protect the integrity of the database. The database will rarely change if records are not added or deleted frequently. Since add and delete operations can occur, even if only rarely, the database must use a synchronization primitive. Obtaining a mutex lock to perform a search operation causes severe serialization of the database because a mutex allows only one search at a time.

Read-write locks were designed specifically for situations where shared data is read often and rarely written. A read-write lock is similar to a mutex except that it allows multiple threads to acquire the lock for reading. Only one thread at a time is allowed to acquire the lock for writing. In the database scenario, the add and delete operations acquire a read-write lock for writing while the search operation acquires the lock for reading. This strategy allows the database to provide parallel search operations.

Whereas read-write locks provide for more parallelism when data is read more often than written, they do have a drawback. Read-write lock operations take more time than mutex operations. Because of this, choose your locking strategy carefully to maximize application performance. In general, if a lock is held for short durations (a few instructions), use mutexes. If a lock is held for long durations and there are many read-only operations but few write operations, use a read-write lock.

In the rest of this section, we'll explore how to use read-write locks.

Read-Write Lock Attributes

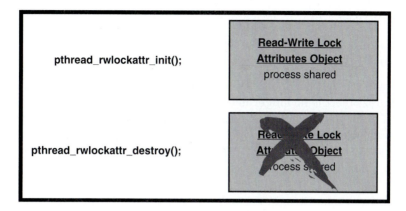

Fig. 10–7 Just like the attributes objects for a thread, a mutex, or a condition variable, the attributes object for a read-write lock can be initialized, shared among multiple read-write locks, and destroyed when no longer needed.

Overview

As with thread creation, read-write locks also have an attributes object that can be used to specify certain characteristics for a read-write lock. The read-write lock attributes object is passed to the read-write lock initialization function to specify a desired type of lock. Read-write lock attributes are optional. A default read-write lock will be created if specialized attributes are not specified.

Initializing Read-Write Lock Attribute Objects

An attributes object must be initialized before its attributes can be accessed. To initialize a read-write lock attributes object, use the function:

```
int pthread_rwlockattr_init(
    pthread_rwlockattr_t    *attr
);
```

This function initializes the read-write lock attributes object *attr*. After initialization is complete, all attributes in *attr* have the system default values. If a read-write lock attribute does not specify a default value, portable applications should not rely on a particular system's default attribute value.

Once the attributes object has been initialized, the read-write lock attributes may be changed to nondefault values. A single read-write lock attributes object can be used to initialize multiple read-write locks. If all read-write locks in an application are going to possess the same attributes, only one read-write lock attributes object is needed for all read-write locks.

After a read-write lock has been initialized with an attributes object [through the `pthread_rwlock_init()` function], the attributes for the read-write lock cannot be changed.

Destroying Read-Write Lock Attribute Objects

After all read-write locks needing the attributes object *attr* have been initialized, the attributes object is no longer needed. Therefore, from a resource conservation viewpoint, it is a good idea to destroy the attributes object. Destroying the attributes object will not affect read-write locks that have been initialized with the attributes object. Destroy an attributes object by using the following function:

```
int pthread_rwlockattr_destroy(
    pthread_rwlockattr_t            *attr
);
```

An application should not rely upon the value of *attr* after it has been destroyed. In fact, `pthread_rwlockattr_destroy()` may set *attr* to an invalid value. After an attributes object has been destroyed, it can later be reinitialized with `pthread_rwlockattr_init()`.

Note: `pthread_rwlockattr_t` is an opaque object; it is not guaranteed to be the same on all systems. It may be a data structure, a pointer, a descriptor similar to a file descriptor, or some other data type. Do not copy *attr* into another variable. Referring to copies of *attr* results in undefined behavior.

Read-Write Lock Attributes

Only one attribute has been defined for creating customized read-write locks:

- `process-shared`: This attribute allows an application to specify whether a read-write lock is to be used only by threads within the process or shared by threads in multiple processes. If the value **PTHREAD_PROCESS_PRIVATE** is specified for this attribute, the read-write lock will be used only by threads within the calling process (this is the default value). If the value of this attribute is set to **PTHREAD_PROCESS_SHARED**, the read-write lock is intended to be used by threads in multiple processes. It is the application's responsibility to allocate the read-write lock in memory that is shared between these multiple processes.

Note: If an application's read-write locks are not going to be shared by multiple processes, do not use the **PTHREAD_PROCESS_SHARED** option. The performance of read-write locks created with the **PTHREAD_PROCESS_PRIVATE** option will generally be faster on most systems.

If a process terminates while one of its threads has a process-shared read-write lock acquired, the lock is never released. This will cause deadlock in other processes using the read-write lock. If process-shared read-write locks are used, always release any acquired read-write locks before calling exit().

Setting/Getting Read-Write Lock Attributes

The process-shared attribute can be retrieved from or set in the read-write lock attributes object with the functions described below. The *attr* parameter represents the read-write lock attributes object that must have been previously initialized with the pthread_rwlockattr_init() function. The second parameter contains either the attribute value being set or a pointer to where the retrieved attribute value is returned (depending on whether it is a set or a get function).

```
int pthread_rwlockattr_getpshared(
    pthread_rwlockattr_t    *attr,
    int                     *pshared
);

int pthread_rwlockattr_setpshared(
    pthread_rwlockattr_t    *attr,
    int                     pshared
);
```

Example

The following code fragment shows how to allocate and initialize a read-write lock that is shared with other processes. A read-write lock attributes object is initialized with the process-shared attribute set to shared. The read-write lock must be allocated in shared memory that all processes needing the read-write lock can access. Once allocated, the read-write lock is initialized and the attributes object destroyed. Remember, only one thread should initialize the read-write lock. All other threads can use the read-write lock once it has been initialized.

```
pthread_rwlock_t    *rw;    /* global process shared R/W lock */

#define RW_SIZE     sizeof(pthread_rwlock_t)
#define KEY         8254

extern void fatal_error(int err, char *func);

#define     check_error(return_val, msg) {              \
                if (return_val != 0)                    \
                        fatal_error(return_val, msg); \
            }

main()
{
        pthread_rwlockattr_t    rw_attr;
        int                     ret_val;
        key_t                   shmid;

        /* Initialize the R/W lock attributes */
        ret_val = pthread_rwlockattr_init(&rw_attr);
        check_error(ret_val, "rwlockattr_init failed");

        /* Set pshared to process shared */
        ret_val = pthread_rwlockattr_setpshared(&rw_attr,
                                        PTHREAD_PROCESS_SHARED);
        check_error(ret_val, "rwlockattr_setpshared failed");

        /* Allocate the R/W lock in shared memory */
        shmid = shmget(KEY, RW_SIZE, 0666|IPC_CREAT);
        if (shmid == -1) {
                perror("shmget():");
                exit(-1);
        }

        rw = (pthread_rwlock_t *) shmat(shmid, (char *)0, 0);
        if ((int)rw == -1) {
                perror("shmat():");
                exit(-1);
        }

        /* Initialize the R/W lock and destroy the attributes */
        ret_val = pthread_rwlock_init(rw, &rw_attr);
        check_error(ret_val, "rwlock_init failed");

        ret_val = pthread_rwlockattr_destroy(&rw_attr);
        check_error(ret_val, "rwlockattr_destroy failed");

        /* Rest of application code here */
        ...
}
```

Initializing and Destroying Read-Write Locks

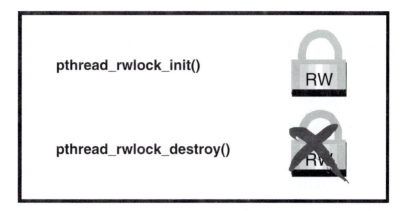

pthread_rwlock_init()

pthread_rwlock_destroy()

Fig. 10–8 Similar to mutexes and condition variables, a read-write lock can be initialized statically or dynamically. To change the attributes for a read-write lock, it must be initialized dynamically.

Overview

Each read-write lock in an application must be initialized before it can be used. An application has two choices for read-write lock initialization: static initialization or dynamic initialization. If a read-write lock is statically allocated [e.g., it was not allocated via `malloc()`], either method can be used. If the read-write lock is dynamically allocated, the dynamic initialization method must be used.

Initializing Read-Write Locks

To statically initialize a read-write lock with default read-write lock attributes, use the macro:

```
pthread_rwlock_t rwlock = PTHREAD_RWLOCK_INITIALIZER;
```

To dynamically initialize a read-write lock (possibly with nondefault read-write lock attributes), use the function:

```
int pthread_rwlock_init(
     pthread_rwlock_t        *rwlock,
     pthread_rwlockattr_t    *attr
);
```

The `pthread_rwlock_init()` function initializes *rwlock* with the read-write lock attributes specified in *attr*. If *attr* is **NULL**, the read-write lock is initialized with the default read-write lock attributes. After a read-write lock has been initialized, the read-write lock is in the unlocked state and ready for use.

A default read-write lock may be statically allocated and initialized with the macro **PTHREAD_RWLOCK_INITIALIZER**. The read-write lock will be initialized with the system default read-write lock attribute values. If the default read-write lock attributes are not acceptable, the application should dynamically initialize the read-write lock with the appropriate attributes.

A read-write lock should be initialized only once. Initializing a read-write lock multiple times may result in incorrect program behavior. Some systems return an error if an application tries to initialize an already initialized read-write lock; others may not. Some systems may not return an error if a locked read-write lock is reinitialized (this can have disastrous results on an application).

Destroying Read-Write Locks

Once an application is finished with a read-write lock, the read-write lock should be destroyed as the system may have allocated resources for it. These resources should be released when the read-write lock is no longer needed.

To destroy a read-write lock, use the function:

```
int pthread_rwlock_destroy(
    pthread_rwlock_t         *rwlock
);
```

An application should not rely on the value of *rwlock* after *rwlock* has been destroyed; in fact, pthread_rwlock_destroy() may set *rwlock* to an invalid value. After this read-write lock has been destroyed, it can later be reinitialized with pthread_rwlock_init().

A locked read-write lock should never be destroyed. Some systems detect this and return an error. Others may allow the destruction to proceed and the application to eventually "fall on its face."

Read-Write Locks and Undefined Behavior

Why is there so much "undefined" behavior with read-write locks? X/Open wanted to leave as much room as possible for implementations to optimize read-write lock performance at the expense of reduced error checking. Read-write locks reduce the amount of parallelism within an application. Consequently, read-write lock operations need to be as fast as possible so that the reduction in parallelism is for the shortest time possible. Many systems optimize for performance by having fewer error checks. For maximum portability, initialize a read-write lock only once, and destroy a read-write lock only when it is in the unlocked state.

Example

The code fragment below shows how to initialize and destroy read-write locks. Three different read-write locks are allocated. The first read-write lock has an attributes object and is dynamically initialized. The second read-write lock is dynamically initialized with default attributes. The third read-write lock is statically initialized with default attributes.

```
pthread_rwlock_t    *rw1;  /* global process shared R/W lock */
pthread_rwlock_t    rw2;
pthread_rwlock_t    rw3 = PTHREAD_RWLOCK_INITIALIZER;

extern void         fatal_error(int err, char *func);

#define    check_error(return_val, msg) {                 \
               if (return_val != 0)                       \
                       fatal_error(return_val, msg); \
           }

main()
{
        pthread_rwlockattr_t    rw_attr1;
        pthread_t               tid1;
        pthread_t               tid2;
        int                     ret_val;
        extern void             start_routine();

        /*
         * Initialize the attributes for rw1
         */
        ret_val = pthread_rwlockattr_init(&rw_attr1);
        check_error(ret_val, "rwlockattr_init failed");

        /*
         * rw1 is shared between multiple processes
         */
        ret_val = pthread_rwlockattr_setpshared(&rw_attr1,
                                    PTHREAD_PROCESS_SHARED);
        check_error(ret_val, "setpshared failed");

        /*
         * Allocate rw1 in shared memory
         */
        ...

        /*
         * Initialize rw1, then destroy the attributes
         */
        ret_val = pthread_rwlock_init(rw1, &rw_attr1);
        check_error(ret_val, "rwlock_init 1 failed");
```

```
          ret_val = pthread_rwlockattr_destroy(&rw_attr1);
          check_error(ret_val, "rwlockattr_destroy failed");

          /*
           * Initialize rw2 with default attributes.
           * rw3 has already been statically initialized.
           */
          ret_val = pthread_rwlock_init(&rw2,
                                  (pthread_rwlockattr_t *)NULL);
          check_error(ret_val, "rwlock_init 2 failed");

          /*
           * Create two threads to do the work
           */
          ret_val = pthread_create(&tid1, (pthread_attr_t *)NULL,
                        (void *(*)())start_routine, (void *)NULL);
          check_error(ret_val, "pthread_create 1 failed");

          ret_val = pthread_create(&tid2, (pthread_attr_t *)NULL,
                        void *(*)())start_routine, (void *)NULL);
          check_error(ret_val, "pthread_create 2 failed");

          /*
           * Wait for the threads to finish
           */
          ret_val = pthread_join(tid1, (void **)NULL);
          check_error(ret_val, "pthread_join: tid1");

          ret_val = pthread_join(tid2, (void **)NULL);
          check_error(ret_val, "pthread_join: tid2");

          /*
           * Destroy the R/W locks
           */
          ret_val = pthread_rwlock_destroy(rw1);
          check_error(ret_val, "rwlock_destroy rw1");

          ret_val = pthread_rwlock_destroy(&rw2);
          check_error(ret_val, "rwlock_destroy rw2");

          ret_val = pthread_rwlock_destroy(&rw3);
          check_error(ret_val, "rwlock_destroy rw3");

          /* Release shared memory from rw1 and exit */
          ...

          exit(0);
     }
```

Locking and Unlocking Read-Write Locks

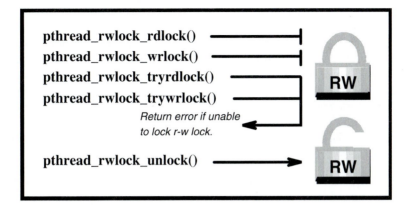

Fig. 10–9 Read-write locks can be locked for reading or for writing. Preference may be given to readers, writers, or preference can be equal. The preference is system-dependent.

Overview

There are five functions for locking and unlocking read-write locks. Each function takes one parameter - a pointer to the read-write lock to be locked or unlocked. The read-write lock must have been previously initialized before using these functions. As read-write lock operations can fail, make sure to check for error return values.

The functions used to lock and unlock read-write locks are not async-signal safe. They should not be called from a signal handler.

Locking a Read-Write Lock for Reading

To lock a read-write lock for reading, use the function:

```
int pthread_rwlock_rdlock(
    pthread_rwlock_t        *rwlock
);
```

This function does not return until *rwlock* has been locked for reading by the calling thread. The read-write lock remains locked until it is unlocked by the calling thread.

If *rwlock* is not currently locked for writing, and there are no writers waiting for *rwlock*, this function acquires the lock for reading immediately. If *rwlock* is currently locked for writing by another thread, the calling thread blocks until the lock can be acquired for reading.

If a thread tries to acquire a read lock while the lock is in the read-locked state but there are writers waiting for the lock, the system has three choices for when the thread acquires the read lock:

- **Reader Preference:** In this method, the system allows readers to continue to acquire a read lock even when writers are currently blocked on the read-write lock. Once all readers have released the read-write lock, a writer will be allowed to acquire the lock. After the writer releases the lock, if there are both readers and writers blocked, the readers acquire the lock next. This method allows writer starvation. If enough readers continually lock the read lock before it is completely released, the writers will never be able to acquire the lock.

- **Writer Preference:** In this method, the system causes all threads trying to acquire a read lock to block if there are writers currently blocked. Once all the current readers release the lock, a writer acquires the lock. After all writers have acquired and released the lock, any blocked readers will be allowed to acquire the lock. This method allows reader starvation if enough writers continually lock and unlock the read-write lock. However, if an application has enough write locks occurring to produce reader starvation, it should probably be using mutexes instead of read-write locks.

- **Equal Preference:** In this method, when the lock is held for reading and there are writers currently blocked, any threads attempting to acquire the lock are blocked in order (whether they want a read lock or a write lock). For example, suppose two threads currently own the read lock and there is one writer blocked. The next reader attempting to acquire the lock blocks on a list after the writer. Other readers will block with the same reader. When another writer must block, it blocks on the list after the set of blocked readers. When the lock is released, the first blocked writer acquires it, followed by the set of blocked readers, followed by the last blocked writer. In this method, neither readers nor writers are starved from acquiring the read-write lock. Readers (in groups) and writers acquire the lock in a specified order, according to when they blocked.

Most systems use the Writer Preference method for read-write locks. A portable application should not rely on this behavior.

A thread may lock a read-write lock for reading multiple times. A read lock is, in a way, similar to a recursive mutex. If a thread locks a read lock multiple times, it must unlock the read lock the same number of times.

If a thread tries to acquire a read lock when it currently owns the write lock, the resulting behavior is undefined. Some systems return an error to the caller, others may allow the caller to deadlock on itself.

If a signal is delivered to a thread waiting for a read-write lock, the signal is handled by the waiting thread. After the signal has been handled, the thread will continue waiting for the read-write lock. An error of **EINTR** is not returned.

Conditionally Locking a Read-Write Lock for Reading

To conditionally lock a read-write lock for reading, use the function:

```
int pthread_rwlock_tryrdlock(
        pthread_rwlock_t          *rwlock
);
```

This function attempts to lock *rwlock* for reading (according to the preference method implemented by the system). If *rwlock* cannot be locked for reading, the function returns immediately with an error of **EBUSY**. The calling thread does not block and wait for the read-write lock. Otherwise, the read-write lock is locked for reading by the calling thread. Conditional locking is useful when implementing a spinning read lock or when attempting to acquire read locks out of order (see Chapter 12, *Writing Thread-Safe Code*).

Locking a Read-Write Lock for Writing

To lock a read-write lock for writing, use the function:

```
int pthread_rwlock_wrlock(
        pthread_rwlock_t          *rwlock
);
```

This function does not return until *rwlock* has been locked for writing by the calling thread. The read-write lock remains locked until it is unlocked by the calling thread. If *rwlock* is currently locked for reading or writing, the calling thread blocks until the lock becomes available for writing. If there are both readers and writers blocked on the read-write lock, whether a reader acquires the lock next or a writer acquires the lock next depends on the preference method implemented by the system.

If a thread tries to acquire a write lock on *rwlock* when it currently has the lock for reading or writing, the resulting behavior is undefined. Some systems return an error to the caller, others may allow the caller to deadlock.

If a signal is delivered to a thread waiting for a read-write lock, the signal is handled by the waiting thread. After the signal has been handled, the thread will continue waiting for the read-write lock. An error of **EINTR** is not returned.

Conditionally Locking a Read-Write Lock for Writing

To conditionally lock a read-write lock for writing, use the function:

```
int pthread_rwlock_trywrlock(
        pthread_rwlock_t         *rwlock
);
```

This function attempts to lock *rwlock* for writing. If *rwlock* cannot be locked, the function returns immediately with an error of **EBUSY**. The calling thread does not block and wait for the read-write lock. Otherwise, the read-write lock is locked for writing by the calling thread. Conditional locking is useful when implementing a spinning write lock or when attempting to acquire write locks out of order (see Chapter 12, *Writing Thread-Safe Code*).

Unlocking a Read-Write Lock

To unlock a read-write lock, use the function:

```
int pthread_rwlock_unlock(
        pthread_rwlock_t         *rwlock
);
```

This function unlocks *rwlock*, whether it was locked for reading or for writing. If this function releases a read lock, the lock remains in the locked state unless the caller is the last reader to unlock *rwlock*.

If this function causes *rwlock* to become unlocked and readers are waiting to lock the read lock, the scheduling policies and priorities of the blocked readers determine the order in which the readers acquire the lock. If writers are waiting to lock the write lock, the scheduling policies of the waiting threads determine which thread acquires the lock for writing next. For threads with realtime scheduling policies, the highest priority, longest waiting writer acquires the lock next. If readers and writers are both blocked, whether readers acquire the lock next or writers acquire the lock next depends on the preference method implemented by the system.

Do not attempt to unlock a read-write lock that is locked by a different thread. Some systems return an error; others may simply unlock the read-write lock. In either case, this action can lead to incorrect application behavior as another thread assumes it has the read-write lock acquired. Do not attempt to unlock an unlocked read-write lock.

Performance

The read-write lock strategy a programmer chooses can make or break the application when it comes to performance. A poor synchronization strategy can lead to excessive serialization of a parallel application. Later in this book we'll discuss some different synchronization strategies to help you maximize the performance of your application.

Example

The following example shows how a read-write lock can be used in a module that maintains a list of data structures. In this module, the `list_lookup()` function is called often. The `list_add()` and `list_delete()` functions are called infrequently. Because of the potential length of time involved in searching the list and the fact that most operations are lookup operations, a read-write lock is a good choice as a synchronization primitive. A read-write lock allows the most parallelism for the common operation, `list_lookup()`.

```
pthread_rwlock_t        rw = PTHREAD_RWLOCK_INITIALIZER;
struct list             *list_head = NULL;
extern void             fatal_error(int err, char *func);

#define      check_error(return_val, msg) {             \
             if (return_val != 0)                       \
                      fatal_error(return_val, msg); \
        }

void
list_add(struct list *add)
{
        struct list   *curr, *prev;
        int           ret_val;

        /* We are modifying the list, get the write lock */

        ret_val = pthread_rwlock_wrlock(&rw);
        check_error(ret_val, "add: write lock failed");

        if (list_head == (struct list *)NULL) {
            add->list = (struct list *)NULL;
            add->list = (struct list *)NULL;
            list_head = add;
        } else {
            /* Find insertion point for add */
            for (curr=list_head; curr!=NULL; curr=curr->next) {
                     if (curr->list_id > add->list_id)
                             break;
                     prev = curr;
            }

            if (curr == list_head) {
                     /* new head of list */
                     add->prev = (struct list *)NULL;
                     add->next = list_head;
```

```
                    list_head->prev = add;
                    list_head = add;
            } else if (curr == (struct list *)NULL) {
                    /* new tail of the list */
                    add->next = (struct list *)NULL;
                    add->prev = prev;
                    prev->next = add;
            } else {
                    /* somewhere in between */
                    add->next = curr;
                    add->prev = prev;
                    prev->next = add;
                    curr->prev = add;
            }
        }

        /* Release the write lock and return */
        ret_val = pthread_rwlock_unlock(&rw);
        check_error(ret_val, "add: write unlock failed");
}


struct list *
list_delete(int delete_id)
{
        struct list   *curr, *prev, *tmp;
        int           ret_val;

        /* We are modifying the list, get the write lock */
        ret_val = pthread_rwlock_wrlock(&rw);
        check_error(ret_val, "delete: write lock failed");

        /* Find delete_id in list*/
        for (curr = list_head; curr != NULL; curr = curr->next) {
            if (curr->list_id >= delete_id)
                    break;
            prev = curr;
        }

        /* Did we find it? */
        if (curr != NULL) {
            if (curr->list_id != delete_id) {
                    curr = (struct list *)NULL;
            } else {
                    if (curr == list_head) {
                        /* new head of list */
                        list_head = curr->next;
                        list_head->prev = (struct list *)NULL;
                    } else {
```

```
                            /* somewhere in between */
                            tmp = curr->next;
                            prev->next = tmp;
                            tmp->prev = prev;
                    }
              }
        }

        /* Release the write lock and return */
        ret_val = pthread_rwlock_unlock(&rw);
        check_error(ret_val, "delete: write unlock failed");

        return(curr);
}



struct list *
list_lookup(int lookup_id)
{
        struct list    *curr;
        int            ret_val;

        /* We are only reading the list, get the read lock */
        ret_val = pthread_rwlock_rdlock(&rw);
        check_error(ret_val, "lookup: read lock failed");

        /* Find lookup_id in list*/
        for (curr = list_head; curr != NULL; curr = curr->next) {
            if (curr->list_id >= lookup_id)
                    break;
        }

        /* Did we find it? */
        if ((curr != NULL) && (curr->list_id != lookup_id))
            curr = (struct list *)NULL;

        /* Release the read lock and return */
        ret_val = pthread_rwlock_unlock(&rw);
        check_error(ret_val, "lookup: read unlock failed");

        return(curr);
}
```

The Timeshare Scheduling Policy

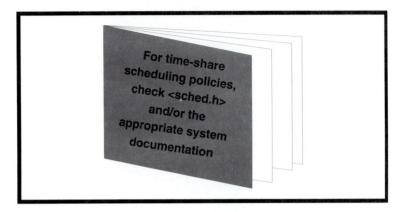

Fig. 10–10 The **SCHED_OTHER** scheduling policy may be mapped to **SCHED_FIFO**, **SCHED_RR**, or perhaps to a timeshare policy. Check your system's documentation.

Overview

POSIX.1b and POSIX.1c specify only the realtime scheduling policies **SCHED_RR** and **SCHED_FIFO**. The policy **SCHED_OTHER** is an implementation-defined scheduling policy intended for threads to indicate that they no longer need realtime scheduling. The problem with this definition is that **SCHED_OTHER** is not required to be defined as a nonrealtime scheduling policy. In fact, a system can map the **SCHED_OTHER** policy to **SCHED_RR** or **SCHED_FIFO**. If **SCHED_OTHER** can be a realtime policy, how does a thread request a nonrealtime scheduling policy?

The Timeshare Scheduling Policy

Every major UNIX system contains a priority-based timeshare scheduling policy. The timeshare scheduling policy is the default policy on most UNIX systems. This policy guarantees that each thread in the system receives some share of the processor's time. A thread using this policy is allowed to execute until it relinquishes the processor (voluntarily or by blocking) or until its time-slice expires.

A priority is associated with each thread using the timeshare policy. This priority is adjusted dynamically throughout the lifetime of the thread. As the thread executes, its priority is lowered. While a thread is waiting to execute, its priority is raised. The automatic adjustment of a thread's priority prevents the thread from monopolizing the system. Exactly how a thread's priority is adjusted may vary from one system to another.

As with the realtime scheduling policies, do not rely on the interactions between the timeshare policy and other scheduling policies. While it is not specified how threads with a timeshare policy are scheduled relative to threads with the real-time policies, most systems always schedule realtime threads before timeshare threads (i.e., realtime policies have higher priorities). Portable applications should not rely on this behavior.

The timeshare scheduling policy is known as **SCHED_TIMESHARE**. On some systems it may be known as **SCHED_TS**. The exact name used by your system can be found in the header file <sched.h>. The **SCHED_TIMESHARE** policy can be specified in calls to any of the POSIX.1b and POSIX.1c scheduling functions. Many systems cause **SCHED_OTHER** to be mapped to **SCHED_TIMESHARE**.

Timeshare Scheduling and Synchronization Primitives

The scheduling policies and priorities of threads blocked on synchronization objects determine the order in which threads are unblocked. For threads using the **SCHED_FIFO** and **SCHED_RR** scheduling policies, the highest priority, longest waiting thread is unblocked when the object is released (or signaled in the case of condition variables). The unblocked thread is guaranteed to acquire the synchronization object next.

Threads using the **SCHED_OTHER** and **SCHED_TIMESHARE** scheduling policies are not required to be unblocked in any specified order. Some systems unblock the longest waiting thread, others may unblock a random thread. With these policies, there is also no guarantee that the thread unblocked will acquire the synchronization object next. Consider the case where thread A is blocked on a mutex. When thread B unlocks the mutex, thread A is allowed to attempt to acquire the mutex. However, before thread A acquires the mutex, thread B (or another thread) locks the mutex, and thread A must block on the mutex again.

Some systems may guarantee that unblocked threads in the timeshare policy acquire the synchronization object next. Portable applications should not rely on this behavior. If a system does not make this guarantee and your application exhibits the false wake-up behavior presented earlier, call sched_yield() after certain calls to pthread_mutex_unlock(). This can be useful in loops that acquire a mutex, perform work, and then release the mutex. The mutex is released and reacquired for each iteration to allow another thread access to the mutex. Placing a call to sched_yield() at the bottom of the loop will give any blocked threads a better chance at acquiring the mutex. Remember, this is an issue only for timeshare-scheduled threads. Threads with realtime scheduling policies will not experience this behavior.

Thread to Processor Binding

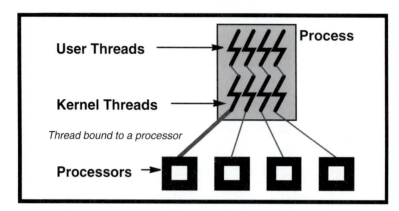

Fig. 10–11 Binding threads to a processor may be the right solution if your application is suffer-ing from cache thrashing. The binding scheme you will use, if any, largely depends on the applica-tion design.

Overview

Most multiprocessor systems have hardware caches so that memory accesses are not always required to go directly to the physical memory location. These caches can provide significant performance improvements for an application. At the same time, they can also provide a performance degradation for multithreaded applications if the application is not designed carefully.

Consider the case where thread A is executing on processor 1 and blocks, waiting for an event. When the event occurs, thread A starts executing on processor 2. If the event occurred quickly, it's possible that some of the data modified by thread A is still in the hardware cache of processor 1. To access this data, the data must be flushed from the hardware cache of processor 1 and placed in the cache for processor 2 (possibly through the physical memory location). This is an expen-sive operation and is known as *cache thrashing*.

In an attempt to minimize cache thrashing, many multiprocessor systems always run a thread on the same processor. If data is left in the cache from the previous time the thread executed, cache thrashing is avoided, and performance gains may occur. This works well for single-threaded applications, but does not always work for multithreaded applications.

Since threads share the process address space, it is possible that different threads may be modifying the same data simultaneously on different processors. When this occurs, data is constantly moving in and out of the hardware caches of multiple processors, causing severe performance degradation. Sometimes cache thrashing will negate any benefit of parallelism in an application. The caching issues with multiprocessor systems are discussed in much more detail in Chapter 15, *Parallel Programming Models and Issues.*

What can you do about this? Hopefully you will not have these problems. Many systems will try to schedule threads accessing the same data on the same processor to avoid cache thrashing. For the cases when cache thrashing occurs, several functions have been provided to allow the application to control which processors a thread is allowed to execute on. A thread can be bound to a specific processor or allowed to execute on any processor. When bound to a processor, the thread will execute only on that processor, even if other processors are idle.

How do you make the most effective use of processor binding? The answer is application- and system-dependent. There are two issues to consider: (1) If several threads synchronize on shared resources often, it may be wise to bind those threads to the same processor. This reduces physical parallelism but takes advantage of the system's hardware cache. (2) If several threads are completely disjoint and share no data, it may be wise to bind those threads to different processors. As these threads will not experience cache thrashing, they can take advantage of the parallelism offered by multiple processors.

Should you make use of these processor binding features? Maybe. Make sure you really have a problem before you bind threads to processors. Most systems do a pretty good job of effectively utilizing the multiprocessor hardware to provide your application with the best performance.

Number of Processors

To obtain the number of processors currently on the system, use the function:

```
int pthread_num_processors_np(void);
```

This function will return the number of processors on the system. It always returns a value greater than or equal to one (there must be at least one processor!). This function does not have any potential error return values.

Processor IDs

To obtain the ID of a specific processor on the system, use the function:

```
int pthread_processor_id_np(
    int              request,
    pthread_spu_t    *answer,
    pthread_spu_t    spu
);
```

This function returns the processor ID for a specific processor on the system. The processor ID of the requested processor is returned in the *answer* parameter. The *request* parameter determines which processor ID is returned. The legal values for the *request* parameter are:

PTHREAD_GETCURRENTSPU_NP: This request causes the ID of the processor that the caller is currently executing on to be returned in *answer*. Be careful, this is not the processor binding of the caller (see **Thread to Processor Binding** below). This information may be out of date at any moment. The calling thread's time-slice may expire, and the next time it is scheduled to run, the thread may be on a different processor. The *spu* parameter is ignored when this option is specified.

PTHREAD_GETFIRSTSPU_NP: This request causes the ID of the first processor in the system to be returned in *answer*. The *spu* parameter is ignored when this option is specified.

PTHREAD_GETNEXTSPU_NP: This request causes the ID of the processor after *spu* to be returned in *answer*. To determine the IDs of all processors in the system, first call this function with the **PTHREAD_GETFIRSTSPU_NP** request. Place the first processor's ID in *spu* and call this function with the **PTHREAD_GETNEXTSPU_NP** request. Repeat this process, storing the previous processor's ID in *spu*, until this function returns **EINVAL**, signifying that there are no more processors on the system.

Thread to Processor Binding

To obtain or change a thread's processor binding, use the function:

```
int pthread_processor_bind_np(
    int                 request,
    pthread_spu_t       *answer,
    pthread_spu_t       spu,
    pthread_t           thread
);
```

The *thread* parameter represents the thread whose processor binding is to be changed or retrieved. The value **PTHREAD_SELFTID_NP** may be specified in *thread* to indicate that the calling thread is the target thread.

To bind *thread* to a specific processor, specify the processor ID in *spu*. To unbind *thread* and allow it to be scheduled on any available processor, specify the value **PTHREAD_SPUFLOAT_NP** in *spu*. To retrieve the current processor binding of *thread*, specify **PTHREAD_SPUNOCHANGE_NP** in *spu*. The thread's processor binding is returned in *answer*. A thread will inherit its initial processor binding values from its creating thread.

Two types of processor binding can be specified in *request*:

> **PTHREAD_BIND_ADVISORY_NP:** This option specifies advisory binding for the target thread. The thread is bound according to the value contained in the *spu* parameter. If the thread's processor binding conflicts with the scheduling policy, the scheduling policy takes precedence. As an example, consider thread *A*, which is bound to processor 1 and is scheduled under the **SCHED_FIFO** scheduling policy. If processor 2 is ready to execute a thread and thread *A* is the highest priority thread, it will choose thread *A*, even though thread *A* is bound to a different processor. The scheduling policy takes precedence over the processor binding. Threads scheduled under **SCHED_TIMESHARE** adhere to the processor binding.

> **PTHREAD_BIND_FORCED_NP:** This option specifies mandatory binding for the target thread. The thread is bound according to the value contained in the *spu* parameter. If the thread's processor binding conflicts with the scheduling policy, the processor binding takes precedence. This may result in a lower priority thread running on a different processor before a higher priority thread is allowed to run. If the highest priority thread is bound to processor 1, when processor 2 is looking for a thread to run, it will not choose a thread that is bound to processor 1.

The ability to bind a thread to a specific processor or to float a thread among the available processors provides an application the ability to set the size of a thread's scheduling allocation domain. By setting a thread's processor binding to the value **PTHREAD_SPUFLOAT_NP**, the thread is given a scheduling allocation domain size equal to the number of available processors. By binding a thread to a specific processor, the thread's scheduling allocation domain size is set to one.

When using this function, make sure your application is dynamic. Your development machine may contain four processors, but the machine(s) on which the application runs may not contain the same number of processors. Your application should be able to execute on a machine with any number of processors. If the application is intended for one specific machine, it should still be dynamic. It's possible that one of the processors may fail and be removed for repair. You will want your application to continue working until the processor is replaced.

Thread `processor` and `binding_type` Attributes

The `processor` and `binding_type` thread attributes allow an application to specify the processor binding for threads created with an attributes object. By setting a thread's processor binding in its attributes object, additional function calls are not required after the thread is created. Additionally, the thread will start executing with the correct processor binding. If the processor binding is performed after the thread is created, the thread may initially execute on the wrong processor.

The `processor` attribute specifies the processor on which the created thread is bound. The following values can be set in the `processor` attribute:

- **PTHREAD_SPUINHERIT_NP:** This value causes the created thread to inherit its processor binding from the creating thread. When this value is set, the `binding_type` attribute is ignored.

- **PTHREAD_SPUFLOAT_NP:** This value causes the created thread to be scheduled on any available processor. No processor binding is maintained for the created thread. When this value is set, the `binding_type` attribute is ignored.

- **<processor_id>:** By setting this attribute to the desired processor ID [obtained from `pthread_processor_id_np()`], the created thread will be bound to the specified processor. The type of processor binding (advisory or forced) is specified in the `binding_type` attribute.

The default value of the `processor` attribute is **PTHREAD_SPUINHERIT_NP**.

The `binding_type` attribute specifies the type of processor binding for the created thread. This attribute is ignored if the `processor` attribute does not contain a processor ID. The following values can be set in the `binding_type` attribute:

- **PTHREAD_BIND_ADVISORY_NP:** This value causes the created thread to have advisory processor binding. Refer to the *Thread to Processor Binding* section above for information on advisory processor binding.

- **PTHREAD_BIND_FORCED_NP:** This value causes the created thread to have forced processor binding. Refer to the *Thread to Processor Binding* section above for information on forced processor binding.

PTHREAD_BIND_ADVISORY_NP is the default value of the `binding_type` attribute.

Note: the `processor` and `binding_type` attributes are not affected by the setting of the `inheritsched` attribute.

Getting/Setting Thread to Processor Binding Attributes

The `processor` and `binding_type` attributes can be retrieved from or set in the thread attributes object with the functions described below. The *attr* parameter represents the thread attributes object, which must have been previously initialized with the function `pthread_attr_init()`. The second parameter contains either the attribute values being set or a pointer to where the retrieved attribute values are returned (depending on whether it is a set or a get function).

```
int pthread_attr_getprocessor_np(
        pthread_attr_t          *attr,
        pthread_spu_t           *processor,
        int                     *binding_type
);


int pthread_attr_setprocessor_np(
        pthread_attr_t          *attr,
        pthread_spu_t           processor,
        int                     binding_type
);
```

Example

The following example obtains the processor IDs of the first four processors on the system. The four elements of the `spu_nums[]` array are filled with the processor IDs. If four processors are not found, the unfilled elements of the array are evenly filled with the existing processor IDs. If the system is a multiprocessor (i.e., we found more than one processor), the four threads in the process are bound to the different processors. If only one processor is available, there's no point in taking the time to bind threads to the only processor.

```
pthread_t    threads[4];     /* IDs of the four running threads */
extern void fatal_error(int err, char *func);
#define      check_error(return_val, msg) {                  \
                  if (return_val != 0)                        \
                        fatal_error(return_val, msg);   \
              }

void
bind_threads()
{
    pthread_spu_t      answer, spu_nums[4], spu = (pthread_spu_t)-1;
    int                i, ret;

    /* Get the ID of the first processor */
    ret = pthread_processor_id_np(PTHREAD_GETFIRSTSPU_NP,
                                  &answer, spu);
    check_error(ret, "get_first_spu");
    spu_nums[0] = answer;

    /* Get the ID of the next 3 processors */
    for (i = 1; i < 4; i++) {
        spu = answer;
        ret = pthread_processor_id_np(PTHREAD_GETNEXTSPU_NP,
                                      &answer, spu);
        if (ret == EINVAL)
            break;
        spu_nums[i] = answer;
    }

    /* Did we find four processors? Spread out the IDs if not. */
    if (i == 2) {                        /* found two processors */
        spu_nums[2] = spu_nums[0];
        spu_nums[3] = spu_nums[1];
    } else if (i == 3) {                 /* found three processors */
        spu_nums[3] = spu_nums[0];
    }

    /* Bind each of the threads if we have multiple processors. */
    if (i > 1) {
        for (i = 0; i < 4; i++) {
            ret = pthread_processor_bind_np(PTHREAD_BIND_FORCED_NP,
                                            &answer, spu_nums[i],
                                            threads[i]);
            check_error(ret, "pthread_processor_bind_np()");
        }
    }

    /* Rest of application here. */
    ...
}
```

Thread Concurrency and MxN Threads

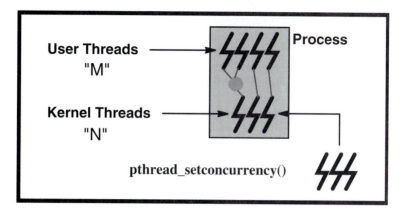

Fig. 10–12 In the MxN Model, you can adjust the number of kernel entities available to the unbound threads in your process.

Overview

In the MxN Threads Model, POSIX.1c allows an application to control the number of user threads that it creates. However, no mechanism was provided to control the number of kernel entities used by unbound threads. A system that supports the MxN Threads Model will guarantee that enough active kernel entities are available so that the process will not deadlock.

In most cases, the system will provide the optimal number of active kernel entities to provide the best performance for an application. This cannot be guaranteed for all applications. Sometimes an application may have better performance if the number of active kernel entities used by unbound threads is increased or decreased from what the system provides.

Two functions are available that allow an application to control the number of active kernel entities used by unbound threads. Note that this is the number of active kernel entities, not the total number of kernel entities. By *active*, we mean the number of running kernel entities. If a kernel entity is blocked in a system call, it is not considered active.

Active Kernel Entities

Each time an unbound thread executes, it is scheduled on top of a kernel entity (usually a kernel thread or lightweight process). The thread uses the kernel entity until its time-slice expires or until it has to block, waiting for an event to occur. If the thread's time-slice has expired, the thread is placed back on the scheduling queue, and the kernel entity is given to another unbound thread.

If the thread blocks on a synchronization primitive such as a mutex or condition variable, most systems will block the thread in user-space (for process private synchronization primitives). The kernel is never called to arbitrate contention. The thread is placed on a blocked queue in the threads library, and the kernel entity is given to another unbound thread.

If the thread makes a system call that blocks, both the thread and the kernel entity are blocked in the kernel. At this point, the kernel entity is no longer considered active. The kernel entity is not available for use until the system call completes.

If all of the kernel entities block inside the kernel, the application can no longer make progress. In fact, there are certain situations where the blocking of all kernel entities could result in application deadlock. Each system that supports the MxN Thread Model will guarantee that the application will not deadlock. This is usually accomplished by the system through the creation of additional active kernel entities when some or all of the active kernel entities block.

As you can see, the system will have to work hard to ensure that the proper number of active kernel entities is maintained to provide the best application performance. Sometimes the application may be able to determine the optimal number of active kernel entities (or concurrency level) for the system. This is where informing the system of the desired concurrency level becomes useful.

Setting the Thread Concurrency Level

To inform the system of the desired concurrency level, use the function:

```
int pthread_setconcurrency(
    int      new_level
);
```

This function informs the system of how many active kernel entities, *new_level*, the application would like to have available for use by unbound threads. The *new_level* parameter is essentially the N in the MxN Threads Model. To let the system decide how many kernel entities should be used by unbound threads, specify zero in *new_level*.

The concurrency level is only a *hint* to the system. A system may choose to ignore this value if it would result in deadlock to the application. Depending on how the system implements the MxN Threads Model, the actual number of active kernel entities may change dynamically in a process' lifetime.

If a system does not support the MxN Threads Model, it saves the value passed in *new_level* for compatibility with MxN Threads Model systems, but ignores the concurrency request.

Getting the Thread Concurrency Level

To obtain the current concurrency level, use the function:

```
int pthread_getconcurrency(void);
```

This function returns the concurrency level (i.e., the number of active kernel entities used by unbound threads). This value is equal to the value specified in a previous call to `pthread_setconcurrency()`. A return value of zero indicates that the system is controlling the application's concurrency level. The actual number of simultaneously running kernel entities may change over time, depending on application needs.

Optimal Concurrency Level

How do you determine an optimal concurrency level? The answer is completely application-dependent. In most cases, the system will provide the optimum concurrency level, and you will never need to worry about it.

What if the system doesn't provide the optimum concurrency level? Usually, an application wants the concurrency level set to the number of processors available on the system. If there are only four processors, having more than four active kernel entities doesn't make sense. At any given time, no more than four kernel entities can be running. However, in actual practice this may not always provide the best performance. Sometimes an application may want to have more processing time than other processes. Adding additional kernel entities will help achieve that additional processing time. You, as the programmer, must experiment and analyze your application's performance to determine the optimal concurrency level.

The concurrency level is highly system-dependent. What is optimal on one system may not be appropriate on another system. While the function is portable, the value specified in *new_level* may need to be different on different systems.

Example

The following example shows how an application using unbound threads might want to set the thread concurrency level. This example creates 40 unbound threads and sets the thread concurrency level to 10. Notice that the concurrency is set before the threads are created. This is because threads could terminate before all the threads have been created.

```
pthread_t      threads[40];
extern void    fatal_error(int err, char *f);
extern void    start_routine();

#define         check_error(return_val, msg) {                      \
                    if (return_val != 0)                            \
                            fatal_error(return_val, msg);   \
                }

main()
{
        pthread_attr_t         attr;
        int                    ret, i;

        /* Set the concurrency level before we create any threads */
        ret = pthread_getconcurrency();
        printf("Concurrency level is initially %d\n", ret);

        ret = pthread_setconcurrency(10);
        check_error(ret, "pthread_setconcurrency()");

        /* Initialize a thread attributes object */
        ret = pthread_attr_init(&attr);
        check_error(ret, "pthread_attr_init()");

        /* Each thread is unbound */
        ret = pthread_attr_setscope(&attr, PTHREAD_SCOPE_PROCESS);
        check_error(ret, "pthread_attr_setscope()");

        /* Create 40 threads to perform the work */
        for (i = 0; i < 40; i++) {
                ret = pthread_create(&threads[i], &attr,
                                    (void *(*)())start_routine,
                                    (void *)NULL);
                check_error(ret, "pthread_create()");
        }

        /* Destroy the attributes. */
        ret = pthread_attr_destroy(&attr);
        check_error(ret, "pthread_attr_destroy()");

        /* Rest of application code */
        ...
}
```

Scheduling Unbound Kernel Entities

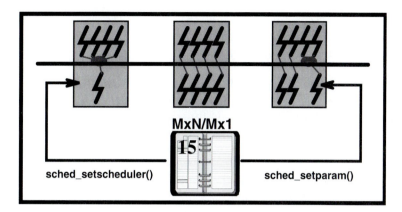

Fig. 10–13 Using the `sched_setscheduler()` and `sched_setparam()` functions, you can effect the scheduling of unbound threads and kernel entities in a process relative to other threads in the system.

Overview

POSIX.1c provides the application with the ability to control the scheduling policy and priority of user threads, whether bound or unbound. However, for unbound threads, there is no mechanism to control the scheduling policy and priority of the underlying kernel entities. POSIX.1c states that how unbound threads compete for system resources (e.g., the processor) with bound threads in the system is undefined.

According to POSIX.1c, the `sched_setscheduler()` and `sched_setparam()` functions *may* affect the scheduling of unbound threads in relation to other threads in the system. A system is not required to have these functions affect the system-wide scheduling of unbound threads. X/Open has extended the behavior of these functions to define required scheduling behavior of unbound threads with these functions.

Scheduling Functions

The `sched_setscheduler()` function changes the scheduling policy and parameters of the target process. It does not change the scheduling policy and parameters of threads in the target process. Since a process is no longer scheduled, this function only causes a new child process to inherit the specified policy and parameters. X/Open has extended the behavior of this function to also change the scheduling policy and parameters of the kernel entities used by unbound threads in the process. The scheduling attributes of unbound threads are not affected by this function.

The `sched_setparam()` function operates like the `sched_setscheduler()` function, except that it changes only the scheduling parameters of the target process. The X/Open extensions also cause this function to change the scheduling parameters of the kernel entities used by unbound threads in the process. The scheduling attributes of unbound threads are not affected by this function.

How do these functions help an application with unbound threads? The scheduling of unbound threads, relative to one another within the process, can be controlled through the Pthread scheduling functions. The `sched_setscheduler()` and `sched_setparam()` functions allow an application to specify how the unbound threads, as a whole, compete with the bound threads in the system.

As an example, consider a system where all bound threads are realtime threads with high priority. Your application uses only unbound threads, and the default scheduling policy of the underlying kernel entities is a timeshare policy. Even though your user threads' scheduling policies and priorities may be extremely high, your process will rarely, if ever, be allowed to execute. Remember, the kernel schedules kernel entities, not user threads. In this situation, the kernel entities used by your application have a low priority compared with all other kernel entities in the system.

To resolve this problem, the application can call the `sched_setscheduler()` and `sched_setparam()` functions to change the scheduling policy and priority of the underlying kernel entities. The scheduling values can be changed to something that allows the application its fair share of processing time on the system.

Example

The following example shows how to change the scheduling policy and priority of kernel entities used by unbound threads in a process. The current scheduling policy and priority is first obtained. If the scheduling policy is not **SCHED_RR**, `sched_setscheduler()` is called to change the policy to **SCHED_RR** and to set the priority to the maximum priority. If the current policy is **SCHED_RR** but the current priority is not the maximum priority, `sched_setparam()` is called to raise the priority.

Notice that the example changes the scheduling policy and priority only if they are not currently set to the required values. Whenever a thread's scheduling policy or priority is changed, the thread is context switched out and placed at the tail of its new priority queue, even if the values are not changed [remember our discussion of `sched_yield()`]. Because of this behavior, we do not want to change the scheduling values if they are already correct.

```
#include <sched.h>
#include <pthread.h>

main()
{
        int                   policy, max_prio;
        pid_t                 my_pid;
        struct sched_param    param;

        my_pid = getpid();

        /*
         * Get our current scheduling policy
         */
        policy = sched_getscheduler(my_pid);
        if (policy == -1)
                perror("sched_getscheduler()");

        /*
         * Get our current scheduling priority
         */
        if (sched_getparam(my_pid, &param) != 0)
                perror("sched_getparam()");

        /*
         * We want to be at this priority
         */
        max_prio = sched_get_priority_max(SCHED_RR);

        /*
         * If we are not RR, change our policy and priority
         */
        if (policy != SCHED_RR) {
                param.sched_priority = max_prio;
                if (sched_setscheduler(my_pid, SCHED_RR, &param) == -1)
                        perror("sched_setscheduler()");

        /*
         * If we are RR but the wrong priority, change the priority
         */
        } else if (param.sched_priority != max_prio) {
                param.sched_priority = max_prio;
                if (sched_setparam(my_pid, &param) != 0)
                        perror("sched_setparam()");
        }

        /* Rest of application code here */
        ...
}
```

Summary

This chapter furnished information about HP and X/Open extensions to the POSIX.1c standard. These extension include an additional thread stack attribute, thread suspension/resumption, four types of mutexes, read-write locks, concurrency and scheduling control in the MxN model, a timeshare scheduling policy, and processor affinity. These features bring powerful enhancements to multithreaded applications.

- The `pthread_attr_setguardsize()` function is used to control the size of the stack overflow (guard) area for a thread. If overflow protection is used and the thread overflows its stack during execution, a signal is delivered to the thread. Not using the stack overflow feature saves system resources. It is more difficult to debug an application that has stack protection disabled.

- Thread suspension is often used to implement a garbage collector. Threads involved in a task are suspended until the "garbage" has been cleaned up. Once this is done, the suspended threads are allowed to resume execution. A thread can suspend itself and be resumed by another thread. A thread can be suspended multiple times.

- The mutex synchronization primitive has been enhanced to support four types of mutexes: normal, recursive, error-checking, and default. A normal mutex provides the best performance but provides no error checking. If a thread locks a normal mutex twice, it will deadlock on itself. A recursive mutex may be locked by a thread multiple times. To release a recursive mutex, the mutex must be unlocked the same number of times it was locked. An error-checking mutex is a good debugging tool. If a thread attempts to lock an error-checking mutex twice, an error is returned. Only the thread "owning" an error-checking mutex can unlock the mutex. The default mutex follows the POSIX.1c guidelines for mutexes: the results of recursively locking the mutex, unlocking an unlocked mutex, and unlocking a mutex locked by another thread result in undefined behavior.

- The `get_expiration_time()` function provides a convenient way to construct an absolute time based on a time interval. When used in conjunction with `pthread_cond_timedwait()`, the wait becomes relative to when the thread starts the condition wait, as opposed to an absolute time.

- Read-write locks are designed for the situation in which reading is done often and writing is done rarely. Using read-write locks, as opposed to mutexes, allows for parallel read operations, but enforces serialized write operations.

- Attributes objects are used to define the specific characteristics of read-write locks. By default, a read-write lock can be used only by threads within the calling process. However, a read-write lock attributes object can be configured to allow threads from other processes to use the lock. To conserve process and system resources, destroy unneeded attributes objects immediately.

- A read-write lock must be initialized before it can be used. Read-write locks can be initialized statically or dynamically. If nondefault attributes are required, you must use dynamic initialization. Once an application is finished with a read-write lock, it should be destroyed to conserve resources.

- Read-write locks may be locked for reading or writing. A preference may be given to readers or writers. Multiple readers may acquire a read lock, but only one writer at a time is allowed to acquire the write lock.

- The **SCHED_OTHER** policy is an implementation-defined policy. Some systems map **SCHED_OTHER** to the realtime scheduling policies **SCHED_FIFO** or **SCHED_RR**. **SCHED_OTHER** can also be mapped to a timeshare policy such as **SCHED_TIMESHARE** (or **SCHED_TS**). Check your system's header file, <sched.h>, to find more information.

- The **SCHED_TIMESHARE** scheduling policy is a nonrealtime priority-based scheduling policy. Threads using this policy execute until their time-slice expires or until they voluntarily release the processor. The system controls the priority of each thread scheduled under this policy to guarantee that no thread is starved from execution.

- Cache thrashing is a situation in which a thread executes on different processors, causing cached data to be moved among the processors. Cache thrashing can cause severe performance degradation. To prevent this problem, a thread can be bound to a specific processor. The benefit of binding threads to processors depends largely on the characteristics of the application and the system on which it will run. As a guideline, threads that synchronize on shared data often should be bound to the same processor. Threads that do not share data are generally better off if they are bound to different processors. However, binding a thread to a processor may not always be necessary. Most systems effectively utilize the multiprocessor hardware to provide optimum application performance.

- The pthread_setconcurrency() function allows you to set the N in the MxN Model for a particular process. N is the number of kernel-scheduled entities that will be available for use by unbound user threads within the process.

- An application can control how unbound threads are scheduled relative to one another in a process with the Pthread scheduling functions. The functions sched_setscheduler() and sched_setparam() allow an application to specify how the unbound threads, as a whole, compete with all the bound threads in the system.

Exercises

1. Write a program where thread *A* suspends itself. When thread *A* is resumed, it should print "I'm awake now!" Thread *B* should also suspend thread *A*. Then thread *B* should print a message saying "Thread *B* lives!" Thread *B* should then call `pthread_continue()` on thread *A*, print "Resumed thread A once," then sleep for 10 seconds. Then thread *B* should resume thread *A* a second time and print "Resumed thread A twice." Check the results, then run the same program with the thread attribute **PTHREAD_FORCE_RESUME_NP** turned on.

2. To observe relocking behavior, write a program that uses the four mutex types: normal, recursive, error-checking, and default. Threads *A*, *B*, *C*, and *D* should lock one of the mutex types. Each thread should print a message indicating that it has successfully locked its respective mutex. The mutex type (normal, recursive, error-checking, default) should be identified in the message. Then each thread should attempt to relock its mutex. Again, each thread should print out an appropriate message. What happens?

3. Write a program where thread *A* uses `get_expiration_time()` to construct a 10-second, relative wait time. Allow thread *A* to immediately wait on the condition using `pthread_cond_timedwait()`. Thread *B* should then signal the condition. If thread *A* successfully awakens from the condition, it should print "success"; otherwise, it should print the error message. What happens? Modify the program by placing a sleep(10) call between the calls to `get_expiration_time()` and `pthread_cond_timedwait()`. What happens? Why?

4. Write a program with a read-write lock protecting a global variable that has been initialized to zero. Create one writer thread and two reader threads. The reader threads should read and print the value of the global variable. The writer thread should change the value of the global variable and print the new value. Allow the writer thread and each of the reader threads about 100 iterations. Measure the execution time of the program. Replace the read-write lock with a mutex, run the program, and measure again. Which synchronization primitive worked best? Why?

5. Check your system's documentation to determine the characteristics of the **SCHED_OTHER** policy. Is **SCHED_OTHER** mapped to **SCHED_FIFO**, **SCHED_RR**, or a timeshare policy?

6. Write a program with two threads that uses a mutex to synchronize access to a global variable. For the length of time the program will run, the two threads should take turns writing to the global variable. Run the program in the following configurations: no thread binding, binding both threads to one processor and, binding each thread to a different processor. Measure the completion time for each instance of program execution. What, if any, conclusions do you reach?

7. Using the same program in #6, determine how many kernel threads are available in your process.

8. Determine whether the `sched_setscheduler()` and `sched_setparam()` functions affect the scheduling of unbound threads on your system.

Thread F/X

This chapter discusses the behavior of common library functions when they are used in multithreaded programs. For example, what happens when a thread calls `fork()`? If a thread locks a file, will other threads in the same process still have access? Are there performance or portability considerations when common library functions are used in multithreaded programs? Questions such as these are answered in this chapter.

In this chapter, we make frequent reference to the *process level*. When we refer to the process level, we are speaking of functions whose actions affect the process, as opposed to the calling thread or a target thread. For example, if a thread uses the `pthread_kill()` function, a signal is sent to the target thread. However, if a thread uses the `kill()` function, a signal is sent to the target process.

Topics Covered...

- `fork()`, `exec()`, `exit()`, and `wait()`
- File and Message-Passing Operations
- Signals
- Locale State
- Timers and Sleepers
- NonLocal Jumps
- Scheduling
- Other Functions

fork(), exec(), exit(), and wait()

Fig. 11–1 The `fork()`, `exec()`, `exit()`, and `wait()` functions can all be used in multithreaded programs. However, the behavior of these functions when used by threads may not be intuitive.

Table 11–1 Process Creation, Exec, Exit, and Wait

Function	Thread F/X
fork()	This function produces a child *process* that contains exactly one thread (which is a duplicate of the calling thread). The address space of the calling process is duplicated in the child process, including the state of all mutexes, semaphores, and so on.
	The child of a multithreaded process should call only async-signal safe functions until an `exec` function is called (refer to: Chapter 4, *Basic Thread Management*; Chapter 5, *Writing Thread-Safe Code*; and Chapter 7, *Threads and Signals*.
execl() **execle()** **execlp()** **execv()** **execve()** **execvp()**	In a multithreaded process, if a thread calls one of the `exec` functions, all threads are terminated and the new image will be single-threaded. As a result, when the `exec` function returns, the state of mutexes or resources held by the previous image is lost.
exit()	When a thread calls `exit()`, all threads within the process are terminated, then the process is terminated.

Table 11–1 Process Creation, Exec, Exit, and Wait

Function	Thread F/X
wait() **waitpid()** **waitid()**	If a thread in the Mx1 Model calls a wait function, the *process* is suspended and a context switch takes place. The process remains suspended on behalf of the calling thread until the target process terminates or until a signal is delivered to the calling thread's process.
	In the 1x1 or MxN models, the calling *thread* is suspended until the target process terminates or until a signal is delivered to the calling thread. Other threads within the process are unaffected.
	If multiple threads call a wait function on a particular target process, all waiting threads will return, but only one thread receives the status information. Which thread receives the status information is undefined.
vfork()	The calling thread will block until the single-threaded child process calls exit() or one of the exec functions.

File and Message-Passing Operations

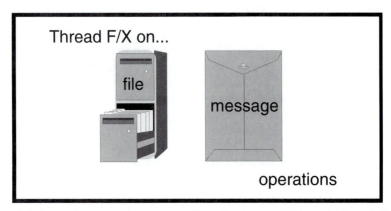

Fig. 11–2 Files and message queues are shared resources in a multithreaded process. Most functions that operate on files and messages do so at the process level.

Table 11–2 File and Message-Passing Operations

Function	Thread F/X
`dup()` `dup2()`	The file descriptor table is a process-wide resource. Therefore, the effect of using these functions is visible to all threads within the process.
`flockfile()`	This function is used by a thread to lock a file. This lock provides file synchronization only for threads within the calling process. If the file is already locked, the calling thread will block until `funlockfile()` is called by the thread owning the lock on the file. For interprocess synchronization, use the `fcntl()` or `lockf()` functions. **Note:** These functions operate on `FILE *` objects, not file descriptors returned via `open()`.
`fnctl()` `lockf()`	Locks on a file via `fnctl()` or `lockf()` are maintained on a per-process basis. If thread *A* locks a file, thread *B* from the same process has access. `fnctl()` and `lockf()` prevent only threads in other processes from accessing the file.
`ftrylockfile()`	This function is used by a thread to attempt to lock a file. If the file is already locked, `ftrylockfile()` returns an error to the caller.

Table 11–2 File and Message-Passing Operations

Function	Thread F/X
`funlockfile()`	This function is used by the thread to unlock a lock on a file. The thread must own the lock, having called either the `flockfile()` or the `ftrylockfile()` function earlier.

`getc()`
`putc()`
`getchar()`
`putchar()`
	These functions are used by threads for reading and writing characters. Note that in order to be *thread-safe*,[1] these functions acquire a lock on each call. Depending on how they are used (e.g., in a loop), performance concerns may arise.

`getc_unlocked()`
`getchar_unlocked()`
`putc_unlocked()`
`putchar_unlocked()`
	These functions are the *unlocked* versions of the functions named above. They are called when character I/O operations need to be performed in a loop. They do not acquire a lock to perform the I/O operation. To synchronize access to files and remain thread-safe, use the `flockfile()` and `funlockfile()` functions in conjunction with the `*_unlocked()` functions.

`getmsg()`
`putmsg()`
`getpmsg()`
`putpmsg()`
	These functions perform operations on streams. Like files, streams are visible to all threads within the process. Therefore, the effect of using these functions is visible to all threads within the process.

`lseek()`	The file offset for a particular file is shared by all threads within the process. To maintain correct I/O, use synchronization.

`msgctl()`
`msgget()`
`msgop()`
`msgsnd()`
`msgrcv()`
	Message queues are per-process resources. Actions taken by threads on a message or the message queue are visible to all threads within the process. However, threads can wait to receive a message independently of one another.
	
	Note: Only one thread should open or close a message queue. Each call to open a message queue returns a *unique* message descriptor.

`open()` `close()`	Again, the file descriptor table is a process-wide resource. When a file is open, it is accessible for reading or writing by all threads within the process. When a file is closed by a thread, all threads within the process lose access to the file.

Table 11–2 File and Message-Passing Operations

Function	Thread F/X
`pipe()`	As threads within the same process share access to the file descriptor table, all threads in the process have access to the two file descriptors opened when this function is called.
`poll()`	Threads within the same process can use this function to query the I/O conditions of any open file descriptors, process-wide.

POSIX.1b message passing functions:
 	
`mq_open()`
`mq_close()`
`mq_send()`
`mq_receive()`
`mq_notify()`
`mq_getattr()`
`mq_setattr()`
`mq_unlink()`
	Again, message queues are per-*process* resources. Any thread within the process can send or receive messages using the open message descriptors and the appropriate message functions.
	
	When receiving, if a message is not available, only the calling thread blocks.
	
	Note: Only one thread should open or close a message queue. Each call to open a message queue returns a *unique* message descriptor.

`read()` `write()`	Because threads within the same process share access to the file descriptor table, they have access to all open file descriptors, including stdin, stdout, and stderr. As the file offset is shared by all threads within a process, you need to synchronize access to file descriptors to avoid interleaved I/O. If a read() or write() call blocks, only the calling thread blocks.
`umask()`	The file mode creation mask is set at the process level. All threads within the process share the same umask() setting.
`utime()`	This function makes access and modification times visible to all threads within the process.

[1]See Chapter 12 or the Glossary for the definition of *thread-safe*.

Signals

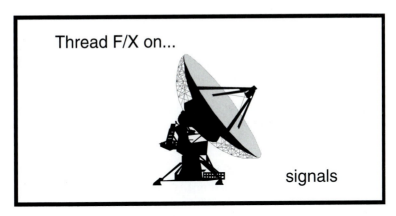

Fig. 11–3 The `sigprocmask()` function should not be used in a multithreaded application. The other signal functions listed here will work fine in multithreaded applications, as long as you know the Thread F/X!

Table 11–3 Signal Functions

Function	Thread F/X
`alarm()`	Alarm signals are sent to the process, not to the calling thread. There is no guarantee which thread will handle the alarm signal when the process receives it. If a particular thread should act upon a signal, all other threads in the process should block that signal. For more information, see the *Waiting for a Signal* section in Chapter 7.
`kill()`	This function sends a signal to one or more processes. If the target process is multithreaded, one thread in the target process receives the signal and acts upon it. Which thread acts on the signal is undefined.
`pause()`	This function suspends the calling thread until a signal is received.
`raise()`	This function sends a signal to the calling thread. Specifically, POSIX.1c states that *"the effect of the raise() function shall be equivalent of calling* `pthread_kill(pthread_self(), sig)`*."*[1]

Table 11–3 Signal Functions

Function	Thread F/X
`sigaction()`	This function is used to examine and/or specify the action to be taken for a signal. If a signal mask is specified for use when invoking a signal handler, only the thread executing the signal handler will have its signal mask changed. Signal handlers are shared by all threads within a process. Per-thread signal handlers are not supported.
`sigaltstack()`	This function is used to give the calling thread's kernel-scheduled entity an alternate signal stack.
`sighold()` `sigpause()` `sigpending()` `sigprocmask()` `sigrelese()`	These functions affect only the kernel scheduled entity of the calling thread. Note on `sigprocmask()`: This function is used to examine or set the signal mask for the calling process. Most systems use `sigprocmask()` to change the signal mask of the calling thread. However, applications should not rely on this behavior (i.e., this is not guaranteed to be portable). To change a thread's signal mask, use the `pthread_sigmask()` function.
`sigignore()` `signal()` `sigset()`	These functions affect the signal actions for all threads within the process.
`sigqueue()`	This function causes the specified *signal* and *value*, to be sent to the target *process*. The information is queued in the process. If the target process is multi-threaded, one thread in the process will receive the signal; which thread is undefined.
`sigsend()` `sigsendset()`	These functions send signals to the process. Which thread handles the signal is undefined.
`sigsuspend()`	This function replaces the signal mask of the calling thread and suspends the thread. The thread remains suspended until a signal is delivered causing a handler to execute or the process to terminate.

[1]P1003.1c Draft 10, September 1994, section 8.1

Locale State

Fig. 11–4 POSIX states that *"the local state is common to all threads within a process."*[1]

The setlocale(int *category*, char **locale*) function is used to query or set the locale of a *process* according to the values of the *category* and *locale* arguments. The possible values for *category* determine how regular expressions, dates, monetary units, etc., will be expressed. For example, in the U.S., the date is expressed as *MM/DD/YY*. The *locale* argument allows you to specify a setting for an international environment. For example, "Fr_FR.8859" represents the French language as spoken in France, according to the ISO 8859 code set. Alternatively, if the *locale* argument is a **NULL** pointer, the setlocale() function returns the current locale for the *category* setting.

The return value from setlocale() is a pointer to a static data area within the function. This static data area contains a string that corresponds to the current international environment. The static data areas within the function can be overwritten through subsequent calls to setlocale(). This string can be copied into a *char* array within the process if you need to reset the locale at a later time.

Threads can call setlocale() to query the current international environment without affecting other threads within the process. If necessary, the return string can be copied into a *char* array and shared with other threads. However, when a thread modifies the locale, all threads within the process see the modification. The static data area inside the setlocale() function is global to the process.

Note: Because setlocale() maintains a static data area within the function, setlocale() is not thread-safe.[2]

---

[1] P1003.1c Draft 10, September 1994, section 8.1.2.2
[2] The term *thread-safe* is defined in the Glossary and in Chapter 12, *Writing Thread-Safe Code.*

Timers and Sleepers

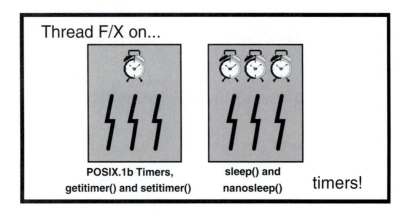

Fig. 11–5 The POSIX.1b timer functions, getitimer() and setitimer(), work at the process level. sleep() and nanosleep() work at the thread level.

Table 11–4 Timers and Sleepers

Function	Thread F/X
getitimer() **setitimer()**	These functions maintain per-process timers. When the timer expires, a signal is sent to the process. Which thread handles the signal is undefined. You can direct a signal to a particular thread using the blocking techniques described in the *Waiting for a Signal* section, Chapter 7.
POSIX.1b timers: timer_create() timer_delete() timer_gettime() timer_settime() timer_getoverrun()	The POSIX.1b timer functions maintain per process timers. When any of the timers expire, a signal is sent to the process. Which thread handles the signal is undefined. Again, the signal can be directed to a particular thread using the blocking techniques described in Chapter 7. If multiple threads set the same timer, only the last timer value set is in effect. The previous values are overwritten.
sleep() **nanosleep()**	The sleep() and nanosleep() functions cause the calling thread, not the process, to suspend execution for the requested time period.

NonLocal Jumps

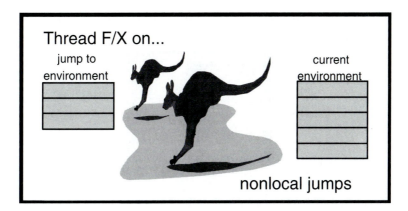

Fig. 11–6 The same thread that performs the `setjmp()` should perform the `longjmp()`.

The nonlocal jump functions are helpful for managing errors and interrupts that may occur during program execution. These functions allow a thread to jump to another area in the code, manage the particular situation, then jump back to the place from which it left off.

The `setjmp(`*jmp_buf *env*`)` and `sigsetjmp(`*sigjmp_buf *env,* `int` *savemask*`)` functions are used to save thread context and jump to another part of the program. Both functions save the environment of the calling thread in *env*. If the *savemask* parameter is not zero, the `sigsetjmp()` function also saves the signal mask of the calling thread in *env*. The `longjmp()` and `siglongjmp()` functions are used to restore the saved environment, respectively. These functions return the calling thread back to the place from which it performed the corresponding `setjmp`.

POSIX.1c states that *"the effect of a call to `longjmp()` where the initialization of the jmp_buf argument was not performed in the calling thread is undefined."* Similarly, POSIX.1c also states that *"the effect of a call to `siglongjmp()` where the initialization of the sigjmp_buf argument was not performed in the calling thread is undefined."*[3]

After a `longjmp()` or `siglongjmp()` has been performed, the local variables saved at the time of the `setjmp()` or `sigsetjmp()` call are undefined. For application portability, and to ensure correct behavior, you should **not** write code with dependencies on such variables. The **same** thread that calls a `setjmp()` function should also call the corresponding `longjmp()` function.

---

[3] P1003.1c Draft 10, September 1994, section 8.3.1

Scheduling

Fig. 11–7 The POSIX.1b scheduling functions listed below operate on the process level. Threads with a *process scheduling contention scope* will be scheduled according to the relative priorities of other processes on the system.

When a process is created, it inherits its scheduling policy and priority from the parent process, not from the thread calling `fork()`. The functions in Table 11-5 obtain and change the scheduling policy and priority of a process or kernel-scheduled entity.

Table 11–5 Process Level Scheduling Policy and Parameters

Function	Thread F/X
nice()	This function affects the kernel-scheduled entity of the calling thread.
sched_getscheduler() **sched_setscheduler()**	These functions retrieve and set the scheduling policy and parameters for the process.
sched_getparam() **sched_setparam()**	These functions retrieve and set the scheduling parameters for the process.
sched_get_rr_interval()	This function is used to obtain the time-slice interval value for a process running under the **SCHED_RR** policy.

The scheduling of bound threads is not affected by the sched_*() functions. However, the scheduling of unbound threads in the calling process *may* be affected, relative to other unbound threads in other processes on the system, when using these functions.

Other Functions

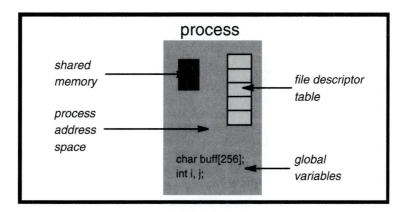

Fig. 11–8 The effect of calling functions that operate on shared resources (e.g., process address space, file descriptors, global variables, and shared memory) is generally visible to all threads within the process.

The table below mentions a few "other functions" and describes the Thread F/X. All of these functions can be found in Section 2 of your system's manual pages.

Table 11–6 Thread F/X on Other Functions

Functions	Thread F/X
`acct()`	This is a process level function. When the process terminates, the accounting records are written.
`acl()`	Authorization and authentication security attributes are implemented at the process level. The same attributes apply to all threads within the host process.
`brk()` `sbrk()`	These functions affect the address space of the host process. Therefore, changes are visible to all threads within the process.
`chdir()`	The current directory setting is shared by all threads within the process.
`chroot()`	Similarly, the same root directory is shared by all threads within the process.
`getcontext()` `setcontext()`	These functions work at the thread level. They get or set information in the kernel-scheduled entity associated with the calling thread.

Table 11–6 Thread F/X on Other Functions

Functions	Thread F/X
getgroups() setgroups()	Threads within a host process share the same group ID (GID).
getpid() getpgrp() getppid() getpgid()	Process ID (PID) is the same for all threads within the host process. PID information is kept with the kernel-scheduled entity(ies).
getrlimit()	Resource limits are governed at the process level. Resource limitation information is kept with the kernel-scheduled entities.
getuid() geteuid() getgid() getegid()	User ID (UID) is the same for all threads within the host process. UID information is kept with the kernel-scheduled entity(ies).
mmap()	Similar to the brk() and sbrk() explanation, address space changes are visible to all threads.
mprotect()	Access protection changes are visible to all threads within the process. Threads within a process will have equal access.
munmap()	Threads within a process share the same address space. The effect of using this function is visible to all threads in the host process.
plock()	Because threads within a process share the process address space, the effects of a call to this function is visible to all threads.
profil()	The execution time profile is done at the process level.
semctl() semget() semop()	Semaphores, as well as other synchronization primitives, are visible to all threads. The effect of using these functions is visible to all threads in the host process.
setpgid() setpgrp() setsid() setuid()	The effect of using these functions is visible to all threads in the host process.
times()	This returns time accounting information for the process. The times reported are a summation of the time accounting information for each thread in the process.

Summary

The Thread Effects ("F/X") chapter presented the specific behaviors you will find when using common functions in a multithreaded application. It discussed how some functions perform on the process level and others perform on the thread level:

- The `fork()` function produces a child *process* that contains exactly one thread (a duplicate of the calling thread). The address space of the calling process is duplicated, and the state of mutexes, read-write locks, etc., is inherited across the `fork()` call.

- When an `exec` function is called, all threads in the calling process are terminated and a new, single-threaded image is created. The state of mutexes or resources in the previous image is lost.

- A call to `exit()` terminates all threads within the host process, after which the process is terminated.

- A call to `wait()` suspends the calling thread until the target process terminates or until the calling thread receives a signal.

- In a multithreaded process, files and message queues are shared resources. Threads within a process share the same view of these resources.

- `getc()`, `putc()`, `getchar()`, and `putchar()` can cause multithreaded applications unexpected performance problems as locks are acquired on each call. The `*_unlocked()` versions of these routines are available to help performance. However, these functions should be used in conjunction with `flockfile()`, `ftrylockfile()`, and `funlockfile()` to avoid interleaved I/O.

- `sigprocmask()` should not be used in a multithreaded application to set the signal mask of a thread. Use `pthread_sigmask()` instead.

- If multiple threads call `alarm()`, the value for seconds is overwritten. The last value written is used.

- The locale state is shared by all threads within a process.

- The POSIX.1b timers are per-process timers. The `sleep()` and `nanosleep()` functions cause the calling thread to sleep.

- The thread that performs an environment save, using a `setjmp()` function, should perform the corresponding environment restore, using the `longjmp()` function. Otherwise, the resulting behavior is undefined.

- `sched_get_rr_interval()`, `sched_getparam()`, `sched_setparam()`, `sched_getscheduler()`, and `sched_setscheduler()` operate on the process level.

- Operations on shared resources are generally visible to all threads in the process.

Exercises

1. Write a multithreaded program that uses getc() and putc() to move characters. The two threads in this program should have equal priority. Designate an input file and an output file. Time how long it take to move the data. Use the *_unlocked() version of getc() and putc() in the second test. In test three, use the f*lock-file() functions. Describe your observations.

2. In a program with two threads, have thread *A* set the alarm for 20 seconds. Have thread *B* call alarm() with a value of 60 seconds. When the alarm signal is sent to the process, thread *A* should handle the signal. What happens? When?

3. In a "two-threaded" program, have thread *A* print the date. Thread *B* should then set the German locale. Then, thread *A* should print the date again.

4. Write a "two-threaded" program that tests the following undefined behavior: Thread *A* performs a setjmp() and thread *B* performs a longjmp() using the *jmp_buf* initialized by thread *A*.

5. In a program with one bound thread and two unbound threads, have each thread print out its scheduling policy and priority. Next, use the sched_setscheduler() function to make the process's priority better. Then print the priority values of the threads once again. Has anything has changed?

Writing Thread-Safe Code

This chapter defines thread-safing terminology and describes several important facets of writing thread-safe code. At the end of this chapter, we provide a preflight checklist for designing a thread-safe library.

Topics Covered...

- Reentrant, Thread-Safe, and Unsafe Functions
- How to Manage Shared Objects
- How to Avoid Deadlock
- How to Find Thread-Safe Library Interfaces
- How to Write Cancel-Safe Functions
- How to Write Fork-Safe Functions
- How to Write a Thread-Safe Library

Reentrant, Thread-Safe, and Unsafe Functions

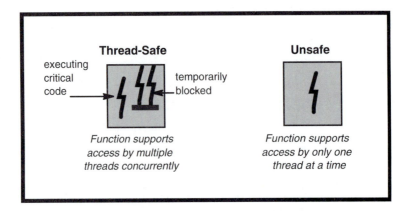

Fig. 12–1 Reentrant and thread-safe functions allow access by multiple threads in an undefined and/or interleaved manner while maintaining logically correct operation. Unsafe functions can be used safely by single-threaded applications or by serializing access in multithreaded applications.

Overview

A **reentrant** function can be used by multiple threads sharing the same address space and process resources. Such functions are guaranteed to work correctly, yielding consistent and predictable results, regardless of the order of execution of threads within the process.

POSIX.1c defines a reentrant function as follows: *"a function whose effect, when called by two or more threads, is guaranteed to be as if the threads each executed the function one after another in an undefined order, even if the actual execution is interleaved."*[1]

Reentrant functions use synchronization primitives, such as mutexes, to protect *critical sections* of code. An example of a critical section of code is a place where a shared object is modified. Shared objects include such things as global data, file descriptors, and shared memory.

A **thread-safe** function is reentrant by default. However, such functions may have additional restrictions or responsibilities. For example, a thread-safe function may be restricted from using asynchronous signal handlers. A thread-safe function may also be responsible for guaranteeing the state of mutexes in the child process after a `fork()`.

An **unsafe** function may be called safely by single-threaded programs or, in some cases, by multithreaded applications when access to the function is serialized.

[1] P1003.1c Draft 10, September 1994, section 2.2.2.157.

Guidelines

- If you want to use a library function in your program, check that function's documentation. **Avoid** using functions that are not thread-safe. Generally speaking, functions are either thread-safe or not thread-safe. However, some systems define more than two levels of thread safety. The documentation for a function may indicate that it is:

  - unsafe

  - safe only when called by the initial (or main) thread

  - safe to be called by any thread if access to the function is serialized

  - safe to be called by any thread

- In addition to checking the thread safety of a library function, see if the function has any **restrictions** or **responsibilities** that may be of concern. For example, if a function contains a cancellation point, how will this affect your application? You should install cancellation cleanup handlers to cleanup thread state in the event a thread is canceled in the function.

- If you are creating a thread-safe function, either from scratch or from an existing unsafe function, use synchronization primitives to **protect access** to shared objects and/or critical code sections.

- The manner in which synchronization primitives are used can have an impact on performance. Manage the use of synchronization primitives for application **performance** as well as for correct behavior:

  - If synchronization is not performed when needed, several race conditions may be introduced that will corrupt the integrity of data.

  - If the synchronization strategy is too course-grained, excessive serialization results, causing application performance to decline.

  - If the synchronization strategy is too fine-grained, the additional locking will cause a decrease in performance.

  - Start with coarse-grained synchronization. Then examine your locking strategy to see if locking can be done at a finer granularity. Optimum performance is achieved when the maximum amount of concurrency is supported without introducing race conditions or spending too much time acquiring synchronization primitives.

Example

This example explores both thread-safing and performance. There are three functions that perform the same task: write to a file. The first function is unsafe, whereas the latter two functions are thread-safe through the proper use of locking. Notice that the second function serializes all access whereas the last function serializes access only at the file level. Because we guarantee that only one thread writes to a file at a time, the unlocked version of putc() is used to avoid the per-call locking overhead penalty.

```
/*
 * This is an unsafe function. Two or more threads
 * executing this function concurrently would produce
 * unpredictable/interspersed results.
 */
void my_fputs(const char *s, FILE *stream)
{
        char    *posn;

        for (posn = s; *posn; posn++)
                putc((int) *posn, stream);
}


/*
 * This function is thread-safe, but access is serialized.
 */
pthread_mutex_t m = PTHREAD_MUTEX_INITIALIZER;

void my_fputs(const char *s, FILE *stream)
{
        char    *posn;

        (void) pthread_mutex_lock(&m);
        for (posn = s; *posn; posn++)
                putc_unlocked((int) *posn, stream);
        (void) pthread_mutex_unlock(&m);
}


/*
 * Multiple threads can use this function concurrently
 * to write to different files. This function serializes access
 * when more than one thread attempts to write to the same file.
 */
void my_fputs(const char *s, FILE *stream)
{
        char    *posn;

        flockfile(stream);
        for (posn = s; *posn; posn++)
                putc_unlocked((int) *posn, stream);
        funlockfile(stream);
}
```

How to Manage Shared Objects

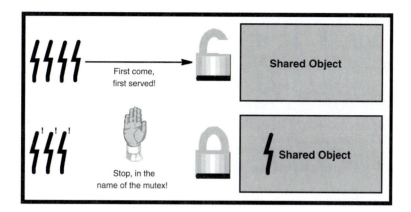

Fig. 12–2 Use a synchronization primitive to synchronize access to shared objects.

Managing Objects

Resources that are accessible by all threads within a process can collectively be called *shared objects*. Some examples of shared objects include global data, message queues, and file descriptors.

In a multithreaded process, threads must synchronize access to shared objects or the program may experience incorrect or unpredictable behavior. Consider the following example, where G is an unprotected global variable:

Table 12–1 Race Condition Scenario

Time	Thread A	Thread B
Time 1	G = G + 5;	
Time 2	Context switch to Thread B	
Time 3		G = (a**2) + (b**2);
Time 4		Context switch to Thread A
Time 5	val = G;	

This type of situation is known as a *race condition*. The example shows that the context switch allowed thread B to "race" ahead of thread A. Because the threads executed in an unanticipated order, an incorrect value for G was assigned to val. The result of this operation was affected by unpredictable timing factors. The same situation can occur without context switches on a multiprocessor machine. If thread A executes `G = G + 5;` and thread B executes `G = (a**2) + (b**2);` simultaneously on different processors, a race condition still exists. When the operations complete, it is unknown what value is contained in the variable `G`.

Managing I/O

File and `stdio` offsets are shared by all threads within a process. Single calls to functions such as `fread()`, `fwrite()`, `printf()`, etc. will complete as atomic operations. If two threads simultaneously call `printf()`, one string will be printed first, followed by the other string. The two strings will not be interleaved in the output. However, without some form of synchronization, you cannot guarantee which string will be printed first.

Sometimes a thread needs to call `printf()` several times and have the calls complete as one atomic operation. If `printf()` is called three times, another thread's `printf()` should be printed either before or after the three strings, not in the middle of the strings. This can be guaranteed by using the `flockfile()`, `ftrylockfile()`, and `funlockfile()` interfaces. These functions provide locks to coordinate access to all `FILE *` objects. For example, the previous situation can be protected by:

```
flockfile(stdout);
printf("This is string 1\n");
printf("This is string 2\n");
printf("This is string 3\n");
funlockfile(stdout);
```

The three printed strings are guaranteed to be printed atomically in one chunk. These functions can be used to synchronize access to any `FILE *` object, not just `stdin`, `stdout`, and `stderr`.

On a similar note, recall from Chapter 11, *Thread F/X,* the discussion on the functions `getc_unlocked()`, `putc_unlocked()`, `getchar_unlocked()`, and `putchar_unlocked()`. These functions provide optimum performance when blocks of characters must be read or written at once. This is because locks are not acquired with each call to a `*_unlocked()` function. Instead, the application is responsible for calling the `f*lockfile()` functions to facilitate atomic I/O operations. For example:

```
flockfile(stdout);
for (posn = s, *posn, posn++)
        putc_unlocked((int) *posn, stdout)
funlockfile(stdout);
```

Guidelines

- Thread-safe code **must** manage shared objects.

- A shared object that is modified during program execution should be **protected** by a mutex or some other appropriate synchronization primitive.

- Locks (e.g., mutexes, semaphores, etc.) should be held for the entire **duration** of the operation to be performed; no longer, no shorter. If a mutex is unlocked too soon, corruption in the application may result. If a mutex is held too long, the excessive serialization will decrease the parallelism benefit of programming with threads.

- Use thread-specific data when appropriate. Global thread-specific data does not need the protection of a lock as the data is specific to each thread. Thread-specific data may be dynamically allocated or allocated from stack memory. Remember, dynamically allocated data is available until the memory is freed. Stack memory generally has a very short life (that of a function call).

- All `stdio` objects (`FILE *` objects) provide locking at the function call level. Locks are acquired internally by functions like `printf()` and `fread()` to guarantee atomic I/O operations.

- If several I/O function calls must be treated as one atomic function call, use the `flockfile()` and `funlockfile()` interfaces to prevent other threads from producing interleaved I/O.

Example

By serializing access to shared objects, race conditions can be prevented. To illustrate this point, we revisit the race condition example. By using a mutex to protect access to global variable G, Thread *A* is guaranteed to store the correct value in `val`. After Thread *A* locks the mutex, Thread *B* will block when it tries to access variable G.

```
int G = 0; /* Global variable. */
pthread_mutex_t Glock;

/*
 * Somewhere in the code...
 * Protecting access to global variable G.
 */
(void) pthread_mutex_lock(&Glock);
G = G + 5;
val = G;
(void) pthread_mutex_unlock(&Glock);
```

How to Avoid Deadlock

```
                    How to Avoid Deadlock

     Method # 1                 Method #2
     ...;                       ...;
     lock mutex 1;              lock mutex 2;
     lock mutex 2;              if ( ! (trylock mutex 1)) {
     lock mutex 3;                  unlock mutex 2;
     ...;                           lock mutex 1;
     unlock mutex 3;                lock mutex 2;
     unlock mutex 2;            }
     unlock mutex 1;            lock mutex 3;
     ...;                       ...;
                                /* Unlock in reverse order later. */
```

Fig. 12–3 One way to avoid *recursive* and *interactive* deadlocks is to lock mutexes in a defined sequence. Never attempt to lock a mutex with a lower sequence number than the mutex currently owned.

Overview

Deadlock arises when one or more threads within a multithreaded application become permanently blocked. There are two types of deadlocks: *recursive* (or self) and *interactive*.

A **recursive** deadlock is the most common type of deadlock. A common scenario for recursive deadlock occurs when a thread tries to lock the same mutex twice. A recursive deadlock can occur when a thread holds a mutex and calls an external function that tries to lock the same mutex. When this happens, the thread becomes deadlocked on itself.

An **interactive** deadlock can occur based on the mutex locking actions of two or more threads. For example, Thread *A* locks mutex m1 and Thread *B* locks mutex m2. As they continue to execute, Thread *B* tries to lock mutex m1 (before releasing m2) and Thread *A* tries to lock mutex m2 (before releasing m1). Both threads are now permanently blocked on each other. Neither thread can execute to release the mutex it has acquired.

Thread A
```
pthread_mutex_lock(&m1);
pthread_mutex_lock(&m2);
```

Thread B
```
pthread_mutex_lock(&m2);
pthread_mutex_lock(&m1);
```

A multithreaded program that has one or more threads in a deadlocked state can have other threads that are still making progress; however, the application will never complete.

Guidelines

- Use error-checking (**debug**) mutexes rather than normal or default mutexes during program development. If a thread tries to recursively lock this type of mutex, an error is returned. However, if a thread recursively locks a normal or default mutex, the thread may become permanently blocked. Once the program has been debugged, use normal or default mutexes for maximum efficiency (unless, of course, you need the functionality of error-checking debug mutexes in your program).

- If more than one mutex is required, first try to rearrange the code so that only one mutex is required. This removes any possibility of interactive deadlock. If this is not possible, **associate a sequence number** with each mutex. Use this numbering system to lock each mutex in sequence. A thread should **never** attempt to lock a mutex with a lower sequence number than any mutex it currently has locked.

- An **alternative** to locking mutexes in sequence is to do the following:
    - The thread locks the mutex it needs.
    - If later, the thread needs a lower-sequence numbered mutex, it calls `pthread_mutex_trylock()` to attempt to lock the other mutex.
    - If the trylock was successful, the thread can continue. Otherwise, the thread should unlock the higher sequence numbered mutexes and relock all mutexes in order.
    - If the first mutex was unlocked to acquire the mutexes in order, the state of the objects protected by those mutexes must be re-verified when the mutexes are reacquired. These objects may have changed state (or gone away if they are dynamic objects) when the mutex was released.

- `FILE` objects locked with `flockfile()` and `ftrylockfile()` need to be locked in predefined order for the same reasons that mutexes require lock ordering. The trylock method can also be used with `FILE` objects.

- Carefully **analyze** the code paths that threads will traverse to see whether recursive or interactive deadlock may occur.

- **Avoid** holding mutexes across long operations, such as I/O. Mutexes should be locked for the shortest time possible. If threads block waiting for a mutex, the application is serialized, and performance suffers.

Example

Two different strategies for mutex locking are presented below. Method #1 locks mutexes in a predefined order. Method #2 acquires a higher sequence lock first. When a lower-sequence mutex is needed later, `pthread_mutex_trylock()` is called. If the mutex is acquired, the thread continues. If it is not acquired, the higher-sequence numbered mutex is unlocked and relocked in sequence.

```
/* Mutex definitions for either method. */
pthread_mutex_t lock1 = PTHREAD_MUTEX_INITIALIZER;
pthread_mutex_t lock2 = PTHREAD_MUTEX_INITIALIZER;
pthread_mutex_t lock3 = PTHREAD_MUTEX_INITIALIZER;


/* Method #1 - Lock mutexes in a predefined order */
void
thread_a_func()
{
        /* Somewhere in the code */
        ...
        (void) pthread_mutex_lock(&lock1);
        (void) pthread_mutex_lock(&lock2);
        (void) pthread_mutex_lock(&lock3);
        ...
        (void) pthread_mutex_unlock(&lock3);
        (void) pthread_mutex_unlock(&lock2);
        (void) pthread_mutex_unlock(&lock1);

        /* Rest of the code */
        ...
}


/* Method #2 - Try to lock the out of order mutex. If the */
/* trylock fails, release all locks and acquire in order. */
void
thread_b_func()
{
        /* Somewhere in the code... */
        (void) pthread_mutex_lock(&lock2);
        ...
        if (pthread_mutex_trylock(&lock1) != 0) {
                (void) pthread_mutex_unlock(&lock2);
                (void) pthread_mutex_lock(&lock1);
                (void) pthread_mutex_lock(&lock2);
                /*
                 * Verify that the state of the data protected by
                 * lock2 has not changed. The data may have
                 * changed while the lock was released.
                 */
        }
        (void) pthread_mutex_lock(&lock3);

        /* We have all the locks now */
        ...
        (void) pthread_mutex_unlock(&lock3);
        (void) pthread_mutex_unlock(&lock2);
        (void) pthread_mutex_unlock(&lock1);
}
```

How to Find Thread-Safe Library Interfaces

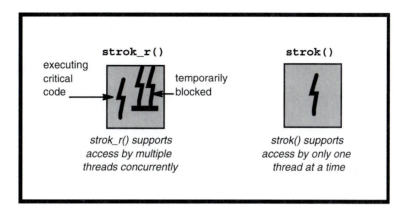

Fig. 12–4 According to POSIX.1c, a reentrant version of an unsafe library interface will have an "_r" suffix.

Overview

Traditional systems supported single-threaded applications. Consequently, these systems did not require support for thread-safe library functions. To support multithreaded applications, thread-safe library functions are required.

Most library functions have been made thread-safe without modifying the function interface. However, a few functions contain interfaces that precluded thread-safing. Generally, these functions maintain or return pointers to static data. New versions of these functions have been created that contain thread-safe interfaces. The new functions are identical to their nonthread-safe counterparts except for their _r suffix and an additional parameter. The additional parameter is usually a pointer to application-allocated space where the results can be returned. For example, the strok() interface is unsafe, but its counterpart, strok_r(), is thread-safe.

The following _r functions are defined by POSIX.1c. Various systems provide other _r functions; however, their use results in a non-portable application:

- asctime_r()
- ctime_r()
- getgrgid_r()
- getgrnam_r()
- getlogin_r()
- getpwnam_r()
- getpwuid_r()
- gmtime_r()
- localtime_r()
- rand_r()
- readdir_r()
- strtok_r()
- ttynam_r()

The following functions may be called by multithreaded applications, as long as the functions are passed a non-**NULL** parameter: ctermid() and tmpnam(). All other functions defined by POSIX and the C standard are thread-safe.

Guidelines

- Do **not** use unsafe code (or library functions) in multithreaded applications. Check your system's documentation; look for and use only thread-safe functions.

- Function characteristics, such as multithreaded **restrictions or responsibilities**, may be important to your application. Look for this information in your system's documentation (generally in the manual pages).

- When using or designing a thread-safe function, remember the *weakest link in the chain* analogy. If the interface calls one or more functions in order to do its work, the thread-safety of the interface will be equivalent to the **least** thread-safe function called.

- Thread-safe functions may contain cancellation points. Not all thread-safe functions are async-cancel safe, async-signal safe, and fork-safe. In fact, most functions are not safe for async-cancel, async-signal, or fork operations.

- If you must use an unsafe function or library interface in your multithreaded application:

    - Use mutexes to **synchronize** access to unsafe functions.

    - **Check the documentation** for any restrictions when using the unsafe function. Some unsafe functions may be safe only when called by a single, dedicated thread. Other unsafe functions may advertise that they are safe only when called by the initial (or main) thread.

    - Remember, a function that calls an unsafe function is itself an **unsafe** function.

    - Note that if a function is not thread-safe, it is probably not **cancel-safe** or **fork-safe**.

Example

Although this section has focused on how to *find* functions with thread-safe interfaces, you might be interested to know how to *write* one. In this example, func() is an unsafe function. However, by cleaning up the global variable *rtn* (i.e., putting it in the parameter list), func() can be made thread-safe. Naturally, we want to follow POSIX.1c's guidelines, so we'll give the thread-safe interface the _r suffix.

```
/*
 * This version of func() in not thread-safe. A global static data
 * structure is returned as the functions return value.
 */
struct rtn_struct      rtn;

struct rtn_struct *
func(char *str, char *arg1)
{
        int     error = 0;

        /* Function code goes here */
        ...

        if (error)
                return((struct rtn_struct *)NULL);
        else
                return(&rtn);
}


/*
 * This version, func_r(), is thread-safe. The caller must pass the
 * space for returning the structure.
 */
int
func_r(char *str, char *arg1, struct rtn_struct *ret)
{
        int                    error = 0;
        struct rtn_struct tmp_rtn;

        /* Function code goes here */
        ...

        if (error) {
                return(-1);
        } else {
                bcopy(&tmp_rtn, ret, sizeof(struct rtn_struct));
                return(0);
        }

}
```

Note that the thread-safe version of func() behaves exactly the same as the unsafe version. As you can see, most of the code is unchanged. The only difference is that the thread-safe version can support many threads accessing it concurrently and still provide logically correct behavior.

This example shows how it is possible to keep an unsafe function interface while still providing thread safety. A new `func()` routine, with the original two parameters, allocates the return data as thread-specific data. It then calls `func_r()`. The thread-specific data structure is returned to the caller.

```
/*
 * This version of func() is thread-safe. It allocates a
 * thread-specific data structure for the return value.
 */
void              func_init(), func_key_destroy(void *value);
pthread_key_t     func_key;
pthread_once_t    func_initialized = PTHREAD_ONCE_INIT;

struct rtn_struct *
func(char *str, char *arg1)
{
        int    error = 0;
        struct rtn_struct *tmp_rtn;

        /* Allocate the TSD return value. */

        (void) pthread_once(&func_initialized, func_init);

        tmp_rtn = (struct rtn_struct *)pthread_getspecific(func_key);
        if (tmp_rtn == NULL) {
                tmp_rtn = (struct rtn_struct *)
                        malloc(sizeof(struct rtn_struct));
                if (tmp_rtn == NULL)
                        return((struct rtn_struct *)NULL);
                pthread_setspecific(func_key, (void *)tmp_rtn);
        }

        /* Call the thread-safe version of this routine. */
        error = func_r(str, arg1, tmp_rtn);
        if (error)
                return((struct rtn_struct *)NULL);
        else
                return(tmp_rtn);
}

void
func_init()
{
        (void) pthread_key_create(&func_key, func_key_destroy);
}

void
func_key_destroy(void *value)
{
        free(value);
}
```

How to Write Cancel-Safe Functions

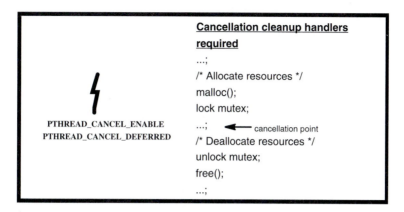

Fig. 12–5 An async-cancel safe function can be called when the asynchronous form of cancellation is enabled.

Overview

A function is **cancel-safe** if a thread executing the function is canceled and no state is left behind from the canceled thread. Consider a situation where a function acquires a lock. If a thread executing this function is canceled while the lock is acquired, the application will eventually deadlock because no other thread will be able to acquire the lock. This function is not cancel-safe.

The problem described above can be avoided by using cancellation cleanup handlers to make the function cancel-safe. The cleanup handlers are responsible for unlocking the mutex and releasing any other resources the canceled thread has acquired.

To determine what the cancellation cleanup handlers should do, the function must be examined closely. Look at all of the functions that are called. If none of these functions are cancellation points, the function is cancel-safe as it is and nothing needs to be done. If functions that are cancellation points are called, it's possible that a thread will never return from one of these calls.

When calling a function that is a cancellation point, examine all of the resources that the thread has acquired. These are the resources that must be released in the cancellation cleanup handlers. The most obvious task that cleanup handlers must perform is to unlock the mutexes that were acquired in the function. However, cancellation cleanup is not limited to unlocking mutexes. The thread may have allocated memory or may have been in the middle of modifying a linked list. If these other resources are not cleaned up, deadlock will not result; however, memory leaks or a loss of data integrity will result.

Guidelines

- Applications which do not call `pthread_cancel()` do not need to install cancellation cleanup handlers; threads in the application are never canceled. Libraries must **always** prepare for cancellation as the library does not know whether the application will ever call `pthread_cancel()`.

- One option to installing cancellation cleanup handlers is to **disable** a thread's **cancelability** state while it is executing the function. Whereas this makes the function cancel-safe, it also works against the reason for having a cancellation facility. This method is **not** recommended for functions that block indefinitely (e.g., waiting for data to arrive on the network). For function calls that complete in a short amount of time, this option may be desirable to avoid writing complicated cleanup handlers.

- Not all thread-safe functions need to disable cancellation or install cleanup handlers. Only functions that contain **cancellation points** within sections of code that acquire resources need to take these measures.

- Be sure to carefully **analyze** all resources that a thread has acquired in a function. These resources need to be released if the thread is canceled while inside the function.

- Carefully analyze functions that are called from this function. If any of these functions contain cancellation points that are called while resources are acquired, **cleanup handlers should be installed**.

- Be careful about leaving **data in an inconsistent state** when calling a function that is a cancellation point. It may be difficult to write a cancellation cleanup handler to restore the state of inconsistent data if the thread is canceled.

- The function `pthread_cleanup_push()` installs cleanup handlers onto the calling thread's cancellation stack. The `pthread_cleanup_pop()` function removes the cancellation cleanup handler from the top of the calling thread's cancellation stack. The installed handlers are **automatically** called when the thread terminates.

- If the function you are writing is a library function, be sure to **document** whether or not the function is a cancellation point. If the function calls a function that is a cancellation point, the function is a cancellation point.

- For more information, see Chapter 8, *Thread Cancellation*.

Example

The following code fragment shows how to use cancellation cleanup handlers within a function. In this example, a thread has acquired a mutex and allocated memory. If the thread is canceled while in this function, the cleanup handler releases the memory and unlocks the mutex.

```
void                    cleanup_func();
extern size_t           alloc_len;
extern pthread_mutex_t  mtx = PTHREAD_MUTEX_INITIALIZER;

void
csafe_function()
{
        char    *ptr;

        /* Allocate memory for a buffer. */
        ptr = (char *) malloc((size_t)1024);
        if (ptr == NULL) {
                fprintf(stderr, "Out of memory\n");
                exit(-1);
        }

        /* Lock the mutex */
        (void) pthread_mutex_lock(&mtx);

        /* Install the cancellation cleanup handler */
        pthread_cleanup_push(cleanup_func, ptr);

        /*
         * Code to do things to ptr goes here. This code contains
         * a cancellation point, hence the need for the
         * cancellation cleanup handler.
         */
        ...

        /*
         * Finished with ptr, free() it up, unlock the mutex,
         * and remove the cancellation cleanup handler.
         */
        pthread_cleanup_pop(0);
        (void) pthread_mutex_unlock(&mtx);
        free(ptr);

        pthread_exit((void *)NULL);
}

/*
 * Cancellation cleanup handler for csafe_function().
 */
void
cleanup_func(void *ptr)
{
        (void) pthread_mutex_unlock(&mtx);
        free(ptr);
}
```

How to Write Fork-Safe Functions

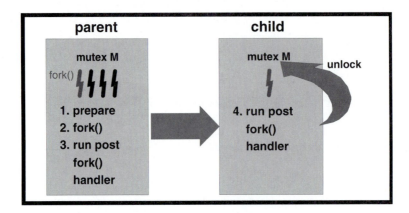

Fig. 12–6 A thread in the parent process calling `fork()` creates a single-threaded process. The state of any shared resources, such as mutexes, is retained across a call to `fork()`. Therefore, a deadlock could occur in the child process. To prevent problems, an `exec` function should be called immediately after the call to `fork()`.

Overview

When a thread calls `fork()`, POSIX.1c states that *"the new process contains a replica of the calling thread and its entire address space, possibly including the states of mutexes and other resources."*[2] Because the child process retains the state of shared objects across a call to `fork()`, there is a high probability that a deadlock could occur in the child process. A mutex that is locked in the parent process is also locked in the child process. If the thread calling `fork()` was not the thread locking the mutex, no one can unlock the mutex in the child process. Therefore, fork safety is a concern. This is especially true if you are designing library routines.

A function is **fork-safe** if it can be called by the child process before one of the `exec` functions is called. If a function does not lock mutexes, the function is usually considered fork-safe. To be fork-safe, a function should not leave any resources in an inconsistent state in the child process after a `fork()`.

For functions that always acquire a mutex before modifying global data or resources, fork handlers should be installed to make the function fork-safe. If a function cheats by modifying global data or resources without the protection of a lock, it cannot be made fork-safe. Many functions cannot easily be made fork-safe. POSIX.1c states that the only POSIX functions that are fork-safe are those functions that are also async-signal safe (refer to Chapter 7, *Threads and Signals*, for a list of async-signal safe functions).

[2] P1003.1c Draft 10, September 1994, section 3.1.1.2.

Recall from Chapter 4, *Basic Thread Management*, that the function `pthread_atfork()` is used to install fork handlers. There are three actions taken by the fork handlers. If the *prepare* handler is used, all of the necessary locks surrounding critical code sections should be acquired. These locks will remain locked until the call to `fork()` completes. After the call to `fork()` completes, the *parent* handler executes in the parent process and unlocks the mutexes acquired by the *prepare* handler. The *child* handler executes in the child process and unlocks the mutexes acquired by the *prepare* handler. Now, if a thread in the child process attempts to acquire one of these mutexes, it will not deadlock.

Guidelines

- First determine whether a function should be made **fork-safe**. Because many functions cannot be called in the child process, the time required to make a function fork-safe may not be worth the effort involved. If the function will not be made fork-safe, it should not be called by a child process.

- If a function should be made fork-safe, **install fork handlers** to acquire and release any mutexes or read-write locks that are normally acquired by the function.

- Be careful about the **order** in which the fork handlers are installed. Remember our earlier discussion of lock acquisition order? This applies to fork handlers also. The handlers should be installed so that all locks are acquired in the same order that they are acquired in normal execution. If the order is reversed, an interactive deadlock will occur.

- Because of lock order acquisition, it may not be possible to install fork handlers for a function or module. Consider a module that acquires mutex A. While this mutex is held, function `abc()` is called. This function acquires mutex B. The lock order for mutexes A and B has already been determined. A thread must first acquire mutex A and then acquire mutex B. This also determines the installation order for the fork handlers. The fork handler for mutex B must be installed first, followed by the fork handler for mutex A (the *prepare* handlers are called in LIFO order). When analyzing lock order dependencies, it may be determined that fork handlers cannot be installed for a module without introducing interactive deadlock.

- If the function you are writing is a library function, be sure to **document** whether or not it is fork-safe. If it is not fork-safe, an application should not call it from the child process of a multithreaded application.

How to Write a Thread-Safe Library

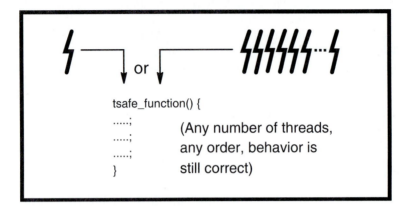

tsafe_function() {
.....;   (Any number of threads,
.....;   any order, behavior is
.....;   still correct)
}

Fig. 12–7 Use the guidelines below to write thread-safe library interfaces.

Overview

The previous sections in this chapter have provided the background information required to write thread-safe code. The following preflight checklist should act as a reminder of the steps required to write thread-safe code in an application or a library.

Guidelines

- Make each function **reentrant**. If it is not possible to make a function's interface reentrant, create a functionally equivalent _r version of the function.

- Make each function **thread-safe**. This may require the use of mutexes to protect global data in critical sections of code.

- Make each function **cancel-safe**. Library functions do not know if an application is going to cancel threads. Therefore, each library function needs to be prepared for a thread to be canceled while in the function. This may require the installation of cancellation cleanup handlers. The cancellation cleanup handlers will release resources (like mutexes or allocated memory) that were acquired by the canceled thread.

- Make each function **fork-safe** if the function is to be called in a child process after fork().

- Obtain the errno declaration only from the file <errno.h>. There should be no explicit declarations of the form extern int errno; in the source code.

- All components of a library should be compiled according to your system's requirements for compiling multithreaded applications. Many systems require multithreaded applications and the libraries used by multithreaded applications to be compiled with the **-D_REENTRANT** compile flag.

- Document whether or not each function is **thread-safe**. Document any restrictions on the use of the function by multithreaded applications.

- Document whether or not each function is a **cancellation point**.

- Document whether or not each function is **async-signal safe**.

- Document whether or not each function is **async-cancel safe**.

- Document whether or not each function is **fork-safe**.

- Document whether or not the interface anonymously creates threads. An application that is seemingly single-threaded may become multithreaded because a library function anonymously creates threads. This will help the application developer determine how to effectively handle signals and calls to `fork()`.

- Develop tests to validate the interface in a multithreaded environment and **thoroughly** test each function.

Summary

In this chapter, we provided guidelines for developing thread-safe code. Here they are: The function must be reentrant, access to shared objects must be managed, deadlock must be avoided, thread-safe library functions must be used, and the application should be cancel-safe and fork-safe. Finally, the function should be documented and thoroughly tested.

- The use of an unsafe function in a multithreaded program is highly discouraged for safety and performance reasons. However, an unsafe function can be called in a multithreaded application when access is serialized. There may also be additional restrictions.

- A thread-safe function may be called by any number of threads in any order–even interleaved–without sacrificing the logical correctness of the function.

- A thread-safe function is reentrant at minimum. A thread-safe function may have additional restrictions or responsibilities when compared to purely reentrant functions.

- Access by threads to shared objects must be serialized.

- Use error-checking (debug) mutexes during application development and testing. Then switch to normal or default mutexes for performance.

- In an application that will use more than one mutex, associate a sequence number with each mutex. Lock mutexes in sequential order to prevent deadlock. Alternatively, use the `pthread_trylock()` method described in the *How to Avoid Deadlock* section.

- Avoid holding mutexes over long operations, such as I/O.

- Some unsafe library functions have a thread-safe counterpart. The thread-safe counterpart uses the original interface name with a `_r` suffix.

- When using or designing a thread-safe function, remember the *weakest link in the chain* analogy. The thread safety of an interface is equivalent to the least thread-safe function called.

- Cancel-safe functions may use cancellation cleanup handlers to release any resources acquired during execution of the function.

- If a thread in a multithreaded process calls `fork()`, a single-threaded child process is created. The child process contains a replica of the calling thread and a copy of the parent process's address space. The address space contains the state of any resources, such as mutexes, that are in the parent process. If a function should be made fork-safe, install fork handlers to acquire and release any mutexes or read-write locks that are normally acquired by the function.

Exercises

1. Compare and contrast thread-safe, reentrant, and unsafe functions.

2. Describe how to use synchronization for performance as well as for correctness. Provide an example.

3. Function `func_unsafe(char *str)` evaluates an argument and returns 1 or 0 in a global static data structure called *rtn*. Make the function safe but retain its calling convention (one argument).

4. Why is cancel safety a concern for a thread-safe function? When is cancel safety an issue? How can a function be made cancel-safe? Is a cancel-safe function the same as an async-cancel safe function? Why or why not?

5. Why is fork safety a concern? Describe two ways that a function can be made fork-safe.

Programming Guidelines

This chapter is designed to provide specific guidelines for programming with threads based upon the information presented in the previous chapters. These guidelines include best practices, performance and portability tips, and constructs to avoid.

This material is rather terse. If you need a refresher on a particular topic, you can use the section and subsection titles in this chapter as pointers to chapters and sections containing more detailed information.

Topics Covered...

- Basic Thread Management
- Thread Synchronization
- Thread Scheduling
- Threads and Signals
- Thread Cancellation
- Thread-Specific Data
- Thread Extensions
- Thread F/X

Basic Thread Management

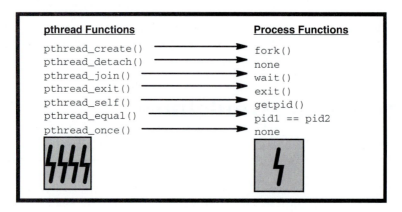

Fig. 13–1 POSIX.1c leaves a number of basic thread management behaviors unde-fined. Understanding the design and function of the basic thread management func-tions will help you design applications that perform well and are portable.

Creating a Thread

- Pthread functions do **not** set the `errno` variable when an error occurs. All Pthread functions return a value of zero for success or an error number indicating the error.
- Do **not** assume that a newly created thread is running (or going to run) after a call to `pthread_create()`. It is possible for the new thread to exe-cute and terminate before the call to `pthread_create()` returns.
- If *arg* is a pointer, it should **not** point to one of the creating thread's local variables. When the creating thread returns from the current function, this local variable is no longer valid.

Waiting for a Thread

- It is good practice to join with all joinable threads. Joined threads have their resources returned to the system. This provides performance and resource conservation benefits.
- Multiple threads should **not** call `pthread_join()` specifying the same thread ID; the resulting behavior is **undefined**. The calling thread may or may not receive an error. For maximum portability, `pthread_join()` should be called only once for a particular thread ID.
- Each process has a limit on the number of threads that can be created. POSIX.1c does not specify whether a thread that has terminated, but not yet been joined, counts against this limit. For maximum portability, use the `pthread_join()` function for all threads that an application creates.
- If a thread returns an exit status to an allocated data structure or resource, release that data structure or resource when the joining thread is finished with it.

Detaching a Thread

- An application should **not** call `pthread_join()` on a detached thread; an error will be returned. You cannot obtain the exit status of a detached thread. A thread that is **not** detached is a joinable thread.
- Do **not** call `pthread_detach()` on the same thread more than once. Most systems return an error of **EINVAL**, but the result of calling `pthread_detach()` on the same thread more than once is **undefined**.
- Before communicating or synchronizing with a detached thread, the application should ensure that the detached thread has not terminated.
- When an application does not care about the return status of a terminated thread, use `pthread_detach()`. Initialization and termination performance is better with `pthread_detach()` than with `pthread_join()`. The latter function has incremental overhead for suspending the calling thread and eventually returning exit status.
- An application should not return until all of its threads have terminated. Because a detached thread is not joinable, you must choose another method to ensure that detached threads complete before the application terminates.

Terminating a Thread

- Use `pthread_exit()` to terminate the calling thread. The `exit()` function terminates all of the threads in a process and then the process itself.
- When a thread terminates, its resources are **not** returned to the system. Use `pthread_join()` or `pthread_detach()` to ensure that the resources of a terminated thread are returned to the system.
- Do **not** attempt to access the local variables of a thread after it has terminated. Similarly, the exit status of a terminated thread should not be a pointer to one of the terminated thread's local variables. Attempting to access the local variables or exit status of a terminated thread is **undefined** by POSIX.
- A detached thread should **not** exit with a status other than **NULL** because its return status cannot be retrieved by calling `pthread_join()`.

Finding a Thread's ID

- Use `pthread_self()` and o **not** rely on system-wide unique thread IDs. Thread IDs are guaranteed to be unique only within a process.

Comparing Thread IDs

- Use `pthread_equal()` to compare thread IDs. `pthread_t` is an opaque data type that is **not** guaranteed to be a long or short.
- `pthread_equal()` does not verify that the two thread IDs to be compared refer to valid threads.

Performing One-Time Initialization

- Use `pthread_once()` when you must **guarantee** that an initialization function is called once, and only once. If this method is not used, multiple threads can call an initialization function, producing a race condition.
- The *once_control* variable should be a **global** variable.
- Each initialization function should have its **own** *once_control* variable. Similarly, a *once_control* variable should be passed to `pthread_once()` only with its associated initialization function.

Establishing Fork Handlers

- Resources, such as mutexes and memory, not needed in a child process should be released after a call to `fork()`. Use `pthread_atfork()` to prepare for a `fork()` and to clean up the parent and child processes after a `fork()`.
- A fork handler should **not** try to lock a mutex currently owned by the calling thread.
- The child process should call async-signal safe functions only before calling one of the `exec` functions (refer to Chapter 7, *Threads and Signals*, for a list of async-signal safe functions).

Creating Specialized Thread Attributes

- Most thread attributes have a default value. If POSIX.1c does not specify a default value for an attribute, do **not** rely on the attribute's consistency across platforms.
- `pthread_attr_t` is an opaque object that is **not** guaranteed to be the same on all systems. Do **not** copy *attr* into another variable. Referring to copies of *attr* results in **undefined** behavior.
- If you set the `stackaddr` attribute in an attributes object, the attributes object should be used only for creating **one** thread. If multiple threads are created with an attributes object having `stackaddr` set, all threads will share the same stack.
- To **conserve** resources, thread attributes objects should be destroyed when they are no longer needed. Destroying a thread attributes object has no effect on the threads already created with that attributes object.
- Do **not** rely on the value of *attr* after it has been destroyed. However, after the attributes object has been destroyed, it may be later reinitialized.

Thread Synchronization

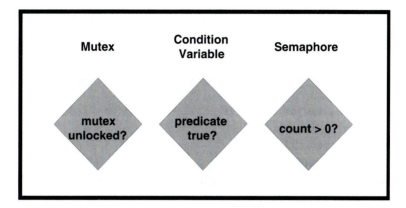

Fig. 13–2 Thread synchronization is perhaps the most difficult area in multithreaded programming. You will spend most of your time designing synchronization strategies to protect access to shared objects such as global data and file descriptors. Synchronization primitives include mutexes, condition variables, and semaphores.

Mutexes

- Shared data and resources, such as global variables and linked lists, should be protected by some form of synchronization. A mutex is one form of a synchronization primitive.
- It is possible to avoid using a lock around a shared object if you can guarantee the object will not be modified after threads are created. Locking is necessary only when a shared object may change.

Mutex Attributes

- Most mutex attributes have a default value. If POSIX.1c does not specify a default value for an attribute, do **not** rely on the attribute's consistency across platforms.
- Do **not** rely on the value of a mutex attributes object after it has been destroyed. `pthread_mutexattr_destroy()` may set *attr* to an invalid value. However, after the attributes object has been destroyed, it can later be reinitialized with `pthread_mutexattr_init()`.
- To **conserve** resources, mutex attributes objects should be destroyed when they are no longer needed. Destroying a mutex attributes object has no effect on the mutexes already initialized with that attributes object.
- `pthread_mutexattr_t` is an opaque object that is **not** guaranteed to be the same on all systems. Do **not** copy *attr* into another variable. Referring to copies of *attr* results in **undefined** behavior.

- Watch out for the following situation: A mutex is shared among processes (using the **PTHREAD_PROCESS_SHARED** attribute). A thread within one of the processes locks the mutex, then the process terminates. If another thread from one of the remaining processes attempts to lock this mutex, it will **deadlock**. Process and thread termination do not cause locked mutexes to be unlocked.
- For optimal performance, use the **PTHREAD_PROCESS_SHARED** attribute only when the mutex will be shared among multiple processes.

Initializing and Destroying Mutexes

- To prevent a thread from attempting to acquire an uninitialized mutex, mutexes should be initialized **before** any threads are created.
- A mutex should be initialized only **once**. Initializing a mutex more than once can result in incorrect program behavior. Some systems may return an error, others may not. Some systems may not return an error, even if a locked mutex is reinitialized. This can have detrimental effects on an application.
- To **conserve** resources, mutexes should be destroyed when they are no longer needed.
- A locked mutex should **never** be destroyed. Some systems may detect this and return an error. Other systems may allow the destruction to proceed, in which case the application eventually fails.

Locking and Unlocking Mutexes

- Do **not** attempt to relock a mutex. The resulting behavior is **undefined**. Some systems return an error; others allow the thread to deadlock. (See the *Thread Extensions* section for more information.)
- Do **not** attempt to unlock a mutex that has been locked by a different thread. Some systems may return an error; others may simply unlock the mutex. In either case, incorrect application behavior results.
- Similarly, do **not** attempt to unlock an unlocked mutex.
- For optimal performance, a mutex should be held for only **short** durations (a few instructions). Holding a mutex over long operations, such as I/O, can hurt performance.

Condition Variables

- Due to the possibility of spurious wakeups, predicate evaluation should **always** be done in a loop. Always re-evaluate the predicate when returning from pthread_cond_wait() or pthread_cond_timedwait().
- A mutex should **always** be associated with a condition variable. When changing the state of a condition predicate, the associated mutex should **always** be locked.

Condition Variable Attributes

- Most condition variable attributes have a default value. If POSIX.1c does not specify a default value for an attribute, do **not** rely on the attribute's consistency across platforms.
- Do **not** rely on the value of a condition variable attributes object after it has been destroyed. `pthread_condattr_destroy()` may set *attr* to an invalid value. However, after the attributes object has been destroyed, it can later be reinitialized with `pthread_condattr_init()`.
- To **conserve** resources, condition variable attributes objects should be destroyed when they are no longer needed. Destroying a condition variable attributes object has no effect on the condition variables already initialized with that attributes object.
- `pthread_condattr_t` is an opaque object that is **not** guaranteed to be the same on all systems. Do **not** copy *attr* into another variable. Referring to copies of *attr* results in **undefined** behavior.
- If a condition variable is initialized with the **PTHREAD_PROCESS_SHARED** attribute, the associated mutex should also be given this attribute. Otherwise, threads in other processes will not be able to lock the condition variable's mutex.
- Watch out for the following situation: A condition variable is shared among processes (using the **PTHREAD_PROCESS_SHARED** attribute). Threads from the sharing processes wait on the condition variable. If the process containing the thread that will signal the condition terminates, **deadlock** has occurred for the threads waiting on the condition variable. Process and thread termination do not cause locked mutexes to be unlocked or condition variables to be signaled.
- For optimal performance, use the **PTHREAD_PROCESS_SHARED** attribute only when the condition variable will be shared among multiple processes.

Initializing and Destroying Condition Variables

- When a condition variable is shared among multiple processes, only **one** process should perform the initialization.
- To prevent a thread from attempting to wait on an uninitialized condition variable, condition variables should be initialized **before** any threads are created.
- A condition variable should be initialized only **once**. Initializing a condition variable more than once can result in incorrect program behavior. Some systems may return an error, others may not. Some systems may not return an error, even if a condition variable in use is reinitialized. This can have detrimental effects on an application.
- To **conserve** resources, destroy condition variables when they are no longer needed.

- A busy condition variable (one with waiting threads) should **never** be destroyed. Some systems may return an error if this is attempted. Other systems may allow the destruction, and the application will eventually fail.

Waiting on a Condition

- Due to the possibility of spurious wakeups, condition predicate evaluations should **always** be done in a loop. Always re-evaluate the predicate when returning from `pthread_cond_wait()` or `pthread_cond_timedwait()`.
- `pthread_cond_wait()` and `pthread_cond_timedwait()` are cancellation points. If an application is using cancellation and condition variables, it should **install** cancellation cleanup handlers so that, upon cancellation, the condition variable's associated mutex is released.

Signaling a Condition

- The `pthread_cond_signal()` function signals **one** thread waiting on the specified condition. The `pthread_cond_broadcast()` function signals **all** threads waiting on the specified condition. If no threads are waiting on the specified condition, no action is taken. Condition signals are **not** held pending if there are no waiters.

Semaphores

- Do **not** copy *sem* into another variable. Referring to copies of *sem* results in **undefined** behavior with the semaphore operations.
- Use **named** semaphores when synchronizing multiple processes. Named semaphores do not require the use of shared memory.
- Use **unnamed** semaphores to synchronize threads within a multithreaded process or threads within a multithreaded, multiprocess application. In the latter case, shared memory must be allocated for the semaphore. Unnamed semaphores are similar to mutexes and are easy to use.
- Watch out for the following situation: A semaphore is shared among processes. A thread within one of the sharing processes acquires the semaphore, then the process terminates. If another thread from one of the remaining processes attempts to acquire the semaphore, it will **deadlock**. Process and thread termination do not cause locked semaphores to be unlocked.

Initializing and Destroying Semaphores

- To prevent a thread from attempting to access an uninitialized semaphore, semaphores should be initialized **before** any threads are created.
- If a semaphore is shared among multiple processes, only **one** process should initialize the semaphore.

- A semaphore should be initialized only **once**. Initializing a semaphore more than once can result in incorrect program behavior. Some systems may return an error, others may not. Some systems may not return an error even if a locked semaphore is reinitialized. This can have detrimental effects on an application.
- To **conserve** resources, destroy semaphores when they are no longer needed.
- A busy semaphore (one that has threads using it) should **never** be destroyed. Some systems may return an error if this is attempted. Other systems may allow the destruction, and the application will eventually fail.

Locking and Unlocking Semaphores

- The `sem_wait()` function will **not** return until the semaphore has been locked. The `sem_trywait()` function returns immediately, with either a lock on the semaphore or an error of **EBUSY**.

Handling Synchronization Errors

- Depending on the error returned from a call to a synchronization primitive, it may be appropriate to try the call again rather than to allow the application to terminate. For example, when calling `pthread_mutex_init()`, the system may be temporarily low on memory, causing the call to return **ENOMEM**. Alternatively, the call could return **EAGAIN**, indicating that the system is out of resources. A robust application detects errors like these and tries some reasonable number of times to complete the function call successfully or gracefully bubbles the error back to higher levels in the application.

Memory Models and Synchronization

- Use the POSIX functions listed in the *Memory Models and Synchronization* section to synchronize memory with respect to other threads.
- Read-only global data does not require synchronization.

Thread Scheduling

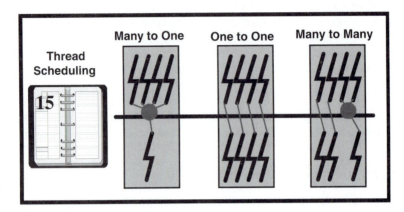

Fig. 13–3 In multithreaded programming, you have much more control and responsibility for scheduling. Using one scheduling policy in your application helps simplify your scheduling strategy.

Thread Scheduling Contention Scopes

- The scheduling behavior of threads using *process* versus *system scheduling contention scope* is **undefined**.
- The decision to use bound or unbound threads should be based on the specific characteristics of the application. To make the right determination, ask the following questions:

    + How many threads will the application require? Keep in mind that bound threads are more **expensive** than unbound threads in terms of the resources they require. A user thread is very lightweight and exists only in user space. However, a bound thread has a user and a kernel component, and the kernel is involved in all thread management operations.

    + How long will particular threads be needed? **Short-term** threads are typically better off when they are unbound. Because unbound threads are of lighter weight, operations such as thread creation, context switching, and termination do not have to cross expensive user/kernel boundaries. The "expense" of crossing the user/kernel boundary comes from switching to the kernel stack and calling the library functions necessary to invoke the proper kernel function. For operations other than thread termination, the overhead of switching back to user mode is also part of this "expense."

    + What **types of operations** will the threads be executing? Threads that spend most of their time using synchronization primitives to share data tend to perform better as unbound entities. The user space scheduler is involved in the thread management operations, obviating the need to cross user/kernel boundaries to involve the kernel scheduler. On the other hand, bound threads are usually better for compute-bound functions. There is a higher probability that compute-bound threads will use their entire time-slice without performing an operation that will cause a context switch.

+   Will I require **profiling** information? Unbound threads may not carry enough context for detailed profiling. For example, if four threads are multiplexed on top of one kernel thread, it is difficult to determine how much CPU time each thread is receiving.

+   How **often** will each thread need to run? Strike the right balance between optimum performance and efficient/effective resource utilization.

+   Is true **realtime** scheduling required? If so, use a bound thread.

Thread Scheduling Policies and Priorities

* If your application uses the **SCHED_OTHER** scheduling policy, **always** check your system's documentation to see how it has been implemented. **SCHED_OTHER** may not be the same on different systems.

Thread Scheduling Allocation Domains

* Check your system's documentation to determine the thread scheduling allocation domain(s).

Thread Creation Scheduling Attributes

* Remember this when choosing scheduling attributes: Systems are required to support process or system scheduling contention scope, but not both. MxN Model systems support both. 1x1 Model systems support only threads with the **PTHREAD_SCOPE_SYSTEM** contention scope. Mx1 Model systems support only threads with the **PTHREAD_SCOPE_PROCESS** contention scope.
* POSIX.1c does not specify a default scheduling inheritance policy. Most systems default to **PTHREAD_INHERIT_SCHED**.
* Your system may support scheduling policies other than **SCHED_FIFO**, **SCHED_RR**, and **SCHED_OTHER**. Care must be taken when using other policies if portability is a concern.
* If your scheduling policy is **SCHED_FIFO** or **SCHED_RR**, only the `sched_priority` member of the `schedparam` scheduling attribute is required to be set. If your scheduling policy is **SCHED_OTHER** or some other scheduling policy, check your system's documentation to see whether and how the `schedparam` attribute should be set.

Dynamic Thread Scheduling

- Use the following function to dynamically change a thread's priority, scheduling policy, or both: pthread_setschedparam().

Scheduling Priority Values

- How threads with different scheduling policies interact with one another is **undefined** by POSIX.1c. Each system defines and documents this behavior. Do not rely on a particular system's behavior to be portable across different systems.
- Care must be taken when trying to mix scheduling policies with different threads in your application. There is **no** guarantee that scheduling priority ranges will be the same across vendor systems. Typically, the **SCHED_FIFO** priority range is higher than **SCHED_OTHER**.

Yielding the Processor

- Remember that sched_yield() yields the processor to another thread only of equal or higher priority.

Priority Inversion and Mutexes

- To prevent priority inversion, the priority inheritance or priority ceiling protocol should be used. The protocol mutex attribute allows you to specify which protocol to use. POSIX.1c does not specify a default value for protocol, but most systems default to **PTHREAD_PRIO_NONE**. There is also **PTHREAD_PRIO_INHERIT** and **PTHREAD_PRIO_PROTECT**.
- For maximum portability, only threads having the **SCHED_FIFO** scheduling policy should use **PTHREAD_PRIO_PROTECT** mutexes. If threads with other scheduling policies use such a mutex, the priority specified in the prioceiling attribute may not be a valid priority for the locking thread's scheduling policy. The prioceiling attribute must have a value that is valid for **SCHED_FIFO**.
- For maximum portability, only threads with the **same** scheduling policy should use **PTHREAD_PRIO_INHERIT** mutexes. This prevents problems if the blocking thread's scheduling policy is not the same as that of the thread owning the mutex.

Threads and Signals

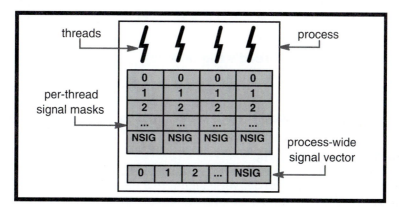

Fig. 13–4 Threads can send signals to each other. When a signal is sent to the process, there is no guarantee which thread will handle the signal. However, a signal can be directed to a particular thread. All threads except one can block the signal in their signal masks.

Signals in the Thread Model

- Some functions [e.g., `kill()`, `alarm()`, etc.] deliver asynchronous signals to the process rather than individual threads. One thread, and only one thread, will handle a signal delivered to the process; however, exactly which thread is **undefined**. If you would like a particular signal to be handled by a particular thread, all other threads in the process should block the signal.
- A thread should use one of the `sigwait()` functions to wait for an asynchronous signal to be sent to the process. (See *Waiting for a Signal* in this section.)
- When a thread handles a signal, if the action for that signal causes the thread to be terminated, stopped, or continued, the entire **process** will be terminated, stopped, or continued. This behavior is the same, whether the signal is sent to a thread or to the process.

Synchronous and Asynchronous Signals

- Synchronously generated signals are delivered to the **thread** based on some action performed by the thread, such as *division by zero*. Asynchronous signals, such as those delivered by `kill()`, timers, or asynchronous I/O operations, are delivered to the **process**.
- Use `pthread_kill()` to deliver an asynchronous signal to a thread.
- If you want a particular thread within a process to handle an asynchronous signal, all other threads within the process should block that signal. (The signal handling thread can be used to dispatch tasks to other threads based on the signal received.)

- If more than one thread is allowed to handle a particular signal, the associated signal handler should be generic. Remember that signal handlers are per-process resources, and signal masks are per-thread resources.

Examining/Changing a Thread's Signal Mask

- Use `pthread_sigmask()`, **not** `sigprocmask()`, to change the signal mask of a thread. Although some systems support using `sigprocmask()` to change the signal mask of a thread, this functionality is not portable.

Sending Signals to Threads

- Use `pthread_kill()` to deliver a signal to a particular thread.
- Remember, when a thread handles a signal, if the action for that signal causes the thread to be terminated, stopped, or continued, the entire **process** will be terminated, stopped, or continued. This behavior is the same, whether the signal is sent to a thread or to the process.

Waiting for a Signal

- Signals specified in the *set* parameter of the `sigwait()` functions should be **blocked** prior to calling a `sigwait()` function. If this is not done, the resulting behavior is **undefined**.
- Application behavior is **undefined** if an application uses `sigaction()` and one of the `sigwait()` functions concurrently.

Async-Signal Safe Thread Functions

- **None** of the `pthread_*` functions are async-signal safe. Do **not** call any of these functions from within a signal handler.
- If an application is a library that is supplied to other application developers, the library should specify whether each of its routine is async-signal safe.

SIGEV_THREAD

- Use **SIGEV_THREAD** (an extension to the `sigevent` structure) for event handling. When the event occurs, the system creates a *notification thread* to execute a handler. Only functions using `sigevent` structures can make use of this feature.
- By default, notification threads have their detach state set to the value **PTHREAD_CREATE_DETACHED**.
- For maximum portability, do **not** rely on the signal mask of an event notification thread being initialized to any value. Initialize the mask yourself.

Thread Cancellation

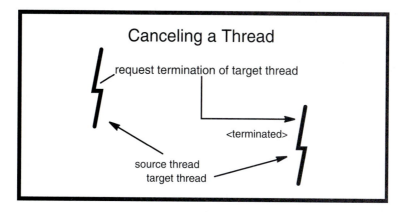

Fig. 13–5 The use of signals within multithreaded applications can have negative effects. You can use the thread cancellation feature, with cleanup handlers, to cleanly and asynchronously terminate a thread.

Thread Cancelability States

- Cancellation requests should be **held pending** (i.e., disabled) when a thread starts an operation that cannot or should not be terminated.
- Care should be taken when disabling thread cancellation. You do **not** want a thread indefinitely blocked with no clean way to be terminated.
- When using **PTHREAD_CANCEL_ASYNCHRONOUS**, a thread should call **only** async-cancel safe functions. A thread should not acquire or allocate any resources while the asynchronous form of cancellation is enabled.

Thread Cancellation Points

- `pthread_mutex_lock()` is not a cancellation point. Consequently, applications should **not** leave mutexes locked for an indefinite period of time. Threads blocked on mutexes cannot be canceled.
- If a thread unblocks from a function that allows cancellation and a cancellation request is received at the same time, POSIX.1c does **not** specify whether the thread should return from the function or act on the cancellation request first. Most systems return from the function and hold the cancellation request pending. Portable applications should not rely on this behavior.
- If an application is a library supplied to other application developers, the library should **specify** every routine that contains a cancellation point.
- If threads in your application use deferred cancellation, it is important for you to know where cancellation can take place. Consult the list of cancellation points given in Chapter 8, *Thread Cancellation*.

Setting Thread Cancelability States

- Use `pthread_setcancelstate()` to enable or disable thread cancellation. Thread cancellation should be **disabled** when a thread is performing an operation that should not be terminated.
- Use `pthread_setcanceltype()` to choose deferred or asynchronous cancellation. When cancellation is deferred, cancellation requests are **held pending** until the thread reaches a cancellation point. Asynchronous cancellation can take place at **any** time.

Creating a Cancellation Point

- If a thread disables cancellation for a long period of time, it should first use `pthread_testcancel()` to **check** for any pending cancellation requests.

Installing Cancellation Cleanup Handlers

- A thread using **PTHREAD_CANCEL_ASYNCHRONOUS** should call **only** async-cancel safe functions. It should not acquire any resources while asynchronous cancellation is enabled. However, if it is necessary for the thread to acquire resources, **install** cleanup handlers for each resource acquired.
- Cleanup handlers are installed on a stack and executed in **LIFO** order.
- A thread's cancellation cleanup handlers are executed under the following conditions: when the thread calls `pthread_exit()`, when the thread is canceled as the result of a call to `pthread_cancel()`, or if the thread calls `pthread_cleanup_pop()` with a non-zero *execute* parameter.
- `pthread_cleanup_push()` and `pthread_cleanup_pop()` are generally implemented as macros. Both must appear in pairs within the same lexical scope.

Cancelling a Thread

- When `pthread_cancel()` returns, do **not** assume that the target thread has been canceled. Cancellation request may be held pending.

Async-Cancel Safety

- An async-cancel safe function may be safely called by a thread with the cancelability state set to **PTHREAD_CANCEL_ENABLE** and the cancelability type set to **PTHREAD_CANCEL_ASYNCHRONOUS**. If a thread is canceled in one of these functions, no resources are left in an inconsistent state.
- If an application is a library supplied to other application developers, it should **specify** every routine that is async-cancel safe.
- Threads with asynchronous cancelability enabled should call **only** library functions that are async-cancel safe. Otherwise, when a thread is canceled, a resource could be left in an inconsistent state.

Thread-Specific Data

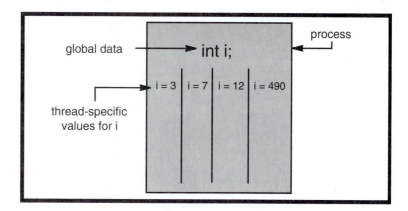

Fig. 13–6 In a multithreaded application, data can be global and synchronized using synchronization primitives, or global data can be specific to each thread. Use thread-specific data to avoid the need for synchronization and allow global data to be specific to each thread.

Creating Thread-Specific Data Keys

- Thread-specific data keys should **always** be created in global memory. It is wise to create thread-specific data in `main()` before any threads have been created. Otherwise, a thread may attempt to access a thread-specific data key before it has been created.

Deleting Thread-Specific Data Keys

- Once a thread-specific data key has been removed, threads in the application will not be able to use that key.
- If a thread allocates a resource and associates the resource with a thread-specific data key, when the key is deleted, the resource will be lost. Delete a key only after **all** threads have finished using the key.

Accessing Thread-Specific Data Elements

- If a thread attempts to access thread-specific data with an invalid *key*, the resulting behavior is **undefined**. Most systems return **NULL** in this situation, but portable applications should not rely on this.
- If an application makes use of several thread-specific data keys, it may be wise to **consolidate** them into a single data structure for performance. One key is associated with the entire data structure. When a thread needs thread-specific data values, it calls `pthread_getspecific()` with the appropriate key. A pointer to the data structure is returned, and the thread-specific data values are accessed through this pointer.

Thread Extensions

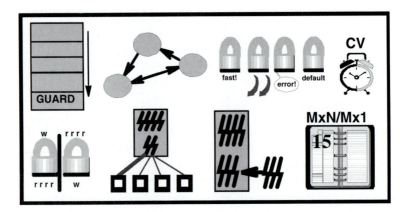

Fig. 13–7 Thread extensions include additional thread stack attributes, thread suspension/resumption, four new mutexes, read-write locks, concurrency and scheduling control in the MxN model, a new scheduling policy, and processor affinity. These are powerful features that can enhance multithreaded programs.

HP and X/Open Thread Extensions

- X/Open thread extensions are portable. HP-only thread extensions are **not** portable. If you write an application that is intended to run on multiple platforms, you may not want to use these features. If similar features are provided on the "port to" system(s), you will need to #ifdef your code.
- Remember, **all** functions containing _np or _NP suffixes are not portable.

Thread Stack Attributes

- Stack overflow protection causes a "guard page" to be created that detects stack overflow. When stack overflow occurs, a signal is delivered to the thread. This is a useful **debugging** feature. It is enabled on most systems by default.
- The size of the guard area can be controlled with the guardsize (stack protection) thread attribute. If an application contains thousands of threads, the guard page may become too expensive (#_threads * guardsize = memory consumed). Therefore, you may consider turning stack protection off in an application that has been **thoroughly** tested. Applications should be developed and tested with stack protection enabled.
- If your application allocates large arrays on the stack, consider increasing the size of the guard area to help detect stack overflow.

Suspending and Resuming Threads

* The `pthread_suspend()` function causes the target thread to **suspend** its execution. A thread can suspend itself or another thread. A thread may also be suspended multiple times by one or more threads.
* The `pthread_continue()` function causes the target thread to **resume** execution, regardless of how many times it was suspended.
* The `pthread_resume_np()` function causes the target thread to be **resumed**. If the target thread suspended itself, another thread must resume the suspended thread. If a thread was suspended multiple times, it must be resumed an equal number of times with **PTHREAD_COUNT_RESUME_NP** or once with **PTHREAD_FORCE_RESUME_NP** before it will continue. For portability, **use pthread_continue()**.
* The suspend and resume functions should **not** be used for thread synchronization. The application cannot control exactly when the target thread is suspended or resumed.
* It is usually **not** wise to have one thread issue a suspend and a different thread issue the resume. Resuming a thread that is not suspended has no effect. If the two threads issuing the suspend and resume are not synchronized, it is possible that the resume could be issued before the suspend. In this situation, the target thread is left suspended.
* It is possible to use synchronization primitives rather than suspension, obviating the need for these functions. When faced with the choice, **use synchronization primitives** for better application portability.
* When using the `pthread_resume_np()` function, it is strongly recommended that the **PTHREAD_COUNT_RESUME_NP** flag be used instead of the **PTHREAD_FORCE_RESUME_NP** flag. If multiple threads suspend a target thread simultaneously and one thread issues a resume, the other threads may continue on the assumption that the target thread is still suspended. Use a force resume **only** when a thread must respond to an event immediately.

Mutex Extensions

* Four mutex types are defined: **PTHREAD_MUTEX_NORMAL, PTHREAD_MUTEX_ RECURSIVE, PTHREAD_MUTEX_ERRORCHECK,** and **PTHREAD_MUTEX_ DEFAULT.** Use the "normal" version for the fastest synchronization. Use the "recursive" version when a thread must recursively lock a mutex. Use the "error-check" version during development and/or debugging. The "default" version is typically mapped to one of the former three versions. Otherwise, relocking a default mutex or unlocking a default mutex with a thread that is not the owner results in undefined behavior. Portable applications should **not** rely on default mutex behavior being the same across platforms.
* Operations on normal mutexes do **not** provide error checking. If a thread relocks a normal mutex, it deadlocks on itself.

- A recursive mutex has an owner field. A recursive mutex can be locked **multiple** times by the owning thread, without causing deadlock. To unlock a recursive mutex, it must be unlocked the same number of times it was locked. Use a recursive mutex when you have recursive functions needing mutex locks or multiple code paths that enter a function sometimes with the lock held and sometimes without the lock held.
- An error-checking mutex also maintains an owner field. An error checking mutex is sometimes known as a **debug** mutex because it returns an error if a thread attempts to relock it. Use an error-checking mutex during application development and debugging. After the application has been thoroughly tested, switch to a normal or default mutex for better performance.
- Default mutexes contain undefined behavior in relation to error-checking and recursive locking. Some systems map the default mutex to the normal mutex, but portable applications should not rely on this behavior.
- Use the `pthread_mutexattr_settype()` function to set the mutex type.
- See the discussion on mutex attributes in the *Thread Synchronization* section of this chapter for more information on attributes in general.

Condition Variable Expiration Time

- After calling `get_expiration_time()`, the *abstime* parameter should be used in a call to `pthread_cond_timedwait()` to perform a relative condition wait. The timed wait should be performed **immediately** after constructing *abstime*. If the thread performs other operations after *abstime* has been constructed, *abstime* may pass before the timed wait function is called. In this case, an **ETIMEDOUT** error is returned rather than waiting for the delta time interval.

Read-Write Locks

- The advantage of using a read-write lock is that an application can allow multiple reader threads access to a shared object **concurrently**. However, read-write locks have higher overhead than do mutexes. Therefore, if a lock is held for only a short duration (a few instructions), use mutexes. If a lock is held for long durations and there are many read-only operations but few write operations, use a read-write lock.

Read-Write Lock Attributes

- If a default value for a read-write lock attribute is not specified, do **not** rely on the attribute's consistency across platforms.
- Once a read-write lock attributes object has been initialized, the attributes **can** be changed. The attributes object can be used to initialize multiple read-write locks, where you desire each one to have the same attributes.

- After a read-write lock has been initialized, its attributes **cannot** be changed.
- To **conserve** resources, a read-write lock attributes object should be destroyed when it is no longer needed. Destroying a read-write attributes object has no effect on the read-write locks already initialized.
- Do **not** rely upon the value of *attr* after the read-write attributes object has been destroyed. The function `pthread_rwlockattr_destroy()` may set *attr* to an invalid value. However, after this attributes object has been destroyed, `pthread_rwlockattr_init()` can be used to reinitialize *attr* at a later time.
- `pthread_rwlockattr_t` is an opaque object; it is **not** guaranteed to be the same on all systems. Therefore, do **not** copy *attr* into another variable. Referring to copies of *attr* results in undefined behavior.
- Watch out for the following situation: A read-write lock is shared among processes (using the **PTHREAD_PROCESS_SHARED** attribute). A thread within one of the sharing processes locks the read-write lock (let's say for reading), then the process terminates. The writer threads will wait indefinitely. Process and thread termination do not cause locked read-write locks to be unlocked.
- Use the **PTHREAD_PROCESS_PRIVATE** option with read-write locks. Read-write locks created with this attribute generally perform better than do the process-shared variety.

Initializing and Destroying Read-Write Locks

- If you need to change a read-write lock's default attributes, the read-write attributes object must be **dynamically** initialized using the function `pthread_rwlock_init()`.
- A read-write lock should be initialized only **once**. Initializing a read-write lock multiple times may result in incorrect program behavior. Some systems may return an error if an application tries to initialize an already initialized read-write lock; others may not. Some systems may not even return an error if a locked read-write lock is reinitialized. This can have detrimental results on an application.
- To **conserve** resources, a read-write lock should be destroyed when it is no longer needed.
- An application should **not** rely on the value of *rwlock* after *rwlock* has been destroyed. In fact, `pthread_rwlock_destroy()` may set *rwlock* to an invalid value. However, `pthread_rwlock_init()` can be used to reinitialize *rwlock* at a later time.
- A locked read-write lock should **never** be destroyed. Some systems may detect this and return an error. Others may allow the destruction to proceed, and the application will eventually fail. A read-write lock should be destroyed only when it is in the unlocked state.

Locking and Unlocking Read-Write Locks

- **Before** using a lock or unlock function, the target read-write lock must have been previously initialized.
- Read-write lock operations can fail. Therefore, make sure to **check** for potential error values.
- The functions used to lock and unlock a read-write lock are **not** async-signal safe.
- In general, a lock operation blocks the calling thread until it can lock the read-write lock. If the read-write lock is unlocked, the locking function returns immediately with the read-write locked for reading or for writing. However, it is **unspecified** as to whether a writer thread immediately acquires the write lock when readers are blocked on the lock.
- Use `pthread_rwlock_[rd|wr]lock()` to block the calling thread's execution until the read-write lock can be acquired. Use the functions `pthread_rwlock_try[rd|wr]lock()` to return either with the lock acquired or with an error if the read-write lock could not be acquired.
- A thread should **not** attempt to acquire a write lock on a *rwlock* when it currently holds the read lock. The resulting behavior is **undefined**.
- If a signal is delivered to a thread waiting on a read-write lock, the thread continues waiting for the read-write lock after handling the signal. The **EINTR** error is **not** returned.
- Do **not** attempt to unlock a read-write lock that has been locked by a different thread. Some systems may return an error, others may simply unlock the read-write lock. In either case, this can lead to incorrect application behavior as another thread assumes it has the read-write lock acquired.
- Do **not** attempt to unlock an unlocked read-write lock.

The Timeshare Scheduling Policy

- **Check** your system's documentation to see how **SCHED_OTHER** is defined. Look in `<sched.h>` to determine the name for any timeshare policy supported on your system. It may be called **SCHED_TIMESHARE** or **SCHED_TS**.

Thread to Processor Binding

- If several threads synchronize on shared resources often, it may be wise to bind them to the **same** processor. Although this reduces parallelism, it takes advantage of the system's hardware cache. This *trade-off* may *pay off*.
- If several threads are completely disjointed and share no data, it may be wise to bind those threads to **different** processors. Because these threads have no problem with cache thrashing, they can take advantage of the parallelism offered by multiple processors.

- Most systems do a pretty good job of effectively utilizing the multiprocessor hardware to provide your application with optimum performance. You may **not need to bind** threads to processors at all.
- Use **PTHREAD_GETCURRENT_SPU_NP** as the *request* parameter in a call to pthread_processor_id_np() to determine on which processor the target thread is currently executing. Remember, however, that the information returned may be **out of date** at any moment. A context switch can take place, and the thread may later be scheduled to run on a different processor.
- If a thread is using **PTHREAD_BIND_ADVISORY_NP**, **scheduling policy takes precedence over a thread's binding**. If a realtime thread that is bound to processor *A* is the highest priority thread, it is scheduled to run on processor *B* if processor *A* is not available. On the other hand, if a thread is using **PTHREAD_BIND_FORCED_NP**, the **thread's binding takes precedence over its scheduling policy**. By setting a thread's processor binding to **PTHREAD_SPUFLOAT_NP**, the thread is given a scheduling allocation domain equal to the number of available processors (i.e., it can be scheduled on any processor).
- When considering a binding strategy, **remember** that the **allocation domain** may change. The development system may have more or fewer processors than does the run-time system.

Thread Concurrency and MxN Threads

- Most systems provide the optimum number of kernel-scheduled entities in a process by default. However, should you need to **change** this number, use the pthread_setconcurrency() function. The *new_level* parameter essentially represents the **N** in MxN. Remember, however, that the concurrency level is only a *hint* to the system. The system may choose to ignore a value for *new_level* that would result in deadlock.
- If the pthread_setconcurrency() function is issued in an application running on a non-MxN Model system, it saves the value in *new_level* but **ignores** the concurrency request.
- Setting the optimum number of kernel-scheduled entities is an application- and system-dependent exercise. You need to **experiment** and analyze the application's performance to determine the optimal concurrency level.
- The concurrency level required to achieve optimum performance is **system-dependent**.

Scheduling Unbound Kernel Entities

- X/Open has extended the behavior of the sched_setscheduler() and sched_setparam() functions. Use these functions to specify how unbound threads, as a whole, will **compete** with all bound threads in the system.

Thread F/X

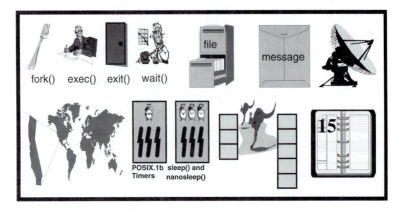

Fig. 13–8 Thread Effects (F/X) presents the specific behavior found when using common functions in a multithreaded environment. Some functions act at the process level, other functions act at the thread level. In either case, it is important for you to understand the thread f/x!

`fork()`, `exec()`, `exit()`, and `wait()`

- If a thread within a multithreaded process calls `fork()` to create a new process, the new process will be single-threaded. The state of all mutexes, condition variables, etc. are **inherited** across the `fork()` call. To prevent the possibility of deadlock, use `pthread_atfork()` or have the child call an `exec` function immediately.
- In a multithreaded process, if a thread calls one of the `exec` functions, **all** threads are terminated, and the new image will be single-threaded. The state of any mutexes, condition variables, etc. is **lost** after returning from an `exec` function.
- The `exit()` function operates at the **process level**. Calling `exit()` terminates all threads in the process, then the process itself.
- The `wait()` function operates at the **thread level**. The calling thread is suspended until the target process terminates or receives a signal.
- When using `vfork()`, the calling thread will **block** until the single-threaded child process calls `exit()` or one of the `exec` functions.

File and Message-Passing Operations

- When one thread calls a function like `dup()`, `open()`, `close()`, `pipe()`, etc., the effect is visible to **all** threads. This is because the file descriptor table is a global (process-wide) resource.
- When using `lseek()`, `read()`, or `write()`, the file offset is shared by **all** threads.

- On blocking system calls such as `read()`, `mq_receive()`, etc., **only** the calling thread will block (except on a Mx1 Model system where the whole process may block).
- When a thread closes a file or a message queue, that resource is closed for **all** threads in the process.
- **Avoid** interleaved I/O by synchronizing access to open file descriptors.
- Locks on a file via `fnctl()` or `lockf()` are maintained on a **per process** basis. If thread *A* locks a file, thread *B*, from the same process, can access the file.
- Use the `flockfile()`, `funlockfile()`, and the `ftrylock()` functions to perform file locking at the **thread level**.
- The `getc()`, `putc()`, `getchar()`, and `putchar()` functions acquire a lock each time they are called. This can decrease performance. Therefore, you should **explore** the use of `getc_unlocked()`, `putc_unlocked()`, `getchar_unlocked()`, and `putchar_unlocked()`.
- The functions `flockfile()`, `funlockfile()`, and `ftrylock()` **should** be used with the `*_unlocked()` functions to prevent corrupted I/O.
- Message queues are **per process** resources. Once a message queue is opened, all threads within the process have access. To preserve integrity, only **one** thread should open and close a message queue. If a thread attempts to access an unopened message queue or if a message queue is closed while in use, this has detrimental effects on the application.

Signals

- When using the `alarm()` function, the alarm signal is sent to the **process**. Which thread handles the signal is **undefined**. If you would like only one thread to handle the alarm signal, all threads but that one should block the signal. If `alarm()` is called multiple times, the *sec* value is overwritten. The last value written is used (unless a previous value times out before a subsequent value is written).
- Remember that using the `raise()` function is equivalent to calling `pthread_kill(pthread_self(), sig)`.
- The `sigaction()` function should **not** be used in conjunction with one of the `sigwait()` functions.
- The `sigprocmask()` function should **not** be used to examine or change the signal mask of a thread-this is not guaranteed to be portable. Use `pthread_sigmask()` for this purpose.
- The `sigqueue()` function sends a signal to the specified **process**. Which thread handles this signal is **undefined**. You can use the blocking technique described above to direct a signal to a particular thread.

Locale State

- The locale state for a process should be set by only **one** thread making a call to `setlocale()`. Any thread within the process can read the value. Because this function is **not** thread-safe, only one thread should write the value. If multiple threads call this function to set the *locale*, the last value written is used.

Timers and Sleepers

- The POSIX.1b timer functions maintain **per-process** timers. When a timer expires, the signal is set to the process. Which thread handles this signal is **undefined**. If you would like only one thread to handle a timer expiration signal, all threads but one should block the signal. If multiple threads set the timer, the last value written is used (unless a previous value times out before a subsequent value is written).
- `setitimer()` and `getitimer()` also reference additional **per-process** timers.
- The `sleep()` and `nanosleep()` functions cause the calling **thread** to suspend execution for the requested time period.

Nonlocal Jumps

- Do **not** call `longjmp()` or `siglongjmp()` using a jump buffer initialized by another thread. The resulting behavior is **undefined**.
- After a `longjmp()` or `siglongjmp()` has been performed, the local variables saved at the time of the `setjmp()` or `sigsetjmp()` call are **undefined**. For application portability and to ensure correct application behavior, you should **not** write code with dependencies on local variables.

Scheduling

- Use `sched_setscheduler()` and `sched_setparam()` to effect the scheduling of threads with a process scheduling contention scope. Threads with a system scheduling contention scope will **not** be affected.

Summary

Perhaps the most challenging aspect in multithreaded programming is to manage access to shared objects by threads. The results of timing and interaction among threads may be difficult to judge. This chapter has provided guidelines for thread synchronization and many other areas essential to programming with threads. Here is a summary:

- POSIX.1c leaves a number of thread management behaviors undefined. Understanding the design and function of the basic thread management functions will help design applications that perform well and are portable.

- Thread synchronization is perhaps the most difficult area in multithreaded programming. You will spend most of your time designing synchronization strategies to protect access to shared objects such as global data and file descriptors. Synchronization primitives include mutexes, condition variables, and semaphores.

- In multithreaded programming, you have much more control and responsibility for scheduling. Using one scheduling policy in your application helps simplify your scheduling strategy.

- Threads can send signals to each other. When a signal is sent to the process, there is no guarantee which thread will handle the signal. However, a signal can be directed to a particular thread. All threads but one can block the signal in their signal masks.

- The use of signals within multithreaded applications can have negative effects. A signal that causes a thread to terminate causes the entire process to terminate. POSIX.1c has provided thread cancellation facilities. You can use the thread cancellation feature, with cleanup handlers, to cleanly and asynchronously terminate a thread.

- In a multithreaded application, access to global data can be synchronized using synchronization primitives, or global data can be specific to each thread. Use thread-specific data to avoid the need for synchronization and allow global data to be specific to each thread.

- The thread extensions provided on HP-UX include additional thread stack attributes, thread suspension/resumption, four new mutexes, read-write locks, concurrency and scheduling control in the MxN model, a new scheduling policy, and processor affinity. These are powerful features that can enhance multithreaded programs.

- Thread Effects (F/X) presents the specific behavior found when using common functions in a multithreaded environment. Some functions act at the process level; other functions act at the thread level. In either case, it is important for you to understand the thread f/x!

Exercises

1. Develop your own methodology for creating multithreaded programs. At a minimum, your methodology should clearly outline design, performance, resource conservation, and portability considerations.
2. Test your development methodology on several multithreaded programs.
3. Teach your development methodology to one or two others and get their feedback.
4. Update your methodology as you learn more.
5. Use it!

Debugging Threaded Applications

You have written your multithreaded application. It compiles. But when running the application, you notice some unexpected behavior. Perhaps a value from a calculation is incorrect, I/O is interleaved, or performance is poor. Alternatively, you may notice that certain tasks are incomplete or maybe the whole program hangs. This chapter presents *symptoms*, *probable causes*, and *possible solutions* for you to consider during your systematic program debugging process.

Topics Covered...

- Deadlock
- Inconsistent Behavior Across Platforms
- Out of Resources (**EAGAIN/ENOMEM**)
- Poor Performance
- Unexpected Behavior, Value, or Output

Deadlock

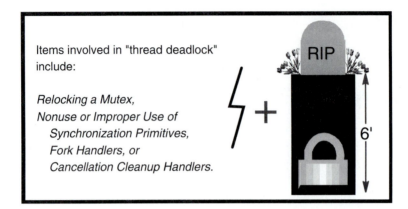

Items involved in "thread deadlock"
include:

Relocking a Mutex,
Nonuse or Improper Use of
Synchronization Primitives,
Fork Handlers, or
Cancellation Cleanup Handlers.

Fig. 14–1 Common causes of thread deadlock include non-use or improper use of fork handlers, synchronization primitives (including read-write locks), and cancellation cleanup handlers. The most common cause of deadlock is a thread relocking a mutex. Solution? Use error checking mutexes during application development. Switch to normal mutexes (as appropriate for your application) when the application is bug free.

Table 14–1 Deadlock Symptoms, Probable Causes, and Possible Solutions

Symptom	Probable Cause(s)	Possible Solution(s)
Child process deadlocks after a call to `fork()`.	A thread in the child process is blocked on a locked mutex inherited from the parent process.	**Install** a fork handler. Use `pthread_atfork()`. Call an `exec` function **immediately** after the call to `fork()`. Ref: *Establishing Fork Handlers*, Chapter 4.
Threads in the parent process deadlock after a call to `fork()`.	The *"parent"* portion of the fork handler is not releasing the mutex(es) acquired. The *"parent"* fork handlers are called in the wrong order.	**Check** the *"parent"* portion of the fork handler. Make sure it is installed and functional. Remember, *"parent"* handler functions are called in **FIFO** order. Check/reorder handler calls if necessary. Ref: *Establishing Fork Handlers*, Chapter 4.

Table 14–1 Deadlock Symptoms, Probable Causes, and Possible Solutions

Symptom	Probable Cause(s)	Possible Solution(s)
A thread does not complete execution or it receives an **EDEADLK** error.	A thread attempts to lock a mutex or semaphore that is shared among processes, but the process containing the thread that has the resource locked terminates.	In this case...
	A thread waits on a condition variable that is shared among processes, but the process containing the thread that should signal the condition terminates.	...or in this case, determine whether the terminated process should have terminated. If not, troubleshoot the process. If so, the terminating process should restore resources to a consistent state **before** terminating. Refs: *Mutex Attributes* and *Condition Variable Attributes*, Chapter 5.
	A thread attempted to relock a POSIX.1c mutex (or a normal mutex).	Use **debug mutexes** while debugging. They will return a helpful error message if relocked. Convert to normal mutexes after debugging is complete. Ref: *Locking and Unlocking Mutexes*, Chapter 5.
	A mutex, condition variable, semaphore, or readwrite lock is destroyed while in use.	Do **not** destroy these synchronization primitives while they are in use by threads. Refs: *Initializing and Destroying Condition Variables* and *Initializing and Destroying Unnamed Semaphores*, Chapter 5.

Table 14–1 Deadlock Symptoms, Probable Causes, and Possible Solutions

Symptom	Probable Cause(s)	Possible Solution(s)
A thread does not complete execution or it receives an **EDEADLK** error.		Ref: *Initializing and Destroying Read-Write Locks*, Chapter 10.
	A canceled thread did not release a mutex or signal a condition.	**Install** cancellation cleanup handlers. Ref: *Installing Cancellation Cleanup Handlers*, Chapter 8.
	A thread fails to resume after it is suspended.	A thread can be suspended multiple times. Ensure that a suspended thread is resumed (or continued) the **same** number of times. Make sure the suspend and the resume calls are **ordered** properly, such that the resume will not occur before the suspend. Ref: *Suspending and Resuming Threads*, Chapter 10.
	A process has terminated while a read-write lock was locked by one of its threads.	If the process did not terminate as expected, find out why. Otherwise, make sure resources and synchronization objects are left in a consistent state **before** process termination. Ref: *Read-Write Lock Attributes*, Chapter 10.
A thread does not complete execution or it receives an **EDEADLK** error.	A signal handler is using a `pthread_*` function.	Do **not** call `pthread_*` functions from a signal handler as they are not async-signal safe. Ref: *Async-Signal Safe Thread Functions*, Chapter 7.

Inconsistent Behavior Across Platforms

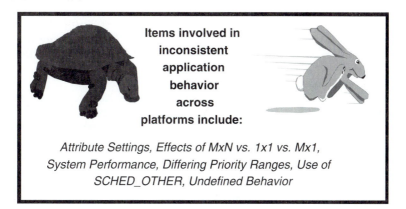

Items involved in
inconsistent
application
behavior
across
platforms include:

*Attribute Settings, Effects of MxN vs. 1x1 vs. Mx1,
System Performance, Differing Priority Ranges, Use of
SCHED_OTHER, Undefined Behavior*

Fig. 14–2 Applications that are ported to different platforms may experience behaviors that are not consistent with your development system. Causes for inconsistent behavior include attribute settings that do not have a POSIX.1c default value, the system's Thread Model (Mx1, 1x1, MxN), and scheduling priority ranges. Attributes that do not have a default value as specified by POSIX.1c should be defined for maximum portability.

Table 14–2 Inconsistent Behavior Across Platforms

Symptom	Probable Cause(s)	Possible Solution(s)
Behavior of a thread, mutex, condition variable, or read-write lock changes when the application is executed on different platforms.	One or more attributes within the appropriate attributes object does not have a default value specified by POSIX.1c. `pthread_attr_t,` `pthread_mutex_attr_t,` `pthread_cond_attr_t,` or `pthread_rwlockattr_t,` object has been used improperly.	In the appropriate attributes object, **define** the attribute values that are not given a default value by POSIX.1c. Attributes objects are opaque data types that may be implemented differently across platforms. Do not copy `*attr_t` objects. **Use the proper functions** to manage these objects. Do **not** rely on the value of `*attr_t` objects after they have been destroyed. (Reinitialize the object if it is needed again.)

Table 14–2 Inconsistent Behavior Across Platforms

Symptom	Probable Cause(s)	Possible Solution(s)
Behavior of a thread, mutex, condition variable, or read-write lock changes when the application is executed on different platforms.		Ref: *Creating Specialized Thread Attributes*, Chapter 4. Refs: *Mutex Attributes* and *Condition Variable Attributes*, Chapter 5. Ref: *Read-Write Lock Attributes*, Chapter 10.
Thread execution behavior varies across platforms.	Application is using the **SCHED_OTHER** scheduling policy. The **SCHED_OTHER** scheduling policy may be implemented differently on across platforms.	If possible or practical, choose another scheduling policy: **SCHED_FIFO** or **SCHED_RR**. Ref: *Thread Scheduling Policies* and *Thread Scheduling Priority Values*, Chapter 6.
	The scheduling allocation domains are different.	If possible or practical, **adjust** the scheduling allocation domain. POSIX.1c does not specify a mechanism for changing the scheduling allocation domain. Each system may have a non-portable mechanism for adjusting the scheduling allocation domain. Check the system's documentation. Ref: *Thread Scheduling Allocation Domains*, Chapter 6.
	PTHREAD_INHERIT_SCHED varies on the "port to" platform(s).	**Set** this attribute explicitly in the thread attributes object. Ref: *Thread Creation Scheduling Attributes*, Chapter 6.

Table 14–2 Inconsistent Behavior Across Platforms

Symptom	Probable Cause(s)	Possible Solution(s)
Thread execution behavior varies across platforms.	Threads within the application use different scheduling policies.	Threads in applications intended to be portable should use the **same** scheduling policy. Priority ranges for scheduling policies may vary among vendors. Ref: *Thread Scheduling Priority Values*, Chapter 6.
A high-priority thread does not react or execute in a timely manner in response to an event.	Priority inversion is taking place.	Use the **priority inheritance** or **priority ceiling** protocol mutex attribute. Ref: *Priority Inversion and Mutexes*, Chapter 6.
The behavior is inconsistent across systems.	The priority ranges for the scheduling policies on various platforms are different. The scheduling policies are different.	For maximum portability, threads should have the **same** scheduling policy. When using the priority ceiling protocol, threads should use the **SCHED_FIFO** scheduling policy. Ref: *Thread Scheduling Priority Values*, Chapter 6.
The degree of parallelism varies across platforms.	Different scheduling contention scopes are in use on the different platforms. The Mx1 Model does not support parallel thread execution within a process.	Different platforms may support different scheduling contention scopes (i.e., Mx1, 1x1, or MxN). Ref: *Thread Scheduling Contention Scopes*, Chapter 6.

Table 14–2 Inconsistent Behavior Across Platforms

Symptom	Probable Cause(s)	Possible Solution(s)
The degree of parallelism varies across platforms.	The concurrency level of each platform is different.	It may be possible to **set** the concurrency level using the function `pthread_setconcurrency()`. (For MxN Model systems only.) Ref: *Thread Concurrency and MxN Threads*, Chapter 10.
Threads, that the application dedicates for signal handling do not handle signals in a consistent manner.	The signal handler is not generic.	Signal handlers are process-wide resources. If more than one thread will execute a signal handler, the signal handler should be written **generically**. Ref: *Synchronous and Asynchronous Signals*, Chapter 7.
Signal blocking does not work correctly or works inconsistently across platforms.	Application is using `sigprocmask()` to change the signal mask of threads.	Use **`pthread_sigmask()`**. Ref: *Examining / Changing a Thread's Signal Mask*, Chapter 7.
Event notification thread does not react to correct signal or does not react the same across platforms.	The signal mask of the event notification thread has not been initialized.	Do **not** rely on the signal mask being initialized to any value. **Initialize** the signal mask yourself. Ref: *A New Signal Delivery Method— SIGEV_THREAD*, Chapter 7.

Table 14–2 Inconsistent Behavior Across Platforms

Symptom	Probable Cause(s)	Possible Solution(s)
General behavior that is **undefined** by POSIX.1c (resulting in an error, invalid results, or unpredictable behavior).	`pthread_join()` or `pthread_detach()` is called more than once on the same thread ID.	**Avoid** calling these functions more than once on the same thread ID. Refs: *Waiting for a Thread* and *Detaching a Thread*, Chapter 4.
	Attempting to access local variables of a terminated thread.	Do **not** attempt to access local variables of a terminated thread. At the very least, this action is not portable. Ref: *Terminating a Thread*, Chapter 4.
Undefined behavior with attributes objects.	`pthread_attr_t`, `pthread_mutexattr_t`, `pthread_condattr_t`, `pthread_rwlockattr_t` or `sem_t` objects are used improperly.	`*attr_t` and `sem_t` objects are opaque. They should **not** be copied or used after they are destroyed. However, they may be reinitialized after being destroyed. Ref: *Creating Specialized Thread Attributes*, Chapter 4. Refs: *Mutex Attributes, Condition Variable Attributes,* and *Semaphores*, Chapter 5. Ref: *Read-Write Lock Attributes*, Chapter 10.

Table 14–2 Inconsistent Behavior Across Platforms

Symptom	Probable Cause(s)	Possible Solution(s)
Undefined behavior leading to deadlock.	A POSIX.1c (or normal) mutex has been relocked.	Some systems will report an error, others will allow the deadlock to take place. Use **error-checking** mutexes during application development. Switch to normal mutexes after the application has been thoroughly tested. Ref: *Locking and Unlocking Mutexes*, Chapter 5.
	A thread called `longjmp()` or `siglongjmp()` using a `jmp_buf` or `sigjmp_buf` initialized by another thread.	**Only** the thread that calls `setjmp()` or `sigsetjmp()` should make the call to `longjmp()` or `siglongjmp()`. Ref: *Nonlocal Jumps*, Chapter 11.
Undefined behavior with scheduling characteristics.	The scheduling characteristics of threads using *process* versus *system* scheduling contention scope is different across the "port to" platforms.	This is system-dependent. **Check** the system's documentation and your application's use of `sched_setscheduler()` and `sched_setparam()`. Ref: *Thread Scheduling Contention Scopes*, Chapter 6. Ref: *Scheduling Unbound Kernel Entities*, Chapter 10.

Table 14–2 Inconsistent Behavior Across Platforms

Symptom	Probable Cause(s)	Possible Solution(s)
Undefined behavior with scheduling characteristics.	Threads within the application are using different scheduling policies.	The priority ranges for different scheduling policies may vary on different platforms. **Investigate** using one scheduling policy or setting thread's scheduling priority. Ref: *Thread Scheduling Priority Values*, Chapter 6.
Undefined behavior with signals.	Threads that should not handle a signal are not blocking the signal.	Some functions (e.g., kill(), alarm(), etc.) deliver asynchronous signals to the process; which thread handles an asynchronous signal is **undefined**. If a signal should be handled by a particular thread, the other threads in the process should **block** the signal. Ref: *Signals in the Thread Model,* and *Synchronous and Asynchronous Signals*, Chapter 7.
Undefined behavior with signals.	The signal was not blocked before calling the sigwait() function.	If the signal is not blocked before calling sigwait(), the thread may miss the signal. **Always** block the signals you intend to catch before calling sigwait().
	sigaction() and one of the sigwait() calls has been used concurrently.	Do **not** call sigaction() while a thread is blocked in a sigwait() function. Ref: *Waiting for a Signal*, Chapter 7.

Table 14–2 Inconsistent Behavior Across Platforms

Symptom	Probable Cause(s)	Possible Solution(s)
Undefined behavior with thread cancellation.	The thread received a cancellation request at the same time that it was about to return from the function call.	Most systems return to the function and hold the cancellation request pending. If this does not happen on a particular system, do **not** rely on the event still being available (i.e., data can still be read). Ref: *Thread Cancellation Points*, Chapter 8.
Undefined behavior with thread-specific data.	The key is invalid.	The key may not have been initialized or may have been deleted. If one thread removes a thread-specific data key, that key is invalid for all threads in the application. Do **not** remove the key until the thread-specific data is no longer needed in the application. Ref: *Accessing Thread-Specific Data Elements*, Chapter 9.
Undefined behavior with read-write locking.	A thread, that currently holds the read lock attempts to lock the read-write lock for writing.	**Unlock** the read lock before attempting to lock the write lock. Ref: *Locking and Unlocking Read-Write Locks*, Chapter 10.

Out of Resources

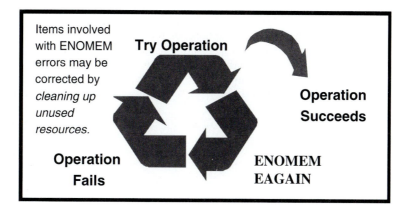

Fig. 14–3 When a system or process is out of resources, the application can fail. Typically, memory is the resource in question. Application performance can be affected if memory is low. In the most severe case, such as being *out* of memory, applications can fail. Sometimes, this problem can be corrected by cleaning up unused resources, such as attributes objects or thread context.

Table 14–3 Out of Resources

Symptom	Probable Cause(s)	Possible Solution(s)
ENOMEM or **EAGAIN**	Thread context is not cleaned up in an application that creates and terminates many threads during execution.	Use **pthread_join()** or **pthread_detach()** to ensure that resources from terminated threads are cleaned up.
		Ref: *Waiting for a Thread* and *Detaching a Thread,* Chapter 4.
	Bound threads use more system resources than do unbound threads.	**Investigate** the use of unbound threads in the application (MxN Model only).
		Ref: *Thread Scheduling Contention Scopes,* Chapter 6.

Table 14–3 Out of Resources

Symptom	Probable Cause(s)	Possible Solution(s)
ENOMEM or **EAGAIN**	Mutex, condition variable, semaphore, or read-write lock resources are not cleaned up when the application is through with them.	Use the appropriate **destroy** function to conserve memory. Refs: *Initializing and Destroying Mutexes, Initializing and Destroying Condition Variables,* and *Initializing and Destroying Unnamed Semaphores,* Chapter 5. Ref *Initializing and Destroying Read-Write Locks,* Chapter 10.
	Attributes objects for threads, mutexes, condition variables, or read-write locks have not been cleaned up.	**Destroy** any attributes objects that are no longer needed. Ref: *Creating Specialized Thread Attributes,* Chapter 4. Ref: *Mutex Attributes* and *Condition Variable Attributes,* Chapter 5. Ref: *Read-Write Lock Attributes,* Chapter 10.
	Application using a *very large* number of threads is low on memory.	To save memory, you can **turn off** stack overflow protection. This will decrease memory usage by page_size * number of threads. However, this should be done only after the application has been **thoroughly** tested. Ref: *Thread Stack Attributes,* Chapter 10.

Table 14–3 Out of Resources

Symptom	Probable Cause(s)	Possible Solution(s)
ENOMEM or **EAGAIN**	Low on memory or processes.	**ENOMEM** and **EAGAIN** errors may be **recoverable**. In the event that an application receives such errors, you may be able to clean up resources or wait for some amount of time, then try the operation again. Ref: *Handling Synchronization Errors*, Chapter 5.
Thread stack overflow occurs.	Stack size not sufficient.	**Increase** the `stacksize` attribute in the thread attributes object. Ref: *Creating Specialized Thread Attributes*, Chapter 4.

Poor Performance

**Items involved in
poor application
performance
include:**

*Low on Memory, Effects of MxN vs. 1x1 vs. Mx1
Attribute Settings, Improper use of Synchronization, Scheduling,
Bound/Unbound Threads, or Processor Binding*

Fig. 14–4 Experts tend to agree that performance tuning is both a science and an art. Solutions can be elusive; the location of a performance bottleneck can change as you are fixing the problem. Some causes and solutions for memory bottlenecks were covered in the previous section. This section provides debug advice for other areas, including scheduling, overhead, and the use of bound versus unbound threads.

Table 14–4 Poor Performance

Symptom	Probable Cause(s)	Possible Solution(s)
Bound thread performance is poor.	Bound thread is used for a short-term task or is used in a task where a lot of synchronization is required.	Use an **unbound** thread. (You have this choice only when using the MxN Model.) Unbound threads have less overhead for thread creation, termination, and context switches. Ref: *Many-to-Many (MxN)*, Chapter 2. Ref: *Thread Scheduling Contention Scopes*, Chapter 6.
Unbound thread performance is poor.	Unbound thread is used for a realtime or compute-intensive task (where there are few context switches).	Use a **bound** thread. (You have this choice only when using the MxN Model.) Ref: *Many-to-Many (MxN)*, Chapter 2.

Table 14–4 Poor Performance

Symptom	Probable Cause(s)	Possible Solution(s)
Unbound thread performance is poor.		Ref: *Thread Scheduling Contention Scopes*, Chapter 6.
Cannot profile threads in the application.	Insufficient thread context.	Bound threads carry enough **context** for profiling. Unbound threads may not. Ref: *Many-to-One (Mx1)*, Chapter 2.
Synchronized access to an object is slow or inefficient.	A thread locks a mutex, then performs a long operation, such as I/O.	Do **not** perform long operations while holding a lock on a mutex.
	A mutex is used where read-write lock should be used.	If multiple threads in the application require read-only access, and writing of the object is done less frequently, use a **read-write lock**.
	Using recursive or error checking mutexes when not needed.	Use default or normal mutexes for optimal performance unless error checking is always required.
	A read-write lock is used where mutex should be used.	If random reads and modification of an object will take place and/or few instructions are executed while the lock is held, use a **mutex**. Ref: *Mutexes*, Chapter 5. Ref: *Mutex Extensions* and *Read-Write Locks*, Chapter 10.

Table 14–4 Poor Performance

Symptom	Probable Cause(s)	Possible Solution(s)
Threads using a read-write lock realize poor performance.	There are not many parallel read operations or there are too many parallel write operations.	Use a **mutex** instead of a read-write lock. Ref: *Locking and Unlocking Read-Write Locks*, Chapter 10.
Threads using non-default processor binding experience poor performance.	Threads synchronize on shared resources often.	Use the system's default binding or try binding these threads to the **same** processor.
	Threads perform disjointed activities and share no data.	Use system's default binding or try binding these threads to **different** processors.
	A thread's scheduling policy is taking precedence over its processor binding.	**Convert** from using an "advisory" binding to a "forced" binding in the thread attributes object. Ref: *Thread to Processor Binding*, Chapter 10.
Level of parallelism is insufficient. (MxN Model only)	Thread concurrency level is set too low.	Use **pthread_setconcurrency()** to add more kernel-scheduled entities (kernel threads) to the process. Ref: *Thread Concurrency and MxN Threads*, Chapter 10.

Unexpected Behavior, Value, or Output

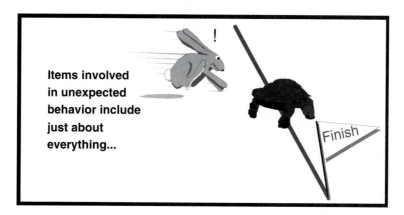

Items involved in unexpected behavior include just about everything...

Fig. 14–5 The Unexpected Behavior section is a catch-all for items that are not represented in the other sections. Unexpected behaviors include surprises, such as the application quitting in midstream, an event happening that should not happen, or an event not happening that should happen. Problems may arise because Process Model practices are used in Thread Model applications. Other problems may result from lack of synchronization or programming practices that lead to behavior that is undefined by POSIX.1c.

Table 14–5 Unexpected Behavior, Value, or Output

Symptom	Probable Cause(s)	Possible Solution(s)
Cannot join with a thread nor reap status information.	The target thread is detached.	Investigate why the target thread is detached. If the thread can be made joinable, **create** the thread with a joinable detach state. Ref: *Detaching a Thread*, Chapter 4.
Process terminates unexpectedly.	A thread called `exit()` when it should have called `pthread_exit()`.	Use **`pthread_exit()`** to terminate a single thread.
	When the `main()` thread returns, an implicit call to `exit()` is made.	The main thread should call `pthread_exit()` if the application is to continue after the main thread terminates. Ref: *Terminating a Thread*, Chapter 4.

Table 14–5 Unexpected Behavior, Value, or Output

Symptom	Probable Cause(s)	Possible Solution(s)
Initialization of a module fails.	A race condition has occurred–two or more threads executed the initialization function.	**Use pthread_once()** to ensure initialization is performed only once. Ref: *Performing One-Time Initialization*, Chapter 4.
One or more threads terminate unexpectedly or do not execute as expected.	A thread attributes object, with stackaddr defined, was used to create two or more threads.	If stackaddr is defined in a thread attributes object, that thread attributes object should be used to create **one** thread only. Ref: *Creating Specialized Thread Attributes*, Chapter 4.
Unexpected value or output (including data corruption).	Shared data or resources (such as a linked list) do not have access by threads serialized.	**Protect** shared objects with some form of synchronization primitive. (e.g., mutex). Refs: *Mutexes* and *Semaphores*, Chapter 5.
	A mutex, condition variable, semaphore, or read-write lock is... ...used before initialized.	Initialize all synchronization primitives **before** starting the threads that will use them.
	...destroyed while in use by threads.	Do **not** destroy these synchronization primitives while they are in use by threads.
	...initialized more than once.	Do **not** initialize synchronization primitives more than once. Refs: *Initializing and Destroying Mutexes, Initializing and Destroying Condition Variables,* and *Initializing and Destroying Unnamed Semaphores,* Chapter 5.

Table 14–5 Unexpected Behavior, Value, or Output

Symptom	Probable Cause(s)	Possible Solution(s)
Unexpected value or output (including data corruption).		Ref: *Initializing and Destroying Read-Write Locks,* Chapter 10.
One or more threads either execute before the condition is signaled or miss a condition signal.	The condition predicate is not re-evaluated when the condition is signaled.	Always **re-evaluate** the condition predicate in a loop in case of spurious wakeups.
	Race condition. A mutex has not been associated with the condition variable.	To prevent missed condition signals, **always** associate a mutex with a condition variable. The mutex should be locked whenever checking or changing the state of the condition predicate. Ref: *Condition Variables,* Chapter 5.
	A process-shared condition variable (one that is created with the **PTHREAD_PROCESS_SHARED** attribute set) is used in a multiprocess application where the thread that should signal the condition is in a process that has terminated.	When sharing a condition variable across processes, make sure any terminating processes leave the condition variable in a consistent state **before** they terminate.
	The mutex associated with a process-shared condition variable does not have the **PTHREAD_PROCESS_SHARED** attribute set.	The **PTHREAD_PROCESS_SHARED** attribute **must** be set in the mutex attributes object of the mutex associated with a process-shared condition variable. Ref: *Condition Variable Attributes,* Chapter 5.

Table 14–5 Unexpected Behavior, Value, or Output

Symptom	Probable Cause(s)	Possible Solution(s)
One or more threads either execute before a condition is signaled or miss a condition signal.	Thread(s) were canceled [pthread_cond_wait() and pthread_cond_timedwait() are cancellation points].	**Install** cancellation cleanup handlers or temporarily disable cancellation as necessary. Ref: *Waiting on a Condition*, Chapter 5.
	The initialization of a process-shared condition variable takes place more than once.	Only **one** process should perform process-shared condition variable initialization. Ref: *Initializing and Destroying Condition Variables*, Chapter 5.
Unable to yield the processor to another thread.	The application is using threads with different priorities and/or scheduling policies.	The sched_yield() function will yield the processor only to a thread with **equal or higher priority**. Ref: *Yielding the Processor*, Chapter 6.
A high-priority thread does not react or execute in a timely manner in response to some event.	Priority inversion is taking place.	Use the **priority inheritance** or **priority ceiling** protocol mutex attribute. (For maximum portability, only threads with the **same** scheduling policy should use the priority inherit protocol. Alternatively, threads should use the **SCHED_FIFO** scheduling policy when using the priority ceiling protocol.) Ref: *Priority Inversion and Mutexes*, Chapter 6.

Table 14–5 Unexpected Behavior, Value, or Output

Symptom	Probable Cause(s)	Possible Solution(s)
Process terminates, stops or continues unexpectedly.	A thread sent an asynchronous signal that caused the process to react.	Remember that when a thread handles a signal, if the action for the signal causes the thread to terminate, stop, or continue, the entire **process** will terminate, stop, or continue.
	`kill()` was used when `pthread_kill()` should have been used.	Use **pthread_kill()** to deliver an asynchronous signal to a thread. Refs: *Signals in the Thread Model* and *Sending Signals to Threads*, Chapter 7.
Desired thread does not handle an asynchronous signal.	The other threads in the application are not blocking the signal.	To direct a signal delivered to the process to a specific thread, the other threads within the process must **block** the signal. Refs: *Signals in the Thread Model* and *Synchronous and Asynchronous Signals*, Chapter 7.
A thread missed an asynchronous signal when it was sent.	The signal to be waited for was not blocked when the call to a `sigwait()` function occurred.	**Always** block the "wait for" signals prior to calling a `sigwait()` function. Ref: *Waiting for a Signal*, Chapter 7.
Unable to join with or obtain the exit status of an event thread.	An attempt has been made to obtain the status of a detached thread. (Event threads are created detached by default.)	**Change** the thread attributes object so that the event thread is joinable. Ref: *A New Delivery Method— SIGEV_THREAD*, Chapter 7.

Table 14–5 Unexpected Behavior, Value, or Output

Symptom	Probable Cause(s)	Possible Solution(s)
A thread terminates unexpectedly (perhaps while executing a critical section of code).	A pending cancellation request was acted upon when the thread reached a cancellation point or when asynchronous cancellation was enabled.	**Determine** whether the canceled thread: (1) should have had cancellation disabled, or (2) was using asynchronous rather than deferred cancellation. Install cancellation cleanup handlers as necessary.
A thread does not react to a cancellation request.	Cancellation requests are deferred or cancellation is disabled.	If cancellation is **deferred**, the thread will not respond to a cancellation request until a cancellation point is reached. If appropriate, you can use `pthread_testcancel()` to insert a cancellation point. If cancellation is **disabled**, cancellation requests will be held pending. Refs: *Thread Cancelability States,* and *Thread Cancellation Points*, Chapter 8.
Thread deadlock, lost resources, or data corruption occur after thread cancellation.	A thread that had acquired a lock or resources was canceled without calling cancellation cleanup handlers.	For cancel-safe code, **install** cleanup handlers. When asynchronous cancellation is used, do **not** acquire resources.
Thread deadlock, lost resources, or data corruption occur after thread cancellation.	Cancellation cleanup handlers are called in the wrong order.	Cancellation cleanup handlers are called in **LIFO** order. Check the order in which resources are released to see if there are any logic problems. Refs: *Setting Thread Cancelability States* and *Installing Cancellation Cleanup Handlers*, Chapter 8.

Table 14–5 Unexpected Behavior, Value, or Output

Symptom	Probable Cause(s)	Possible Solution(s)
Thread deadlock, lost resources, or data corruption occur after thread cancellation.	A thread with asynchronous cancellation enabled has called a function that is not async-cancel safe.	Check the execution path of the thread(s) with asynchronous cancellation enabled (*including calls to libraries*). Do **not** call code modules that are not async-cancel safe (e.g., modules that acquire resources) while the asynchronous form of cancellation is enabled. Refs: *Installing Cancellation Cleanup Handlers* and *Async-Cancel Safety*, Chapter 8.
Thread continues indefinitely after it has been canceled.	This is normal.	When the function `pthread_cancel()` returns, this does **not** mean the target thread has been terminated. **Verify** your cancellation strategy. Ref: *Canceling a Thread*, Chapter 8.
Thread-specific data keys are unavailable to all threads...	The keys were not created in global memory.	Thread-specific data keys should **always** be created in global memory.
...and access to the resources associated with a key is lost.	The thread-specific data key has been deleted by a thread.	Do **not** remove a thread-specific data key until all threads are finished with it. Ref: *Deleting Thread-Specific Data Keys*, Chapter 9.

Table 14–5 Unexpected Behavior, Value, or Output

Symptom	Probable Cause(s)	Possible Solution(s)
A thread does not resume after being suspend.	Two or more threads are involved in suspending and resuming a target thread. The calling order is not synchronized and the resume function is called before the suspend function, leaving the thread suspended.	Use **one** thread to suspend and resume a target thread.
	The target thread has been suspended more times than it has been resumed.	A thread must be resumed the **same** number of times that it has been suspended or the force resume option must be used.
A thread resumes unexpectedly.	A thread suspended itself and no other thread resumed the suspended thread.	**Another** thread will have to resume a thread that suspends itself.
	The thread attribute **PTHREAD_FORCE_RESUME _NP** may have been used or `pthread_continue()` was used.	Use **PTHREAD_COUNT_RE-SUME_NP** if this behavior is not acceptable. Ref: *Suspending and Resuming Threads*, Chapter 10.
A recursive mutex is not unlocked after being used by a thread.	The recursive mutex has not been unlocked the proper number of times.	A thread must unlock a recursive mutex the **same** number it times that it was locked in order to actually unlock the mutex. Ref: *Mutex Extensions*, Chapter 10.

Table 14–5 Unexpected Behavior, Value, or Output

Symptom	Probable Cause(s)	Possible Solution(s)
A thread fails to wait on a condition variable (**ETIMEDOUT** is received).	*abstime* has expired when the condition timed wait function is called.	Call the timed wait **immediately** after the *abstime* is constructed to ensure that *abstime* does not expire. Ref: *Condition Variable Expiration Time*, Chapter 10.
A read-write lock does not work correctly–error or unexpected behavior when calling the lock or unlock functions.	The read-write lock was not initialized before calling the lock or unlock functions.	Initialize the read-write lock **before** calling the lock or unlock functions. Ref: *Locking and Unlocking Read-Write Locks*, Chapter 10.
A thread's signal mask is not set correctly.	The sigprocmask() function was used.	Use the **pthread_sigmask()** function, not sigprocmask().
The alarm and timer signals are not handled by the designated thread.	The alarm signal is delivered to the process. Similarly, the POSIX.1b and X/Open timer functions, are all per-process timers. There is no guarantee which thread will handle a signal generated from these sources.	All threads but the designated thread in the process should **block** the appropriate signal(s). This will allow the signal(s) to be directed toward the designated thread. Refs: *Signals* and *Timers and Sleepers*, Chapter 11.

Summary

This chapter presented information, previously learned, in a format usable for debugging a multithreaded application. Certainly, this is not an exhaustive list of symptoms, probable causes, and possible solutions. However, the information provided may assist you in narrowing down a problem.

- Common causes of thread deadlock include non-use or improper use of fork handlers, synchronization primitives (including read-write locks), and cancellation cleanup handlers. The most common cause of deadlock is a thread relocking a mutex. Solution? Use error-checking mutexes during application development. Switch to normal mutexes (as appropriate for your application) when the application is bug free.

- Applications that are ported to different platforms may experience behaviors that are not consistent with your development system. Causes for inconsistent behavior include attribute settings that do not have a POSIX.1c default value, the system's Thread Model (Mx1, 1x1, MxN), and scheduling priority ranges. Attributes that do not have a default value, as specified by POSIX.1c, should be defined for maximum portability.

- When a system or process is out of resources, the application can fail. Typically, memory is the resource in question. Application performance can be effected if memory is low. In the most severe case, such as being *out* of memory, applications can fail. Sometimes, this problem can be corrected by cleaning up unused resources such as attributes objects or thread context.

- Experts tend to agree that performance tuning is both a science and an art. Solutions can be elusive; the location of a performance bottleneck can change as you are fixing the problem. Some causes and solutions for memory bottlenecks were covered in the *Out of Resources* section. The *Poor Performance* section provides debug advice for other areas, including scheduling, overhead, and the use of bound versus unbound threads.

- The *Unexpected Behavior, Value, or Output* section is a catch-all for items that are not represented in the other sections. Unexpected behaviors include surprises such as the application quitting in midstream, an event happening that should not happen, or an event not happening that should happen. Problems may arise because Process Model practices are used in Thread Model applications. Other problems may result from lack of synchronization or programming practices that lead to behavior that is undefined by POSIX.1c.

Exercises

1. Create your own troubleshooting methodology. At a minimum, your methodology should clearly outline a methodical process for narrowing down various bugs or anomalies in multithreaded applications. In this process, identify any tools you might use along the way, such as a multithreaded debugger.

2. Test your troubleshooting methodology on several multithreaded programs.

3. Teach your troubleshooting methodology to one or two others and get their feedback.

4. Use it!

Parallel Programming Models and Issues

This chapter discusses several software models suitable for multithreaded programs. Some models are suitable for I/O-bound applications whereas others are suitable for compute-bound applications. The former exploits the concurrency benefit whereas the latter uses parallelism to exploit the power of multiprocessor systems. A discussion of parallel programming issues follows. Several important issues relating to thread creation, thread synchronization, and multiprocessor cache thrashing are identified. Specific techniques, guidelines, and solutions are also presented.

Topics Covered...

- Parallel Programming
- The Work-Crew Model
- The Boss-Worker Model
- The Pipeline Model
- The Master-Slave Model
- Thread Creation Issues
- Thread Synchronization Issues
- Multiprocessor Cache Thrashing Issues

Parallel Programming

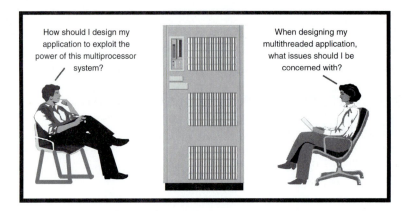

Fig. 15–1 The parallel programming models discussed in this chapter include models that are suited for applications desiring parallelism or concurrency. Parallel programming issues include thread creation, thread synchronization, and multiprocessor cache thrashing.

Overview

Two aspects of programming with threads that have a profound effect on performance are the synchronization strategy and the parallel programming model chosen by an application. This chapter is provides a discussion of some basic parallel models and their associated synchronization strategies.

An application that relies on parallelism for performance improvement does not benefit from multithreading when executing on a single-processor system. These applications are usually compute-bound and require multiple threads to execute simultaneously across multiple processors. Other applications are really seeking concurrency - when one thread blocks, another thread in the application can continue to make forward progress. The distinction between parallelism and concurrency is important to keep in mind as you read this chapter. Applications requiring parallelism will often use a parallel model and synchronization strategy that differs from applications requiring concurrency only.

Parallel Programming Models

The first half of this chapter discusses some basic parallel programming models that can be used to solve a wide range of problems. Each parallel model presented contains the following sections: (a) an **overview** section that describes the parallel model, (b) a **synchronization** section that discusses the synchronization primitives and techniques used to synchronize threads, (c) a **terminating threads** section that describes how to terminate threads in the model, (d) a **balance problems** section that discusses scheduling and workload balance issues with the model, and (e) an **algorithm** section that provides a code template that can be used to implement the model in an application.

Four parallel models are presented in this chapter: the *work-crew* model, the *boss-worker* model, the *pipeline* model, and the *master-slave* model. These are logically parallel models; some suitable for parallel processing, others suitable for concurrent processing. A variety of different problems can be solved by using one of these models or a combination of different models. A discussion of all parallel models is beyond the scope of this book. However, several good books are available that are devoted to parallel programming models. These books describe numerous parallel models and techniques that may be applied to multithreaded applications. Refer to the *Bibliography* for a list of books on parallel programming.

Parallel Programming Issues

The last half of this chapter discusses some common issues programmers must resolve when parallel programming with threads. Several questions and problems that commonly occur with thread creation, synchronization, and multiprocessor cache thrashing are presented, along with the techniques that can be used to resolve the problem. Some of the questions and problems discussed include:

- *How many threads should I create?*
- *Should I dynamically create threads as needed or cache threads?*
- *Should I use bound or unbound threads?*
- *How do I minimize lock contention?*
- *Where should I place my synchronization points?*
- *How do I avoid the need for synchronization?*
- *How do I prevent cache thrashing?*
- *How do I prevent false data sharing?*
- *Should I bind threads directly to processors? If so, which processors?*

This chapter attempts to make you aware of the issues and different techniques that can be used to resolve the issues. The resolution in many cases will be application- and system-dependent.

The Work-Crew Model

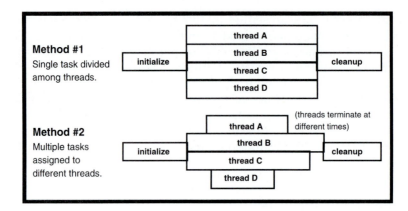

Fig. 15–2 The Work-Crew Model provides two methods for threading an application. Method 1, for compute bound tasks, divides a single task into multiple parts and relies on parallel computation. Method 2, for disjoint tasks, uses a thread for each task and relies on concurrency.

Overview

The Work-Crew Model is the easiest parallel model to implement. In this model, a control thread divides up the work, creates worker threads to perform the work, then waits for those threads to finish. The control thread may also process part of the work. Once all the work has been processed, the control thread performs any final cleanup tasks.

This model can be used in two different ways: (a) divide up one task among several different threads or (b) divide up several tasks among different threads.

The first method is used when there is one task that may take a long time to process. The task is evenly divided among the available threads. All threads finish processing their portion of the task at the same time. This method is often used to parallelize loops or large compute-bound tasks and relies on threads executing in parallel on multiple processors.

The second method is used when an application has several tasks (possibly disjoint tasks) that need to be processed. Each thread is assigned a different task to perform. These tasks may or may not take the same amount of time to process. This method is often used to break up large applications containing different tasks. Concurrency in the application, not parallelism, is the goal in this situation. If one thread blocks, another thread in the application may continue executing. If parallelism is achieved due to multiprocessor hardware, it's an extra added bonus.

Synchronization

All synchronization in this model is performed through the basic thread management functions `pthread_create()`, `pthread_exit()`, and `pthread_join()`. The control thread partitions the work before creating each work thread. Each thread's work is passed as a parameter to its start routine. Once the worker thread has finished processing the work, any output results are passed as the thread's exit status. When the control thread joins with the terminated worker, the results of the work are retrieved, and any final processing is performed.

The control thread only accesses the work (i.e., data) before the worker threads are created and after they have terminated. Consequently, no additional synchronization is needed between the control thread and worker threads. The worker threads operate only on the data passed to their *start_routine*, hence, no synchronization is needed between the worker threads.

Terminating Threads

Unlike other parallel models, terminating worker threads in the work-crew model is simple. Because each worker thread has only one task to process, it calls `pthread_exit()` when the task is complete. The control thread waits for the workers to finish their work and terminate by calling `pthread_join()`.

Balance Problems

When the Work-Crew Model is used to divide up one task evenly among many threads, a balance problem may occur if the division of work is done improperly. The goal of this method is to perform one task in the shortest time possible by having the threads execute in parallel on different processors. The most logical division of work for compute-bound applications is to create one thread per processor. If the application is I/O bound, enough threads should be created to have one running or runnable thread per processor at all times. If one thread blocks waiting for I/O, another thread in the application should be able to take its place (two threads per processor is a good starting point). When the processors are kept busy at all times, the task will complete in the shortest time possible.

In a compute-bound application seeking parallelism, the scheduler may decide to context switch one of the running threads (e.g., its time-slice has expired or it has been preempted). Consider an application that has divided up work among four threads. All four threads are running in parallel when the scheduler preempts one of the threads. By the time the preempted thread is allowed to run, the other three threads have completed their work and terminated. Eventually, the fourth thread completes its work and terminates. It has now taken at least twice as long to process the work. This scenario can be further applied to each of the worker threads, creating severe balance and performance problems.

Any of the following techniques can be applied to attempt to prevent or minimize balance problems:

- Guarantee that the application is the only process on the system. If no other processes are running, there are no other threads that can preempt one of the worker threads. This may be feasible for some applications, but not many.

- Assign the worker threads scheduling attributes which make them the highest priority **SCHED_FIFO** threads on the system. The **SCHED_FIFO** policy will ensure that a time-slice does not occur for the worker threads. Because the worker threads are the highest priority threads on the system, they will never be preempted by other threads. Because many systems restrict the **SCHED_FIFO** and **SCHED_RR** policies for use only by privileged applications, this option may not be viable. Additionally, if each thread must process a large task, it may not be wise to monopolize the system for the duration of the task.

- Some systems provide a gang scheduling policy. Under the gang scheduling policy, an application-defined gang of threads are scheduled together. All threads in the gang execute at the same time and are time-sliced at the same time. Because the threads are scheduled together and execute together, they will terminate together (assuming the task is evenly divided among the threads). A gang scheduling policy allows an application to truly take advantage of the physical parallelism available in multiprocessor systems. However, not all systems support a gang scheduling policy.

- The final option to prevent or minimize balance problems is to break up the task into smaller pieces and to create more than one thread per processor. At the finest granularity, each piece of the task completes within one time-slice. This will guarantee that each thread completes its task without being time-sliced. Be careful, the overhead associated with creating, terminating, and synchronizing large numbers of threads for small tasks may cause a significant performance penalty. It's best to experiment with different numbers of threads to find the optimal combination of balance and performance. We suggest starting with one thread per processor. Increase the number of threads until the proper balance is determined for your application.

When the Work-Crew Model is used to divide up several tasks among different threads, balance may not be an issue. Analyze your application and determine whether it matters that one thread takes significantly longer to complete than another thread. If you're using the Work-Crew Model to break up large disjointed parts of an application, chances are that balance will not be an issue. If balance is an issue, break up the application into parts that take the same amount of time to process. You may also need to use one of the above techniques to minimize or prevent balance problems.

Algorithm

The following template can be used to implement the Work-Crew Model in an application. The control thread initializes an array of work structures, one structure for each worker thread. This structure contains the thread ID, start routine, argument, and exit status. Depending on the use of this template, the start routine for each thread may be the same function (i.e., one task divided among multiple threads) or it may be a different function for each thread (i.e., several tasks divided among multiple threads).

Any data needed by a worker thread is passed as an argument to the thread's start routine. While the worker is processing the data, the control thread is not allowed to examine the data. Once the worker thread has finished the task, the control thread joins with the worker and can then safely examine the results of the task. The results can be passed as the worker thread's exit status or modified directly in the *arg* parameter (which the control thread can access through the work[] array).

This template creates a static number of threads. Depending on your needs, you may need to make this dynamic in your application. The number of threads to create can be passed as a parameter to control_thread() or based on the number of processors on the system.

```
struct wc_work_struct {
        pthread_t         thread;
        pthread_attr_t    attr;
        void              (*func)();
        int               exit;
};


void
control_thread()
{
        int                    i, ret_val;
        struct wc_work_struct   work[NUM_THREADS];

        /* Perform any initialization */
        ...

        /* Setup work structure for each thread */
        for (i = 0; i < NUM_THREADS; i++) {
            (void) pthread_attr_init(&work[i].attr);
            /* Set thread start_routine */
            ...
        }
```

```
            /* Create each of the threads */
            for (i = 0; i < NUM_THREADS; i++) {
                ret_val = pthread_create(&work[i].thread, &work[i].attr,
                                          (void *(*)())work[i].func,
                                          (void *)i);
                check_error(ret_val, "pthread_create()");
                (void) pthread_attr_destroy(&work[i].attr);
            }

            /* The initial thread can also be a work thread if desired */
            ...

            /* Wait for each of the threads */
            for (i = 0; i < NUM_THREADS; i++) {
                ret_val = pthread_join(work[i].thread,
                                        (void **)work[i].exit);
                check_error(ret_val, "pthread_join()");
            }

            /* Perform any final processing from thread exit stats. */
            for (i = 0; i < NUM_THREADS; i++) {
                /* Process work[i].exit */
                ...
            }

            return;
}

void work_thread1(void *arg)
{
        int     processing_result;

        /* Process work */
        ...

        /* Return any exit information or processing results */
        pthread_exit((void *)processing_result);
}

void work_thread2(void *arg)
{
        int     processing_result;

        /* Process work */
        ...

        /* Return any exit information or processing results */
        pthread_exit((void *)processing_result);
}
```

The Boss-Worker Model

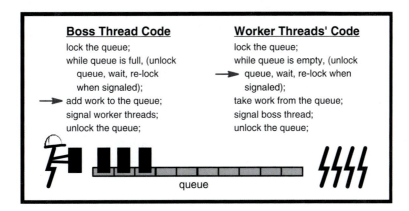

Fig. 15–3 The Boss-Worker Model may be ideal for client/server applications. A *boss* thread creates and adds work to the work queue. *Worker* threads are signaled to perform the work that has been added to the queue.

Overview

The Boss-Worker Model is most suitable for producer-consumer type problems. In this model, one thread is designated as the *Boss* thread. All other threads are *Worker* threads. The boss thread produces or obtains work and places it on a work queue. The worker threads remove and process work from the work queue. This model is useful in a variety of situations that include: applications receiving input from external sources (i.e., servers and user interfaces), search algorithms, divide-and-conquer algorithms, and parallel loop processing.

Usually there is only one boss thread in the Boss-Worker Model. Nothing restricts an application from creating more than one boss thread. A server with multiple input sources may allocate one thread per input source to act as boss threads and several worker threads to process the input. Additionally, each worker thread may also act as a boss thread by placing additional work on the queue (e.g., as part of processing work, a worker thread creates additional work).

Synchronization

The Boss-Worker Model is generally implemented with two condition variables, one mutex, a queue, and several counters. The mutex protects the queue, condition variables, and counters. One condition variable is used by waiting worker threads when the queue is empty. The other condition variable is used by the boss thread when the queue is full. A minimum of three counters are needed to keep track of: (1) the number of work requests on the queue, (2) the number of waiting worker threads, and (3) the number of waiting boss threads.

To place work on the queue, the boss thread must first acquire the queue's mutex. If there is room on the queue for additional work, the work is added to the queue, and any waiting worker threads are signaled. If the queue is full, the boss thread waits on a condition variable until there is room on the queue for additional work requests. Once the work has been queued, the mutex is released, and the boss thread returns to create more work.

To remove work from the queue, a worker thread must first acquire the queue's mutex. If work is available, a work request is removed from the queue, and any waiting boss threads are signaled. If work is not available, the worker thread waits on a condition variable until work is available. Once work has been removed from the queue, the mutex is released and the worker thread processes the work.

Synchronization is needed only when work requests are added to or removed from the queue. This is the only place where work (i.e., shared data) can be accessed by multiple threads. While the boss is creating work, none of the worker threads can access that work or its associated data. Once a worker thread obtains work, none of the other worker threads (or the boss thread) can access that work or its associated data.

Static or Dynamic Length Queues

When the work queue has a static or maximum queue size, two condition variables must be used (one for worker threads and one for boss threads). There are situations where the queue length can be infinitely long. In these cases, only one condition variable is needed for waiting worker threads. The boss thread continually adds work to the queue, regardless of the queue length.

Static queues with a maximum size have the advantage that the boss thread does not overrun the worker threads by creating too much work. A certain balance is guaranteed with maximum queue lengths. However, the boss thread must block when the queue is full, impacting the user or network responsiveness of the application.

Terminating Threads

In the Boss-Worker Model, each of the worker threads is in a continuous loop of obtaining and processing work. At some point, all work requests will have been processed, and the worker threads should terminate. The worker threads need to be instructed to terminate, they cannot simply terminate when the queue is empty. There are two techniques for terminating worker threads in this model:

- Create an "exit" work request for each worker thread and place it on the queue. When a worker thread receives one of the exit tasks, it will terminate. This method depends on the queue order being **FIFO**. The exit requests must be the last work requests queued by the boss thread.

- Associate an "exit" flag with the work queue. When the boss thread wants the worker threads to terminate, the queue's exit flag is set to **EXIT**. When workers try to dequeue work, if the queue is empty and the queue's exit flag is set, they call `pthread_exit()`. Note that the queue must be empty. If worker threads terminate whenever the flag is set, they may terminate before all work has been processed.

Once all worker threads have been instructed to terminated, the boss thread calls `pthread_join()` to wait for each worker to terminate.

Balance Problems

For applications using this model to achieve parallelism on multiprocessors, scheduling balance is an issue. These applications divide up work to take advantage of multiprocessor hardware to solve a problem in the shortest time possible. Refer back to *The Work-Crew Model* section of this chapter for a list of techniques to minimize scheduling balance problems for applications seeking parallelism on multiprocessor systems.

For applications using this model to achieve concurrency, scheduling balance may not be a concern. These applications use the Boss-Worker Model to break up tasks so that when one thread blocks, another thread in the application can continue to make progress. This is often the case when this model is used for servers and user interfaces where the amount of work is controlled by external events. The boss thread accepts tasks and passes them on to worker threads. Scheduling balance is not a concern for these applications.

A different kind of balance is important in the Boss-Worker Model: queue balance. An efficient application will maintain queues that never cause the boss or worker threads to block (i.e., the queue is never empty or full). For applications that maintain control over the amount of work to be produced, you can experiment and tune the application for optimum performance. If the boss thread is blocking because the queue is full, try increasing the maximum queue length or adding additional worker threads. If worker threads are blocking because the queue is empty, try increasing the number of boss threads or decreasing the number of worker threads.

For applications that are controlled by external events (e.g., user- or network-generated input), a balanced queue will never be completely possible. There are times when external conditions cause either too much work or no work. These applications should consider having a dynamic number of boss and worker threads. When the workload is light, use one boss thread and a few worker threads. As the workload increases beyond an application-defined threshold, increase the number of worker threads (and potentially boss threads). You'll need to experiment with different workloads to determine when to add additional threads and when to terminate excess threads.

Algorithm

The following template can be used to implement the Boss-Worker Model in an application. The boss thread initializes the work queue and creates worker threads to process work. You'll need to create the fields for the work structures and the code specific to your application to obtain work in the boss thread and process work in the worker threads.

The following functions are provided in the template:

- `queue_init()`: This function initializes a queue structure. It provides synchronization to ensure that two threads do not initialize the same queue and that an initialized queue is not reinitialized. The queue is initialized with a maximum queue length.

- `enqueue()`: This function is called by the boss thread to add work requests to the queue. If the queue is full, the caller waits on a condition variable until more work can be added to the queue. Once the work has been added to the queue, if there are workers waiting, one worker is signaled.

- `dequeue()`: This function is called by the worker threads to obtain a work request. If the queue is empty, the caller waits on a condition variable until work is available. After a work request has been removed from the queue, if there are boss threads waiting to add work to the queue, one boss thread is signaled. This function also contains a hook to terminate worker threads. If the queue's exit flag is set and the queue is empty, the worker thread calls `pthread_exit()`.

- `queue_terminate_workers()`: This function sets the terminate field in the queue and issues a condition broadcast to any waiting worker threads. This function is called to request that all worker threads terminate when the queue is empty.

- `queue_wait_workers()`: Though not used in this template, this function may prove useful to your application. The caller waits until the worker threads have finished processing all work requests and have blocked, waiting for further work. It does not terminate the worker threads.

- `process_tasks()`: This function is called to start processing the tasks in the Boss-Worker Model. It initializes the work queue, creates the worker threads, and calls `boss()` to act as the boss thread. When processing is complete, this function waits for each worker to terminate.

- boss(): This function enters a loop, creating work for the worker threads. Each work request is added to the queue. When all work requests have been added to the queue, the boss thread returns.

- worker(): This is the start routine for each of the worker threads. This function enters a loop consisting of: (a) get work request and (b) process work request. The worker thread will call pthread_exit() from inside the dequeue() function when the queue's exit flag is set and the queue is empty.

Tailor this template to the specific needs of your application. Comments in the code explain the application-specific sections that should be implemented.

```
/*
 * Work structure which is placed on the queue and later processed by
 * the worker threads. This data structure should contain all the
 * necessary information for the worker to process the request.
 */
struct q_work_struct {
    struct q_work_struct    *next;
    int                     req_type;

    /* Place application specific task data here */
    ...
};

/* Queue data structure passed to the queue mgmt functions */
#define QUEUE_VALID     5768

struct queue_struct {
    int                     valid;
    pthread_mutex_t         lock;
    pthread_cond_t          boss_cv;
    pthread_cond_t          worker_cv;
    int                     exit;
    int                     boss_waiting;
    int                     worker_waiting;
    int                     queue_len;
    int                     max_queue_len;
    struct q_work_struct    *head;
    struct q_work_struct    *tail;
};

/* Global queue and the mutex protecting its initialization */
struct queue_struct     thr_queue;
pthread_mutex_t             queue_init_mtx = PTHREAD_MUTEX_INITIALIZER;
```

```
int
queue_init(struct queue_struct *queue, int max_len)
{
     if (queue == NULL)
          return(EINVAL);

     /* Use a lock to make sure two threads don't init the queue */
     (void) pthread_mutex_lock(&queue_init_mtx);

     /* Already valid? */
     if (queue->valid == QUEUE_VALID) {
          (void) pthread_mutex_unlock(&queue_init_mtx);
          return(EBUSY);
     }

     /* Initialize the queue */
     (void) pthread_mutex_init(&queue->lock, NULL);
     (void) pthread_cond_init(&queue->boss_cv, NULL);
     (void) pthread_cond_init(&queue->worker_cv, NULL);
     queue->exit = 0;
     queue->boss_waiting = 0;
     queue->worker_waiting = 0;
     queue->queue_len = 0;
     queue->max_queue_len = max_len;
     queue->head = NULL;
     queue->tail = NULL;
     queue->valid = QUEUE_VALID;
     (void) pthread_mutex_unlock(&queue_init_mtx);

     return(0);
}


int
enqueue(struct queue_struct *queue, struct q_work_struct *elem)
{
     if ((queue == NULL) || (queue->valid != QUEUE_VALID))
          return(EINVAL);

     (void) pthread_mutex_lock(&queue->lock);

     /*
      * Note: If more than one boss thread exists, either a) the
      * application must ensure that a boss does not add work to
      * the queue after calling queue_terminate() or b) should
      * add a check here to disallow adding requests after the
      * exit field has been set.
      */
```

```
        /* If the queue is full, wait until we can add more work */
        while (queue->queue_len == queue->max_queue_len) {
                queue->boss_waiting++;
                pthread_cond_wait(&queue->boss_cv, &queue->lock);
                queue->boss_waiting--;
        }

        /* We can now add the work to the queue. */
        elem->next = NULL;
        if (queue->queue_len == 0) {
                queue->head = queue->tail = elem;
        } else {
                queue->tail->next = elem;
                queue->tail = elem;
        }
        queue->queue_len++;

        /* Do we have a worker to wake-up? */
        if (queue->worker_waiting)
                (void) pthread_cond_signal(&queue->worker_cv);

        (void) pthread_mutex_unlock(&queue->lock);
        return(0);
}


struct q_work_struct *
dequeue(struct queue_struct *queue)
{
        struct q_work_struct*ptr;

        if ((queue == NULL) || (queue->valid != QUEUE_VALID))
                return(NULL);

        (void) pthread_mutex_lock(&queue->lock);

        /* Is there work on the queue? */
        while (queue->queue_len == 0) {
                /* Are we supposed to terminate? */
                if (queue->exit) {
                        (void) pthread_mutex_unlock(&queue->lock);
                        pthread_exit(NULL);
                }

                /* Wait for data */
                queue->worker_waiting++;
                (void) pthread_cond_wait(&queue->worker_cv,&queue->lock);
                queue->worker_waiting--;
        }
```

```
    /* Take the work off the queue */
    ptr = queue->head;
    queue->head = ptr->next;
    queue->queue_len--;
    if (queue->queue_len == 0)
            queue->tail = NULL;

    /* Do we have any waiting boss threads? */
    if (queue->boss_waiting)
            (void) pthread_cond_signal(&queue->boss_cv);

    (void) pthread_mutex_unlock(&queue->lock);
    return(ptr);
}


int
queue_terminate_workers(struct queue_struct *queue)
{
    if ((queue == NULL) || (queue->valid != QUEUE_VALID))
            return(EINVAL);

    (void) pthread_mutex_lock(&queue->lock);
    queue->exit = 1;

    /* Wakeup any waiting workers */
    (void) pthread_cond_broadcast(&queue->worker_cv);
    (void) pthread_mutex_unlock(&queue->lock);

    return(0);
}


void
queue_wait_workers(struct queue_struct *queue, int nthreads)
{
    if ((queue == NULL) || (queue->valid != QUEUE_VALID))
            return;

    (void) pthread_mutex_lock(&queue->lock);
    while (queue->worker_waiting != nthreads) {
            queue->boss_waiting++;
            (void) pthread_cond_wait(&queue->boss_cv, &queue->lock);
            queue->boss_waiting--;
    }
    (void) pthread_mutex_unlock(&queue->lock);
}
```

```c
void process_tasks()
{
#define MAX_THREADS        64
    int                    i, ret, nthreads, max_queue_len;
    pthread_t              threads[MAX_THREADS];
    pthread_attr_t         attr;
    void                   worker(), boss();

    /* Initialization code */
    ...

    /* Determine number of threads to create and max queue length*/
    nthreads = ...
    max_queue_len = ...

    /* Initialize the queue*/
    if (queue_init(&thr_queue, max_queue_len) != 0) {
        fprintf(stderr, "queue_init() error\n");
        exit(-1);
    }

    /* Initialize any special thread attributes (if needed) */
    (void) pthread_attr_init(&attr);
    ...

    /* Create worker threads */
    for (i = 1; (i < nthreads) && (i < MAX_THREADS); i++) {
        ret = pthread_create(&threads[i], &attr,
                             (void *(*)())worker, NULL);
        check_error(ret, "pthread_create()");
    }
    (void) pthread_attr_destroy(&attr);

    /* We are the boss thread */
    boss();

    /* Request the workers terminate when all work is processed */
    if (queue_terminate_workers(&thr_queue) != 0) {
        fprintf(stderr, "dequeue() error\n");
        exit(-1);
    }

    /* Wait for the workers to terminate */
    for (i = 1; (i < nthreads) && (i < MAX_THREADS); i++) {
        ret = pthread_join(threads[i], NULL);
        check_error(ret, "pthread_join()");
    }

    /* Perform any final processing and return */
}
```

```
void boss()
{
      struct q_work_struct*ptr;
      int                   ret;

      /* Obtain work. Return when complete. */
      for ( ; ; ) {
             /* allocate a work structure */
             ptr = (struct q_work_struct *)malloc(
                                   sizeof(struct q_work_struct));
             if (ptr == NULL)
                    break;

             /* Create/obtain work and fill in work structure */
             ret = get_work(ptr);
             if (ret == 0) {
                    free((void *)ptr);
                    break;
             }

             /* Queue up the work */
             if (enqueue(&thr_queue, ptr) != 0) {
                    fprintf(stderr, "enqueue() error\n");
                    exit(-1);
             }
      }
}

void worker()
{
      struct q_work_struct*ptr;

      /* Go into an infinite loop processing work received from */
      /* the work queue. If we are supposed to terminate, we    */
      /* will never return from one of the calls to dequeue().  */
      for ( ; ; ) {
             /* Obtain the next work request */
             ptr = dequeue(&thr_queue);
             if (ptr == NULL) {
                    fprintf(stderr, "dequeue() error\n");
                    exit(-1);
             }

             /* Process the work request */
             ...

             /* Release memory for work request*/
             free((void *)ptr);
      }
}
```

The Pipeline Model

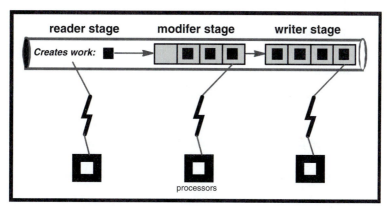

Fig. 15–4 The Pipeline Model is analogous to an assembly line. Threads are stationed at successive points along the assembly line. As the task moves down the assembly line, it is modified at each stage. The task is complete when the data has passed through the last stage.

Overview

The Pipeline Model is similar to an assembly line where data passes from one stage to the next. Each stage performs a specific operation on the data. This model works well when data must go through a read-process-write type operation. The UNIX `awk` program can easily be thought of as a pipeline. An input record is read in the first stage of the pipe, processed in the second stage, and written in the third stage. In its most basic form, with one boss and one worker, the Boss-Worker Model is a pipeline.

Synchronization

The Pipeline Model is implemented with the same queues as the Boss-Worker Model queues. Each stage in the pipeline contains an input and output queue. The output queue for a stage is the input queue for the next stage. As each stage processes data, it places the data on the output queue. The next stage receives this data from the same queue, processes it, and places it on its output queue.

Synchronization is needed only when work is added to or removed from one of the queues. This is the only place where shared data can be accessed by multiple threads. When a chunk of shared data is not on a queue, the thread operating on the data has exclusive access to the data.

Terminating Threads

When all work has been processed, the threads in the pipeline need to terminate. This is accomplished by having the first thread in the pipeline pass an **EOF** or **EXIT** request through the pipeline. As each thread receives this request, it passes it on to the next stage and then terminates. This technique can also be used to pass other requests, such as a reinitialize request, through the pipeline. Each stage of the pipeline should be coded to recognize special requests versus normal processing requests.

Balance Problems

Because pipelines are usually implemented in read-process-write type applications, parallelism is usually not a goal. Threads are used to achieve concurrency within the application. While one thread is blocked reading data, another thread in the pipeline can be processing other data. For applications seeking parallelism in the Pipeline Model, refer back to *The Work-Crew Model* section of this chapter for a list of techniques to minimize scheduling balance problems.

Pipelines need to worry about queue balance. Any time one stage in the pipeline must block, because either its input queue is empty or its output queue is full, performance suffers. The most efficient pipelines contain queues that are never full. The queues for each stage should be large enough that the amount of data processed in one time-slice will not fill up the output queue. If the output queue for a stage is often full and the thread must block, waiting for the next stage to catch up, experiment with adding additional threads to the next stage. This may produce a model that is a combination of the Pipeline and Boss-Worker Models.

Be careful when adding additional threads, in some pipelines there may be one stage where the processing is extremely fast compared with all other stages. Suppose the fast stage is able to process ten blocks of data in the same time that it takes the previous and next stages to process one. Rather than trying to speed up the entire pipe by adding additional threads in the previous and next stages, let the fast thread block. However, instead of the previous stage waking up the thread when it adds one block of data, have the previous stage wake-up the thread when ten blocks of data have accumulated on the queue. When the thread starts executing, it will have enough data to process to (hopefully) consume at least one time-slice.

Algorithm

The following template can be used to implement the pipeline model in an application. The queue management functions and data structures from the Boss-Worker Model are used in this model. The process_pipe() function initializes the pipeline queues, creates threads for each stage of the pipe, and then acts as the stage-1 thread in the pipe. Once all data has been processed and the pipe is shut down, this function waits for the worker threads to terminate.

The stage1(), stage2(), and stage3() functions process the work in the pipeline. These functions pass work requests through the queue functions. If a special **EXIT** task is received, the threads in each stage pass the request along to the next stage and then terminate.

```
struct queue_struct        stage2_queue, stage3_queue;
void                       stage1(), stage2(), stage3();
#define EXIT               -1

void
process_pipe()
{
#define NTHREADS   2
    int                    i, ret, max_queue_len;
    pthread_t              thread[NTHREADS];
    pthread_attr_t         attr;

    /* Initialization code */
    ...

    /* Determine max queue length*/
    max_queue_len = ...

    /* Initialize the queues*/
    if ((queue_init(&stage2_queue, max_queue_len) != 0)
    || (queue_init(&stage3_queue, max_queue_len) != 0)) {
        fprintf(stderr, "queue_init() error\n");
        exit(-1);
    }

    /* Initialize any special thread attributes (if needed) */
    (void) pthread_attr_init(&attr);
    ...

    /* Create worker threads */
    ret = pthread_create(&thread[0], &attr,
                        (void *(*)())stage2, NULL);
    check_error(ret, "pthread_create()");

    ret = pthread_create(&thread[1], &attr,
                        (void *(*)())stage3, NULL);
    check_error(ret, "pthread_create()");

    (void) pthread_attr_destroy(&attr);

    /* We are the stage 1 thread */
    stage1();

    /* Wait for the workers to terminate */
    for (i = 1; i < NTHREADS; i++) {
        ret = pthread_join(thread[i], NULL);
        check_error(ret, "pthread_join()");
    }
    /* Perform any final processing and return */
}
```

```
void
stage1()
{
      struct q_work_struct*ptr;
      int                  req_type;

      /* Obtain work (i.e., wait for user input, requests off the */
      /* network, etc.). Return when complete. */
      for ( ; ; ) {
            /* allocate a work structure */
            ptr = (struct q_work_struct *)malloc(
                                      sizeof(struct q_work_struct));
            if (ptr == NULL) {
                  fprintf(stderr, "Out of Memory\n");
                  exit(-1);
            }

            /* Create/obtain work and fill in work structure */
            ...
            req_type = ptr->req_type;

            /* Process stage 1 of the work */
            if (req_type != EXIT) {
                  ...
            }

            /* Queue up the work for stage 2 */
            if (enqueue(&stage2_queue, ptr) != 0) {
                  fprintf(stderr, "enqueue() error\n");
                  exit(-1);
            }

            if (req_type == EXIT)
                  return;
      }
}

void
stage2()
{
      struct q_work_struct*ptr;
      int                  req_type;

      /* Go into an infinite loop processing work received from */
      /* the work queue.                                        */
      for ( ; ; ) {
            /* Obtain the next work request */
            ptr = dequeue(&stage2_queue);
            if (ptr == NULL) {
                  fprintf(stderr, "dequeue() error\n");
```

```
                        exit(-1);
                }
                req_type = ptr->req_type;

                /* Process the stage 2 work */
                if (req_type != EXIT) {
                        ...
                }

                /* Queue up the work for stage 3 */
                if (enqueue(&stage3_queue, ptr) != 0) {
                        fprintf(stderr, "enqueue() error\n");
                        exit(-1);
                }

                if (req_type == EXIT)
                        return;
        }
}

void
stage3()
{
        struct q_work_struct*ptr;
        int                  req_type;

        /* Go into an infinite loop processing work received from */
        /* the work queue.                                        */
        for ( ; ; ) {
                /* Obtain the next work request */
                ptr = dequeue(&stage3_queue);
                if (ptr == NULL) {
                        fprintf(stderr, "dequeue() error\n");
                        exit(-1);
                }
                req_type = ptr->req_type;

                /* Process the stage 3 work */
                if (req_type != EXIT) {
                        ...
                }

                /* Release memory for work structure */
                free((void *)ptr);

                if (req_type == EXIT)
                        return;
        }
}
```

The Master-Slave Model

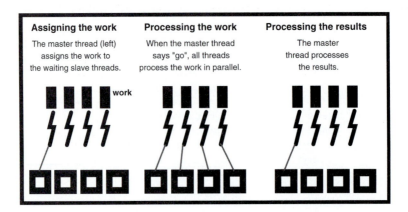

Fig. 15–5 In the Master-Slave Model, the master thread divides work evenly among the slave threads. All threads, including the master thread, start processing the work in parallel. After the work has been processed, the slave threads rendezvous and wait for more work while the master thread processes the results. This process repeats until all work has been processed. The Master-Slave Model should be used only for compute-intensive applications on multiprocessor systems.

Overview

In the Master-Slave Model, one master thread divides work evenly among several slave threads. Each of the slave threads start processing their share of the work simultaneously. After the work has been processed, the slave threads rendezvous and wait for more work to process. While the slaves are waiting, the master thread performs any final processing of the results. This process repeats until all work has been processed.

The Master-Slave Model is used most often when an application needs to process a compute-intensive task and wants the task processed in the shortest time possible. This model is used to take advantage of multiprocessor hardware so that multiple threads can process work in parallel. While this model can be used to solve problems where threads block waiting for I/O, it is most effective for solving compute-intensive problems.

Because of the desire to solve a compute intensive-problem in parallel, this model should be used only on multiprocessor machines. On a single-processor machine, breaking up a compute-intensive task and assigning multiple threads to process the task takes longer than processing the task sequentially. The amount of time required to process the task, whether sequentially or in chunks by different threads, is the same for compute-intensive problems. Breaking up the task and using threads adds the additional overhead of thread creation, termination, and synchronization. On a multiprocessor machine, the performance benefit of parallel computation makes this overhead acceptable (if the task is large enough).

Synchronization

The Master-Slave Model is usually implemented with barriers. The barriers provide the necessary synchronization between the master and slave threads. All slaves wait at a barrier until they are allowed to proceed and process a task. Once the task is finished, the slaves rendezvous at another barrier. The following pseudocode shows the flow of control in the Master-Slave Model. Note that the master thread is also a slave and processes part of the task:

```
Master                          Slave
master() {                      slave(index) {
    initialization
    create N slaves
    while (work to do) {            while (work to do) {
        create work
        barrier 1                       barrier 1
        process work                    process work
        barrier 2                       barrier 2
        process results
    }                              }
    join N slaves               pthread_exit()
}                               }
```

The master thread allocates an array of work structures. Each thread is assigned an index into this work array. When slave threads start processing, they receive any input data from their work structure in the array. After a slave has finished processing its work, any output is stored in this work structure.

The barriers provide the necessary synchronization between the master and the slaves. The master is allowed to access the work structures only when the slaves are blocked in a barrier (i.e., either before processing work or after processing work). The slaves are allowed to access their work structures only when they are processing work (i.e., between `barrier 1` and `barrier 2`). Each slave is allowed to access only its own work structure. Consequently, through the use of barriers, only one thread at a time is allowed to access one of the work structures.

If the time it takes the master to either set-up the work or process the results is extremely small, you may want to consider making one or both of the barriers a spinning or limited spin barrier. The barrier example we presented in Chapter 5, *Thread Synchronization*, is an example of a blocking barrier. If the time it takes to set-up or process work is less than the time it takes to perform a context switch, a spinning or limited spin barrier may be a better alternative. With a blocking barrier, the master may have finished processing the results and setting up more work just as the slaves have finished blocking in the barrier. The time required to schedule and context switch the slaves back in is wasted, causing additional overhead and delays. A spinning barrier would prevent the overhead of scheduling and context switching each slave as the slaves do not block.

Be careful when using spinning or limited spin barriers. Spinning, whether in a loop or for a limited amount of time, wastes CPU cycles that another thread could be using. Spinning should be used only when you can guarantee that the master thread is currently executing and will allow the slaves to proceed shortly. If this cannot be guaranteed, it is possible to severely waste CPU cycles because the master thread may block or be context switched by the scheduler. There are three ways to guarantee the controlling thread is running and will allow the slaves to continue shortly: (a) monopolize the machine (i.e., this is the only application), (b) use the highest priority scheduling parameters on the system, or (c) use a gang scheduling policy (if available).

Terminating Threads

After all work has been processed, the slave threads are no longer needed and should be terminated. The master thread can terminate the slave threads with either of the following methods:

- Create a special "exit" task in the work structure for each slave thread. When the slave threads are allowed to proceed past the first barrier, they will see the exit task and call `pthread_exit()`.

- If the barriers used by the slave threads are based on condition variables, the master thread can call `pthread_cancel()` for each of the slave threads. Since the slaves are blocked on a condition variable and a condition wait is a cancellation point, all slaves will be terminated. Be careful with this technique; when a thread is cancelled during a condition wait, the canceled thread reacquires the condition's associated mutex before terminating. The barrier implementation should install a cancellation cleanup handler to release the barrier's mutex before the thread terminates.

Once all slave threads have been instructed to terminate, the master thread should call `pthread_join()` to wait for each slave thread to terminate.

Balance Problems

In the Master-Slave Model, work must be divided equally among all slave threads. This model is used to take advantage of multiple processors to process a compute-intensive task in parallel. If the threads are not executing in parallel, a balance problem occurs in the application. It's possible that the scheduler will choose to schedule the slave threads sequentially on the same processor or time-slice one of the threads, or that one of the slaves may block waiting for I/O. All of these conditions create a balance problem for applications seeking parallel computation on multiprocessor systems. Refer back to *The Work-Crew Model* section of this chapter for a list of techniques to minimize scheduling balance problems.

Algorithm

The following template can be used to implement the Master-Slave Model in an application. The master thread initializes an array of work structures, one structure for each slave thread. This structure contains the thread ID, thread exit status, and input/output fields for passing data between the master and the slave. You will need to modify the contents of the work structure to reflect how data is to be passed between the master and slaves in your application. This can be accomplished with pointers to dynamically allocated memory, a copy of the actual data, a pointer to the original location of the data to be processed, or a pointer to a function for the slave to execute.

Any input data needed by a slave thread is stored in the slave's work structure. While the slave is processing the data, the master thread is not allowed to examine the data. Once the slave thread has finished the task, the master thread can safely examine the results of the task. The results of the task are returned to the master thread in the work structure. This template uses barriers to synchronize both the slave thread's execution and the master thread's access to the work structure of each slave.

```
/*
 * Each slave thread is allocated a work structure.
 * The work structure contains all input data (or instructions
 * on the work to be performed). Additionally, each structure
 * contains a place for any output data or results that need
 * to be returned to the master thread when processing completes.
 * Tailor this data structure as needed for your application.
 */
struct ms_work_struct {
    pthread_t       id;
    void            *return_status;
    void            *slave_input;
    void            *slave_output;
};

/*
 * Array of work structures, one for each thread
 */
struct ms_work_struct *work;

/*
 * Each thread, master included, synchronizes on this barrier.
 * The barrier determines who is allowed to access the work
 * data structures at what time as well as rendezvouzing
 * slave threads after processing work.
 */
barrier_t       sync_barrier;

void            process_work(), master(int nthr), slave(int index);
```

```
void
process_work()
{
      int                  i, ret, nthreads;
      pthread_attr_t       attr;

      /* Initialization code */
      ...

      /* Determine number of threads to create */
      nthreads = ...

      work = (struct ms_work_struct *)malloc(nthreads *
                                    sizeof(struct ms_work_struct));
      if (work == NULL) {
            fprintf(stderr, "Out of Memory\n");
            exit(-1);
      }

      /* Initialize the barrier */
      if (barrier_init(&sync_barrier, nthreads) != 0)
            return;

      /* Initialize thread attributes (if needed) */
      (void) pthread_attr_init(&attr);
      ...

      /* Create slave threads (we are a slave thread: index = 0 */
      for (i = 1; i < nthreads; i++) {
            ret = pthread_create(&work[i].id, &attr,
                              (void *(*)())slave,(void *)i);
            check_error(ret, "pthread_create()");
      }
      (void) pthread_attr_destroy(&attr);

      /* We are the master thread */
      master(nthreads);

      /* Join slave threads (we are a slave thread: index = 0 */
      for (i = 1; i < nthreads; i++) {
            ret = pthread_join(work[i].id, &work[i].return_status);
            check_error(ret, "pthread_join()");
      }

      /* Perform any final processing and return */
      ...

      return;
}
```

```
void master(int nthreads)
{
      int    i, more_work;

      for ( ; ; ) {
              /* Initialize work structure for each slave.      */
              /* When we are here, slaves are not accessing      */
              /* the work[] array.                               */

              for (i = 0; i < nthreads; i++) {
                      /*
                       * Store input work in work[i].slave_input. If we
                       * do not have any more work, set this field to
                       * NULL to indicate to the slave threads to
                       * terminate.
                       */
                      if (more_work) {
                              work[i].slave_input = ...
                      } else {
                              work[i].slave_input = NULL;
                      }
              }

              /* Let all the slave go now */
              barrier_wait(&sync_barrier);
              if (!more_work)
                      return

              /*
               * We are a slave thread also. Process the work in
               * work[0].slave_input. Store any results in
               * work[0].slave_output. When we are here, each slave is
               * accessing its own work[] structure so we cannot
               * globally access any work[] structure but our own.
               */
              ...

              /* Synchronize when all slaves have finished */
              barrier_wait(&sync_barrier);

              /* Process any returned data from the slaves       */
              /* When we are here, slaves are not accessing work. */
              for (i = 0; i < nthreads; i++) {
                      /* Output results are in work[i].slave_output */
                      ...
              }

              /* Loop back for more tasks to process in parallel */
      }
}
```

```
void slave(int index)
{

     /* Initialization code */
     ...

     /* Process the work */
     for ( ; ; ) {
            /*
             * Wait until the master thread has our work[] structure
             * ready for us to proceed. We are prohibited from
             * accessing it until we leave the barrier.
             */
            barrier_wait(&sync_barrier);

            /*
             * Process the work in work[index].slave_input. Store any
             * results in work[index].slave_output. If the input field
             * is NULL, we are supposed to terminate. When we are
             * here, the master thread cannot access our work[]
             * structure.
             */
            if (work[index].slave_input == NULL)
                  break;

            /* Process work in work[index].slave_input */
            ...

            /* Return any results in work[index].slave_output */
            work[index].slave_output = ...

            /* Wait for all other slave to finish */
            barrier_wait(&sync_barrier);

            /*
             * At this point, only the master thread can access
             * our work[index] structure. Loop back for more tasks to
             * process in parallel.
             */
     }

     /* Perform any final processing and terminate */
     ...

     pthread_exit((void *)NULL);
}
```

Thread Creation Issues

Issues	Answers
How many threads are required?	- Compute-bound applications should start with one thread per processor. - I/O-bound applications should create enough threads to keep the processor(s) busy as other threads block waiting for I/O to complete.
Should I use static or dynamic thread creation?	- Use statically created threads when the workload is known in advance. When the workload is unknown and blocking may occur, use a combination of statically and dynamically created threads.
Should I use bound or unbound threads?	- For real-time behavior, or compute-bound threads, use bound threads. - For most I/O activities, use unbound threads.
Should I use cached threads?	- This may be useful if thread creation/termination occurs often in an application. A thread caching module can be implemented with the Boss-Worker Model..

Fig. 15–6 The number of threads required for optimal performance is application-dependent. As a rule of thumb, compute-bound applications perform best with one thread per processor. If threads are assigned to work on very small tasks, the benefit of threads may be outweighed by thread management overhead. Performance tuning is a science and an art. Experimentation is required.

How Many Threads?

The most common question a programmer asks when writing a multithreaded application is: How many threads should I create? The answer is application-dependent. We cannot tell you the correct answer; however, we can provide you with some questions to ask yourself to help determine the right answer. You may need to experiment with many different situations and workloads to determine the optimal number of threads for your application.

Are you using threads to achieve parallelism or concurrency within your application?

The most obvious answer is: both. Before you decide, let's revisit concurrency and parallelism. Applications using threads to achieve parallelism tend to be compute-bound applications that want to use multiple processors to complete a task in a shorter amount of time. Adding more processors increases application performance, whereas removing processors decreases application performance. These applications are often single-threaded on a single-processor system as they cannot run faster without additional processors (i.e., the application does not block often). These applications depend on the ability to execute in parallel for performance improvements.

Applications using threads to achieve concurrency want the ability for the application to continue to make forward progress when one thread in the application blocks (i.e., waiting for user input or a message from the network). These applications can obtain a performance improvement even on a single-processor system, as other threads in the application are allowed to execute while one thread is blocked. Multiple processors on the system are an added bonus, potentially allowing threads within the application to execute in parallel and the application to complete faster.

Is your application compute-bound?

Compute-bound applications desire physical parallelism and generally want to allocate one thread per processor. Your application should be robust and should determine the number of processors on the system before creating threads. One thread per processor is theoretically the optimal number of threads. However, as we've seen earlier in this chapter, balance problems may arise due to scheduling algorithms of the system or threads in the application blocking. Depending on how successful you are at preventing or minimizing balance problems, you may need more than one thread per processor. Start with one thread per processor and increase the number of threads until you determine the optimal number of threads that provide the best performance. Generally, the best performance is achieved when the application allocates between one and two threads per processor.

For small tasks, one thread per processor may be excessive. If the task assigned to each thread is extremely small, the costs associated with creating, terminating, and synchronizing the threads may be too high. In your experiments, you should determine both the minimum and maximum number of threads that should be used to process a task. Make your application robust so that it does not create threads beyond these limits.

Applications that are not compute-bound should determine how many running/ runnable threads need to be present at any time. For example, suppose all worker threads in the Boss-Worker Model spend 50% of their time running and 50% of their time blocked, waiting for I/O to complete. In this situation, allocating two threads per processor may be optimal. While one thread is blocked, another thread can be running. Again, you'll need to experiment to find the correct number of threads for your application.

On what types of hardware will your application run?

Is your application going to be restricted to one machine or going to run on a variety of different machines? Make sure your application is robust enough to recognize when it should and shouldn't create additional threads. An application with 64 threads may perform extremely well on a 32-processor system but poorly on a single-processor desktop workstation.

How large are the tasks each thread will process?

Each task assigned to a thread needs to be large enough to warrant the additional overhead associated with creating, terminating, and synchronizing the thread. Quite obviously, creating one thread to execute 10 or 20 instructions is a waste of time and system resources. If each task is relatively small, consider having one thread perform several tasks, rather than creating one thread per task.

The final result

In the end, you must experiment to find the optimal number of threads. The most common mistake made by programmers learning multithreaded programming is to create too many threads. Start small and then add threads to see how the performance of your application changes. Take into consideration the number of processors on the system and make your application robust. Don't overload the system with too many threads. Your application may run faster, but other applications may slow down if they don't get their fair share of CPU time.

Static or Dynamic Thread Creation?

Many applications know the amount of work to be processed at the beginning of the task. These applications can calculate the number of threads needed to process the task (in relation to the number of processors on the system). However, many applications do not know the amount of work in advance. Applications that are servers or have user interfaces fall into this category. These applications are usually implemented with the Boss-Worker Model.

These applications usually have a good idea of the average workload. The workload changes dynamically - sometimes higher, sometimes lower. Consider making the application dynamic in response to these workload changes. If the workload increases beyond a certain threshold, add additional worker threads to help process the extra work. If threads are idle for long periods, terminate the excess idle threads to free up system resources.

Bound or Unbound Threads?

Applications needing true realtime behavior should use bound threads. Only the kernel can guarantee true system-wide realtime scheduling behavior. Unbound threads are only prioritized relative to other unbound threads within the process. Compute-bound applications should also use bound threads. These applications allocate one thread per processor to execute in parallel. The kernel needs to schedule each thread in order to guarantee parallelism.

Applications that are completely I/O-bound (i.e., they spend the majority of their time blocked, waiting for I/O to complete) should also use bound threads. Most systems will allocate an additional kernel-scheduled entity when one (or sometimes all) of the threads block. When an application using unbound threads spends most of its time blocked, waiting for I/O, it ends up as a 1x1 model application because of the way the system operates. The overhead of maintaining the proper number of kernel-scheduled entities may become too expensive if the application is constantly causing kernel entities be created and destroyed.

All other applications (i.e., partially I/O-bound, partially compute-bound) should consider using unbound threads when they are available on the target system.

Unbound threads are faster to create, terminate, and synchronize. In addition, it's not as critical to determine the optimal number of threads with the MxN threads model. The system will attempt to maintain the optimal level of concurrency within your application. For example, your application may have ten runnable threads, but since the system has only four processors, only four kernel-scheduled entities may be allocated. The ten user threads will be scheduled on top of the four kernel-scheduled entities. As long as the system maintains one running kernel-scheduled entity per processor, the application cannot run faster. There is one exception to this statement: if your application runs on a system shared by many applications, by having more than one kernel-scheduled entity per processor, your application receives more scheduling time than other applications receive.

Caching Threads

While threads are extremely cheap to create, relative to creating processes, threads are not completely free. If your application is designed to dynamically create and terminate threads as needed, the thread creation, termination, and synchronization overhead may be too high. Consider caching or pooling threads in your application. Compilers often use this technique when threads are not needed after executing a loop in parallel.

After a thread has finished processing a task and is no longer needed, have it wait for work rather than terminating. When a new thread is needed, dispatch the work to one of the waiting threads. The Boss-Worker Model is useful for this type of thread caching. When a thread has finished its task, it waits for a new task to arrive on the queue. When the thread dequeues a work request, part of the request will contain the thread's *start_routine* and *arg*ument parameter.

Be cautious when caching threads. It's possible to have threads cached that will never be used. Make sure your application contains high-water marks so that only a certain number of threads are cached. When this mark has been reached, other threads that terminate will actually terminate rather than being cached. In addition, consider putting time limits on cached threads. If a cached thread has not been used after a certain time, have the thread terminate. The dequeue function can use `pthread_cond_timedwait()` to determine when a thread has been idle for too long. Remember, each thread that is cached is essentially unused and consuming system resources.

Thread Synchronization Issues

Issues	Answers
How do I minimize data sharing?	- Where possible, use existing functions, like pthread_join(), etc., to pass data between threads. - If a thread is synchronized for other reasons (i.e., barrier), try to use this synchronization point for data access also.
How do I decrease synchronization overhead?	- Obtain more than one task at a synchronization point. - For a task that currently requires synchronization, see if one thread can perform the job better than two or more threads.
Where do I place synchronization primitives?	- Place synchronization primitives as close to the shared object as possible. - Do not to hold a lock while performing a system call, especially a blocking system call.
How do I handle lock contention?	- Check lock granularity: too fine means too much synchronization overhead, too coarse means too much serialization. - Hold the lock for the shortest time possible, - Investigate the use of read-write locks and spinlocks.

Fig. 15–7 Synchronization primitives carry overhead and serialize thread execution. Structure your application to minimize the sharing of data among threads. This reduces the need for the use of synchronization primitives and increases application performance.

Minimize Data Sharing

Data that is shared by multiple threads must be protected by some form of synchronization. Whenever threads synchronize on data, the application is serialized, reducing parallelism and performance. Structure your application so that data sharing between threads is kept to a minimum. Use existing functions like pthread_create(), pthread_exit(), and pthread_join() to pass data between threads where possible. If your application needs to use primitives like barriers, use the barriers to also provide synchronized access to shared data. The Master-Slave Model provides a good example of this technique. While the slave threads are blocked in the barrier, only the master thread can access the shared data. Consequently, further synchronization of the shared data is not required.

Keep in mind that you will never be able to remove the need for synchronization. Synchronization is inherent in parallel programming and cannot be avoided. You can however, design a parallel application which minimizes the amount of data sharing between threads.

Synchronization Overhead

Synchronization in parallel applications is expensive. Even if a thread can acquire a lock without blocking, it must still spend time acquiring and releasing the lock. This synchronization overhead decreases the overall application performance. By minimizing data sharing, your application contains less synchronization overhead.

An application may minimize data sharing but still experience too much overhead with synchronization primitives. It's possible that the amount of work performed between synchronization points is small enough that the threads spend excessive amounts of time synchronizing. If this occurs, consider increasing the amount of work threads process between synchronization points. Try having each thread obtain multiple tasks at each synchronization point so that more processing is performed in relation to the synchronization overhead.

Another cause of high synchronization overhead is when a task is divided among threads when one thread should really process the task. If two threads spend a significant amount of time sharing data, consider folding the tasks of the two threads into one thread to avoid the need for synchronization. The amount of time spent waiting for locks can negate the benefit of multiple threads when data is shared too often.

Synchronization Placement

Place calls to synchronization functions in the lower layers of your application. For example, the queue management functions in the **Example** sections of this chapter are the synchronization points for threads. The locks protecting the queue are contained within the queue management functions. The outer layers of the application have no idea that locks are needed when accessing the queue. In fact, they shouldn't need to know. By placing the synchronization primitives at the lowest possible layers, two benefits arise: (1) the locks are held for the shortest time possible and (2) because there are fewer calls to synchronization primitives, fewer bugs can occur, and debugging is easier. If calls to synchronization functions are scattered throughout the code, it's easier for something to go wrong and harder to make modifications to the application.

Lock Contention

Lock contention occurs when a thread tries to acquire a lock, but because the lock is acquired by another thread, the thread must block. During the time the thread is blocked, the application has been delayed and its execution serialized. Additionally, the application must pay the extra cost of blocking and unblocking the thread. Lock contention can create severe performance penalties for an application.

Lock contention can never be completely prevented. If it could, there would be no need to synchronize access to shared data. If lock contention occurs frequently, any of the following techniques can be used to attempt to minimize contention:

- *Break up the locks*: A common cause of lock contention is large lock granularity. Analyze your locks to determine which data is protected by the lock. If a single lock is protecting several data structures, consider breaking up the lock into multiple locks.

For example, a single lock that protects a linked list and the data contained in each structure on the list can be broken up into one lock which protects the list and one lock per structure which protects the data contained in the structure. By breaking up the lock this way, the list lock needs to be acquired only while performing list operations like add, delete, and lookup. Once a structure has been obtained, the structure's lock is acquired to protect the data contained in the structure, and the list lock is released. This technique allows other threads to add, delete, or look up structures on the list while another thread is modifying the contents of a structure on the list.

Be careful when breaking up locks. It's possible to go to the other extreme and create so many locks that application performance decreases due to the excessive synchronization overhead. An application that performs: (lock x, modify a, unlock x), (lock y, modify b, unlock y), (lock z, modify c, unlock z), has probably gone too far.

- *Shorten the amount of work performed while the lock is held*: Sometimes lock contention develops because locks are held too long. Analyze each of your locks and ensure that the lock is held for the shortest duration possible. If extra work not requiring protection is performed while the lock is held, try to move the work outside of the protection of the lock. If possible, avoid making system calls while a lock is acquired, especially blocking system calls. System calls are expensive and take a significant amount of time to complete. Additionally, if the thread blocks, receives a signal, or is time-sliced while in the system call, the lock is held for an extremely long duration, causing further lock contention.

- *Use read-write locks*: If the data protected by a lock is usually accessed as read-only data and rarely changed, consider using read-write locks to allow read access by multiple threads. Multiple threads can acquire the read lock in parallel to access the data for reading. When the data needs to be written or updated, a write lock around the data serializes access so that the update completes atomically.

- *Use spinlocks*: Sometimes, when a thread tries to acquire a lock and it is not currently available, the lock may be available in a few machine cycles. If the thread tries to acquire the lock once and then blocks; by the time the blocking is complete, the lock is available. The overhead of blocking on a lock is expensive. Consider using a limited-spin spinlock. Spin on the lock for a certain time and, if still not acquired, block on the lock. As we've previously seen, this technique can be dangerous if the thread owning the lock is not currently running or is holding the lock for long periods. True spinlocks which spin forever are the most dangerous if the lock is not held for short durations. Limited-spin spinlocks are generally safer. You'll need to tune the amount of time spent spinning, but studies have shown that allowing the thread to spin for 50-100% of the time it takes to block or context switch a thread is most effective.

Multiprocessor Cache Thrashing Issues

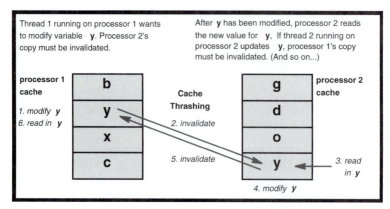

Fig. 15–8 Cache thrashing takes place when multiple threads running on different processors are modifying the same cache line. Cache thrashing can reduce performance significantly. One technique for preventing cache thrashing is to minimize the amount of data sharing among threads. Another technique is to bind threads that share data to the same processor.

Multiprocessor Caches

As we discussed in Chapter 10, *Thread Extensions*, multiprocessor systems use hardware caches to cache chunks of memory for faster access. Cache sizes vary from system to system, some as small as 32K, others 4M or larger. When memory locations are accessed and copied into the cache, they are copied in chunks called *cache lines*. Just as cache sizes vary, so do cache line sizes. Cache lines sizes are generally 8, 16, 32, or 64 bytes. The first memory location of a cache line is always an address which is aligned to a multiple of the cache line size. When a memory location is accessed, the entire cache line which contains that location is loaded into the cache. When a processor must go out to main memory to retrieve a memory location, it's called a *cache miss*. When a processor obtains a memory location from its cache, it's called a *cache hit*. The more cache hits an application achieves, the better the performance (the process spends less time accessing main memory).

A cache line is allowed to exist in the caches of multiple processors, as long as the data contained in the cache line is only being read. If data in a cache line is modified, the same cache line in other processors is now inconsistent. One processor has a cache line that contains the new data and the other processors have a cache line with old invalid data. To prevent inconsistent processor caches, systems use a *cache coherency* or *cache consistency* protocol. Several different protocols are used to implement cache coherency, but all protocols have the same final result: Data in a processor cache is consistent with data in other processor's cache.

The most common cache coherency protocol is the *write-invalidate* model. In this model, when a cache line is modified (i.e., written to), the processor must first invalidate copies of the cache line that exist in other processors. Once all copies of the cache line have been invalidated or deleted, the data in the cache line can be modified. Only one copy of the data is allowed to exist in multiprocessor caches if the data is being modified. Invalidating cache lines in other processor caches takes time, uses up the processor interconnect network bandwidth, and decreases application performance.

Some systems group cache lines into *cache blocks*. Usually two or four cache lines are placed into a cache block. The cache coherency protocol will then keep track of cache blocks instead of cache lines. Any time data is modified, the entire block of cache lines containing that data in other processors is invalidated. By using blocks of cache lines, the cache coherency protocol has smaller tables to maintain in order to keep the processor caches consistent.

As you can see, data sharing can be an expensive and time-consuming operation on multiprocessor systems when multiple threads are modifying the same data. Consider a situation where two threads on different processors each want to modify the variable y. Both processors have the cache line containing y in their processor cache. The processor of the first thread to perform the modification must invalidate y's cache line in the second processor. Once the modification is complete, the second thread's processor must read the new value of y, then invalidate the first processor's cache line containing y. This situation, known as *cache thrashing*, gets worse as multiple threads on different processors modify the same data.

False Sharing and Data Allocation

The first way to prevent caching performance problems is to minimize the amount of data shared between threads. We've already explored several options to minimize data sharing. However, a certain amount of data must be shared. The next step toward preventing caching performance problems is to be smart about how shared data is allocated.

As an example, in the Master-Slave Model, an array of work structures is allocated, one for each thread. Let's suppose that our system's cache line size is 64 bytes and that the work structure size is 48 bytes. When the first slave accesses its work structure, the first 64 bytes (a cache line) of the array are copied into the processor cache. This data includes the first work structure in the array and a portion of the second work structure (16 bytes) in the array. When the second thread (on a different processor) accesses its work structure, part of the work structure is in the cache of another processor. If the first thread has modified its work structure, the cache line containing the structure must be removed from the processor cache of the first thread and loaded into the processor cache of the second thread. This situation is known as *false sharing*. The threads are not sharing data, but since their unshared data resides on the same cache line, the processors must keep the cache data consistent. False sharing of data can create severe performance problems as threads read and write data in their work structures.

To solve false data sharing problems, allocate shared data in chunks that are multiples of the cache line size and aligned on cache line boundaries (i.e., the start address is a multiple of a cache line size). In our example, the array of work structures would be allocated to start at an address that is a multiple of the cache line size, and the work structure would contain padding to make the size of each structure a multiple of the cache line size. If your system implements cache coherency with blocks of cache lines, you'll need to allocate data that is aligned on cache block boundaries and padded to the cache block size.

You may have noticed that the solution to false data sharing isn't very portable. Each machine your application is designed to execute on may have a different cache line size. What do you do? You've got a few choices: (a) don't worry about cache lines and pay the performance penalties (maybe they won't be high), (b) #ifdef your code to work for any of the general cache line sizes and compile it appropriately, depending on the system running the application, or (c) assume the worst case and design your application to work with large cache lines (i.e., 64 bytes). If the cache line is smaller, this technique still works, you've just wasted a little extra space.

Preventing Cache Thrashing

There is one last technique that can be used to prevent cache thrashing: the brute force method: bind threads to specific processors (see Chapter 10, *Thread Extensions*). Depending on how your application was designed and the parallel model used, you may want to bind threads to specific processors. In the master-slave model, the desired goal is parallelism: one thread executing on each processor. The pthread_processor_bind_np() function can be used to guarantee that each thread executes on a different processor.

Other models, like the Pipeline Model, may experience cache thrashing if the threads execute on different processors. Again, this depends on how your application was designed. If threads are used to gain concurrency (i.e., threads in the pipeline block, waiting on I/O) and the pipeline is fast enough that data always stays in the cache, it may be best to bind the threads in the pipeline to the same processor. The application will not achieve parallelism or benefit from multiple processors, but it will benefit from concurrency if threads in the pipeline block. Cache thrashing may prohibit increased performance on multiple processors (i.e., the application runs faster on a single processor).

Before you try binding threads to processors, first verify that your application is actually experiencing cache thrashing problems and that you have no alternative. Many systems will try to schedule threads in a way that avoids cache thrashing. Once all other courses of action have been tried, consider processor binding and experiment until you find the proper solution. As you experiment, take into consideration how data is shared by the threads and, as a result, moved around between processors.

Summary

In this chapter, we discussed several software models that are suitable for multi-threaded applications. Models that are more suitable for compute-bound applications exploit parallelism. Such applications run best on multiprocessor systems. I/O-bound applications can exploit the models that are geared toward concurrent processing. The goal of the concurrent processing models is to allow the application to continue to make forward progress, even if one or more threads must block. Along with the models discussion, we presented a number of best practices for thread creation, thread synchronization, and prevention of cache trashing. The detailed summary follows:

- The Work-Crew Model provides two methods for threading an application. Method 1, for compute-bound tasks, divides a single task into multiple parts and relies on parallel computation. This model is really a simplified version of the Master-Slave Model. Method 2, for disjoint tasks, uses a thread for each task and relies on concurrency. Synchronization is provided by the thread creation, termination, and joining functions. Termination is accomplished by a simple call to `pthread_exit()`. Balancing can be achieved by having one thread per processor and by taking steps to ensure that all threads are free to execute in parallel (important mainly for Method #1).

- The Boss-Worker Model may be ideal for client/server applications. One or more *boss* threads load the work queue. *Worker* threads are signaled to perform work that has been loaded in the queue. Synchronization is typically done with two condition variables (one for the boss and the other for the workers) and a mutex that protects the queue. The type of queue selected (static or dynamic) will have an effect on performance. Termination can be accomplished with a special exit task or a flag in the dequeue function. Balance issues for the Boss-Worker Model are the same as for the Work-Crew Model when it comes to parallelism. Concurrency is not an issue.

- The Pipeline Model is analogous to the assembly line. Threads are stationed at successive points along the assembly line. As the task moves down the assembly line, it is modified at each stage. The task is complete when the data has passed through the last stage. A good application for the Pipeline Model is an application that reads, modifies, and then writes out the modified data. Such an application could have three threads - one for each stage of the pipe: read, modify, write. Synchronization for the Pipeline Model is similar to the Boss-Worker Model. When work is added to or removed from a queue, synchronization is required. Termination is achieved by having the first thread in the pipe pass and **EOF** or **EXIT** request through the pipeline. If parallelism is a goal, refer to the Work-Crew Model discussion on balancing. Queue length and the number of threads applied to each stage of the pipe are the primary concerns for balancing (or tuning) the Pipeline Model.

- In the Master-Slave Model, the master thread divides work evenly among the slave threads. All threads, including the master thread, process the task in parallel. After the work has been processed, the slave threads rendezvous and wait for more work while the master thread processes the results. This process repeats until all work has been processed. The Master-Slave Model should be used only for compute-intensive applications on multiprocessor systems. Synchronization for this model is usually implemented with barriers: The slaves wait for the master to say "go" before processing work. The slaves also rendezvous at a second barrier when processing is complete.

- The number of threads required for the best application performance is application-dependent. As a rule of thumb, compute-bound applications perform best when there is one thread per processor. I/O-bound applications should create just enough threads to keep the processors busy as other threads block, waiting for I/O to complete. Use statically created threads when the workload is known in advance. Otherwise, consider a combination of statically and dynamically created threads. For realtime behavior or compute-bound threads, use bound threads. Consider thread caching, which can be implemented with the Boss-Worker Model. If threads are assigned to work on very small tasks, the benefit of threads may be outweighed by thread management and synchronization overhead. Performance tuning is a science and an art. Experimentation is required.

- Synchronization primitives carry overhead and serialize thread execution. Structure your application to minimize the sharing of data among threads. This reduces the need to use synchronization primitives and increases application performance. Where possible, use existing functions such as pthread_join() to pass data between threads. If a thread is synchronized for other reasons (i.e., barriers), try to use this synchronization point for data access also. Obtain more than one task at a synchronization point (if appropriate). If a task requires synchronization, see if one thread performs better than two or more threads plus synchronization overhead. Place synchronization primitives as close to the shared object as possible. Do not hold a lock over a system call, especially a blocking system call. Hold locks for the shortest duration possible. Check locking granularity: too coarse means too much serialization, too fine means too much synchronization overhead. Investigate the use of read-write or spinlocks.

- Cache thrashing takes place when multiple threads running on different processors are modifying the same data. Cache thrashing can reduce performance significantly. One technique for preventing cache thrashing is to minimize the amount of data sharing among threads. Another technique is to bind threads that share data to the same processor.

Exercises

1. Write a program that implements Method #1 of the Work-Crew Model (all threads run in parallel). What kind of program did you choose for this model? Why?

2. Write a program that implements the Boss-Worker Model. What kind of program did you choose for this model? Why?

3. Write a program that implements the Pipeline Model. What kind of program did you choose for this model? Why?

4. Write a single-threaded, compute-bound program for the Master-Slave Model. Run the program on a single-processor system and measure the execution time. Multi-thread the same program, run it on the same single-processor system, and measure the execution time. Finally, run the multithreaded version of the program on a multiprocessor machine and measure the execution time. What are your findings?

5. Practice tuning the Boss-Worker Model program created in #2 by adjusting the queue length. Practice tuning the Pipeline application created in #3 by adjusting the number of threads at each stage of the pipe. In both programs, record your methodology and results.

6. In the Master-Slave program created in #4, practice modifying and printing a piece of shared data using the barriers as synchronization points. In the Pipeline program created in #3, put a system call inside the protection of synchronization primitives and measure the execution time. What happens to the performance of your program?

7. Write a program where two threads continuously modify a data element. If your system supports processor affinity, run the program with each thread locked on a different processor. Run the program again with both threads locked on the same processor. Finally, run the program "as is" and see how the system manages cache thrashing. Measure the execution times. Which scenario had the best results? Why?

Pthread Manual Pages

The pthread manual pages in this appendix come directly from Hewlett-Packard's HP-UX Release 10.30. They appear in this book exactly as they appear on-line. Many thanks to Hewlett-Packard for allowing us to publish these manual pages.

Be careful when reading the pthread manual pages (whether they are from the POSIX.1c specification or from this book). Under the **ERRORS** sections, there are two different types of descriptions.

When you see the statement:

If any of the following occur,

It indicates that this error condition must be checked for and, if it occurs, the proper error returned. All POSIX.1c-compliant systems must check for this error condition.

When you see the statement:

For each of the following conditions, if the condition is detected,

It indicates that this error condition may optionally be checked for on POSIX.1c-compliant systems. A system is not required to check for these error conditions. Some systems will ignore the optional error checks to provide better performance. The mutex lock and unlock functions are good examples of where certain error conditions may not be detected.

All optional error conditions that are not detected on HP-UX are specially noted in the manual pages. For maximum portability, do not rely on optional error conditions being detected on all systems.

If the **_POSIX_THREADS** feature test macro is defined, the following functions are available. This macro is defined on HP-UX Release 10.30:

pthread_atfork()	pthread_attr_getdetachstate()
pthread_attr_setdetachstate()	pthread_attr_destroy()
pthread_attr_getschedparam()	pthread_attr_init()
pthread_attr_setschedparam()	pthread_cancel()
pthread_cleanup_pop()	pthread_cleanup_push()
pthread_condattr_destroy()	pthread_condattr_init()
pthread_cond_broadcast()	pthread_cond_destroy()
pthread_cond_init()	pthread_cond_signal()
pthread_cond_timedwait()	pthread_cond_wait()
pthread_create()	pthread_detach()
pthread_equal()	pthread_exit()
pthread_getspecific()	pthread_join()
pthread_key_create()	pthread_key_delete()
pthread_kill()	pthread_mutexattr_destroy()
pthread_mutexattr_init()	pthread_mutex_destroy()
pthread_mutex_init()	pthread_mutex_lock()
pthread_mutex_trylock()	pthread_mutex_unlock()
pthread_once()	pthread_self()
pthread_setcancelstate()	pthread_setcanceltype()
pthread_attr_setschedparam()	pthread_setspecific()
pthread_sigmask()	pthread_testcancel()

If the **_POSIX_THREAD_ATTR_STACKADDR** feature test macro is defined, the following functions are available. This macro is defined on HP-UX Release 10.30:

pthread_attr_getstackaddr()	pthread_attr_setstackaddr()

If the **_POSIX_THREAD_ATTR_STACKSIZE** feature test macro is defined, the following functions are available. This macro is defined on HP-UX Release 10.30:

pthread_attr_getstacksize()	pthread_attr_setstacksize()

If the **_POSIX_THREAD_PRIORITY_SCHEDULING** feature test macro is defined, the following functions are available. This macro is defined on HP-UX Release 10.30:

pthread_getschedparam()	pthread_setschedparam()
pthread_attr_getinheritsched()	pthread_attr_getschedpolicy()
pthread_attr_getscope()	pthread_attr_setinheritsched()
pthread_attr_setschedpolicy()	
pthread_attr_setscope() (**PTHREAD_SCOPE_SYSTEM** only on HP-UX)	

If the **_POSIX_THREAD_PROCESS_SHARED** feature test macro is defined, the following functions are available. This macro is defined on HP-UX Release 10.30:

pthread_condattr_getpshared()   pthread_condattr_setpshared()
pthread_mutexattr_getpshared()   pthread_mutexattr_setpshared()

If the **_POSIX_THREAD_SAFE_FUNCTIONS** feature test macro is defined, the following functions are available. This macro is defined on HP-UX Release 10.30:

asctime_r()	ctime_r()	gmtime_r()
flockfile()	ftrylockfile()	funlockfile()
getc_unlocked()	getchar_unlocked()	getgrgid_r()
getgrnam_r()	getlogin_r()	getpwuid_r()
getpwnam_r()	localtime_r()	putc_unlocked()
putchar_unlocked()	rand_r()	readdir_r()
strtok_r()	ttyname_r()	

If the **_POSIX_THREAD_PRIO_PROTECT** feature test macro is defined, the following functions are available. This macro is not defined on HP-UX Release 10.30. This macro may be defined on a future release of HP-UX:

pthread_mutexattr_getprioceiling()   pthread_mutexattr_setprioceiling()
pthread_mutex_getprioceiling()   pthread_mutex_setprioceiling()

If the **_POSIX_THREAD_PRIO_INHERIT** or **_POSIX_THREAD_PRIO_PROTECT** feature test macros are defined, the following functions are available. Neither of these macros are defined on HP-UX Release 10.30. These macros may be defined on a future release of HP-UX:

pthread_mutexattr_setprotocol()   pthread_mutexattr_setprotocol()

The following list of functions are **extensions** provided on HP-UX Release 10.30:

get_expiration_time()	pthread_attr_getguardsize()
pthread_attr_setguardsize()	pthread_attr_getprocessor_np()
pthread_attr_setprocessor_np()	pthread_continue()
pthread_default_stacksize_np()	pthread_getconcurrency()
pthread_mutexattr_gettype()	pthread_mutexattr_settype()
pthread_num_processors_np()	pthread_rwlockattr_destroy()
pthread_rwlockattr_init()	pthread_rwlockattr_getpshared()
pthread_rwlockattr_setpshared()	pthread_rwlock_destroy()
pthread_rwlock_init()	pthread_rwlock_rdlock()
pthread_rwlock_tryrdlock()	pthread_rwlock_trywrlock()
pthread_rwlock_wrlock()	pthread_rwlock_unlock()
pthread_processor_bind_np()	pthread_processor_id_np()
pthread_resume_np()	pthread_setconcurrency()
pthread_suspend()	

NAME

flockfiile() – stdio lock function.
ftrylockfile() - stdio trylock function.
funlockfile() - stdio unlock function.

SYNOPSIS

#include <stdio.h>

void flockfile(FILE   *file);

int   ftrylockfile(FILE   *file);

void funlockfile(FILE   *file);

PARAMETERS

file   File to be locked.

DESCRIPTION

These functions provide for explicit application-level lock of stdio (**FILE ***) objects. They can be used by any thread within the application to delineate a sequence of I/O instructions that are to be executed as a unit atomically.

The **flockfile()** function is used by a thread to lock (acquire ownership of) a **FILE *** object. If the object is not available, the calling thread is suspended until it can lock the object.

The **flocktryfile()** function is identical to the **ftrylock()** function except that if the object could not be locked after one attempt an error is returned to the calling thread.

The **funlockfile()** function releases a lock (relinquishes ownership of) on a **FILE *** object. Undefined behavior results if a thread releases a lock on an object that it does not own.

Logically, there is a lock count associated with each (**FILE ***) object. The count is implicitly initialized to zero when the object is created. When the lock count is zero, the object is in the unlocked state without an owner. When the lock count is positive, the object is in the locked state with an owning thread. When the **flockfile()** function is called, if either the lock count is zero, or the lock count is positive with the calling thread as the owner, the lock count is incremented and the function returns. Otherwise, the calling thread suspends itself, waiting for the lock count to reach zero. Each call to **funlockfile()** decrements the lock count. When the count reaches zero, the object is unlocked and available to be locked by other threads.

All functions that reference **FILE *** objects behave as if they use **flockfile()** and **funlockfile()** internally to obtain ownership of the **FILE *** objects.

RETURN VALUE

The **flockfile()** and **funlockfile()** functions do not have return values. The **ftrylockfile()** returns zero on success and non-zero if the lock could not be acquired.

ERRORS

No errors are defined for these functions.

AUTHOR

flockfile(), **ftrylockfile()**, and **funlockfile()** were developed by POSIX.

SEE ALSO

getc_unlocked(3), getchar_unlocked(3), putc_unlocked(3), putchar_unlocked(3).

NAME

get_expiration_time() – add a specific time interval to the current absolute system time.

SYNOPSIS

#include <time.h>

int get_expiration_time(
        struct timespec   ***delta,**
        struct timespec   ***abstime**
);

PARAMETERS

delta   Number of seconds and nanoseconds to add to the current system time.

abstime   Output parameter for the absolute system time after adding *delta* to the current absolute system time.

DESCRIPTION

The **get_expiration_time()** function adds a specific time interval to the current absolute system time and returns the new absolute time. This new absolute time is used as the expiration time in a call to *pthread_cond_timedwait*(3T).

The *delta* argument represents the number of seconds and nanoseconds to add to the current system time. On return from this function, the *abstime* argument contains the absolute system time that will be used in a call to *pthread_cond_timedwait*(3T).

RETURN VALUE

Upon successful completion, **get_expiration_time()** returns zero.
Otherwise, an error number is returned to indicate the error (the **errno** variable is not set).

ERRORS

If any of the following occur, the **get_expiration_time()** function returns the corresponding error number:

[EINVAL]   The value specified by *delta* or *abstime* is invalid.

AUTHOR

get_expiration_time() was developed by X/Open.

SEE ALSO

pthread_cond_timedwait(3T).

STANDARDS CONFORMANCE

get_expiration_time():X/Open.

NAME

pthread_atfork() – register fork handlers.

SYNOPSIS

#include <pthread.h>

int pthread_atfork(
>   **void   (*prepare)(void),**
>   **void   (*parent)(void),**
>   **void   (*child)(void)**
);

PARAMETERS

prepare   This function is called before performing the *fork*().

parent   This function is called in the parent process after performing the *fork*().

child   This function is called in the child process after performing the *fork*().

DESCRIPTION

The **pthread_atfork()** function allows an application to install fork handlers. These fork handlers will be called before and after a *fork()* operation. These handlers will be called in the context of the thread calling *fork()*. Similar to the *atexit()* handlers, the application does not need to do anything special for these fork handlers to be called. They will be invoked by the system when a *fork()* operation occurs.

The *prepare()* function is called before the *fork*() operation in the parent process. The *parent()* function is called after the *fork*() operation in the parent process. The *child()* function is called after the *fork*() operation in the child process.

If a fork handler is not needed in one or more of these three places, the appropriate fork handler parameter may be set to **NULL**.

A process may install multiple fork handling functions. The *parent()* and *child()* fork handlers will be called in the order in which they were installed (i.e., First-In, First-Out). The *prepare()* fork handlers will be called in the opposite order (i.e., Last-In, First-Out).

RETURN VALUE

Upon successful completion, **pthread_atfork()** returns zero. Otherwise, an error number is returned to indicate the error (the **errno** variable is not set).

ERRORS

If any of the following occur, the **pthread_atfork()** function returns the corresponding error number:

[ENOMEM]   There is insufficient table space to install the fork handlers.

AUTHOR

pthread_atfork() was derived from the IEEE POSIX P1003.1c standard.

SEE ALSO

atexit(3), fork(2).

STANDARDS CONFORMANCE

pthread_atfork():POSIX 1003.1c.

NAME

pthread_attr_init() – initialize a thread attributes object.
pthread_attr_destroy() – destroy a thread attributes object.

SYNOPSIS

#include <pthread.h>

int pthread_attr_init(
        pthread_attr_t   *attr
);

int pthread_attr_destroy(
        pthread_attr_t   *attr
);

PARAMETERS

attr   Pointer to the thread attributes object to be initialized or destroyed.

DESCRIPTION

pthread_attr_init() initializes a thread attributes object *attr* with the default value for all the thread attributes.

When a thread attributes object is used to create a thread, the values of the individual attributes determine the characteristics of the new thread. Attributes objects act like additional parameters to object creation. A single attributes object can be used in multiple calls to *pthread_create()*.

After a thread attributes object has been used to initialize one or more threads, any function affecting the attributes object does not affect the previously created threads.

The thread attributes and their default values are:

stacksize	POSIX.1c does not define a default value. On HP-UX release 10.30, the default value is 64K.
guardsize	The default value is **PAGESIZE** bytes.
stackaddr	The default value is **NULL**.
detachstate	The default value is **PTHREAD_CREATE_JOINABLE**.
contentionscope	POSIX.1c does not define a default value. On HP-UX release 10.30, the current default value is **PTHREAD_SCOPE_SYSTEM**. Note: This default value will change to **PTHREAD_SCOPE_PROCESS** when HP-UX supports the MxN Threads Model.
inheritsched	POSIX.1c does not define a default value. On HP-UX, the default value is **PTHREAD_INHERIT_SCHED**.
schedpolicy	POSIX.1c does not define a default value. On HP-UX, the default value is **SCHED_TIMESHARE**.
schedparam	POSIX.1c does not define a default value.
processor	The default value is **PTHREAD_SPUINHERIT_NP**.
binding_type	The default value is **PTHREAD_BIND_ADVISORY_NP**.

If an initialized thread attributes object is reinitialized, the initialization results in undefined behavior.

pthread_attr_destroy() destroys the thread attributes object *attr*. The destroyed thread attributes object ceases to exist and its resources are reclaimed. Referencing the object after it has been destroyed results in undefined behavior. A destroyed thread attributes object can be reinitialized using thread attribute initialization routine **pthread_attr_init**().

Threads that have already been created using this attributes object are not affected by the destruction of the thread attributes object.

RETURN VALUE

Upon successful completion, **pthread_attr_init**() and **pthread_attr_destroy**() return zero. Otherwise, an error number is returned to indicate the error (the **errno** variable is not set).

ERRORS

If any of the following occur, the **pthread_attr_init**() function returns the corresponding error number:

[ENOMEM]   There is insufficient memory available in which to initialize the pthread attributes object.

[EINVAL]   The value specified by *attr* is invalid.

If any of the following occur, the **pthread_attr_destroy**() function returns the corresponding error number:

[EINVAL]   The value specified by *attr* is invalid.

AUTHOR

pthread_attr_init() and **pthread_attr_destroy**() were derived from the IEEE POSIX P1003.1c standard.

SEE ALSO

pthread_create(3T).

STANDARDS CONFORMANCE

pthread_attr_init():POSIX 1003.1c.
pthread_attr_destroy():POSIX 1003.1c.

NAME

pthread_attr_setdetachstate() – set the detachstate attribute
pthread_attr_getdetachstate() – get the detachstate attribute

pthread_attr_setstacksize() – set the stacksize attribute
pthread_attr_getstacksize() – get the stacksize attribute

pthread_attr_setstackaddr() – set the stackaddr attribute
pthread_attr_getstackaddr() – get the stackaddr attribute

pthread_attr_setguardsize() – set the guardsize attribute
pthread_attr_getguardsize() – get the guardsize attribute

pthread_attr_setinheritsched() – set the inheritsched attribute
pthread_attr_getinheritsched() – get the inheritsched attribute

pthread_attr_setschedpolicy() – set the schedpolicy attribute
pthread_attr_getschedpolicy() – get the schedpolicy attribute

pthread_attr_setschedparam() – set the schedparam attributes
pthread_attr_getschedparam() – get the schedparam attributes

pthread_attr_setscope() – set the contentionscope attribute
pthread_attr_getscope() – get the contentionscope attribute

pthread_attr_setprocessor_np() – set the processor and binding_type attributes
pthread_attr_getprocessor_np() – get the processor and binding_type attributes

SYNOPSIS

#include <pthread.h>

```
int pthread_attr_setdetachstate(pthread_attr_t    *attr,    int  detachstate);
int pthread_attr_getdetachstate(pthread_attr_t    *attr,    int *detachstate);

int pthread_attr_setstacksize(pthread_attr_t      *attr,    size_t  stacksize);
int pthread_attr_getstacksize(pthread_attr_t      *attr,    size_t *stacksize);

int pthread_attr_setstackaddr(pthread_attr_t      *attr,    void  *stackaddr);
int pthread_attr_getstackaddr(pthread_attr_t      *attr,    void **stackaddr);

int pthread_attr_setguardsize(pthread_attr_t      *attr,    size_t  guardsize);
int pthread_attr_getguardsize(pthread_attr_t      *attr,    size_t *guardsize);

int pthread_attr_setinheritsched(pthread_attr_t   *attr,    int  inheritsched);
int pthread_attr_getinheritsched(pthread_attr_t   *attr,    int *inheritsched);

int pthread_attr_setschedpolicy(pthread_attr_t    *attr,    int  policy);
int pthread_attr_getschedpolicy(pthread_attr_t    *attr,    int *policy);

int pthread_attr_setscope(pthread_attr_t      *attr,    int  contentionscope);
int pthread_attr_getscope(pthread_attr_t      *attr,    int *contentionscope);

int pthread_attr_setprocessor_np(pthread_attr_t   *attr,
                                 pthread_spu_t    processor,
                                 int              binding_type);
int pthread_attr_getprocessor_np(pthread_attr_t   *attr,
                                 pthread_spu_t    *processor,
                                 int              *binding_type);
```

int pthread_attr_setschedparam(pthread_attr_t *attr,
                              struct sched_param *param);

int pthread_attr_getschedparam(pthread_attr_t *attr,
                              struct sched_param *param);

PARAMETERS

attr   Pointer to the thread attributes object whose attributes are to be set/
                   retrieved.

detachstate   This parameter either specifies the new value of the *detachstate*
                   attribute (set function) or it points to the memory location where the
                   detachstate attribute of *attr* is to be returned (get function).

stacksize   This parameter either specifies the new value of the *stacksize*
                   attribute (set function) or it points to the memory location where the
                   stacksize attribute of *attr* is to be returned (get function).

stackaddr   This parameter either specifies the new value of the *stackaddr*
                   attribute (set function) or it points to the memory location where the
                   stackaddr attribute of *attr* is to be returned (get function).

guardsize   This parameter either specifies the new value of the *guardsize*
                   attribute (set function) or it points to the memory location where the
                   guardsize attribute of *attr* is to be returned (get function).

inheritsched   This parameter either specifies the new value of the *inheritsched*
                   attribute (set function) or it points to the memory location where the
                   inheritsched attribute of *attr* is to be returned (get function).

policy   This parameter either specifies the new value of the *schedpolicy*
                   attribute (set function) or it points to the memory location where the
                   schedpolicy attribute of *attr* is to be returned (get function).

param   This parameter either specifies the new values of the *schedparam*
                   attributes (set function) or it points to the memory location where the
                   schedparam attributes of *attr* are to be returned (get function).

contentionscope
                   This parameter either specifies the new value of the *contentionscope*
                   attribute (set function) or it points to the memory location where the
                   contentionscope attribute of *attr* is to be returned (get function).

processor   This parameter either specifies the new value of the *processor*
                   attribute (set function) or it points to the memory location where the
                   processor attribute of *attr* is to be returned (get function).

binding_type   This parameter either specifies the new values of the *binding_type*
                   attributes (set function) or it points to the memory location where the
                   binding_type attributes of *attr* are to be returned (get function).

DESCRIPTION

The attributes object *attr* must have previously been initialized with the function
pthread_attr_init() before these functions are called.

ATTRIBUTE: detachstate

The legal values for the *detachstate* attribute are:

PTHREAD_CREATE_DETACHED

> This option causes all threads created with *attr* to be in the detached state. The resources associated with threads having this state are reclaimed automatically by the system when the threads terminate. Calling the *pthread_detach( )* or *pthread_join( )* function for threads created with this attribute results in an error.

PTHREAD_CREATE_JOINABLE

> This option causes all threads created with *attr* to be in the joinable state. The resources associated with threads having this state are not reclaimed when the threads terminate. An application must call the *pthread_detach( )* or *pthread_join( )* functions for threads created with this attribute to reclaim the system resources.

The default value of *detachstate* is **PTHREAD_CREATE_JOINABLE**.

pthread_attr_setdetachstate() is used to set the *detachstate* attribute in the initialized attributes object *attr*. The new value of the *detachstate* attribute is passed to this function in the *detachstate* parameter.

pthread_attr_getdetachstate() retrieves the value of the *detachstate* attribute from the thread attributes object *attr*. This value is returned in the *detachstate* parameter.

ATTRIBUTE: stacksize

The legal values for the *stacksize* attribute are:

PTHREAD_STACKSIZE_MIN

> This option specifies that the size of the user stack for threads created with this attributes object will be of default stack size. This value is the minimum stack size (in bytes) required for a thread. This minimum value may not be acceptable for all threads.

<stacksize>

> This defines the size (in bytes) of the user stack for threads created with this attributes object. This value must be greater than or equal to the minimum stack size **PTHREAD_STACKSIZE_MIN**.

POSIX.1c does not define a default value. On HP-UX release 10.30, the default value of the *stacksize* attribute is 64K.

pthread_attr_setstacksize() is used to set the *stacksize* attribute in the initialized attributes object *attr*. The new value of the *stacksize* attribute is passed to this function in the *stacksize* parameter.

pthread_attr_getstacksize() retrieves the value of the *stacksize* attribute from the thread attributes object *attr*. This value is returned in the *stacksize* parameter.

ATTRIBUTE: stackaddr

The legal values for the *stackaddr* attribute are:

NULL

> This option specifies that the storage for the user stack of the threads created with this attributes object will be allocated and deallocated by

the threads library. The application does not need to allocate and manage thread stacks.

\<stack_address\>

This option specifies the base address of a stack that any created thread will use. The application is completely responsible for allocating, managing, and deallocating these stacks. Some options for allocation of storage are the *malloc(3)*, *brk(2)*, and *mmap(2)* functions. Note: if this option is used, only one thread should be created with this attributes object. If multiple threads are created, they will all use the same stack.

The default value of the *stackaddr* attribute is **NULL**.

pthread_attr_setstackaddr() is used to set the *stackaddr* attribute in the initialized attributes object *attr*. The new value of the *stackaddr* attribute is passed to this function in the *stackaddr* parameter.

pthread_attr_getstackaddr() retrieves the value of the *stackaddr* attribute from the thread attributes object *attr*. This value is returned in the *stackaddr* parameter.

The *guardsize* attribute is ignored if the storage for the thread's user stack is not allocated by the library (i.e., the *stackaddr* attribute is not **NULL**).

ATTRIBUTE: guardsize

The *guardsize* attribute allows an application to specify the size of the guard area for threads created with this attributes object. The size of the guard area is specified in bytes. Most systems will round up the guard size to a multiple of the system configurable variable **PAGESIZE**. If the value zero is specified, a guard area will not be created.

The default value of *guardsize* is **PAGESIZE** bytes. The actual value of **PAGESIZE** is implementation-dependent and may not be the same on all implementations. The *guardsize* attribute is ignored if the storage for the user stack is not allocated by the pthread library. The application is responsible for protecting against stack overflow.

pthread_attr_setguardsize() is used to set the *guardsize* attribute in the initialized attributes object *attr*. The new value of the *guardsize* attribute is passed to this function in the *guardsize* parameter.

pthread_attr_getguardsize() retrieves the value of the *guardsize* attribute from the thread attributes object *attr*. This value is returned in the *guardsize* parameter. If the guard area is rounded up to a multiple of **PAGESIZE**, a call to this function shall store in the *guardsize* parameter the guard size specified in the previous **pthread_attr_setguardsize()** function call.

ATTRIBUTE: inheritsched

The legal values for the *inheritsched* attribute are:

PTHREAD_INHERIT_SCHED

This option specifies that the scheduling policy and associated attributes are to be inherited from the creating thread. The scheduling policy and associated attributes in the *attr* argument will be ignored when a thread is created with *attr*.

PTHREAD_EXPLICIT_SCHED

This option specifies that the scheduling policy and associated attributes for the created thread(s) are to be taken from this attributes object. These values will not be inherited from the creating thread.

POSIX.1c does not define a default value for the *inheritsched* attribute. On HP-UX, the default value is **PTHREAD_INHERIT_SCHED**.

pthread_attr_setinheritsched() is used to set the *inheritsched* attribute in the initialized attributes object *attr*. The new value of the *inheritsched* attribute is passed in the *inheritsched* parameter.

pthread_attr_getinheritsched() retrieves the value of the *inheritsched* attribute from the thread attributes object *attr*. This value is returned in the *inheritsched* parameter.

ATTRIBUTE: schedpolicy

The *schedpolicy* attribute allows threads created with this attributes object to use a specific scheduling policy. To use this attribute, the *inheritsched* attribute must be set to **PTHREAD_EXPLICIT_SCHED**. For a complete list of valid scheduling policies, refer to *sched_setscheduler*(2) and *<sched.h>*.

POSIX.1c does not specify a default value for the *schedpolicy* attribute. On HP-UX, the default value for system scope threads is **SCHED_TIMESHARE**.

pthread_attr_setschedpolicy() is used to set the *schedpolicy* attribute in the initialized attributes object *attr*. The new value of the *schedpolicy* attribute is passed to this function in the *policy* parameter.

pthread_attr_getschedpolicy() retrieves the value of the *schedpolicy* attribute from the thread attributes object *attr*. This value is returned in the *policy* parameter.

ATTRIBUTE: schedparam

The legal values for the *schedparam* attribute associated with the *schedpolicy* attribute vary depending upon the scheduling policy. For the **SCHED_FIFO** and **SCHED_RR** scheduling policies, only the *sched_priority* member of the *schedparam* attribute is required. Legal values for *sched_priority* can be obtained through *sched_get_priority_max*(2) and *sched_get_priority_min*(2). The required contents of *schedparam* for other scheduling policies is undefined. For a complete list of required and valid scheduling parameters for all scheduling policies, refer to *sched_setparam*(2) and *<sched.h>*.

pthread_attr_setschedparam() is used to set the *schedparam* attribute in the initialized attributes object *attr*. The new value of the *schedparam* attribute is passed to this function in the *param* parameter.

pthread_attr_getschedparam() retrieves the value of the *schedparam* attribute from the thread attributes object *attr*. This value is returned in the *param* parameter.

ATTRIBUTE: contentionscope

The legal values for the *contentionscope* attribute are:

PTHREAD_SCOPE_SYSTEM
> Threads created with this contention scope contend for resources with all other threads in the system (and within the same scheduling domain). This attribute is generally used to indicate that the user thread should be bound directly to a kernel-scheduled entity.

PTHREAD_SCOPE_PROCESS

Threads created with this contention scope contend directly with other threads within their process that were created with this scheduling contention scope. This attribute is generally used to indicate that the user thread should be unbound (in the Mx1 and MxN Threads Model).

This value is currently not supported on HP-UX release 10.30.

The default value of the *contentionscope* attribute is not defined by POSIX.1c. On HP-UX release 10.30, the current default value of the *contentionscope* attribute is **PTHREAD_SCOPE_SYSTEM**. Note: This default value will change to **PTHREAD_SCOPE_PROCESS** when HP-UX supports the MxN Threads Model.

pthread_attr_setscope() is used to set the *contentionscope* attribute in the initialized attributes object *attr*. The new value of the *contentionscope* attribute is passed to this function in the *contentionscope* parameter.

pthread_attr_getscope() retrieves the value of the *contentionscope* attribute from the thread attributes object *attr*. This value is returned in the *contentionscope* parameter.

ATTRIBUTES: processor and binding_type

The legal values for the *processor* attribute are:

PTHREAD_SPUINHERIT_NP

Threads created with this *processor* attribute inherit their processor binding attributes from the creating thread. This is the default value of the *processor* attribute. The *binding_type* attribute is ignored.

PTHREAD_SPUFLOAT_NP

Threads created with this *processor* attribute are allowed to execute on any processor the system chooses. No processor binding is maintained. The *binding_type* attribute is ignored.

(pthread_spu_t) processor_id

Threads created with this *processor* attribute are bound to the processor specified in the *processor* parameter. The type of binding (advisory or mandatory) is specified in the *binding_type* attribute.

The legal values for the *binding_type* attribute (if the *processor* attribute is not **PTHREAD_SPUINHERIT_NP** or **PTHREAD_SPUFLOAT_NP**) are:

PTHREAD_BIND_ADVISORY_NP

Threads created with this *binding_type* attribute have advisory processor binding. Refer to *pthread_processor_bind_np()* for more information on advisory binding. This is the default value of the *binding_type* attribute.

PTHREAD_BIND_FORCED_NP

Threads created with this *binding_type* attribute have forced (or mandatory) processor binding. Refer to *pthread_processor_bind_np()* for more information on forced binding.

The default value of the *processor* attribute is **PTHREAD_SPUINHERIT_NP**. The default value of the *binding_type* attribute is **PTHREAD_BIND_ADVISORY_NP**.

pthread_attr_setprocessor_np() is used to set the *processor* and *binding_type* attributes in the initialized attributes object *attr*. The new values of the *processor* and *binding_type* attributes are passed to this function in the *processor* and *binding_type* parameters, respectively.

pthread_attr_getprocessor_np() retrieves the values of the *processor* and *binding_type* attributes from the thread attributes object *attr*. These values are returned in the *processor* and *binding_type* parameters, respectively.

RETURN VALUE

Upon successful completion, **pthread_attr_setstacksize()**, **pthread_attr_getstacksize()**, **pthread_attr_setstackaddr()**, **pthread_attr_getstackaddr()**, **pthread_attr_setguardsize()**, **pthread_attr_getguardsize()**, **pthread_attr_setdetachstate()**, **pthread_attr_getdetachstate()**, **pthread_attr_setinheritsched()**, **pthread_attr_getinheritsched()**, **pthread_attr_setschedpolicy()**, **pthread_attr_getschedpolicy()**, **pthread_attr_setschedparam()**, **pthread_attr_getschedparam()**, **pthread_attr_setprocessor_np()**, **pthread_attr_getprocessor_np()**, **pthread_attr_setscope()**, and **pthread_attr_getscope()** return zero. Otherwise, an error number is returned to indicate the error (the **errno** variable is not set).

ERRORS

If any of the following occur, the **pthread_attr_setscope()**, **pthread_attr_getscope()**, **pthread_attr_setinheritsched()**, **pthread_attr_getinheritsched()**, **pthread_attr_setschedpolicy()**, and **pthread_attr_getschedpolicy()** functions return the corresponding error number:

[ENOSYS]   **_POSIX_THREAD_PRIORITY_SCHEDULING** is not defined and these functions are not supported.

If any of the following occur, the **pthread_attr_getstackaddr()** and **pthread_attr_setstackaddr()** functions return the corresponding error number:

[ENOSYS]   **_POSIX_THREAD_ATTR_STACKADDR** is not defined and these functions are not supported.

If any of the following occur, the **pthread_attr_getstacksize()** and **pthread_attr_setstacksize()** functions return the corresponding error number:

[ENOSYS]   **_POSIX_THREAD_ATTR_STACKSIZE** is not defined and these functions are not supported.

If any of the following occur, **pthread_attr_setstacksize()**, **pthread_attr_getstacksize()**, **pthread_attr_setstackaddr()**, **pthread_attr_getstackaddr()**, **pthread_attr_setguardsize()**, **pthread_attr_getguardsize()**, **pthread_attr_setdetachstate()**, **pthread_attr_getdetachstate()**, **pthread_attr_setinheritsched()**, **pthread_attr_getinheritsched()**, **pthread_attr_setschedpolicy()**, **pthread_attr_getschedpolicy()**, **pthread_attr_setschedparam()**, **pthread_attr_getschedparam()**, **pthread_attr_setprocessor_np()**, **pthread_attr_getprocessor_np()**, **pthread_attr_setscope()**, and **pthread_attr_getscope()** return the corresponding error number:

[EINVAL]   The value specified by *attr* is invalid.

[EINVAL]   The value specified by *stacksize* is less than the minimum required stacksize of **PTHREAD_STACK_MIN** or exceeds a system-imposed limit.

[EINVAL]   *detachstate*, *guardsize*, *inheritsched*, *policy*, *processor*, *binding_type*, *param*, or *scope* contains an invalid value.

[ENOTSUP]   The value contained in *policy* is not a supported value.

AUTHOR

pthread_attr_setstacksize(), **pthread_attr_getstacksize**(), **pthread_attr_setstackaddr**(), **pthread_attr_getstackaddr**(), **pthread_attr_setdetachstate**(), **pthread_attr_getdetachstate**(), **pthread_attr_setinheritsched**(), **pthread_attr_getinheritsched**(), **pthread_attr_setschedpolicy**(), **pthread_attr_getschedpolicy**(), **pthread_attr_setschedparam**(), **pthread_attr_getschedparam**(), **pthread_attr_setscope**(), and **pthread_attr_getscope**() were derived from the IEEE POSIX P1003.1c standard.

pthread_attr_setguardsize() and **pthread_attr_getguardsize**() were developed by X/Open.

pthread_attr_setprocessor_np() and **pthread_attr_getprocessor_np**() were developed by HP.

SEE ALSO

pthread_create(3T), pthread_attr_init(3T), pthread_attr_destroy(3T).

STANDARDS CONFORMANCE

pthread_attr_setstacksize():POSIX 1003.1c.
pthread_attr_getstacksize():POSIX 1003.1c.
pthread_attr_setstackaddr():POSIX 1003.1c.
pthread_attr_getstackaddr():POSIX 1003.1c.
pthread_attr_setguardsize():X/Open.
pthread_attr_getguardsize():X/Open.
pthread_attr_setdetachstate():POSIX 1003.1c.
pthread_attr_getdetachstate():POSIX 1003.1c.
pthread_attr_setinheritsched():POSIX 1003.1c.
pthread_attr_getinheritsched():POSIX 1003.1c.
pthread_attr_setschedpolicy():POSIX 1003.1c.
pthread_attr_getschedpolicy():POSIX 1003.1c.
pthread_attr_setschedparam():POSIX 1003.1c.
pthread_attr_getschedparam():POSIX 1003.1c.
pthread_attr_setscope():POSIX 1003.1c.
pthread_attr_getscope():POSIX 1003.1c.
pthread_attr_setprocessor_np():None.
pthread_attr_getprocessor_np():None.

NAME

pthread_cancel() – cancel execution of a thread

SYNOPSIS

#include <pthread.h>

int pthread_cancel(
         pthread_t   thread
);

PARAMETERS

thread   Target thread to be canceled.

DESCRIPTION

pthread_cancel() requests that *thread* (hereby referred to as target thread) be canceled. It allows a thread to terminate the execution of any thread in the process in a controlled manner.

The target thread's cancelability state and type determine when the cancellation takes effect. Cancellation only occurs when the target thread's cancelability state is **PTHREAD_CANCEL_ENABLE**. When the target thread's cancelability state is **PTHREAD_CANCEL_DISABLE**, cancellation requests against the target thread are held pending and will be acted upon when cancellation is enabled.

When the cancelability type is **PTHREAD_CANCEL_ASYNCHRONOUS** for the target *thread*, new or pending cancellation requests are acted upon at any time. When the target thread's cancelability type is **PTHREAD_CANCEL_DEFERRED**, cancellation requests are held pending until the target thread reaches a cancellation point (see below).

If the target thread's cancelability state is disabled, the cancelability type is ignored. When cancelability is enabled, the cancelability type will take effect.

When the cancellation is acted on, the cancellation cleanup handlers for *thread* are called. The cancellation cleanup handlers are called in the opposite order in which they were installed. When the last cancellation cleanup handler returns, the thread-specific data destructor functions for *thread* are called. When the last destructor function returns, *thread* shall be terminated.

The caller of **pthread_cancel**() will not wait for the target thread to be canceled.

CANCELLATION POINTS

Cancellation points are points inside of certain functions where a thread must act on any pending cancellation request when cancelability is enabled if the function would block.

RETURN VALUE

Upon successful completion, **pthread_cancel**() returns zero. Otherwise, an error number is returned to indicate the error (the **errno** variable is not set).

ERRORS

For each of the following conditions, if the condition is detected, the **pthread_cancel**() function returns the corresponding error number:

[ESRCH]   No thread could be found corresponding to *thread*.

WARNINGS

Use of asynchronous cancelability while holding resources that need to be released may result in resource loss. Applications must carefully follow static lexical scoping rules in their execution behavior. For instance, the use of *setjmp*(3), return, goto, etc., to leave user-defined cancellation scopes without doing the necessary scope pop will result in undefined behavior.

AUTHOR

pthread_cancel() was derived from the IEEE POSIX P1003.1c standard.

SEE ALSO

pthread_exit(3T), pthread_join(3T), pthread_setcancelstate(3T), pthread_setcanceltype(3T), pthread_cleanup_push(3T), pthread_cleanup_pop(3T), pthread_cond_wait(3T), pthread_cond_timedwait(3T).

STANDARDS CONFORMANCE

pthread_cancel():POSIX 1003.1c.

NAME

pthread_cleanup_push() – register a cancellation cleanup handler
pthread_cleanup_pop() – remove a cancellation cleanup handler

SYNOPSIS

#include <pthread.h>

void   pthread_cleanup_push(void   (*routine)(void *), void   *arg);

void   pthread_cleanup_pop(int   execute);

PARAMETERS

routine   Routine registered as a cancellation cleanup handler.

arg   Parameter to be passed to the cancellation cleanup handler *routine()*.

execute   Indicates if the popped cancellation cleanup handler is to be executed.

DESCRIPTION

pthread_cleanup_push() installs the cancellation cleanup handler *routine* onto the calling thread's cancellation cleanup stack. This handler will be popped from the calling thread's cancellation cleanup stack and called with the *arg* parameter when any of the following occur:

(a) the thread calls *pthread_exit()* or returns from its start routine.

(b) the thread acts upon a cancellation request.

(c) the thread calls **pthread_cleanup_pop()** with a non-zero *execute* argument.

When a thread terminates, it will execute each of the cancellation cleanup handlers on its cancellation cleanup stack. These handlers will be popped and executed in the reverse order that they were installed (Last-In, First-Out).

pthread_cleanup_pop() removes the cancellation cleanup handler at the top of the calling thread's cancellation stack. If *execute* is non-zero, the cancellation cleanup handler is called after it is removed from the cancellation stack. If *execute* is zero, the cancellation cleanup handler is simply removed and will not be called.

pthread_cleanup_push() and **pthread_cleanup_pop()** must appear as statements and in pairs within the same lexical scope. These functions may be macros which contain the opening '}' in the push function and the closing '}' in the pop function.

Calling *longjmp()* or *siglongjmp()* is undefined if there have been any calls to **pthread_cleanup_push()** or **pthread_cleanup_pop()** made without the matching call since the jump buffer was filled.

Calling *longjmp()* or *siglongjmp()* from inside a cancellation cleanup handler results in undefined behavior unless the corresponding *setjmp()* or *sigsetjmp()* was also done inside the cancellation cleanup handler.

RETURN VALUE

The **pthread_cleanup_push()** and **pthread_cleanup_pop()** functions must be used as statements. They do not have return values or errors.

WARNINGS

The functions **pthread_cleanup_push()** and **pthread_cleanup_pop()** must be called in the same lexical scope or the result is undefined behavior.

SEE ALSO

pthread_cancel(3T), pthread_setcancelstate(3T), pthread_setcanceltype(3T).

NAME

pthread_cond_init() – initialize a condition variable.
pthread_cond_destroy() – destroy a condition variable.

SYNOPSIS

#include <pthread.h>

int pthread_cond_init(
        pthread_cond_t   *cond,
        const pthread_condattr_t   *attr
);

pthread_cond_t   cond = PTHREAD_COND_INITIALIZER;

int pthread_cond_destroy(
        pthread_cond_t   *cond
);

PARAMETERS

cond   Pointer to the condition variable to be initialized or destroyed.

attr   Pointer to the attributes object that defines the characteristics of the condition variable to be initialized. If the pointer is **NULL**, default attributes are used.

DESCRIPTION

The **pthread_cond_init()** function initializes the condition variable *cond* with the attributes *attr*. If *attr* is **NULL**, the default condition variable attributes are used to initialize the attributes object. Refer to *pthread_condattr_init( )* for a list of the default condition variable attributes. After successful initialization, the condition variable may be used in condition variable operations. A condition variable should be initialized only once or the resulting behavior is undefined. The *pthread_once( )* function provides a way to ensure that a condition variable is only initialized once.

The macro **PTHREAD_COND_INITIALIZER** can be used to initialize condition variables that are statically allocated. These condition variables will be initialized with default attributes. The **pthread_cond_init()** function does not need to be called for statically initialized condition variables.

If the *process-shared* attribute in the condition variable attributes object referenced by *attr* is defined as **PTHREAD_PROCESS_SHARED**, the condition variable must be allocated such that the processes sharing the condition variable have access to it. This may be done through the memory-mapping functions (see *mmap*(2)) or the shared memory functions (see *shmget*(2)).

The **pthread_cond_destroy()** function destroys the condition variable *cond*. This function may set *cond* to an invalid value. The destroyed condition variable can be reinitialized using the function **pthread_cond_init()**. If the condition variable is used after destruction in any condition variable call, the resulting behavior is undefined.

A condition variable should be destroyed only when there are no threads currently blocked on it. Destroying a condition variable that is currently in use results in undefined behavior.

RETURN VALUE

Upon successful completion, **pthread_cond_init**() and **pthread_cond_destroy**() return zero. Otherwise, an error number is returned to indicate the error (the **errno** variable is not set).

ERRORS

If any of the following occur, the **pthread_cond_init**() function returns the corresponding error number:

[EAGAIN] The system does not have the available resources (other than memory) to initialize the condition variable.

[ENOMEM] There is insufficient memory available in which to initialize the condition variable.

For each of the following conditions, if the condition is detected, the **pthread_cond_init**() function returns the corresponding error number:

[EINVAL] The value specified by *cond* or *attr* is invalid.

[EBUSY] The specified condition variable is an already initialized condition variable.

[EFAULT] The *cond* parameter points to an illegal address.

For each of the following conditions, if the condition is detected, the **pthread_cond_destroy**() function returns the corresponding error number:

[EINVAL] *cond* is not a valid condition variable.

[EBUSY] An attempt to destroy *cond* while it is in use by another thread.

WARNING

The space for condition variable must be allocated before calling **pthread_cond_init**(). Undefined behavior will result if the *process-shared* attribute of *attr* is **PTHREAD_PROCESS_SHARED** and the space allocated for the condition variable is not accessible to cooperating threads.

AUTHOR

pthread_cond_init() and **pthread_cond_destroy**() were derived from the IEEE POSIX P1003.1c standard.

SEE ALSO

pthread_cond_wait(3T), pthread_cond_timedwait(3T), pthread_cond_signal(3T), pthread_cond_broadcast(3T)

STANDARDS CONFORMANCE

pthread_cond_init():POSIX 1003.1c.
pthread_cond_destroy():POSIX 1003.1c.

NAME

pthread_cond_signal() – unblock one thread waiting on a condition variable.
pthread_cond_broadcast – unblock all threads waiting on a condition variable.

SYNOPSIS

#include <pthread.h>

int pthread_cond_signal(
        pthread_cond_t   *cond
);

int pthread_cond_broadcast(
        pthread_cond_t   *cond
);

PARAMETERS

cond   Pointer to the condition variable to be signaled or broadcast.

DESCRIPTION

The **pthread_cond_signal**() function is used to wake-up one of the threads that are
waiting for the occurrence of a condition associated with the condition variable *cond*.
If there are no threads blocked on *cond*, this function has no effect. If more than one
thread is blocked on *cond*, the scheduling policy determines which thread is
unblocked. It is possible that more than one thread can be unblocked due to a spurious
wakeup.

The **pthread_cond_broadcast**() function is used to wake-up all threads that are
waiting for the occurrence of a condition associated with the condition variable *cond*.
If there are no threads blocked on *cond*, this function has no effect. If more than one
thread is blocked on *cond*, the scheduling policy determines the order in which
threads are unblocked.

The condition variable denoted by *cond* must have been dynamically initialized by a
call to *pthread_cond_init()* or statically initialized with the macro
PTHREAD_COND_INITIALIZER.

An unblocked thread will reacquire the mutex it held when it started the condition
wait before returning from **pthread_cond_wait**() or **pthread_cond_timedwait**().
The threads that are unblocked contend for the mutex according to their scheduling
policy and priority.

The **pthread_cond_signal**() or **pthread_cond_broadcast**() functions can be called
by a thread whether or not it currently owns the condition variable's associated
mutex. For predictable scheduling behavior and to prevent lost wake-ups, the mutex
should be held when signaling a condition variable.

RETURN VALUE

Upon successful completion, **pthread_cond_signal**() and
pthread_cond_broadcast() return zero. Otherwise, an error number is returned to
indicate the error (the **errno** variable is not set).

ERRORS

For each of the following conditions, if the condition is detected, the **pthread_cond_signal()** and **pthread_cond_broadcast()** functions return the corresponding error number:

[EINVAL]   *cond* is not a valid condition variable.

[EFAULT]   The *cond* parameter points to an illegal address.

USAGE

When using condition variables, there is a boolean predicate associated with each condition wait. If this predicate is false, the thread should do a condition wait. Spurious wakeups may occur when waiting on a condition variable. Because the return values from **pthread_cond_wait()** and **pthread_cond_timedwait()** do not imply anything about the value of this predicate, the predicate should always be re-evaluated.

Applications using condition variables typically acquire a mutex and enter a loop which checks the predicate. Depending on the value of the predicate, the thread either breaks out of the loop or waits on the condition. On return from the condition wait, the predicate is re-evaluated.

AUTHOR

pthread_cond_signal() and **pthread_cond_broadcast()** were derived from the IEEE POSIX P1003.1c standard.

SEE ALSO

pthread_cond_init(3T), pthread_cond_destroy(3T), pthread_cond_wait(3T), pthread_cond_timedwait(3T).

STANDARDS CONFORMANCE

pthread_cond_signal():POSIX 1003.1c.
pthread_cond_broadcast():POSIX 1003.1c.

NAME

pthread_cond_wait() – wait on a condition variable.
pthread_cond_timedwait() – timed wait on a condition variable.

SYNOPSIS

#include <pthread.h>

int pthread_cond_wait(
        pthread_cond_t   ***cond,**
        pthread_mutex_t   ***mutex**
);

int pthread_cond_timedwait(
        pthread_cond_t   ***cond,**
        pthread_mutex_t   ***mutex,**
        const struct timespec   ***abstime**
);

PARAMETERS

cond   Pointer to the condition variable to be waited on.

mutex   Pointer to the mutex associated with the condition variable *cond*.

abstime   Absolute time at which the wait expires, even if the condition has not been signaled or broadcast.

DESCRIPTION

The **pthread_cond_wait()** function is used to wait for the occurrence of a condition associated with the condition variable *cond.*

The **pthread_cond_timedwait()** function is used to wait a limited amount of time for the occurrence of a condition associated with the condition variable *cond*. The *abstime* parameter specifies the time at which this function should time out. If the absolute time specified by *abstime* passes and the indicated condition has not been signaled, the function returns an error to the caller. NOTE: *abstime* is the time at which the wait expires, NOT the length of time the thread will wait.

The condition variable denoted by *cond* must have been dynamically initialized by a call to *pthread_cond_init()* or statically initialized with the macro **PTHREAD_COND_INITIALIZER**.

Both functions should be called with *mutex* locked by the calling thread. If *mutex* is not locked by the calling thread, undefined behavior will result. These functions atomically release *mutex* and cause the calling thread to block on the condition variable *cond*. If another thread is able to acquire the mutex after the about-to-block thread has released it but before it has actually blocked, a subsequent call to **pthread_cond_signal()** or **pthread_cond_broadcast()** by the other thread will behave as if it were issued after the about-to-block thread has blocked.

When the condition is signaled or the timed wait expires, the caller is unblocked and will reacquire *mutex* before returning. Whether these functions succeed or fail, *mutex* will always be reacquired before returning to the caller.

Using different mutexes for concurrent calls to these functions on the same condition variable results in undefined behavior.

When using condition variables, there is a boolean predicate associated with the condition wait. If this predicate is false, the thread should perform a condition wait.

Spurious wakeups may occur when waiting on a condition variable. A spurious wakeup occurs when a thread returns from a condition wait when it should really continue waiting. A normal signal being delivered to a thread may cause a spurious wakeup during a condition wait. Since the return values from **pthread_cond_wait()** and **pthread_cond_timedwait()** do not imply anything about the value of the predicate, the predicate should always be re-evaluated.

A condition wait is a cancellation point. When the calling thread has deferred cancellation enabled, cancellation requests will be acted upon. If a cancellation request is acted upon while a thread is blocked in one of these functions, *mutex* is re-acquired before calling the cancellation cleanup handlers. The cancellation cleanup handlers should release *mutex* so that application deadlock does not occur. If the condition signal and the cancellation request both occur, the canceled thread will not consume the condition signal (i.e., a different thread will be unblocked due to the condition signal).

If a signal is delivered to a thread waiting for a condition variable, upon return from the signal handler, the thread may return zero due to a spurious wakeup or continue waiting for the condition.

RETURN VALUE

Upon successful completion, **pthread_cond_wait()** and **pthread_cond_timedwait()** return zero. Otherwise, an error number is returned to indicate the error (the **errno** variable is not set).

ERRORS

If any of the following occur, the **pthread_cond_timedwait()** function returns the corresponding error number.

[ETIMEDOUT]   *abstime* has passed and a condition signal has not been received.

For each of the following conditions, if the condition is detected, the **pthread_cond_wait()** and **pthread_cond_timedwait()** functions return the corresponding error number:

[EINVAL]   The value specified by *cond*, *mutex* or *abstime* is invalid.

[EINVAL]   *mutex* is not owned by the calling thread. This error is not returned for a **PTHREAD_MUTEX_NORMAL** or **PTHREAD_MUTEX_DEFAULT** mutex on HP-UX

[EINVAL]   Different mutexes are being used for *cond*. This error is not detected on HP-UX.

[EFAULT]   The *cond*, *mutex*, or *abstime* parameter points to an illegal address.

WARNING

It is important to note that when **pthread_cond_wait()** or **pthread_cond_timedwait()** return without error, the associated predicate may still be false. When **pthread_cond_timedwait()** returns with the timeout error, the associated predicate may be true. It is recommended that a condition wait be enclosed in the equivalent of a "while loop," which checks the predicate.

Undefined behavior results if these functions are called with a **PTHREAD_MUTEX_RECURSIVE** mutex.

EXAMPLES

pthread_cond_wait() is recommended to be used in a loop testing the predicate associated with it. This will take care of any spurious wakeups that may occur.

```
pthread_mutex_t    mutex = PTHREAD_MUTEX_INITIALIZER;
pthread_cond_t     cond = PTHREAD_COND_INITIALIZER;

(void) pthread_mutex_lock(&mutex);
while (predicate == FALSE) {
     (void) pthread_cond_wait(&cond, &mutex);
}
(void) pthread_mutex_unlock(&mutex);
```

pthread_cond_timedwait() is also recommended to be used in a loop. This function can return success even if the predicate is not true. It should be called in a loop while checking the predicate. If the function times out, the predicate may still have become true. The predicate should be checked before processing the timeout case. The example given below does not do any other error checking.

```
pthread_mutex_t    mutex = PTHREAD_MUTEX_INITIALIZER;
pthread_cond_t     cond = PTHREAD_COND_INITIALIZER;
struct timespec    abstime;

(void) pthread_mutex_lock(&mutex);
abstime = absolute time to timeout.

while (predicate == FALSE) {
     ret = pthread_cond_timedwait(&cond, &mutex, &abstime);
     if (ret == ETIMEDOUT) {
          if (predicate == FALSE) {
               /* Code for time-out condition */
          } else {
               /* success condition */
               break;
          }
     }
}
(void) pthread_mutex_unlock(&mutex);
Code for success condition.
```

AUTHOR

pthread_cond_wait() and **pthread_cond_timedwait()** were derived from the IEEE POSIX P1003.1c standard.

SEE ALSO

pthread_cond_init(3T), pthread_cond_destroy(3T), pthread_cond_signal(3T), pthread_cond_broadcast(3T).

STANDARDS CONFORMANCE

pthread_cond_wait():POSIX 1003.1c.
pthread_cond_timedwait():POSIX 1003.1c.

NAME

pthread_condattr_setpshared() – set the process-shared attribute
pthread_condattr_getpshared() – get the process-shared attribute

SYNOPSIS

#include <pthread.h>

int pthread_condattr_getpshared(
        pthread_condattr_t   *attr,
        int   *pshared
);

int pthread_condattr_setpshared(
        pthread_condattr_t   *attr,
        int   pshared
);

PARAMETERS

attr   Pointer to the condition variable attributes object whose *process-shared* attribute is to be set/retrieved.

pshared   This parameter either specifies the new value of the *process-shared* attribute (set function) or it points to the memory location where the *process-shared* attribute of *attr* is to be returned (get function).

DESCRIPTION

The attributes object *attr* must have previously been initialized with the function *pthread_condattr_init( )* before these functions are called.

The functions are used to set and retrieve the *process-shared* attribute in a condition variable attributes object. The legal values for the *process-shared* attribute are:

PTHREAD_PROCESS_SHARED
    This option permits a condition variable to be operated upon by any thread that has access to the memory where the condition variable is allocated. The application is responsible for allocating the condition variable in memory that multiple processes can access.

PTHREAD_PROCESS_PRIVATE
    The condition variable can be operated on only by threads created within the same process as the thread that initialized the condition variable. If threads of differing processes attempt to operate on such condition variable, the behavior is undefined.

The default value of *process-shared* is **PTHREAD_PROCESS_PRIVATE**.

pthread_condattr_setpshared() sets the *process-shared* attribute in *attr*. The new value of the *process-shared* attribute of *attr* is set to the value specified in the *pshared* parameter.

pthread_condattr_getpshared() retrieves the value of the *process-shared* attribute from *attr*. The value of the *process-shared* attribute of *attr* is returned in the *pshared* parameter.

RETURN VALUE

Upon successful completion, **pthread_condattr_getpshared()** and **pthread_condattr_setpshared()** return zero. Otherwise, an error number is returned to indicate the error (the **errno** variable is not set).

ERRORS

If any of the following occur, the **pthread_condattr_getpshared()** and **pthread_condattr_setpshared()** functions return the corresponding error number:

[ENOSYS]   **_POSIX_THREAD_PROCESS_SHARED** is not defined and these functions are not supported.

For each of the following conditions, if the condition is detected, the **pthread_condattr_setpshared()** function returns the corresponding error number:

[EINVAL]   *attr* is not a valid condition variable attributes object.

[EINVAL]   The value specified by *pshared* is not a legal value.

For each of the following conditions, if the condition is detected, the **pthread_condattr_getpshared()** function returns the corresponding error number:

[EINVAL]   The value specified by *attr* or *pshared* is invalid.

WARNING

If a condition variable is created with the *process-shared* attribute defined as **PTHREAD_PROCESS_SHARED**, the cooperating processes should have access to the memory in which the condition variable is allocated.

AUTHOR

pthread_condattr_setpshared() and **pthread_condattr_getpshared()** were derived from the IEEE POSIX P1003.1c standard.

SEE ALSO

pthread_create(3T), pthread_condattr_init(3T), pthread_cond_init(3T), pthread_mutex_init(3T).

STANDARDS CONFORMANCE

pthread_condattr_setpshared():POSIX 1003.1c.
pthread_condattr_getpshared():POSIX 1003.1c.

NAME

pthread_condattr_init() – initialize a condition variable attributes object.
pthread_condattr_destroy() – destroy a condition variable attributes object.

SYNOPSIS

#include <pthread.h>

int pthread_condattr_init(
        pthread_condattr_t   *attr
);

int pthread_condattr_destroy(
        pthread_condattr_t   *attr
);

PARAMETERS

attr   Pointer to the condition variable attributes object to be initialized or destroyed.

DESCRIPTION

pthread_condattr_init() initializes the condition variable attributes object *attr* with the default values for all attributes. The attributes object describes a condition variable in detail and is passed to the condition variable initialization function.

When a condition variable attributes object is used to initialize a condition variable, the values of the individual attributes determine the characteristics of the new condition variable. Attributes objects act like additional parameters to object initialization. A single attributes object can be used in multiple calls to the function *pthread_cond_init()*.

When a condition variable is initialized with an attributes object, the attributes are, in effect, copied into the condition variable. Consequently, any change to the attributes object will not affect any previously initialized condition variables. Once all condition variables needing a specific attributes object have been initialized, the attributes object is no longer needed.

The condition variable attributes and their default values are:

process-shared   The default value is **PTHREAD_PROCESS_PRIVATE**.

If an initialized condition variable attributes object is reinitialized, undefined behavior results.

pthread_condattr_destroy() destroys the condition variable attributes object *attr*. The destroyed condition variable attributes object ceases to exist and its resources are reclaimed. Using *attr* after it has been destroyed results in undefined behavior. A destroyed condition variable attributes object can be reinitialized using the function **pthread_condattr_init**().

Condition variables that have been already initialized using this attributes object are not affected by the destruction of the condition variable attributes object.

RETURN VALUE

Upon successful completion, **pthread_condattr_init**() and **pthread_condattr_destroy**() return zero. Otherwise, an error number is returned to indicate the error (the **errno** variable is not set).

ERRORS

If any of the following occur, the **pthread_condattr_init**() function returns the corresponding error number:

[ENOMEM]   There is insufficient memory available in which to initialize the condition variable attributes object.

[EINVAL]   *attr* is not a valid condition variable attributes object.

For each of the following conditions, if the condition is detected, the **pthread_condattr_destroy**() function returns the corresponding error number:

[EINVAL]   *attr* is not a valid condition variable attributes object.

AUTHOR

pthread_condattr_init() and **pthread_condattr_destroy**() were derived from the IEEE POSIX P1003.1c standard.

SEE ALSO

pthread_create(3T), pthread_condattr_getpshared(3T), pthread_condattr_setpshared(3T), pthread_cond_init(3T).

STANDARDS CONFORMANCE

pthread_condattr_init():POSIX 1003.1c.
pthread_condattr_destroy():POSIX 1003.1c.

NAME

pthread_create() – create a new thread of execution.

SYNOPSIS

#include <pthread.h>

int pthread_create(
pthread_t	***thread,**
const pthread_attr_t	***attr,**
void	***(*start_routine)(void *),**
void	***arg**

);

PARAMETERS

thread   Pointer to the location where the created thread's ID is to be returned.

attr   Pointer to the thread attributes object describing the characteristics of the created thread. If the value is **NULL**, default attributes will be used.

start_routine Function to be executed by the newly created thread.

arg   Parameter to be passed to the created thread's *start_routine*.

DESCRIPTION

The **pthread_create()** function is used to create a new independent thread within the calling process. The thread will be created according to the attributes specified by *attr*. If *attr* is **NULL**, the default attributes will be used. The values of the attributes in *attr* describe the characteristics of the to-be-created thread in detail. Refer to the function *pthread_attr_init()* for a list of the default attribute values. A single attributes object can be used in multiple calls to the function **pthread_create()**.

When a thread is created with an attributes object, the attributes are, in effect, copied into the created thread. Consequently, any change to the attributes object will not affect any previously created threads. Once all threads needing a specific attributes object have been created, the attributes object is no longer needed and may be destroyed.

When the new thread is created, it will execute *start_routine()*, which has only one parameter, *arg*. If *start_routine()* returns, an implicit call to *pthread_exit()* is made. The return value of *start_routine()* is used as the thread's exit status.

The created thread's scheduling policy and priority, contention scope, detach state, stack size, and stack address are initialized according to their respective attributes in *attr*. The thread's signal mask is inherited from the creating thread. The thread's set of pending signals is cleared.

Refer to *pthread_exit()*, *pthread_detach()*, and *pthread_join()* for more information on thread termination and synchronizing with terminated threads.

On success, the ID of the created thread is returned in *thread*. If **pthread_create()** fails, a thread is not created and the contents *thread* are undefined.

Thread IDs are guaranteed to be unique only within a process.

NOTE: If the main thread returns from *main()*, an implicit call to *exit()* is made. The return value of *main()* is used as the process' exit status. The main thread can terminate without causing the process to terminate by calling *pthread_exit()*.

RETURN VALUE

Upon successful completion, **pthread_create()** returns zero. Otherwise, an error number is returned to indicate the error (the **errno** variable is not set).

ERRORS

If any of the following occur, the **pthread_create()** function returns the corresponding error number:

[EINVAL]   *attr* is an invalid thread attributes object.

[EINVAL]   The value specified by *thread* is invalid.

[EAGAIN]   The necessary resources to create another thread are not available, or the number of threads in the calling process already equals **PTHREAD_THREADS_MAX**.

[EINVAL]   The scheduling policy or scheduling attributes specified in *attr* are invalid.

[EPERM]   The caller does not have the appropriate privileges to create a thread with the scheduling policy and parameters specified in *attr*.

NOTES

It is unspecified whether joinable threads that have exited but haven't been joined count against the {**PTHREAD_THREADS_MAX**} limit.

AUTHOR

pthread_create() was derived from the IEEE POSIX P1003.1c standard.

SEE ALSO

pthread_exit(3T), pthread_join(3T), fork(2).

STANDARDS CONFORMANCE

pthread_create():POSIX 1003.1c.

NAME

pthread_default_stacksize_np() – change the default stacksize.

SYNOPSIS

#include <pthread.h>

int pthread_default_stacksize_np(
        size_t   **new_size,**
        size_t   ***old_size**
);

PARAMETERS

    new_size   The new default stack size.

    old_size   Pointer to where the old default stack size is returned.

DESCRIPTION

The **pthread_default_stacksize_np()** function allows an application to change the default value for the *stacksize* attribute. This function must be called before any threads have been created. The new default stack size is passed in the *new_size* parameter. If not **NULL**, the previous default stack size is returned in *old_size*. If *new_size* is zero, this function can be used (at any time) to query the current default stack size.

On HP-UX, threads with default stack sizes are cached after they terminate. The next time a thread is created with a default stack size, a cached thread (and its stack) are reused. This can result in significant performance improvements for *pthread_create()*.

However, if the default stack size is not appropriate for an application, it cannot take advantage of this performance enhancement. By using the **pthread_default_stacksize_np()** function, the threads library will change the default stack size so that it matches the applications needs. This allows the application to utilize the performance benefit of cached threads.

RETURN VALUE

Upon successful completion, **pthread_default_stacksize_np()** returns zero. Otherwise, an error number is returned to indicate the error (the **errno** variable is not set).

ERRORS

If any of the following occur, the **pthread_default_stacksize_np()** function returns the corresponding error number:

    [EINVAL]   The value specified by *new_size* is less than
                        PTHREAD_STACK_MIN.

    [EPERM]   The calling process has already created threads (this must be called before any threads are created).

AUTHOR

pthread_default_stacksize_np() was developed by HP.

SEE ALSO

pthread_attr_getstacksize(3T), pthread_attr_setstacksize(3T).

NAME

pthread_detach() – mark a thread as detached to reclaim its resources when it terminates.

SYNOPSIS

#include <pthread.h>

int pthread_detach(
       pthread_t   thread
);

PARAMETERS

thread   Thread whose resources are to be reclaimed immediately when it terminates.

DESCRIPTION

pthread_detach() is used to detach the thread *thread*. When *thread* terminates, its resources will automatically be reclaimed by the system. If *thread* has already terminated, **pthread_detach()** causes the resources of *thread* to be reclaimed by the system.

pthread_detach() does not cause *thread* to terminate.

Once a detached thread has terminated, its resources, including the thread ID, may be reused by the system. The return status of a detached thread is lost when the thread terminates.

Calling this function multiple times for the same thread results in undefined behavior.

RETURN VALUE

Upon successful completion, **pthread_detach()** returns zero. Otherwise, an error number is returned to indicate the error (the **errno** variable is not set).

ERRORS

If any of the following occur, the **pthread_detach()** function returns the corresponding error number:

[EINVAL]   *thread* does not refer to a joinable thread.

[ESRCH]   No thread could be found corresponding to *thread*.

AUTHOR

pthread_detach() was derived from the IEEE POSIX P1003.1c standard.

SEE ALSO

pthread_create(3T), pthread_join(3T), wait(2).

STANDARDS CONFORMANCE

pthread_detach():POSIX 1003.1c.

NAME

pthread_equal() – compare two thread identifiers.

SYNOPSIS

#include <pthread.h>

int pthread_equal(
       pthread_t   t1,
       pthread_t   t2
);

PARAMETERS

t1   First thread ID to be compared.

t2   Second thread ID to be compared.

DESCRIPTION

pthread_equal() compares the thread IDs *t1* and *t2*. Thread IDs are opaque data types. They should be compared only with this function.

RETURN VALUE

pthread_equal() returns a nonzero value if the two thread IDs are equal; otherwise, zero is returned.

This function does not verify that *t1* or *t2* are valid thread IDs.

ERRORS

None.

AUTHOR

pthread_equal() was derived from the IEEE POSIX P1003.1c standard.

SEE ALSO

pthread_create(3T), pthread_self(3T).

STANDARDS CONFORMANCE

pthread_equal():POSIX 1003.1c.

NAME

   pthread_exit() – cause the calling thread to terminate.

SYNOPSIS

   #include <pthread.h>

   void pthread_exit(
           void   *value_ptr
   );

PARAMETERS

   value_ptr   The calling thread's exit status.

DESCRIPTION

   pthread_exit() terminates the calling thread. The calling thread returns an exit status in *value_ptr*. This value is returned to a joining thread calling *pthread_join()* on the terminating thread. Only threads created with the *detachstate* attribute value **PTHREAD_CREATE_JOINABLE** can return an exit status to *pthread_join()*. The exit status of a detached thread is lost when the thread terminates.

   When a thread terminates, process-shared resources are not released. Examples of process-shared resources include mutexes, condition variables, semaphores, message queue descriptors, and file descriptors. The *atexit()* routines are not called when a thread terminates as this is a process termination action.

   An implicit call to **pthread_exit()** is made when a thread returns from its start routine. The function's return value serves as the thread's exit status (see *pthread_create()*). If the main thread returns from *main()* without calling **pthread_exit()**, the process will exit using the return value from *main()* as the exit status. If the main thread calls **pthread_exit()**, the process will continue executing until the last thread terminates or a thread calls *exit()*. After the last thread in the process terminates, the process will exit with an exit status of zero.

   Any installed cancellation cleanup handlers will be popped and executed in the reverse order that they were installed. After the cancellation cleanup handlers have been executed, if the thread has any non-**NULL** thread-specific data values, the appropriate destructor functions are called. The order in which these destructor functions are called is unspecified.

   Calling **pthread_exit()** from a cancellation cleanup handler or destructor function that was invoked because of thread termination results in undefined behavior.

   After a thread has terminated, the result of access to local (auto) variables of the thread is undefined. The terminating thread should not use local variables for the *value_ptr* parameter value.

RETURN VALUE

   None.

ERRORS

   None, this function does not return.

AUTHOR

   pthread_exit() was derived from the IEEE POSIX P1003.1c standard.

SEE ALSO

   pthread_create(3T), pthread_join(3T), exit(2), wait(2).

NAME

pthread_setconcurrency() – set the concurrency level of unbound threads
pthread_getconcurrency() – get the concurrency level of unbound threads

SYNOPSIS

#include <pthread.h>

int pthread_setconcurrency(
      int   new_level
);

int pthread_getconcurrency();

PARAMETERS

new_level   New concurrency level for the unbound threads in the calling process.

DESCRIPTION

The unbound threads in a process may or may not be required to be simultaneously active. By default, the threads implementation ensures that a sufficient number of threads are active so that the process can continue to make progress. While this conserves system resources, it may not produce the most effective level of concurrency. The **pthread_setconcurrency()** function allows an application to inform the threads implementation of its desired concurrency level, *new_level*. The actual level of concurrency provided by the system as a result of this function call is unspecified.

If *new_level* is zero, it will cause the implementation to maintain the concurrency level at its discretion as if **pthread_setconcurrency()** were never called.

The **pthread_getconcurrency()** function returns the value set by a previous call to **pthread_setconcurrency()**. If the **pthread_setconcuurency()** function was not previously called, the function returns zero to indicate that the system is maintaining the concurrency level.

Note: When an application calls **pthread_setconcurrency()**, it is informing the implementation of its desired concurrency level. The implementation will use this as a hint, not a requirement.

If the system does not support the multiplexing of user threads on top of several kernel-scheduled entities, the functions **pthread_getconcurrency()** and
pthread_setconcurrency() will be provided for source code compatibility, but they shall have no effect when called. To maintain the function semantics, the *new_level* parameter will be saved when **pthread_setconcurrency()** is called so that a subsequent call to **pthread_getconcurrency()** will return the same value.

RETURN VALUE

If successful, **pthread_setconcurrency()** returns zero. Otherwise, an error number is returned to indicate the error (the **errno** variable is not set).

The **pthread_getconcurrency()** function always returns the concurrency level set by a previous call to **pthread_setconcurrency()**. If the **pthread_setconcurrency()** function has never been called, **pthread_getconcurrency()** shall return zero.

ERRORS

If any of the following occur, the **pthread_setconcurrency()** function shall return the corresponding error number.

[EINVAL]   The value specified by *new_level* is invalid.

[EAGAIN]   The value specified by *new_level* would cause a system resource to be exceeded.

APPLICATION USAGE

Use of these functions changes the state of the underlying concurrency level upon which the application depends. Library developers are advised to not use the **pthread_getconcurrency()** and **pthread_setconcurrency()** functions as their use may conflict with an applications use of these functions.

AUTHOR

pthread_getconcurrency() and **pthread_setconcurrency()** were developed by X/Open.

SEE ALSO

pthread_num_processors_np(3T), pthread_processor_bind_np(3T), pthread_processor_id_np(3T).

STANDARDS CONFORMANCE

pthread_getconcurrency():X/Open.
pthread_setconcurrency():X/Open.

NAME

pthread_setschedparam() – set the scheduling policy and associated parameters
pthread_getschedparam() – get the scheduling policy and associated parameters

SYNOPSIS

#include <pthread.h>

int pthread_getschedparam(
pthread_t   **thread,**
int   ***policy,**
struct sched_param   ***param**
);

int pthread_setschedparam(
pthread_t   **thread,**
int   **policy,**
struct sched_param   ***param**
);

PARAMETERS

thread   The thread whose scheduling policy and associated parameters are to be set/retrieved.

policy   This parameter either points to the memory location where the scheduling policy of *thread* is returned (get function) or it specifies the new value of the scheduling policy for *thread* (set function).

param   This parameter either points to the memory location where the scheduling parameters of *thread* are returned (get function) or it specifies the new scheduling parameters for *thread* (set function).

DESCRIPTION

These functions allow the scheduling policy and associated parameters of threads within a multithreaded process to be retrieved and changed. The legal values for the scheduling policy and associated scheduling parameters are defined in <sched.h>.

pthread_setschedparam() changes the scheduling policy and associated scheduling parameters for *thread* to the policy and the associated parameters provided in *policy* and *param*, respectively. On HP-UX, appropriate privileges are required to change the scheduling parameters of a thread. The calling process must have appropriate privileges or be a member of a group having **PRIV_RTSCHED** access to successfully call **pthread_setschedparam()**.

The **pthread_getschedparam()** function retrieves the scheduling policy and associated parameters for *thread* and stores those values in *policy* and *param*, respectively. The values returned represent the actual scheduling values, not any temporary values that may be in effect due to priority inheritance or priority ceiling features.

RETURN VALUE

Upon successful completion, **pthread_setschedparam()** and **pthread_getschedparam()** return zero. Otherwise, an error number is returned to indicate the error (the **errno** variable is not set).

ERRORS

If any of the following occur, the **pthread_getschedparam()** and **pthread_setschedparam()** functions return the corresponding error number:

[ENOSYS]   **_POSIX_THREAD_PRIORITY_SCHEDULING** is not defined and these functions are not supported.

For each of the following conditions, if the condition is detected, the **pthread_setschedparam()** function returns the corresponding error number:

[EINVAL]   *policy* or one of the scheduling parameters in *param* is invalid.

[ENOTSUP]   Either the policy or scheduling parameters contain an unsupported value.

[EPERM]   The caller does not have permission to set either the scheduling policy specified in *policy* or the scheduling parameters specified in *param* for *thread*.

[ESRCH]   No thread could be found corresponding to *thread*.

For each of the following conditions, if the condition is detected, the **pthread_getschedparam()** function returns the corresponding error number:

[ESRCH]   No thread could be found corresponding to *thread*.

[EINVAL]   The value specified by *policy* or *param* is invalid.

NOTES

For the **SCHED_FIFO** and **SCHED_RR** scheduling policies, only the *sched_priority* member of the *sched_param* structure is required in the associated scheduling parameters. All other scheduling policies have implementation-defined scheduling policies. Refer to the documentation for *sched_setscheduler()* and *<sched.h>* for further information on implementation-defined scheduling policies.

AUTHOR

pthread_getschedparam() and **pthread_setschedparam()** were derived from the IEEE POSIX P1003.1c standard.

SEE ALSO

pthread_attr_setschedparam(3T), pthread_attr_setschedpolicy(3T), pthread_attr_getschedparam(3T), pthread_attr_getschedpolicy(3T), sched_setscheduler(2), sched_getscheduler(2), sched_getparam(2), sched_setparam(2).

STANDARDS CONFORMANCE

pthread_getschedparam():POSIX 1003.1c.
pthread_setschedparam():POSIX 1003.1c.

NAME

pthread_getspecific() – get the thread-specific data associated with a key
pthread_setspecific() – set the thread-specific data associated with a key

SYNOPSIS

#include <pthread.h>

void *pthread_getspecific(pthread_key_t key);

int pthread_setspecific(pthread_key_t key, const void *value);

PARAMETERS

key   Thread-specific data key whose value for the calling thread is to be set or retrieved.

value   Value to be assigned to the thread-specific data key for the calling thread.

DESCRIPTION

The **pthread_getspecific()** function returns the thread-specific data value associated with *key* for the calling thread. If no value has been associated with *key* for the calling thread, **NULL** is returned.

The **pthread_setspecific()** function associates the thread-specific data *value* with *key*. Each thread may bind a different value to *key*. The thread-specific data values are usually pointers to memory dynamically allocated by the calling thread.

key must be a valid thread-specific data key created by calling *pthread_key_create()*. If *key* is not a valid thread-specific data key, undefined behavior results when calling these functions.

These functions may be called from a thread-specific data destructor function. However, calling **pthread_setspecific()** from a destructor may result in lost storage.

RETURN VALUE

The function **pthread_getspecific()** returns the thread-specific data value associated with *key*. If no thread-specific data value is currently associated with *key*, the value **NULL** is returned.

If successful, **pthread_setspecific()** returns zero. Otherwise, an error number is returned to indicate the error (the **errno** variable is not set).

ERRORS

No errors are returned by the **pthread_getspecific()** function.

If any of the following occur, the **pthread_setspecific()** function returns the corresponding error number:

[ENOMEM]   There is insufficient memory available in which to associate *value* with *key*.

For each of the following conditions, if the condition is detected, the **pthread_setspecific()** function returns the corresponding error number:

[EINVAL]   *key* is an invalid thread-specific data key.

SEE ALSO

pthread_key_create(3T), pthread_key_delete(3T).

NAME
pthread_join() – wait for the termination of a specified thread.

SYNOPSIS
#include <pthread.h>

int pthread_join(
          pthread_t   thread,
          void   **value_ptr
);

PARAMETERS
thread   Thread whose termination is awaited by the caller.

value_ptr Pointer to the location where the exit status of *thread* is returned.

DESCRIPTION
The **pthread_join()** function waits for the termination of the target *thread*. If the target *thread* has already terminated, this function returns immediately. Only threads created with a *detachstate* attribute value of **PTHREAD_CREATE_JOINABLE** may be specified in the target *thread* parameter. On successful return from **pthread_join()**, the *value_ptr* argument, if it is not a null pointer, will contain the value passed to *pthread_exit()* by the terminating thread.

When a **pthread_join()** call returns successfully, the caller is guaranteed the target thread has terminated. If more than one thread calls **pthread_join()** for the same target thread, one thread is guaranteed to return successfully. Undefined behavior results for other callers specifying the same thread.

If the thread calling **pthread_join()** is canceled, the target thread will not be joined. The exit status of the target *thread* will remain available for another thread to call **pthread_join()**.

If the target *thread* was canceled, its exit status is **PTHREAD_CANCELED**.

It is unspecified whether a thread that has exited, but remains unjoined, counts against the **{_POSIX_THREAD_THREADS_MAX}** limit.

RETURN VALUE
Upon successful completion, **pthread_join()** returns zero. Otherwise, an error number is returned to indicate the error (the **errno** variable is not set).

ERRORS
If any of the following occur, the **pthread_join()** function returns the corresponding error number:

[EINVAL]   The value specified by *thread* does not refer to a joinable thread.

[ESRCH]   No thread could be found corresponding to *thread*.

For each of the following conditions, if the condition is detected, the **pthread_join()** function returns the corresponding error number:

[EDEADLK]   This operation would result in process deadlock or *thread* specifies the calling thread.

AUTHOR
pthread_join() was derived from the IEEE POSIX P1003.1c standard.

SEE ALSO
pthread_create(3T), wait(2).

NAME

pthread_key_create() – create a thread-specific data key.
pthread_key_delete() – delete a thread-specific data key.

SYNOPSIS

#include <pthread.h>

int pthread_key_create(
        pthread_key_t *key,
        void   (*destructor)(void *)
);

int pthread_key_delete(
        pthread_key_t key
);

PARAMETERS

key   This is either a pointer to the location where the new key value will to be returned (create function) or the thread-specific data key to be deleted (delete function).

destructor   Function to be called to destroy a data value associated with *key* when the thread terminates.

DESCRIPTION

pthread_key_create() creates a unique thread-specific data *key*. The *key* may be used by threads within the process to maintain thread-specific data. The same key is used by all threads, but each thread has its own thread-specific value associated with *key*. For each thread, the value associated with *key* persists for the life of the thread.

A process may create up to **PTHREAD_KEYS_MAX** thread-specific data keys. When a new thread-specific data key is created, each thread will initially have the value **NULL** associated with the new key. Each time a thread is created, the new thread will have the value **NULL** for each thread-specific data key that has been created in the process. A thread may use *pthread_setspecific()* to change the value associated with a thread-specific data key. Note: **pthread_key_t** is an opaque data type.

When a thread terminates, it may have non-**NULL** values associated with some or all of its thread-specific data keys. Typically, these values will be pointers to dynamically allocated memory. If this memory is not released when the thread terminates, memory leaks in the process occur. An optional *destructor()* function may be provided at key creation time to destroy the thread-specific data of a terminating thread. When a thread terminates, the thread-specific data values associated with the thread will be examined. For each key that has a non-**NULL** thread-specific data value and a destructor function, the destructor function will be called with the thread-specific data value as its sole argument. The order in which destructor functions are called in unspecified.

Once all the destructor functions have been called, the thread-specific data values for the terminating thread are examined again. If there are still non-**NULL** values in which the associated keys have destructor functions, the process of calling destructor functions is repeated. If after **PTHREAD_DESTRUCTOR_ITERATIONS** iterations of this loop there are still some non-**NULL** values with associated destructors, the system may stop calling the destructors or continue calling the destructors until there are no non-**NULL** values. Note: This may result in an infinite loop.

If a destructor function is not desired for *key*, the value **NULL** may be passed in the *destructor* parameter.

The **pthread_key_delete**() function deletes a thread-specific data *key*. The *key* must have been previously created by **pthread_key_create**(). The thread-specific data values associated with *key* are not required to be **NULL** when this function is called. Using *key* after it has been destroyed results in undefined behavior.

If a destructor function is associated with *key,* it will not be invoked by the **pthread_key_delete**() function. Once *key* has been deleted, any *destructor* function that was associated with *key* is not called when a thread exits. It is the responsibility of the application to free any application storage for each of the threads using *key*.

The **pthread_key_delete**() function can be called from a destructor function.

RETURN VALUE

If successful, **pthread_key_create**() and **pthread_key_delete**() return zero. Otherwise, an error number is returned to indicate the error (the **errno** variable is not set).

ERRORS

If any of the following occur, the **pthread_key_create**() function returns the corresponding error number:

[EINVAL]   The value specified by *key* is invalid.

[EAGAIN]   The necessary resources to create another thread-specific data key are not available, or the total number of keys per process has exceeded **PTHREAD_KEYS_MAX**.

[ENOMEM]   There is insufficient memory available in which to create *key*.

For each of the following conditions, if the condition is detected, the **pthread_key_delete**() function returns the corresponding error number:

[EINVAL]   The value specified by *key* is invalid.

AUTHOR

pthread_key_create() and **pthread_key_delete**() were derived from the IEEE POSIX P1003.1c standard.

SEE ALSO

pthread_getspecific(3T), pthread_setspecific(3T).

STANDARDS CONFORMANCE

pthread_key_create():POSIX 1003.1c.
pthread_key_delete():POSIX 1003.1c.

NAME

pthread_kill() – send a signal to a thread.

SYNOPSIS

#include <signal.h>

int pthread_kill(
 pthread_t thread,
 int sig
);

PARAMETERS

thread Thread to which the signal is to be delivered.

sig Signal to be delivered to *thread*.

DESCRIPTION

The **pthread_kill()** function is used to request that a signal be delivered to *thread*. The signal is asynchronously directed to a thread in the calling process. The signal is handled in the context of the given thread; if the signal action results in the thread terminating or stopping, this action is applied to the whole process.

If *sig* is zero, error checking is performed but a signal is not sent.

RETURN VALUE

Upon successful completion, **pthread_kill()** returns zero. Otherwise, an error number is returned to indicate the error (the **errno** variable is not set).

ERRORS

If any of the following occur, the **pthread_kill()** function returns the corresponding error number:

[EINVAL] *sig* is an invalid or unsupported signal number.

[ESRCH] No thread could be found corresponding to *thread*.

AUTHOR

pthread_kill() was derived from the IEEE POSIX P1003.1c standard.

SEE ALSO

kill(2), sigaction(2), pthread_self(3T), raise(2).

STANDARDS CONFORMANCE

pthread_kill():POSIX 1003.1c.

NAME

pthread_mutex_init() – initialize a mutex.
pthread_mutex_destroy() – destroy a mutex.

SYNOPSIS

#include <pthread.h>

int pthread_mutex_init(
      pthread_mutex_t   ***mutex,**
      pthread_mutexattr_t ***attr**
);

pthread_mutex_t   **mutex = PTHREAD_MUTEX_INITIALIZER;**

int pthread_mutex_destroy(
      pthread_mutex_t   ***mutex**
);

PARAMETERS

mutex   Pointer to the mutex to be initialized or destroyed.

attr   Pointer to the attributes object that defines the characteristics of the mutex to be initialized. If the pointer is **NULL**, default attributes are used.

DESCRIPTION

The **pthread_mutex_init**() function initializes the mutex referenced by *mutex* with the attributes *attr*. If *attr* is **NULL**, the default mutex attributes are used. Refer to *pthread_mutexattr_init()* for a list of the default mutex attributes. After successful initialization, the mutex is initialized, unlocked, and ready to be used in mutex operations. A mutex should be initialized only once or the resulting behavior is undefined. The *pthread_once()* function provides a way to ensure that a mutex is initialized only once.

The macro **PTHREAD_MUTEX_INITIALIZER** can be used to initialize mutexes that are statically allocated. These mutexes will be initialized with default attributes. The **pthread_mutex_init**() function does not need to be called for statically initialized mutexes.

If the *process-shared* attribute in the mutex attributes object referenced by *attr* is defined as **PTHREAD_PROCESS_SHARED**, the mutex must be allocated such that the processes sharing the mutex have access to it. This may be done through the memory-mapping functions (see *mmap*(2)) or the shared memory functions (see *shmget*(2)).

The **pthread_mutex_destroy**() function destroys the mutex referenced by *mutex*. This function may set *mutex* to an invalid value. The destroyed mutex can be reinitialized using the function **pthread_mutex_init**(). If the mutex is used after destruction in any mutex call, the resulting behavior is undefined.

A mutex should be destroyed only when it is unlocked. Destroying a mutex that is currently being used results in undefined behavior.

RETURN VALUE

Upon successful completion, **pthread_mutex_init**() and **pthread_mutex_destroy**() return zero. Otherwise, an error number is returned to indicate the error (the **errno** variable is not set).

ERRORS

If any of the following occur, the **pthread_mutex_init**() function returns the corresponding error number:

[EAGAIN]   The necessary resources (other than memory) to initialize *mutex* were not available.

[ENOMEM]   There is insufficient memory available in which to initialize *mutex*.

[EPERM]   The caller does not have the necessary permission to perform the mutex initialization.

For each of the following conditions, if the condition is detected, the **pthread_mutex_init**() function returns the corresponding error number:

[EINVAL]   The value specified by *mutex* or *attr* is invalid.

[EBUSY]   *mutex* is an already-initialized mutex.

[EFAULT]   The *mutex* parameter points to an illegal address.

For each of the following conditions, if the condition is detected, the **pthread_mutex_destroy**() function returns the corresponding error number:

[EINVAL]   *mutex* is not a valid mutex.

[EBUSY]   *mutex* is currently locked or in use by another thread.

WARNING

The space for the mutex must be allocated before calling **pthread_mutex_init**(). Undefined behavior will result if the *process-shared* attribute of *attr* is **PTHREAD_PROCESS_SHARED** and the space allocated for the mutex is not accessible to cooperating threads.

AUTHOR

pthread_mutex_init() and **pthread_mutex_destroy**() were derived from the IEEE POSIX P1003.1c standard.

SEE ALSO

pthread_mutex_lock(3T), pthread_mutex_unlock(3T), pthread_mutex_trylock(3T).

STANDARDS CONFORMANCE

pthread_mutex_init():POSIX 1003.1c.

pthread_mutex_destroy():POSIX 1003.1c.

NAME

pthread_mutex_setprioceiling() – set the prioceiling of a mutex.
pthread_mutex_getprioceiling() – get the prioceiling of a mutex.

SYNOPSIS

#include <pthread.h>

int pthread_mutex_getprioceiling(
         pthread_mutex_t   *mutex,
         int   *prioceiling
);

int pthread_mutex_setprioceiling(
         pthread_mutex_t   *mutex,
         int   prioceiling,
         int   *old_ceiling
   );

PARAMETERS

mutex   Pointer to the mutex whose *prioceiling* attribute is to be set/
                retrieved.

prioceiling   This parameter either points to the memory location where the
                prioceiling attribute of *mutex* is to be returned (get function) or
                specifies the new value of the *prioceiling* attribute for *mutex* (set
                function).

old_ceiling   This parameter points to the memory location where the old
                prioceiling attribute of *mutex* is to be returned (set function only).

DESCRIPTION

The **pthread_mutex_setprioceiling()** function will first lock *mutex*. If the mutex is
currently locked, the calling thread will block until the mutex can be locked. Once
the mutex has been locked, the *prioceiling* attribute of *mutex* will be changed to the
value specified in the *prioceiling* parameter and *mutex* will be unlocked. The old priority ceiling for the mutex will be returned in *old_ceiling*.

The **pthread_mutex_getprioceiling()** function returns the current value of the *prioceiling* attribute for *mutex* in the *prioceiling* parameter.

Be sure to check for the definition of **_POSIX_THREAD_PRIO_PROTECT**
before using these functions. Not all systems will support these functions.

RETURN VALUE

Upon successful completion, **pthread_mutex_getprioceiling()** and
pthread_mutex_setprioceiling() return zero. Otherwise, an error number is
returned to indicate the error (the **errno** variable is not set).

ERRORS

If any of the following occur, the **pthread_mutex_getprioceiling()** and
pthread_mutex_setprioceiling() functions return the corresponding error number:

[ENOSYS]   **_POSIX_THREAD_PRIO_PROTECT** is not defined and these
                functions are not supported.

For each of the following conditions, if the condition is detected, the **pthread_mutex_getprioceiling**() and **pthread_mutex_setprioceiling**() functions return the corresponding error number:

[EINVAL]   The priority value *prioceiling* is not a legal value.

[EINVAL]   *mutex* is not a valid mutex.

[EFAULT]   The *mutex* parameter points to an illegal address.

[ENOSYS]   The prioceiling protocol is not supported for mutexes.

[EPERM]   The caller does not have the appropriate privileges to change the priority ceiling for *mutex*.

AUTHOR

pthread_mutex_getprioceiling() and **pthread_mutex_setprioceiling**() were derived from the IEEE POSIX P1003.1c standard.

SEE ALSO

pthread_create(3T), pthread_mutex_init(3T), pthread_mutexattr_setprioceiling(3T), pthread_mutexattr_getprioceiling(3T), pthread_mutex_lock(3T), pthread_mutex_trylock(3T), pthread_mutex_unlock(3T).

STANDARDS CONFORMANCE

pthread_mutex_getprioceiling():POSIX 1003.1c.

pthread_mutex_setprioceiling():POSIX 1003.1c.

NAME

pthread_mutex_lock() – lock a mutex.
pthread_mutex_trylock() – attempt to lock a mutex.

SYNOPSIS

#include <pthread.h>

int pthread_mutex_lock(
        pthread_mutex_t   *mutex
);

int pthread_mutex_trylock(
        pthread_mutex_t   *mutex
);

PARAMETERS

mutex   Pointer to the mutex to be locked.

DESCRIPTION

The mutex object *mutex* is locked by calling the **pthread_mutex_lock()** function. How the calling thread acquires the mutex is dependent upon the *type* attribute for the mutex. This operation returns with the mutex object referenced by *mutex* in the locked state with the calling thread as its owner.

If the mutex *type* is **PTHREAD_MUTEX_NORMAL**, deadlock detection is not provided. Attempting to relock the mutex causes deadlock. If a thread attempts to unlock a mutex that it has not locked or a mutex that is unlocked, undefined behavior results.

If the mutex *type* is **PTHREAD_MUTEX_ERRORCHECK**, the mutex maintains the concept of an owner. If a thread attempts to relock a mutex that it has already locked, an error shall be returned. If a thread attempts to unlock a mutex that it has not locked or a mutex that is unlocked, an error shall be returned.

If the mutex *type* is **PTHREAD_MUTEX_RECURSIVE**, the mutex maintains the concept of an owner and a lock count. When a thread successfully acquires a mutex for the first time, the count field shall be set to one. Every time a thread relocks this mutex, the count field shall be incremented by one. Each time the thread unlocks the mutex, the count field shall be decremented by one. When the count field reaches zero, the mutex shall become available for other threads to acquire. If a thread attempts to unlock a mutex that it has not locked, an error shall be returned.

If the mutex *type* is **PTHREAD_MUTEX_DEFAULT**, attempting to recursively lock the mutex results in undefined behavior. Attempting to unlock the mutex if it was not locked by the calling thread results in undefined behavior. Attempting to unlocked the mutex if it is not locked results in undefined behavior.

The function **pthread_mutex_trylock()** is identical to the **pthread_mutex_lock()** function except that if the mutex object referenced by *mutex* cannot be acquired after one attempt, the call returns immediately with an error.

If a signal is delivered to a thread waiting for a mutex, upon return from the signal handler, the thread shall resume waiting for the mutex as if it was not interrupted.

RETURN VALUE

Upon successful completion, **pthread_mutex_lock()** and **pthread_mutex_trylock()** return zero. Otherwise, an error number is returned to indicate the error (the **errno** variable is not set).

ERRORS

If any of the following occur, the **pthread_mutex_lock()** and **pthread_mutex_trylock()** functions return the corresponding error number:

[EINVAL]   *mutex* is a **PTHREAD_PRIO_PROTECT** mutex and the caller's priority is higher than *mutex's* priority ceiling.

If any of the following occur, the **pthread_mutex_trylock()** function returns the corresponding error number:

[EBUSY]   *mutex* is currently locked by another thread.

If any of the following occur, the **pthread_mutex_lock()** and **pthread_mutex_trylock()** functions return the corresponding error number:

[EAGAIN]   *mutex* could not be acquired because the maximum number of recursive locks for *mutex* has been exceeded. This error is not detected on HP-UX.

For each of the following conditions, if the condition is detected, the **pthread_mutex_lock()** and **pthread_mutex_trylock()** functions return the corresponding error number:

[EINVAL]   *mutex* is not an initialized mutex.

[EFAULT]   The *mutex* parameter points to an illegal address.

[EDEADLK]   The current thread already owns the mutex. This error will only be detected for **PTHREAD_MUTEX_ERRORCHECK** mutexes on HP-UX.

WARNING

A recursive mutex can be locked more than once by the same thread without causing that thread to deadlock. Undefined behavior may result if the owner of a recursive mutex tries to lock the mutex too many times.

AUTHOR

pthread_mutex_lock() and **pthread_mutex_trylock()** was derived from the IEEE POSIX P1003.1c standard and X/Open.

SEE ALSO

pthread_mutex_init(3T), pthread_mutex_destroy(3T), pthread_mutex_unlock(3T).

STANDARDS CONFORMANCE

pthread_mutex_lock():POSIX 1003.1c.
pthread_mutex_trylock():POSIX 1003.1c.

NAME

pthread_mutex_unlock() – unlock a mutex.

SYNOPSIS

#include <pthread.h>

int pthread_mutex_unlock(
        pthread_mutex_t   *mutex
);

PARAMETERS

mutex   Pointer to the mutex to be unlocked.

DESCRIPTION

The function **pthread_mutex_unlock**() is called by the owner of the mutex
referenced by *mutex* to unlock the mutex. The manner in which the mutex is released
is dependent upon the mutex's *type* attribute. For normal and default mutexes,
undefined behavior will result if **pthread_mutex_unlock**() is called on an unlocked
mutex or by a thread that is not the current owner. For recursive and error-checking
mutexes, an error is returned if **pthread_mutex_unlock**() is called on an unlocked
mutex or by a thread that is not the current owner.

For recursive mutexes, the owner must call **pthread_mutex_unlock**() as many times
as the mutex was locked before another thread can lock the mutex.

If there are threads blocked on the mutex referenced by *mutex* when
pthread_mutex_unlock() releases the mutex, the scheduling policy is used to
determine which thread will acquire the mutex next.

RETURN VALUE

Upon successful completion, **pthread_mutex_unlock**() returns zero. Otherwise, an
error number is returned to indicate the error (the **errno** variable is not set).

ERRORS

For each of the following conditions, if the condition is detected, the
pthread_mutex_unlock() function returns the corresponding error number:

[EINVAL]   *mutex* is not an initialized mutex.

[EFAULT]   The *mutex* parameter points to an illegal address.

[EPERM]   The calling thread does not own *mutex*. On HP-UX, this error is
                not detected for **PTHREAD_MUTEX_NORMAL** or
                PTHREAD_MUTEX_DEFAULT mutexes.

AUTHOR

pthread_mutex_unlock() was derived from the IEEE POSIX P1003.1c standard
and HP extensions.

SEE ALSO

pthread_mutex_init(3T), pthread_mutex_destroy(3T), pthread_mutex_lock(3T),
pthread_mutex_trylock(3T).

STANDARDS CONFORMANCE

pthread_mutex_unlock():POSIX 1003.1c.

NAME

pthread_mutexattr_init() – initialize a mutex attributes object.
pthread_mutexattr_destroy() – destroy a mutex attributes object.

SYNOPSIS

#include <pthread.h>

int pthread_mutexattr_init(
        pthread_mutexattr_t   *attr
);

int pthread_mutexattr_destroy(
        pthread_mutexattr_t   *attr
);

PARAMETERS

attr   Pointer to the mutex attributes object to be initialized or destroyed.

DESCRIPTION

pthread_mutexattr_init() initializes the mutex attributes object *attr* with the default values for all attributes. The attributes object describes a mutex in detail and is passed to the mutex creation function.

When a mutex attributes object is used to initialize a mutex, the values of the individual attributes determine the characteristics of the new mutex. Attributes objects act like additional parameters to object initialization. A single attributes object can be used in multiple calls to *pthread_mutex_init()*.

When a mutex is initialized with an attributes object, the attributes are, in effect, copied into the mutex. Consequently, any change to the attributes object will not affect any previously initialized mutexes. Once all mutexes needing a specific attributes object have been initialized, the attributes object is no longer needed.

The mutex attributes and their default values are:

process-shared   The default value is **PTHREAD_PROCESS_PRIVATE**.

type   The default value is **PTHREAD_MUTEX_DEFAULT**.

If an initialized mutex attributes object is reinitialized, undefined behavior results.

pthread_mutexattr_destroy() destroys the mutex attributes object *attr*. The destroyed mutex attributes object ceases to exist and its resources are reclaimed. Using *attr* after it has been destroyed results in undefined behavior. A destroyed mutex attributes object can be reinitialized using the **pthread_mutexattr_init**() function.

Mutexes that have been already initialized using this attributes object are not affected by the destruction of the mutex attributes object.

RETURN VALUE

Upon successful completion, **pthread_mutexattr_init**() and **pthread_mutexattr_destroy**() return zero. Otherwise, an error number is returned to indicate the error (the **errno** variable is not set).

ERRORS

For each of the following conditions, if the condition is detected, the **pthread_mutexattr_init**() and **pthread_mutexattr_destroy**() functions return the corresponding error number:

[ENOMEM]   There is insufficient memory available in which to initialize *attr*.

[EINVAL]   The value specified by *attr* is invalid.

AUTHOR

pthread_mutexattr_init() and **pthread_mutexattr_destroy**() were derived from the IEEE POSIX P1003.1c standard.

SEE ALSO

pthread_create(3T), pthread_mutexattr_getpshared(3T), pthread_mutexattr_setpshared(3T), pthread_mutexattr_gettype(3T), pthread_mutexattr_settype(3T), pthread_mutex_init(3T).

STANDARDS CONFORMANCE

pthread_mutexattr_init():POSIX 1003.1c.
pthread_mutexattr_destroy():POSIX 1003.1c.

NAME

pthread_mutexattr_getprioceiling() – get the prioceiling attribute
pthread_mutexattr_setprioceiling() – set the prioceiling attribute

pthread_mutexattr_getprotocol() – get the protocol attribute
pthread_mutexattr_setprotocol() – set the protocol attribute

SYNOPSIS

#include <pthread.h>

int pthread_mutexattr_setprioceiling(pthread_mutexattr_t *attr,
                                      int prioceiling);

int pthread_mutexattr_getprioceiling(pthread_mutexattr_t *attr,
                                      int *prioceiling);

int pthread_mutexattr_setprotocol(pthread_mutexattr_t *attr, int protocol);

int pthread_mutexattr_getprotocol(pthread_mutexattr_t *attr, int *protocol);

PARAMETERS

attr   Pointer to the mutex attributes object whose attributes are to be set/
                retrieved.

prioceiling   This parameter either specifies the new value of the *prioceiling*
                attribute (set function) or points to the memory location where the
                prioceiling attribute of *attr* is to be returned (get function).

protocol   This parameter either specifies the new value of the *protocol*
                attribute (set function) or points to the memory location where the
                protocol attribute of *attr* is to be returned (get function).

DESCRIPTION

Be sure to check for the definitions of **_POSIX_THREAD_PRIO_PROTECT** and
_POSIX_THREAD_PRIO_INHERIT before using these functions. Not all sys-
tems will support these functions.

The attributes object *attr* must have previously been initialized with the function
pthread_mutexattr_init( ) before these functions are called.

ATTRIBUTE: protocol

Mutexes can be initialized with a priority protocol to help avoid or minimize the priority inversion that can be caused by locked mutexes. The *protocol* attribute in a
mutex attributes object describes the priority protocol to be used when the mutex is
locked by a thread. The legal values for the **protocol** attribute are:

PTHREAD_PRIO_NONE
          A thread's scheduling priority is not changed when it locks this type
          of mutex.

PTHREAD_PRIO_PROTECT
          These types of mutexes have an associated priority value in the *prio-
          ceiling* attribute. When a thread locks a mutex of this type, its sched-
          uling priority will be changed to be the value contained in the
          prioceiling attribute. The value of *prioceiling* must be higher than
          the locking thread's scheduling priority. When the mutex is
          unlocked, the thread's previous scheduling priority will be restored.

If a thread owns several mutexes of this type, its scheduling priority will be changed to the higher of all the *prioceiling* attributes for all mutexes of this type that it owns.

PTHREAD_PRIO_INHERIT

When a thread must block waiting for a mutex of this type, the system will change the scheduling priority of the thread that owns the mutex to be the higher of its own priority or the priority of the highest priority thread blocked on the mutex. When the mutex is unlocked, the thread's previous scheduling priority will be restored.

If a thread owns one or more mutexes having the *protocol* attribute value of **PTHREAD_PRIO_PROTECT** or **PTHREAD_PRIO_INHERIT**, the thread will not be moved to the tail of its priority list if its original priority is changed or when it unlocks the mutex(es).

If a thread owns mutexes of different priority protocols, it will execute at the highest of the priorities that would be obtained by each of these protocols. If this thread becomes blocked on another mutex, the priority behavior is recursive and is passed on to the thread that owns the mutex on which this thread is blocked.

POSIX.1c does not define a default value for the protocol attribute. On HP-UX, the default value is **PTHREAD_PRIO_NONE**.

pthread_mutexattr_setprotocol() is used to set the *protocol* attribute in the initialized attributes object *attr*. The new value of the *protocol* attribute of *attr* is set to the value specified in the *protocol* parameter.

pthread_mutexattr_getprotocol() retrieves the value of the *protocol* attribute from the mutex attributes object *attr*. The value of the *protocol* attribute of *attr* is returned in the *protocol* parameter.

ATTRIBUTE: prioceiling

If the *protocol* attribute has a value of **PTHREAD_PRIO_PROTECT**, the *prioceiling* attribute indicates the priority ceiling of the mutex. Otherwise, this attribute is not used when the mutex is initialized.

The priority values that are valid for this attribute are the same values that are valid for the **SCHED_FIFO** scheduling policy.

pthread_mutexattr_setprioceiling() is used to set the *prioceiling* attribute in the initialized attributes object *attr*. The new value of the *prioceiling* attribute of *attr* is set to the value specified in the *prioceiling* parameter.

pthread_mutexattr_getprioceiling() retrieves the value of the *prioceiling* attribute from the mutex attributes object *attr*. The value of the *prioceiling* attribute of *attr* is returned in the *prioceiling* parameter.

RETURN VALUE

Upon successful completion, **pthread_mutexattr_setprioceiling()**, **pthread_mutexattr_getprioceiling()**, **pthread_mutexattr_setprotocol()**, and **pthread_mutexattr_getprotocol()** return zero. Otherwise, an error number is returned to indicate the error (the **errno** variable is not set).

ERRORS

If any of the following occur, the **pthread_mutexattr_setprioceiling()**, **pthread_mutexattr_getprioceiling()**, **pthread_mutexattr_setprotocol()**, and **pthread_mutexattr_getprotocol()** functions return the corresponding error number:

[ENOSYS]   **_POSIX_THREAD_PRIO_PROTECT** is not defined and these functions are not supported.

[ENOTSUP] *protocol* contains an unsupported value.

For each of the following conditions, if the condition is detected, the **pthread_mutexattr_setprioceiling()**, **pthread_mutexattr_getprioceiling()**, **pthread_mutexattr_setprotocol()**, and **pthread_mutexattr_getprotocol()** functions return the corresponding error number:

[EINVAL]   The value specified by *attr*, *prioceiling*, or *protocol* is invalid.

[EPERM]   The caller does not have the appropriate privilege to set the priority ceiling or priority protocol to the specified values.

AUTHOR

pthread_mutexattr_setprioceiling(), **pthread_mutexattr_getprioceiling()**, **pthread_mutexattr_setprotocol()**, and **pthread_mutexattr_getprotocol()** were derived from the IEEE POSIX P1003.1c standard.

SEE ALSO

pthread_create(3T), pthread_mutexattr_init(3T), pthread_mutex_init(3T).

STANDARDS CONFORMANCE

pthread_mutexattr_setprioceiling():POSIX 1003.1c.

pthread_mutexattr_getprioceiling():POSIX 1003.1c.

pthread_mutexattr_setprotocol():POSIX 1003.1c.

pthread_mutexattr_getprotocol():POSIX 1003.1c.

NAME

pthread_mutexattr_getpshared() – get the process-shared attribute
pthread_mutexattr_setpshared() – set the process-shared attribute

pthread_mutexattr_gettype() – get the type attribute
pthread_mutexattr_settype() – set the type attribute

SYNOPSIS

#include <pthread.h>

int pthread_mutexattr_setpshared(pthread_mutexattr_t *attr, int pshared);

int pthread_mutexattr_getpshared(pthread_mutexattr_t *attr,   int *pshared);

int pthread_mutexattr_settype(pthread_mutexattr_t *attr, int type);

int pthread_mutexattr_gettype(pthread_mutexattr_t *attr, int *type);

PARAMETERS

attr   Pointer to the mutex attributes object whose attributes are to be set/
             retrieved.

pshared   This parameter either specifies the new value of the *process-shared*
             attribute (set function) or points to the memory location where the
             process-shared attribute of *attr* is to be returned (get function).

type   This parameter either specifies the new value of the *type* attribute (set
             function) or points to the memory location where the *type* attribute of
             attr is to be returned (get function).

DESCRIPTION

The attributes object *attr* must have previously been initialized with the function
pthread_mutexattr_init( ) before these functions are called.

ATTRIBUTE: pshared

Mutexes can be used by threads only within the a process or shared by threads in
multiple processes. The *process-shared* attribute in a mutex attributes object
describes who may use the mutex. The legal values for the *process-shared* attribute
are:

PTHREAD_PROCESS_SHARED

This option permits a mutex to be operated upon by any thread that
has access to the memory where the mutex is allocated. The
application is responsible for allocating the mutex in memory that
multiple processes can access.

PTHREAD_PROCESS_PRIVATE

The mutex can be operated upon only by threads created within the
same process as the thread that initialized the mutex. If threads of
differing processes attempt to operate on such mutex, the behavior is
undefined.

The default value of *process-shared* is **PTHREAD_PROCESS_PRIVATE**.

pthread_mutexattr_setpshared() is used to set the *process-shared* attribute in *attr*.
The new value of the *process-shared* attribute of *attr* is set to the value specified in
the *pshared* parameter.

pthread_mutexattr_getpshared() retrieves the value of the *process-shared* attribute from *attr*. The value of the *process-shared* attribute of *attr* is returned in the *pshared* parameter.

ATTRIBUTE: type

Mutexes can be created with four different types. The type of a mutex is contained in the *type* attribute of the mutex attributes object. Valid values for the *type* attribute are:

PTHREAD_MUTEX_NORMAL

This type of mutex does not provide deadlock detection. A thread attempting to relock this mutex without first unlocking it shall deadlock. An error is not returned to the caller. Attempting to unlock a mutex locked by a different thread results in undefined behavior. Attempting to unlock an unlocked mutex results in undefined behavior.

PTHREAD_MUTEX_ERRORCHECK

This type of mutex provides error checking. An owner field is maintained. Only the mutex lock owner shall successfully unlock this mutex. A thread attempting to relock this mutex shall return with an error. A thread attempting to unlock a mutex locked by a different thread shall return with an error. A thread attempting to unlock an unlocked mutex shall return with an error. This type of mutex is useful for debugging.

PTHREAD_MUTEX_RECURSIVE

Deadlock cannot occur with this type of mutex. An owner field is maintained. A thread attempting to relock this mutex shall successfully lock the mutex. Multiple locks of this mutex shall require the same number of unlocks to release the mutex before another thread can lock the mutex. A thread attempting to unlock a mutex locked by a different thread shall return with an error. A thread attempting to unlock an unlocked mutex shall return with an error.

PTHREAD_MUTEX_DEFAULT

Attempting to recursively lock a mutex of this type results in undefined behavior. Attempting to unlock a mutex locked by a different thread results in undefined behavior. Attempting to unlock an unlocked mutex results in undefined behavior. An implementation shall be allowed to map this mutex to one of the other mutex types.

The default value of the *type* attribute is **PTHREAD_MUTEX_DEFAULT**.

pthread_mutexattr_settype() is used to set the *type* attribute in *attr*. The new value of the *type* attribute of *attr* is set to the value specified in the *type* parameter.

pthread_mutexattr_gettype() retrieves the value of the *type* attribute from *attr*. The value of the *type* attribute of *attr* is returned in the *type* parameter.

Never use a **PTHREAD_MUTEX_RECURSIVE** mutex with condition variables because the implicit unlock performed for a **pthread_cond_wait**() or **pthread_cond_timedwait**() may not actually release the mutex if it had been locked multiple times. If this situation happens, no other thread can satisfy the condition of the predicate.

RETURN VALUE

Upon successful completion, **pthread_mutexattr_getpshared()**, **pthread_mutexattr_setpshared()**, **pthread_mutexattr_gettype()**, and **pthread_mutexattr_settype()** return zero. Otherwise, an error number is returned to indicate the error (the **errno** variable is not set).

ERRORS

If any of the following occur, the **pthread_mutexattr_getpshared()** and **pthread_mutexattr_setpshared()** functions return the corresponding error number:

[ENOSYS]   **_POSIX_THREAD_PROCESS_SHARED** is not defined and these functions are not supported.

For each of the following conditions, if the condition is detected, the **pthread_mutexattr_getpshared()**, **pthread_mutexattr_setpshared()**, **pthread_mutexattr_gettype()**, and **pthread_mutexattr_settype()** functions return the corresponding error number:

[EINVAL]   *attr* is not a valid mutex attributes object.

[EINVAL]   The value specified by *pshared* or *type* is not a legal value.

[EINVAL]   The value *pshared* or *type* points to an illegal address.

WARNING

If a mutex is created with the *process-shared* attribute defined as **PTHREAD_PROCESS_SHARED**, the cooperating processes should have access to the memory in which the mutex is allocated.

AUTHOR

pthread_mutexattr_setpshared() and **pthread_mutexattr_getpshared()** were derived from the IEEE POSIX P1003.1c standard.

pthread_mutexattr_settype() and **pthread_mutexattr_gettype()** were developed by X/Open.

SEE ALSO

pthread_create(3T), pthread_mutexattr_init(3T), pthread_mutex_init(3T).

STANDARDS CONFORMANCE

pthread_mutexattr_setpshared():POSIX 1003.1c.

pthread_mutexattr_getpshared():POSIX 1003.1c.

pthread_mutexattr_settype():X/Open.

pthread_mutexattr_gettype():X/Open.

NAME

pthread_once() – call an initialization routine only once.

SYNOPSIS

#include <pthread.h>

pthread_once_t   once_control = PTHREAD_ONCE_INIT;

int pthread_once(
        pthread_once_t   *once_control,
        void   (*init_routine)(void)
);

PARAMETERS

once_control Pointer to the once-control object associated with the one-time initialization function *init_routine()*.

init_routine The one-time initialization routine. This routine is called only once, regardless of the number of times it and its associated *once_control* are passed to **pthread_once()**.

DESCRIPTION

The **pthread_once()** function guarantees that *init_routine()* is only called one time in an application. This function will use the *once_control* object to determine if *init_routine()* has previously been called via **pthread_once()**.

The first time **pthread_once()** is called with *once_control* and *init_routine()* causes *init_routine()* to be called with no arguments. Subsequent calls to **pthread_once()** with the same *once_control* will not cause *init_routine()* to be called again. When **pthread_once()** returns, the caller is guaranteed that *init_routine()* has been called (either just now or via a previous call).

The macro **PTHREAD_ONCE_INIT** is used to statically initialize a once control block. This initialization must be done before calling **pthread_once()**.

pthread_once() is not a cancellation point. However, the caller supplied *init_routine()* may be a cancellation point. If the thread executing *init_routine()* is canceled, the *once_control* argument will be set to a state which indicates that *init_routine()* has not been called yet (see *pthread_cancel()*). The next time the **pthread_once()** function is called with *once_control*, the *init_routine()* function will be called.

The behavior of **pthread_once()** is undefined if *once_control* has automatic storage duration or is not initialized by **PTHREAD_ONCE_INIT**.

RETURN VALUE

Upon successful completion, **pthread_once()** returns zero. Otherwise, an error number is returned to indicate the error (the **errno** variable is not set).

ERRORS

For each of the following conditions, if the condition is detected, the **pthread_once()** function returns the corresponding error number:

    [EINVAL]   Either *once_control* or *init_routine* is invalid.

EXAMPLES

Some modules are designed for dynamic initialization, i.e., global initialization is performed when the first function of the module is invoked. In a single-threaded program, this is generally implemented as follows:

static int   initialized = FALSE;
extern void   initialize();

if (!initialized) {
    initialize();
    initialized = TRUE;
}

/* Rest of the code after initialization. */

For a multithreaded process, a simple initialization flag is not sufficient; the flag must be protected against modification by multiple threads. Consequently, this flag has to be protected by a mutex that has to be initialized only once, and so on. A multithreaded program should use initialization similar to:

static pthread_once_t   once_control = PTHREAD_ONCE_INIT;
extern void   initialize();

(void)pthread_once(&once_control, initialize);

/* Rest of the code after initialization. */

AUTHOR

pthread_once() was derived from the IEEE POSIX P1003.1c standard.

SEE ALSO

pthread_create(3T).

STANDARDS CONFORMANCE

pthread_once():POSIX 1003.1c.

NAME

pthread_num_processors_np() – how many processors are installed in the system.
pthread_processor_bind_np() - bind threads to processors.
pthread_processor_id_np() - determine processor IDs.

SYNOPSIS

#include <pthread.h>

int pthread_num_processors_np();

int pthread_processor_bind_np(
       int   **request,**
       pthread_spu_t   ***answer,**
       pthread_spu_t   **spu,**
       pthread_t   **tid**
);

int pthread_processor_id_np(
       int   **request,**
       pthread_spu_t   ***answer,**
       pthread_spu_t   **spu**
);

PARAMETERS

request   This parameter determines the precise action to be taken by these functions.

answer   This parameter is an output parameter in which values are returned. The meaning of *answer* depends on *request* parameter.

spu   This parameter gives the value of the spu for certain requests.

tid   This parameter gives the value of the thread id for certain requests.

DESCRIPTION

These functions provide a means of determining how many processors are installed in the system and assigning threads to run on specific processors.

The **pthread_num_processors_np()** function returns the number of processors currently installed on the system.

The **pthread_processor_id_np()** function obtains the processor ID of a specific processor on the system. The processor ID is returned in *answer*. The *request* parameter determines the precise action to be taken and is one of the following:

PTHREAD_GETFIRSTSPU_NP
This request stores in the *answer* parameter the ID of the first processor in the system. The *spu* argument is ignored.

PTHREAD_GETNEXTSPU_NP
This request stores in the *answer* parameter the ID of the next processor in the system after *spu*. Typically, **PTHREAD_GETFIRSTSPU_NP** is called to determine the first spu. **PTHREAD_GETNEXTSPU_NP** is then called in a loop (until the call returns **EINVAL**) to determine the IDs of the remaining spus.

PTHREAD_GETCURRENTSPU_NP
This request stores in the *answer* parameter the ID of the processor the thread is currently running on. The *spu* argument is ignored. Note: This

option returns the current processor on which the caller is executing, NOT the processor assignment of the caller.

This information may be out-of-date arbitrarily soon after the call completes.

The **pthread_processor_bind_np()** function is expected to be used to increase performance in certain applications to prevent cache thrashing or to cause threads to execute in parallel on different processors. It should not be used to ensure correctness of an application. Specifically, cooperating threads should not rely on processor assignment in lieu of a synchronization mechanism (such as mutexes).

The **pthread_processor_bind_np()** function binds a thread to a specific processor. The thread specified by *tid* is the target thread whose binding is changed. The *spu* parameter specifies the new processor binding for *tid*. The *request* parameter determines the precise action to be taken by **pthread_processors_np()** and is one of the following:

PTHREAD_BIND_ADVISORY_NP

This request assigns thread *tid* to processor *spu*. Since the new spu assignment is returned in the *answer* parameter, the spu **PTHREAD_SPUNOCHANGE_NP** may be passed to read the current assignment. The tid **PTHREAD_SELFTID_NP** can be used to refer to the calling thread. The value **PTHREAD_SPUFLOAT_NP** may be passed in the *spu* parameter to break any specific processor assignment and allow the implementation to choose which processor the thread should execute on when it is scheduled to execute. This allows the thread to run on any processor the implementation chooses.

This request is only advisory. If the scheduling policy for the thread conflicts with this processor assignment, the scheduling policy shall over rule the processor assignment. For example, when a processor is ready to choose another thread to execute, if the highest priority **SCHED_FIFO** thread on the run queue is bound to a different processor, that thread will execute on the available processor rather than waiting for the processor to which it is bound.

PTHREAD_BIND_FORCED_NP

This request is identical to **PTHREAD_BIND_ADVISORY_NP** except that this thread to processor binding will overrule the scheduling policy. For example, when a processor is ready to choose another thread to execute, if the highest priority **SCHED_FIFO** thread on the run queue is bound to a different processor, that thread will not be chosen by the available processor. That thread will wait until the *wanted* processor becomes available. The available processor will choose a lower priority thread to execute instead of completely honoring the scheduling policies.

Note: binding a thread to a specific processor essentially changes the scheduling allocation domain size for that thread to be one. Having a thread float and be scheduled on whatever processor the system chooses sets a thread's scheduling allocation domain size to a value greater than one (it will generally be equal to the number of processors on the system).

RETURN VALUE

pthread_num_processors_np() always returns the number of processors on the system. It never fails.

Upon successful completion, **pthread_processor_id_np()** returns zero. Otherwise, an error number is returned to indicate the error (the **errno** variable is not set).

Upon successful completion, **pthread_processor_bind_np()** returns zero. Otherwise, an error number is returned to indicate the error (the **errno** variable is not set).

ERRORS

If any of the following occur, the **pthread_processor_id_np()** and **pthread_processor_bind_np()** functions return the corresponding error number:

[EINVAL]   The *request* parameter contains an illegal value.

[EINVAL]   The *request* parameter is **PTHREAD_GETNEXTSPU_NP** and *spu* identifies the last processor.

[EINVAL]   The value specified by *answer* is illegal.

[ESRCH]   No thread could be found in the current process that matches the thread ID specified in *tid*.

[EPERM]   *request* is **PTHREAD_BIND_ADVISORY_NP** or **PTHREAD_BIND_FORCED_NP**, *spu* is not **PTHREAD_SPUNOCHANGE_NP**, and the caller does not have the appropriate permission to change a threads binding to a specific processor.

AUTHOR

pthread_num_processors_np(), **pthread_processor_id_np()**, and **pthread_processor_bind_np()** were developed by HP.

SEE ALSO

sleep(3), sched_yield(2).

STANDARDS CONFORMANCE

pthread_num_processors_np():None.
pthread_processor_id_np():None.
pthread_processor_bind_np():None.

NAME

pthread_continue() - continue execution of a thread.
pthread_resume_np() – resume execution of a thread.
pthread_suspend() – suspend execution of a thread.

SYNOPSIS

#include <pthread.h>

int pthread_continue(
        pthread_t   thread
);

 void pthread_resume_np(
        pthread_t   thread,
        int   flags
);

int pthread_suspend(
        pthread_t   thread
);

PARAMETERS

thread   whose execution is to be suspended or resumed.

flags   Flags to be used by **pthread_resume_np()**. The valid values are:

   PTHREAD_COUNT_RESUME_NP
          The target thread's suspension count is decremented by
          one. If the target thread was suspended and has a
          suspend count greater than one, the thread will not
          resume execution.

   PTHREAD_FORCE_RESUME_NP
          The target thread's suspension count is set to zero. The
          target will resume execution even if its suspend count
          was greater than one.

DESCRIPTION

The **pthread_suspend()** function suspends execution of the target thread specified
by *thread*. The target thread may not be suspended immediately (at that exact
instant). On successful return from the **pthread_suspend()** function, *thread* is no
longer executing. Once a thread has been suspended, subsequent calls to the
pthread_suspend() function increment a per thread suspension count and return
immediately.

Calling **pthread_suspend()** with the calling thread specified in *thread* is allowed.
The calling thread shall be suspended from execution. Note that in this case the
calling thread shall be suspended during execution of the **pthread_suspend()**
function call and shall only return after another thread has called the
pthread_resume_np() or **pthread_continue()** function for *thread*.

The **pthread_continue()** function resumes the execution of the target thread
specified by *thread*. If *thread* was suspended by multiple calls to
pthread_suspend(), only one call to **pthread_continue()** is required to resume the
execution of *thread*. Calling **pthread_continue()** for a target thread that is not
suspended shall have no effect and return no errors. A call to **pthread_continue()** is
equivalent to calling **pthread_resume_np()** with the *flags* parameter specified as
PTHREAD_FORCE_RESUME_NP.

The **pthread_resume_np()** function resumes the execution of the target thread specified by *thread*. If the *flags* argument is **PTHREAD_COUNT_RESUME_NP**, the target thread's suspension count is decremented by one. If the *flags* argument is **PTHREAD_FORCE_RESUME_NP,** the target thread's suspension count is set to zero. When the target thread's suspension count reaches zero, the target thread is allowed to continue execution. Calling **pthread_resume_np()** for a target thread that is not suspended shall have no effect and return no errors.

RETURN VALUE

If successful, **pthread_continue(), pthread_suspend()** and **pthread_resume_np()** return zero. Otherwise, an error number shall be returned to indicate the error (the **errno** variable is not set).

ERRORS

If any of the following occur, the **pthread_suspend()** function returns the corresponding error number.

[ESRCH]   The target thread *thread* is not in the current process.

[EDEADLK]   The target thread *thread* is the last running thread in the process. The operation would result in deadlock for the process.

If any of the following occur, the **pthread_continue()** and **pthread_resume_np()** functions return the corresponding error number.

[ESRCH]   The target thread *thread* is not in the current process.

[EINVAL]   The value specified by *flags* is invalid.

APPLICATION USAGE

This functionality enables a process that is multithreaded to temporarily suspend all activity to a single thread of control. When the process is single threaded, the address space is not changing, and a consistent view of the process can be gathered. One example of its use is for garbage collecting. The garbage collector runs asynchronously within the process and assumes that the process is not changing while it is running.

Suspending a thread may have adverse effects on an application. If a thread is suspended while it holds a critical resource, such as a mutex or a read-write lock, the application may stop or even deadlock until the thread is continued. While the thread is suspended, other threads which may contend for the same resource must block until the thread is continued. Depending on application behavior, this may even result in deadlock. Application programmers are advised to either a) only suspend threads which call async-signal safe functions or b) ensure that the suspending thread does not contend for the same resources that the suspended thread may have acquired. Note: this includes resources that may be acquired by libraries.

The **pthread_suspend()**, **pthread_continue()**, and **pthread_resume_np()** functions cannot reliably be used for thread synchronization. Synchronization primitives like mutexes, semaphores, read-write locks, and condition variables should be used instead.

AUTHOR

pthread_suspend() and **pthread_continue()** were developed by X/Open.
pthread_resume_np() was developed by HP.

SEE ALSO

pthread_create(3T).

NAME

pthread_rwlock_init() – initialize a read-write lock.
pthread_rwlock_destroy() – destroy a read-write lock.

SYNOPSIS

#include <pthread.h>

int pthread_rwlock_init(
  pthread_rwlock_t   *rwlock,
  pthread_rwlockattr_t   *attr
);

pthread_rwlock_t   rwlock = PTHREAD_RWLOCK_INITIALIZER;

int pthread_rwlock_destroy(
  pthread_rwlock_t   *rwlock
);

PARAMETERS

rwlock   Pointer to the read-write lock to be initialized or destroyed.

attr   Pointer to the attributes object that defines the characteristics of the read-write lock to be initialized. If the pointer is **NULL**, default attributes are used.

DESCRIPTION

pthread_rwlock_init() initializes the read-write lock referenced by *rwlock* with the attributes *attr*. If *attr* is **NULL**, the default read-write lock attributes are used. Upon successful initialization, the state of the read-write lock becomes initialized and unlocked. Attempting to initialize an already initialized read-write lock object results in undefined behavior.

The macro **PTHREAD_RWLOCK_INITIALIZER** can be used to initialize read-write locks that are statically allocated. The effect is equivalent to dynamic initialization by a call to **pthread_rwlock_init**() with the parameter *attr* specified as **NULL**, except that no error checks are performed. The read-write lock will be initialized with default attributes.

If the *process-shared* attribute in the read-write lock attributes object referenced by *attr* is defined as **PTHREAD_PROCESS_SHARED**, the read-write lock must be allocated such that the processes sharing the read-write lock has access to it. This may be done through the memory-mapping functions (see *mmap*(2)) or shared memory functions (see *shmget*(2)). **pthread_rwlock_destroy**() destroys the read-write referenced by *rwlock*. This function may set *rwlock* to an invalid value. The destroyed read-write lock can be reinitialized using the function **pthread_rwlock_init**(). If the read-write lock is referenced after destruction in any read-write lock call, the resulting behavior is undefined.

A read-write lock should be destroyed only when no threads are currently using it. Destroying a read-write lock which is currently in use results in undefined behavior.

RETURN VALUE

Upon successful completion, **pthread_rwlock_init**() and
pthread_rwlock_destroy() returns zero. Otherwise, an error number is returned to indicate the error (the **errno** variable is not set).

ERRORS

If any of the following occur, the **pthread_rwlock_init**() function returns the corresponding error number:

[EAGAIN]	The necessary resources (other than memory) to initialize *rwlock* are not available.
[ENOMEM]	There is insufficient memory available in which to initialize the read-write lock *rwlock*.
[EPERM]	The caller does not have the privilege to perform the operation.

For each of the following conditions, if the condition is detected, the **pthread_rwlock_init**() function returns the corresponding error number:

[EINVAL]	The value specified by *rwlock* or *attr* is invalid.
[EBUSY]	*rwlock* is an already initialized read-write lock.

For each of the following conditions, if the condition is detected, the **pthread_rwlock_destroy**() function returns the corresponding error number:

[EINVAL]	The value specified by *rwlock* is invalid.
[EBUSY]	*rwlock* is currently locked or being used by other threads.

WARNING

The space for the read-write lock must to be allocated before calling **pthread_rwlock_init**(). Undefined behavior may result if the *process-shared* attribute of *attr* is **PTHREAD_PROCESS_SHARED** and the space allocated for the read-write lock is not accessible to cooperating threads.

AUTHOR

pthread_rwlock_init() and **pthread_rwlock_init**() were developed by X/Open.

SEE ALSO

pthread_rwlock_rdlock(3T), pthread_rwlock_wrlock(3T),
pthread_rwlock_unlock(3T), pthread_rwlock_tryrdlock(3T),
pthread_rwlock_trywrlock(3T).

STANDARDS CONFORMANCE

pthread_rwlock_init():X/Open.
pthread_rwlock_destroy():X/Open.

NAME

pthread_rwlock_rdlock() – lock a read-write lock for reading.
pthread_rwlock_tryrdlock() – attempt to lock a read-write lock for reading.

SYNOPSIS

#include <pthread.h>

int pthread_rwlock_rdlock(
      pthread_rwlock_t   *rwlock
);

int pthread_rwlock_tryrdlock(
      pthread_rwlock_t   *rwlock
);

PARAMETERS

rwlock   Pointer to the read-write lock to be locked for reading.

DESCRIPTION

The **pthread_rwlock_rdlock()** function applies a read lock to the read-write lock object referenced by *rwlock*. The calling thread shall acquire the read lock if a writer does hold the lock and there are no writers blocked on the lock. It is unspecified whether the calling thread acquires the lock when a writer does not hold the lock and there are writers waiting for the lock. If a writer holds the lock, the calling thread shall not acquire the read lock. If the read lock is not acquired, the calling thread blocks (that is, it does not return from the **pthread_rwlock_rdlock()** call) until it can acquire the lock. Results are undefined if the calling thread currently owns a write lock on *rwlock*.

Implementations shall be allowed to favor writers over readers to avoid writer starvation.

A thread may hold multiple concurrent locks on *rwlock* (that is, successfully call the **pthread_rwlock_rdlock()** function *n* times). If so, the thread must perform the matching unlocks (that is, it must call the **pthread_rwlock_unlock()** function *n* times).

The function **pthread_rwlock_tryrdlock()** applies a read lock as in the **pthread_rwlock_rdlock()** function with the exception that the function fails if any thread holds a write lock on *rwlock* or there are writers blocked on *rwlock*.

Results are undefined if any of these functions are called with an uninitialized read-write lock.

If a signal is delivered to a thread waiting for a read-write lock, upon return from the signal handler, the thread shall resume waiting for the read-write lock as if it was not interrupted.

RETURN VALUE

Upon successful completion, **pthread_rwlock_rdlock()** and **pthread_rwlock_tryrdlock()** returns zero. Otherwise, an error number is returned to indicate the error (the **errno** variable is not set).

ERRORS

If any of the following occur, the **pthread_rwlock_tryrdlock()** function returns the corresponding error number:

[EBUSY]   The read-write lock *rwlock* could not be acquired for reading because a writer holds the lock or was blocked on it.

For each of the following conditions, if the condition is detected, the **pthread_rwlock_rdlock()** and **pthread_rwlock_tryrdlock()** functions return the corresponding error number:

[EINVAL]   The value specified by *rwlock* does not refer to an initialized read-write lock.

[EDEADLK]   The current thread already owns the read-write lock for writing.

[EAGAIN]   The read lock could not be acquired because the maximum number of read locks for *rwlock* has been exceeded. This error is not detected on HP-UX.

AUTHOR

pthread_rwlock_rdlock() and **pthread_rwlock_rdlock()** were developed by X/Open.

SEE ALSO

pthread_rwlock_init(3T), pthread_rwlock_destroy(3T), pthread_rwlock_trywrlock(3T), pthread_rwlock_wrlock(3T), pthread_rwlock_unlock(3T).

STANDARDS CONFORMANCE

pthread_rwlock_rdlock():X/Open.
pthread_rwlock_tryrdlock():X/Open.

NAME

pthread_rwlock_unlock() – unlock a read-write lock.

SYNOPSIS

#include <pthread.h>

int pthread_rwlock_unlock(pthread_rwlock_t   *rwlock);

PARAMETERS

rwlock   Pointer to the read-write lock to be unlocked.

DESCRIPTION

The function **pthread_rwlock_unlock()** is called by the owner to release the read-write lock referenced by *rwlock*. Results are undefined if the read-write lock *rwlock* is not held by the calling thread.

If this function is called to release a read lock on the read-write lock *rwlock* and there are other read locks currently held on this read-write lock, the read-write lock shall remain in the read locked state but without the current thread as one of its owners. If this function releases the last read lock for this read-write lock, the object shall be put in the unlocked state with no owners.

If this function is called to release a write lock on the read-write lock *rwlock*, the read-write lock shall be put in the unlocked state with no owners.

If the call to the **pthread_rwlock_unlock()** function results in the read-write lock becoming unlocked and there are threads waiting to acquire the read-write lock for writing, the scheduling policy is used to determine which thread shall acquire the read-write lock for writing. If there are threads waiting to acquire the read-write lock for reading, the scheduling policy is used to determine the order in which the waiting threads shall acquire the read-write lock object for reading. If there are multiple threads blocked on *rwlock* for both read locks and write locks, it is unspecified whether the readers will acquire the lock first or whether a writer will acquire the lock first.

Results are undefined if this function is called with an uninitialized read-write lock.

RETURN VALUE

Upon successful completion, **pthread_rwlock_unlock()** returns zero.
Otherwise, an error number is returned to indicate the error (the **errno** variable is not set).

ERRORS

For each of the following conditions, if the condition is detected, the **pthread_rwlock_unlock()** function returns the corresponding error number:

[EINVAL]   The value specified by *rwlock* does not refer to an initialized read-write lock object.

[EPERM]   The current thread does not own the read-write lock.

AUTHOR

pthread_rwlock_unlock() was developed by X/Open.

SEE ALSO

pthread_rwlock_init(3T), pthread_rwlock_destroy(3T),
pthread_rwlock_rdlock(3T), pthread_rwlock_wrlock(3T),
pthread_rwlock_tryrdlock(3T), pthread_rwlock_trywrlock(3T).

NAME

pthread_rwlock_wrlock() – lock a read-write lock for writing.
pthread_rwlock_trywrlock() – attempt to lock a read-write lock for writing.

SYNOPSIS

#include <pthread.h>

int pthread_rwlock_wrlock(
        pthread_rwlock_t   *rwlock
);

int pthread_rwlock_trywrlock(
        pthread_rwlock_t   *rwlock
);

PARAMETERS

rwlock   Pointer to the read-write lock to be locked for writing.

DESCRIPTION

The **pthread_rwlock_wrlock()** function applies a write lock to the read-write lock object referenced by *rwlock* for writing. The calling thread acquires the write lock if no other thread (reader or writer) holds the read-write lock *rwlock*. Otherwise, the thread blocks (that it, does not return from the **pthread_rwlock_wrlock()** call) until it can acquire the lock. Results are undefined if the calling thread holds the read-write lock (whether a read or a write lock) at the time the call is made.

The function **pthread_rwlock_trywrlock()** applies a write lock as in the **pthread_rwlock_wrlock()** function with the exception that the function fails if any thread currently holds *rwlock* (for reading or writing).

Results are undefined if any of these functions are called with an uninitialized read-write lock.

If a signal is delivered to a thread waiting for a read-write lock, upon return from the signal handler, the thread shall resume waiting for the read-write lock as if it was not interrupted.

RETURN VALUE

Upon successful completion, **pthread_rwlock_wrlock()** and **pthread_rwlock_trywrlock()** return zero. Otherwise, an error number is returned to indicate the error (the **errno** variable is not set).

ERRORS

If any of the following occur, the **pthread_rwlock_trywrlock()** function returns the corresponding error number:

[EBUSY]   The read-write lock *rwlock* could not be acquired for writing because it was already locked for reading or writing.

For each of the following conditions, if the condition is detected, the **pthread_rwlock_wrlock()** and **pthread_rwlock_trywrlock()** functions return the corresponding error number:

[EINVAL]   The value specified by *rwlock* does not refer to an initialized read-write lock.

[EDEADLK]   The current thread already owns the read-write lock for reading or writing.

AUTHOR

pthread_rwlock_wrlock() and **pthread_rwlock_trywrlock**() were
developed by X/Open.

SEE ALSO

pthread_rwlock_init(3T), pthread_rwlock_destroy(3T),
pthread_rwlock_tryrdlock(3T), pthread_rwlock_rdlock(3T),
pthread_rwlock_unlock(3T).

STANDARDS CONFORMANCE

pthread_rwlock_wrlock():X/Open.
pthread_rwlock_trywrlock():X/Open.

NAME

pthread_rwlockattr_init() – initialize a read-write lock attributes object.
pthread_rwlockattr_destroy() – destroy a read-write lock attributes object.

SYNOPSIS

#include <pthread.h>

int pthread_rwlockattr_init(
      pthread_rwlockattr_t   ***attr**
);

int pthread_rwlockattr_destroy(
      pthread_rwlockattr_t   ***attr**
);

PARAMETERS

attr   Pointer to the read-write lock attributes object to be initialized or destroyed.

DESCRIPTION

pthread_rwlockattr_init() initializes the read-write lock attributes object *attr* with the default value for all attributes. The attributes object describes a read-write lock in detail and is passed to the read-write lock initialization function.

When a read-write lock attributes object is used to initialize a read-write lock, the values of the individual attributes determine the characteristics of the new read-write lock. Attributes objects act like additional parameters to object initialization.

After a read-write lock attributes object has been used to initialize one or more read-write lock, any function affecting the attributes object does not affect the previously initialized read-write locks.

The read-write lock attributes and their default values are:

process-shared   The default value is **PTHREAD_PROCESS_PRIVATE**.

If an initialized read-write lock attributes object is reinitialized, undefined behavior results.

pthread_rwlockattr_destroy() destroys the read-write lock attributes object *attr*. The destroyed read-write lock attributes object ceases to exist and its resources are reclaimed. Referencing the object after it has been destroyed results in undefined behavior. A destroyed read-write lock attributes object can be reinitialized using the function **pthread_rwlockattr_init()**.

Read-write locks which have been already initialized using this attributes object are not affected by the destruction of the read-write lock attributes object.

RETURN VALUE

Upon successful completion, **pthread_rwlockattr_init()** and **pthread_rwlockattr_destroy()** return zero. Otherwise, an error number is returned to indicate the error (the **errno** variable is not set).

ERRORS

For each of the following conditions, if the condition is detected, the **pthread_rwlockattr_init**() and **pthread_rwlockattr_destroy**() functions return the corresponding error number:

[ENOMEM]   There is insufficient memory available in which to initialize *attr*.

[EINVAL]   The value specified by *attr* is invalid.

AUTHOR

pthread_rwlockattr_init() and **pthread_rwlockattr_destroy**() were developed by X/Open.

SEE ALSO

pthread_create(3T), pthread_rwlockattr_getpshared(3T), pthread_rwlockattr_setpshared(3T), pthread_rwlock_init(3T).

STANDARDS CONFORMANCE

pthread_rwlockattr_init():X/Open.

pthread_rwlockattr_destroy():X/Open.

NAME

pthread_rwlockattr_getpshared() – get the process-shared attribute
pthread_rwlockattr_setpshared() – set the process-shared attribute

SYNOPSIS

#include <pthread.h>

int pthread_rwlockattr_setpshared(pthread_rwlockattr_t *attr,
**   int pshared);**

int pthread_rwlockattr_getpshared(pthread_rwlockattr_t *attr,
**   int *pshared);**

PARAMETERS

attr   Pointer to the read-write lock attributes object whose attributes are to be set/retrieved.

pshared   This parameter either specifies the new value of the *process-shared* attribute (set function) or points to the memory location where the *process-shared* attribute of *attr* is to be returned (get function).

DESCRIPTION

The attributes object *attr* must have previously been initialized with the function *pthread_rwlockattr_init()* before these functions are called.

Mutexes can be used only by threads within the process or shared by threads in multiple processes. The *process-shared* attribute in a read-write lock attributes object describes who may use the read-write lock. The legal values for the *process-shared* attribute are:

PTHREAD_PROCESS_SHARED
This option permits a read-write lock to be operated upon by any thread that has access to the memory where the read-write lock is allocated. The application is responsible for allocating the read-write lock in memory that multiple processes can access.

PTHREAD_PROCESS_PRIVATE
The read-write lock can only be operated upon by threads created within the same process as the thread that initialized the read-write lock. If threads of differing processes attempt to operate on such read-write lock, the behavior is undefined.

The default value of *process-shared* is **PTHREAD_PROCESS_PRIVATE**.

pthread_rwlockattr_setpshared() is used to set the *process-shared* attribute in the initialized attributes object *attr*. The new value of the *process-shared* attribute of *attr* is set to the value specified in the *pshared* parameter.

pthread_rwlockattr_getpshared() retrieves the value of the *process-shared* attribute from the read-write lock attributes object *attr*. The value of the *process-shared* attribute of *attr* is returned in the *pshared* parameter.

RETURN VALUE

Upon successful completion, **pthread_rwlockattr_getpshared()** and **pthread_rwlockattr_setpshared()** return zero. Otherwise, an error number is returned to indicate the error (the **errno** variable is not set).

ERRORS

If any of the following occur, the **pthread_rwlockattr_getpshared**() and **pthread_rwlockattr_setpshared**() functions return the corresponding error number:

[ENOSYS]   **_POSIX_THREAD_PROCESS_SHARED** is not defined and these functions are not supported.

For each of the following conditions, if the condition is detected, the **pthread_rwlockattr_getpshared**() and **pthread_rwlockattr_setpshared**() functions return the corresponding error number:

[EINVAL]   The value specified by *attr* is invalid.

[EINVAL]   The value specified by *pshared* is not a legal value.

[EINVAL]   The value *pshared* points to an illegal address.

WARNING

If a read-write lock is created with the *process-shared* attribute defined as **PTHREAD_PROCESS_SHARED**, the cooperating processes should have access to the memory in which the read-write lock is allocated.

AUTHOR

pthread_rwlockattr_setpshared() and **pthread_rwlockattr_getpshared**() were developed by X/Open.

SEE ALSO

pthread_create(3T), pthread_rwlockattr_init(3T), pthread_rwlock_init(3T).

STANDARDS CONFORMANCE

pthread_rwlockattr_setpshared():X/Open.

pthread_rwlockattr_getpshared():X/Open.

NAME

pthread_self() – obtain the thread ID for the calling thread.

SYNOPSIS

#include <pthread.h>

pthread_t pthread_self();

PARAMETERS

None.

DESCRIPTION

pthread_self() returns the thread ID of the calling thread. The thread ID returned is the same ID that is returned in the *thread* parameter to the creating thread at thread creation time. Thread IDs are guaranteed to be unique only within a process.

RETURN VALUE

pthread_self() always returns the thread ID of the current thread.

ERRORS

None.

AUTHOR

pthread_self() was derived from the IEEE POSIX P1003.1c standard.

SEE ALSO

pthread_create(3T), pthread_equal(3T), getpid().

STANDARDS CONFORMANCE

pthread_self():POSIX 1003.1c.

NAME

pthread_setcancelstate() – sets and retrieves the current thread's cancelability state.
pthread_setcanceltype() – sets and retrieves the current thread's cancelability type.

SYNOPSIS

#include <pthread.h>

int pthread_setcancelstate(
        int   state,
        int   *oldstate
);

int pthread_setcanceltype(
        int   type,
        int   *oldtype
);

PARAMETERS

state   Value to which the cancelability state of the calling thread is to be set.

oldstate   Pointer to the location where the old cancelability state of the calling thread will be returned.

type   Value to which the cancelability type of the calling thread is to be set.

oldtype   Pointer to the location where the old cancelability type of the calling thread will be returned.

DESCRIPTION

pthread_setcancelstate() atomically sets the calling thread's cancelability state to the value in *state* and returns the previous cancelability state in *oldstate*. The legal values for *state* are:

PTHREAD_CANCEL_DISABLE
Disable cancelability for the calling thread. Cancellation requests against the calling thread are held pending.

PTHREAD_CANCEL_ENABLE
Enable cancelability for the calling thread. Cancellation requests against the calling thread may be acted upon. When a pending cancellation request will be acted upon depends on the thread's cancelability type.

By default, a thread's cancelability state is set to **PTHREAD_CANCEL_ENABLE** when it is created.

pthread_setcanceltype() atomically sets the calling thread's cancelability type to the value in *type* and returns the previous cancelability type in *oldtype*. The legal values for *type* are:

PTHREAD_CANCEL_ASYNCHRONOUS
New or pending cancellation requests against the calling thread may be acted upon at any time (if cancellation is enabled for the calling thread).

PTHREAD_CANCEL_DEFERRED
Cancellation requests for the calling thread are held pending until a cancellation point is reached.

A thread's cancelability type is set to **PTHREAD_CANCEL_DEFERRED** when it is created.

If a thread's cancelability state is disabled, the setting of the thread's cancelability type has no immediate effect. All cancellation requests are held pending. However, once cancelability is enabled again, the new type will be in effect.

RETURN VALUE

Upon successful completion, **pthread_setcancelstate**() and **pthread_setcanceltype**() return zero. Otherwise, an error number is returned to indicate the error (the **errno** variable is not set).

ERRORS

For each of the following conditions, if the condition is detected, the **pthread_setcancelstate**() and **pthread_setcanceltype**() functions return the corresponding error number:

[EINVAL]   *state* contains an invalid value.

[EINVAL]   *type* contains an invalid value.

NOTES

Only functions that are async-cancel safe should be called from a thread that is asynchronously cancelable.

AUTHOR

pthread_setcancelstate() and **pthread_setcanceltype**() were derived from the IEEE POSIX P1003.1c standard.

SEE ALSO

pthread_exit(3T), pthread_join(3T), pthread_cancel(3T), pthread_cond_wait(3T), pthread_cond_timedwait(3T).

STANDARDS CONFORMANCE

pthread_setcancelstate():POSIX 1003.1c.
pthread_setcanceltype():POSIX 1003.1c.

NAME

pthread_sigmask() – examine/change the signal mask of the calling thread.

SYNOPSIS

#include <pthread.h>

int pthread_sigmask(
        int   **how,**
        const sigset_t   ***set,**
        sigset_t   ***oset**
);

PARAMETERS

how   This parameter defines how the signal mask of the calling thread will be changed.

set   Pointer to the set of signals which will be used to change the currently blocked signal set.

oset   Pointer to where the previous signal mask will be returned.

DESCRIPTION

pthread_sigmask() allows the calling thread to examine and/or change its signal mask.

Unless it is a null pointer, the argument *set* points to a set of signals that are to be used to change the currently blocked signal set.

The argument *how* indicates how the set is changed. The legal values are:

SIG_BLOCK
     The resulting set is the union of the current set and the signal set pointed to by *set*.

SIG_UNBLOCK
     The resulting set is the intersection of the current set and the complement of the signal set pointed to by *set*.

SIG_SETMASK
     The resulting set is the signal set pointed to by *set*.

If the argument *oset* is not a null pointer, the previous signal mask is returned in *oset*. If *set* is a null pointer, the value of the argument *how* is insignificant and the thread's signal mask is unchanged; thus, the call can be used to inquire about currently blocked signals.

If there any pending unblocked signals after the call to **pthread_sigmask()**, at least one of those signals is delivered before the call to **pthread_sigmask()** returns.

It is impossible to block the **SIGKILL** or **SIGSTOP** signal. This is enforced by the system without causing an error to be indicated.

The thread's signal mask is not changed if **pthread_sigmask()** fails for any reason.

RETURN VALUE

Upon successful completion, **pthread_sigmask()** returns zero. Otherwise, an error number is returned to indicate the error (the **errno** variable is not set).

ERRORS

If any of the following occur, the **pthread_sigmask**() function returns the corresponding error number:

[EINVAL]   *how* contains an invalid value.

[EFAULT]   *set* or *oset* points to an invalid address. The reliable detection of this error is implementation dependent.

AUTHOR

pthread_sigmask() was derived from the IEEE POSIX P1003.1c standard.

SEE ALSO

sigprocmask(2).

STANDARDS CONFORMANCE

pthread_sigmask():POSIX 1003.1c.

NAME

pthread_testcancel() – process any pending cancellation requests.

SYNOPSIS

#include <pthread.h>

void pthread_testcancel();

PARAMETERS

None.

DESCRIPTION

The **pthread_testcancel()** function checks for any pending cancellation requests against the calling thread. If a cancellation request is pending and the calling thread has its cancelability state enabled, the cancellation request will be acted upon. If the cancelability state of the calling thread is disabled, this function will have no effect.

RETURN VALUE

None, the **pthread_testcancel()** function does not return a value.

If the calling thread acts upon a cancellation request, this function will not return; the calling thread will be terminated.

ERRORS

None.

AUTHOR

pthread_testcancel() was derived from the IEEE POSIX P1003.1c standard.

SEE ALSO

pthread_exit(3T), pthread_join(3T), pthread_setcancelstate(3T), pthread_setcanceltype(3T), pthread_cleanup_push(3T), pthread_cleanup_pop(3T), pthread_cond_wait(3T), pthread_cond_timedwait(3T).

STANDARDS CONFORMANCE

pthread_testcancel():POSIX 1003.1c.

NAME

sched_get_priority_max() – obtain the max priority for a policy
sched_get_priority_min() – obtain the min priority for a policy
sched_yield() – yield the processor

SYNOPSIS

#include <sched.h>

int sched_get_priority_max(int   policy);

int sched_get_priority_min(int   policy);

int sched_yield();

DESCRIPTION

The **sched_get_priority_max()** function returns the maximum priority value for the scheduling policy specified by *policy*.

The **sched_get_priority_min()** function returns the minimum priority value for the scheduling policy specified by *policy*.

The value of *policy* must be one of the scheduling policy values defined in **<sched.h>**.

The **sched_yield()** function forces the running thread to relinquish the processor. When the calling thread is at the head of its priority list, it is allowed to execute again. Note: If the calling thread is using either the **SCHED_FIFO** or **SCHED_RR** scheduling policy, this function only causes the calling thread to yield to another thread of equal or higher priority.

RETURN VALUE

The **sched_yield()** function returns zero on success. It returns -1 on error with *errno* set to the corresponding error.

The **sched_get_priority_max()** and **sched_get_priority_min()** functions return the maximum and minimum priority values, respectively, on success. They return -1 on error with *errno* set to the corresponding error.

ERRORS

If the **sched_yield()** function fails, **errno** is set to one of the following values.

[ENOSYS]   The function is not supported.

If the **sched_get_priority_max()** or **sched_get_priority_min()** functions fail, **errno** is set to one of the following values.

[EINVAL]   The value of the *policy* parameter is not a valid scheduling policy.

[ENOSYS]   These functions are not supported.

AUTHOR

The **sched_get_priority_max()**, **sched_get_priority_min()**, and **sched_yield()** functions were derived from the IEEE POSIX P1003.1b and P1003.1c standards.

SEE ALSO

sched_getparam(2), sched_setparam(2), sched_getscheduler(2), sched_setscheduler(2).

NAME

sem_destroy – destroy an unnamed POSIX semaphore

SYNOPSIS

#include <semaphore.h>

int sem_destroy(sem_t *sem);

DESCRIPTION

sem_destroy() is used to destroy an unnamed semaphore. A successful call to **sem_destroy()** will invalidate the unnamed semaphore referred to by *sem*. The semaphore should have been created by a previous call to *sem_init()*. Destroying a semaphore on which threads are currently blocked results in undefined behavior. A destroyed semaphore can be reinitialized by calling *sem_init()*.

RETURN VALUE

If the semaphore was destroyed, **sem_destroy()** returns 0 to the caller.

If the semaphore could not be destroyed, the call returns -1 and sets **errno** to indicate the error.

ERRORS

If any of the following occur, the **sem_destroy()** function returns -1 and sets *errno* to the corresponding error:

[EINVAL]   *sem* is not a valid unnamed semaphore.

[ENOSYS]   This function is not supported.

For each of the following conditions, if the condition is detected, the **sem_destroy()** function returns -1 and sets *errno* to the corresponding error:

[EBUSY]   There are threads currently blocked on the semaphore.

[EBUSY]   There are outstanding locks held on the semaphore. Note: This is not required by POSIX but is checked on HP-UX.

AUTHOR

sem_destroy() was derived from the IEEE POSIX P1003.1b standard.

SEE ALSO

sem_init(2), sem_open(2), <semaphore.h>

STANDARDS CONFORMANCE

sem_destroy():POSIX.1b

NAME

sem_getvalue – get the value of a POSIX semaphore

SYNOPSIS

#include <semaphore.h>

int sem_getvalue(sem_t *sem,   int *sval);

DESCRIPTION

sem_getvalue() is used to read the value of a semaphore.   The value of the semaphore specified by *sem* is read, at some unspecified time during the call, and then stored into *sval*. If the semaphore value is <= 0, at that time, the semaphore is considered unavailable.   If the semaphore value is > 0, at that time, the semaphore is considered available.

If the value returned in *sval* is positive, it is equal to the number of locks available on the semaphore, at the time the semaphore value was read.   If the value returned in *sval* is negative, its absolute value is equal to the number of blocked threads waiting for the semaphore to become available, at the time the semaphore value was read.

Note: the value returned in *sval* may be out of date at any arbitrary point, possibly even before this call returns.

RETURN VALUE

A successful call to **sem_getvalue()** will return 0. Otherwise, the call to the function **sem_getvalue()** will return -1, with *errno* set to the appropriate value of the error condition.

ERRORS

If any of the following occur, the **sem_getvalue()** function returns -1 and sets *errno* to the corresponding error:

[EPERM]	The caller does not have the privileges necessary to read the semaphore. Note: This is not required by POSIX but is checked on HP-UX.
[EINVAL]	*sem* is not a valid semaphore.
[ENOSYS]	This function is not supported.

AUTHOR

sem_getvalue() was derived from the IEEE POSIX P1003.1b standard.

SEE ALSO

sem_post(2), sem_wait(2), sem_trywait(2), <semaphore.h>

STANDARDS CONFORMANCE

sem_getvalue():POSIX.1b

NAME

sem_init – initialize an unnamed POSIX semaphore

SYNOPSIS

#include <semaphore.h>

int sem_init(sem_t *sem,   int pshared,   unsigned int value);

DESCRIPTION

sem_init() is used to initialize an unnamed semaphore. A successful call to **sem_init**() will initialize the unnamed semaphore referred to by *sem,* The initial value of the semaphore is set to the non-negative value specified by *value.*

The argument *pshared* specifies whether the unnamed semaphore is sharable with other processes. If *pshared* is equal to 0, the unnamed semaphore is not shared with other processes (i.e., it is only used by threads within the calling process). If *pshared* is nonzero, the unnamed semaphore is sharable with any process that can access *sem.* If the calling process may attach to the shared sem_t structure, it is assumed it may operate on the semaphore.

Initializing an already initialized semaphore results in undefined behavior.

RETURN VALUE

If the semaphore was created and initialized, **sem_init**() returns 0 to the caller.

If the semaphore could not be created/initialized, the call returns -1 and sets **errno** to indicate the error.

ERRORS

If any of the following occur, the **sem_init**() function returns -1 and sets *errno* to the corresponding error:

[EPERM]	The caller does not have the privileges necessary to initialize *sem.*
[EBUSY]	There are threads currently blocked on the semaphore.
[EBUSY]	There are outstanding locks held on the semaphore.
[EINVAL]	*value* is greater than **SEM_VALUE_MAX**.
[ENOSPC]	There are insufficient resources to perform the operation or the upper limit on the number of semaphores, **SEM_NSEMS_MAX**, has been reached.
[ENOSYS]	This function is not supported.

AUTHOR

sem_init() was derived from the IEEE POSIX P1003.1b standard.

SEE ALSO

sem_destroy(2), sem_post(2), sem_trywait(2), sem_wait(2), <semaphore.h>

STANDARDS CONFORMANCE

sem_init():POSIX.1b

NAME

sem_post – unlock a POSIX semaphore

SYNOPSIS

#include <semaphore.h>

il. sem_post(sem_t *sem);

DESCRIPTION

sem_post() is used to post the semaphore referenced by *sem*. The **sem_post()** function will perform the semaphore unlock function on *sem*.

If the resulting value of the semaphore is > 0, no threads were blocked on the semaphore. This function will atomically increment the value of *sem* and return immediately.

If the resulting value of the semaphore is 0, the semaphore has blocked threads waiting for the semaphore to become available.

If the semaphore has waiters at the time its value is checked, the semaphore value is not changed. Instead, the calling thread will wake-up a thread waiting on *sem*, thus allowing that thread to return from its call to *sem_wait( )*. If the semaphore has waiters having realtime priorities, the highest priority, longest waiting thread is chosen. Otherwise, the thread that has waited the longest is chosen.

If the specified semaphore referred to by *sem* is a named semaphore, this semaphore must have been opened by the calling process with *sem_open( )*. The calling process must have both read and write permissions on the semaphore to perform this operation. The **sem_post()** routine may be called asynchronously, i.e. from a signal handler.

RETURN VALUE

A successful call to **sem_post()** will return 0 and the calling thread will have posted the semaphore. Otherwise, the call to **sem_post()** will return -1 with *errno* set to the appropriate value of the error condition.

ERRORS

If any of the following occur, the **sem_post()** function returns -1 and sets *errno* to the corresponding error:

[EINVAL]	*sem* is not a valid semaphore.
[ENOSYS]	This function is not supported.
[EPERM]	The caller does not have the privileges necessary to post the semaphore. Note: This is not required by POSIX but is checked on HP-UX.

AUTHOR

sem_post() was derived from the IEEE POSIX P1003.1b standard.

SEE ALSO

sem_wait(2), sem_trywait(2), <semaphore.h>

STANDARDS CONFORMANCE

sem_post():POSIX.1b

NAME

sem_wait, sem_trywait – lock a POSIX semaphore

SYNOPSIS

#include <semaphore.h>

int sem_wait(sem_t *sem);

int sem_trywait(sem_t *sem);

DESCRIPTION

sem_wait() is used to lock the semaphore *sem*. The calling thread will not return from its call to **sem_wait**() until one of the following events occur: it successfully obtains a lock on the semaphore, it is interrupted by a signal, or an error condition occurs.

sem_trywait() is used to lock a semaphore, if it is available. If the semaphore is available, it is locked by the calling thread and the function returns. If the semaphore is not available, **sem_trywait**() returns an error immediately (it does not cause the caller to block waiting for the semaphore).

To lock a semaphore, the value of *sem* is checked at some time during the call. If the semaphore is available at the time its value is checked (the value of the semaphore is > 0), the calling thread will atomically, with respect to the checking of the value, lock the semaphore and decrement the semaphore's value. The thread will now own a lock on the semaphore; the call returns successfully. If the semaphore is not available (the value of the semaphore is 0), **sem_wait**() will block until the semaphore can be locked while **sem_trywait**() will immediately return with an error.

Upon successful return, the semaphore will be locked and will stay locked until it is explicitly released by a call to *sem_post()*.

If *sem* is a named semaphore, this semaphore must have been opened by the calling process with *sem_open()*. The calling process must have both read and write permissions on the semaphore to perform these operations.

RETURN VALUE

A successful call to **sem_wait**() will return 0 and the calling thread will own a lock on the semaphore. Otherwise, the call to **sem_wait**() will return -1 with *errno* set to the appropriate value of the error condition.

A successful call to **sem_trywait**() will return 0, if the semaphore was available and the calling thread was able to lock the semaphore. Otherwise, the call to **sem_trywait**() will return -1 with *errno* set to the appropriate value of the error condition.

ERRORS

If any of the following occur, the **sem_wait**() and **sem_trywait**() functions return -1 and sets *errno* to the corresponding error:

[EINTR]	The function was interrupted by a signal.
[EAGAIN]	The semaphore was not available and hence could not be locked by **sem_trywait**(). [This error occurs only in **sem_trywait**()].
[EINVAL]	*sem* is not a valid semaphore.
[EPERM]	The caller does not have the privileges necessary to lock the semaphore. Note: This is not required by POSIX but is checked on HP-UX.
[ENOSYS]	These functions are not supported.

For each of the following conditions, if the condition is detected, the **sem_wait()** and **sem_trywait()** functions return -1 and set *errno* to the corresponding error:

[EDEADLCK]   The resulting semaphore lock operation would result in deadlock.

AUTHOR

sem_wait() and **sem_trywait()** were derived from the IEEE POSIX P1003.1b standard.

SEE ALSO

sem_post(2), <semaphore.h>

STANDARDS CONFORMANCE

sem_wait():POSIX.1b
sem_trywait():POSIX.1b

NAME

sigwait – synchronously accept a signal

SYNOPSIS

#include <signal.h>

int sigwait(const sigset_t *set,   int *sig);

int sigwaitinfo(const sigset_t *set,   siginfo_t *info);

int sigtimedwait(const sigset_t *set,   siginfo_t *info,   struct timespec *timeout);

DESCRIPTION

The **sigwait**() function atomically selects and clears a pending signal from *set* and returns the signal number in the location pointed to by *sig*. If none of the signals in *set* is pending at the time of the call, the calling thread will be suspended until one or more signals become pending or the thread is interrupted by an unblocked, caught signal. The signals in *set* should be blocked at the time of the call to **sigwait**(); otherwise, the behavior is undefined.

If there are multiple signals queued for the selected signal number, **sigwait**() will return with the first queued signal and the remainder will remain queued. If any of multiple pending signals in the range SIGRTMIN to SIGRTMAX is selected, the lowest numbered signal will be returned.

If more than one thread in a process is in **sigwait**() for the same signal, only one thread will return from **sigwait**() with the signal number; which thread returns is undefined.

sigwaitinfo() has the same behavior as **sigwait**() if the *info* parameter is **NULL.** When the *info* parameter is not **NULL, sigwaitinfo**() returns the selected signal number in the *info* parameter. The selected signal number is returned in the *si_signo* field of the *info* parameter and the cause of the signal is returned in the *si_code* field.

sigtimedwait() has the same behavior as **sigwaitinfo**() except that **sigtimedwait**() will only wait for the time interval specified by the *timeout* parameter. If the *timeout* parameter specifies a zero-valued time interval, then **sigtimedwait**() will return immediately with an error if no signals in *set* are pending at the time of the call. If the *timeout* parameter is **NULL,** undefined behavior will result.

RETURN VALUE

Upon successful completion, **sigwait**() returns the signal number selected in *sig* and returns with a value of zero. Otherwise, it returns an error number to indicate the error. The **errno** variable is NOT set if an error occurs.

Upon successful completion, **sigwaitinfo**() and **sigtimedwait**() will return the selected signal number. Otherwise a value of -1 is returned and *errno* is set to indicate the error.

ERRORS

If any of the following conditions occur, the sigwait family of routines will return the following error number:

[EAGAIN]   **sigtimedwait**() was called and no signal in the *set* parameter was delivered within the time interval specified by the *timeout* parameter.

[EINTR]   This function was interrupted by an unblocked, caught signal.

[ENOSYS]   These functions are not supported.

If any of the following conditions occur, and the condition is detected, the sigwait functions will fail and return the following error number:

[EINVAL]   *set* contains an invalid or unsupported signal number.

[EINVAL]   **sigtimedwait**() was called and the *timeout* parameter specified a *tv_nsec* value less than zero or greater than or equal to 1000 million.

[EFAULT]   At least one of the *set, sig, info,* or *timeout* parameters references an illegal address.

USAGE

For a given signal number, the sigwait family of routines should not be used concurrently with **sigaction(2)** or any other functions that change signal action. If they are used together, the results are undefined.

Threads Considerations

The sigwait family of routines enable a thread to synchronously wait for signals. This makes the sigwait routines ideal for handling signals in a multithreaded process. The suggested method for signal handling in a multithreaded process is to have all threads block the signals of interest and dedicate one thread to call a sigwait function to wait for the signals. When a signal causes a sigwait function to return, the code to handle the signal can be placed immediately after the return from the sigwait routine. After the signal is handled, a sigwait function can again be called to wait for another signal.

In order to ensure that the dedicated thread handles the signal, it is essential that all threads, including the thread issuing the sigwait call, block the signals of interest. Otherwise, the signal could be delivered to a thread other than the dedicated signal handling thread. This could result in the default action being carried out for the signal.

AUTHOR

sigwaitinfo() and **sigtimedwait**() were derived from the IEEE POSIX P1003.1b standard.

sigwait() was derived from the IEEE POSIX P1003.1c standard.

SEE ALSO

pause(2), sigaction(2), sigpending(2), sigsuspend(2), pthread_sigmask(3T), signal(5)

STANDARDS CONFORMANCE

sigwait():POSIX.1c
sigwaitinfo():POSIX.1b
sigtimedwait():POSIX.1b

Glossary

Application Programming Interface (API): An interface is the conduit that provides access to an entity or communication between entities. In the programming world, an interface describes how access (or communication) with a function should take place. Specifically, the number of parameters, their names and purpose describe how to access a function. An API is the facility that provides access to a function.

Async-Cancel Safe: A function that may be called by a thread with the cancelability state set to **PTHREAD_CANCEL_ENABLE** and the cancelability type set to **PTHREAD_CANCEL_ASYNCHRONOUS**. If a thread is canceled in one of these functions, no state is left in the function. These functions generally do not acquire resources to perform the function's task.

Async-Signal Safe: An async-signal safe function is a function that may be called by a signal handler. Only a restricted set of functions may safely be called by a signal handler. These functions are listed in section 3.3.1.3 of the POSIX.1c standard.

Asynchronous Signal: An asynchronous signal is a signal that has been generated due to an external event. Signals sent via `kill()` and signals generated due to timer expiration or asynchronous I/O completion are all examples of asynchronously generated signals. Asynchronous signals are delivered to the process. All signals can be generated asynchronously.

Atfork Handler: Application-provided and registered functions that are called before and after a `fork()` operation. These functions generally acquire all mutex locks before the `fork()` and release these mutex locks in both the parent and child processes after the `fork()`.

Atomic Operation: An operation or sequence of events that is guaranteed to complete as if it were one instruction.

Barrier: A synchronization primitive that causes a certain number of threads to wait or rendezvous at specified points in an application. Barriers are used when a application needs to ensure that all threads have completed some operation before proceeding onto the next task.

Bound Thread: A user thread that is directly bound to a kernel-scheduled entity. These threads contain a system scheduling scope and are scheduled directly by the kernel.

Cache Thrashing: Cache thrashing is a situation in which a thread executes on different processors, causing cached data to be moved to and from the different processor caches. Cache thrashing can cause severe performance degradation.

Cancellation Cleanup Handler: An application-provided and registered function that is called when a thread is canceled. These functions generally perform thread cleanup actions during thread cancellation. These handlers are similar to signal handlers.

Condition Variable: A condition variable is a synchronization primitive used to allow a thread to wait for an event. Condition variables are often used in producer-consumer problems where a producer must provide something to one or more consumers.

Context Switch: The act of removing the currently running thread from the processor and running another thread. A context switch saves the register state of the currently running thread and restores the register state of the thread chosen to execute next.

Critical Section: A section of code that must complete atomically and uninterrupted. A critical section of code is generally one in which some global resource (variables, data structures, linked lists, etc.) is modified. The operation being performed must complete atomically so that other threads do not see the critical section in an inconsistent state.

Deadlock: A deadlock occurs when one or more threads can no longer execute. For example, thread A holds lock 1 and is blocked on lock 2. Meanwhile, thread B holds lock 2 and is blocked on lock 1. Threads A and B are permanently deadlocked. Deadlocks can occur with any number of resource holding threads. An **interactive deadlock** involves two or more threads. A **recursive** (or **self**) **deadlock** involves only one thread.

Detached Thread: A thread whose resources are automatically released by the system when the thread terminates. A detached thread cannot be joined by another thread. Consequently, detached threads cannot return an exit status.

Joinable Thread: A thread whose termination can be waited for by another thread. Joinable threads can return an exit status to a joining thread. Joinable threads maintain some state after termination until they are joined by another thread.

Kernel Mode: A mode of operation where all operations are allowed. While a thread is executing a system call it is executing in kernel mode.

Kernel Space: The kernel program exists in this space. Kernel code is executed in this space at the highest privilege level. In general, there are two privilege levels: one for user code (user mode) and the other for kernel code (kernel mode).

Kernel Stack: When a thread makes a system call, it executes in kernel mode. While in kernel mode, it does not use the stack allocated for use by the application. Instead, a separate kernel stack is used while in the system call. Each kernel-scheduled entity, whether a process, kernel thread or lightweight process, contains a kernel stack. See **Stack** for a generic description of a stack.

Kernel Thread: Kernel threads are created by the thread functions in the threads library. Kernel threads are *kernel-scheduled entities* that are visible to the operating system kernel. A kernel thread typically supports one or more user threads. Kernel threads execute kernel code or system calls on behalf of user threads. Some systems may call the equivalent of a kernel thread a *lightweight process*. See **Thread** for a generic description of a thread.

Lightweight Process: A kernel-scheduled entity. Some systems may call the equivalent of a lightweight process a kernel thread. Each process contains one or more lightweight process. How many lightweight processes a process contains depends on whether and how the process is multithreaded. See **Thread** for a generic description of a thread.

Multiprocessor: A system with two or more processors (CPUs). Multiprocessors allow multithreaded applications to obtain true parallelism.

Multithreading: A programming model that allows an application to have multiple threads of execution. Multithreading allows an application to have concurrency and parallelism (on multiprocessor systems).

Mutex: A mutex is a mutual exclusion synchronization primitive. Mutexes provide threads with the ability to regulate or serialize access to process shared data and resources. When a thread locks a mutex, other threads trying to lock the mutex block until the owning thread unlocks the mutex.

POSIX: Portable Operating System Interface. POSIX defines a set of standards that multiple vendors conform to in order to provide for application portability. The Pthreads standard (POSIX 1003.1c) provides a set of portable multithreading APIs to application developers.

Priority Inversion: A situation where a low-priority thread has acquired a resource that is needed by a higher priority thread. As the resource cannot be acquired, the higher priority thread must wait for the resource. The end result is that a low-priority thread blocks a high-priority thread.

Process: A process can be thought of as a container for one or more threads of execution, an address space, and shared process resources. All processes have at least one thread. Each thread in the process executes within the process' address space. Examples of process-shared resources are open file descriptors, message queue descriptors, mutexes, and semaphores.

Process Control Block (PCB): This structure holds the register context of a process.

Process Structure: The operating system maintains a process structure for each process in the system. This structure represents the actual process internally in the system. A sample of process structure information includes the process ID, the process' set of open files, and the signal vector. The process structure and the values contained within it are part of the context of a process.

Program Counter (PC): The program counter is part of the register context of a process. It holds the address of the current instruction to be executed.

Race Condition: When the result of two or more threads performing an operation depends on unpredictable timing factors, this is a race condition.

Read-Write Lock: A read-write lock is a synchronization primitive. Read-write locks provide threads with the ability to regulate or serialize access to process-shared data and resources. Read-write locks allow multiple readers to concurrently acquire the read lock whereas only one writer at a time may acquire the write lock. These locks are useful for shared data that is mostly read and only rarely written.

Reentrant Function: A reentrant function is one that when called by multiple threads, behaves as if the function was called serially, one after another, by the different threads. These functions may execute in parallel.

Scheduling Allocation Domain: The set of processors on which a thread is scheduled. The size of this domain may dynamically change over time. Threads may also be moved from one domain to another.

Scheduling Contention Scope: The scheduling contention scope defines the group of threads that a thread competes with for access to resources. The contention scope is most often associated with access to a processor. However, this scope may also be used when threads compete for other resources. Threads with the system scope compete for access to resources with all other threads in the system. Threads with the process scope compete for access to resources with other process scope threads in the process.

Scheduling Policy: A scheduling policy is a set of rules used to determine how and when multiple threads are scheduled to execute. The scheduling policy also determines how long a thread is allowed to execute.

Scheduling Priority: A scheduling priority is a numeric priority value assigned to threads in certain scheduling policies. Threads with higher priorities are given preference when scheduling decisions are made.

Semaphore: A semaphore is similar to a mutex. A semaphore regulates access to one or more shared objects. A semaphore has a value associated with it. The value is generally set to the number of shared resources regulated by the semaphore. When a semaphore has a value of one, it is a binary semaphore. A mutex is essentially a binary semaphore. When a semaphore has a value greater than one, it is known as a *counting semaphore*. A counting semaphore can be locked by multiple threads simultaneously. Each time the semaphore is locked, the value is decremented by one. After the value reaches zero, new attempts to lock the semaphore cause the locking thread to block until the semaphore is unlocked by another thread.

Shared Object: A shared object is a tangible entity that exists in the address space of a process and is accessible by all threads within the process. In the context of multithreaded programming, "shared objects" are global variables, file descriptors, and other such objects that require access by threads to be synchronized.

Signal: A signal is a simplified IPC mechanism that allows a process or thread to be notified of an event. Signals can be generated synchronously and asynchronously.

Signal Mask: A signal mask determines which signals a thread accepts and which ones are blocked from delivery. If a synchronous signal is blocked from delivery, it is held pending until either the thread unblocks the signal or the thread terminates. If an asynchronous signal delivered to the process is blocked from delivery by a thread, the signal may be handled by a different thread in the process that does not have the signal blocked.

Signal Vector: A signal vector is a table contained in each process that describes the action that should be taken when a signal is delivered to a thread within the process. Each signal has one of three potential behaviors: ignore the signal, execute a signal-handling function, or perform the default action of the signal (usually process termination).

Single-Threaded means that there is only one *flow of control* (one thread) through the program code; only one instruction is executed at a time.

Spinlock: A synchronization primitive similar to a mutex. If the lock cannot be acquired, instead of blocking, the thread wishing to acquire the lock spins in a loop until the lock can be acquired. Spinlocks can be easily used improperly and can severely degrade performance if used on a single processor system.

Spurious Wakeup: A spurious wakeup occurs when a thread is incorrectly unblocked, even though the event it was waiting for has not occurred. A condition wait that is interrupted and returns because the blocked thread received a normal signal is an example of a spurious wakeup.

Stack: A stack is used by a thread to make function calls (and return from those calls), to pass arguments to a function call, and to create the space for local variables when in that function call. Bound threads have a user stack and a kernel stack. Unbound threads have only a user stack.

Synchronous Signal: A synchronous signal is a signal that has been generated due to some action of a specific thread. For example, when a thread does a divide by zero, causes a floating point exception, or executes an illegal instruction, a signal is generated synchronously. Synchronous signals are delivered to the thread that caused the signal to be sent.

Traditional Process: This is a single-threaded entity that can be scheduled to execute on a processor.

Thread: A thread is an independent flow of control within a process, composed of a context (which includes a register set and program counter) and a sequence of instructions to execute.

Thread Local Storage (TLS): Thread local storage is essentially thread-specific data requiring support from the compilers. With TLS, an application can allocate the actual data as thread-specific data rather than using thread-specific data keys. Additionally, TLS does not require the thread to make a function call to obtain thread-specific data. The thread can access the data directly.

Thread-Safe Function: A thread-safe function is one that may be safely called by multiple threads at the same time. If the function accesses shared data or resources, this access is regulated by a mutex or some other form of synchronization.

Thread-Specific Data (TSD): Thread-specific data is global data that is specific to a thread. All threads access the same data variable. However, each thread has its own thread-specific value associated with this variable. `errno` is an example of thread-specific data.

Thread Structure: The operating system maintains a thread structure for each thread in the system. This structure represents the actual thread internally in the system. A sample of thread structure information includes the thread ID, the scheduling policy and priority, and the signal mask. The thread structure and the values contained within it are part of the context of a thread.

User Mode: A mode of operation where a subset of operations are allowed. While a thread is executing an applications code, it is executing in user mode. When the thread makes a system call, it changes modes and executes in kernel mode until the system call completes.

User Space: The user code exists in this space. User code is executed in this space at the normal privilege level. In general, there are two privilege levels: one for user code (user mode) and the other for kernel code (kernel mode).

User Stack: When a thread is executing code in user space, it needs to use a stack to make function calls, pass parameters, and create local variables. While in user mode, a thread does not use the kernel stack. Instead, a separate user stack is allocated for use by each user thread. See **Stack** for a generic description of a stack.

User Thread: When `pthread_create()` is called, a user thread is created. Whether a kernel-scheduled entity (kernel thread or lightweight process) is also created depends on the user thread's scheduling contention scope. When a bound thread is created, both a user thread and a kernel-scheduled entity are created. When an unbound thread is created, generally only a user thread is created. See **Thread** for a generic description of a thread.

Bibliography

Throughout this book, several references have been referred to for additional reading. The complete references are in this appendix. Additionally, the references for several books that were used when writing this book are also listed.

Alfieri, Robert A.. *An Efficient Kernel-Based Implementation of POSIX Threads*. Proceedings Summer 1994 USENIX Conference, pp. 59-72, June 1994.

Anderson, T.E.; Lazowska, E.D.; Levy, H.M.. *The Performance Implications of Thread Management Alternatives for Shared Memory Multiprocessors*. IEEE Transactions on Computers, December 1989.

Anderson, T.E.. *The Performance of Spin Lock Alternatives for Shared Memory Multiprocessors*. IEEE Transactions on Parallel and Distributed Systems, January 1990.

Anderson, T.E.; Lazowska, E.D.; Bershad, B.N.; Levy, H.M.. *Scheduler Activations: Effective Kernel Support for the User-Level Management of Parallelism*. Thirteenth ACM Symposium on Operating Systems Principles, October 1991.

Bach, Maurice J.. *The Design of the Unix Operating System*. Prentice-Hall. 0-13-201799.

Barton-Davis, Paul; McNamee, Dylan; Vaswani, Raj; Lazowska, Edward D.. *AAdding Scheduler Activations to Mach 3.0*. Proceedings Mach III Symposium, USENIX Association, pp. 119-136, April 1993.

Boykin, J.; Kirschen, D.; Langerman, A.; LoVerso, S.. *Programming Under Mach*. Addison-Wesley Publishing Company, Inc. 0-201-52739-1.

Brinch Hansen, Per. *Studies in Computational Science: Parallel Programming Paradigms*. Prentice Hall. 0-13-439324-4.

Digital Equipment Corporation. *DECthreads*. Digital Equipment Corporation. Part Number AA-PJNEA-TK.

Devarakonda, Murthy; Mukherjee, Arup. *Issues in Implementation of Cache-Affinity Scheduling*. Proceedings Winter 1992 USENIX Conference, pp. 345-357, January 1992.

Ford, Bryan; Lepreau, Jay. *Evolving Mach 3.0 to a Migrating Thread Model*. Proceedings Winter 1994 USENIX Conference, pp. 97-114, January 1994.

Gallomeister, Bill O.. *POSIX.4: Programming for the Real World*. O'Reilly & Associates, Inc.. 1-56592-074-0.

Gharachorloo, K.; Gupta, A.; Hennessy, J.. *Performance Evaluation of Memory Consistency Models for Shared Memory Multiprocessors*. Proceedings of the Fourth International Conference on Architectural Support for Programming Languages and Operating Systems, ACM, April 1991.

Hauser, C.; Jacobi, C.; Theimer, H.M.; Welsh, B.; Weiser, M.. *Using threads in Interactive Systems: A Case Study*. Proceedings of the Fourteenth ACM Symposium on Operating System Principles, December 1993.

Herlihy, M.. *Wait-Free Synchronization*. ACM Transactions on Programming Languages and Systems, January 1991.

Hewlett-Packard Company. *Programming with Threads on HP-UX*. Hewlett-Packard Company. HP Part No. B2355-90060.

Institute of Electrical and Electronics Engineers. *Portable Operating System Interface (POSIX) - Part 1: Application Program Interface (API) [C Language] - Amendment 1: Realtime Extensions*. Institue of Electrical and Electronics Engineers. 1-55937-375-X.

Institute of Electrical and Electronics Engineers. *Portable Operating System Interface (POSIX) - Part 1: Application Program Interface (API) [C Language] - Amendment 2: Threads Extensions*. Institue of Electrical and Electronics Engineers. 1-55937-573-6.

Jones, Michael B., *Bringing the C Libraries with us into a Multi-Threaded Future*. Proceedings Winter 1991 USENIX Conference, pp. 81-92, January 1991.

Kane, Gerry, *PA-RISC 2.0 Architecture*, Prentice Hall. 0-13-182734-0.

Karlin, A.R.; Li, K.; Manasse, M.S.; Owicki, S.. *Empirical Studies of Competitive Spinning for a Shared Memory Multiprocessor*. Proceedings of the Thirteenth ACM Symposium on Operating System Principles, October1991.

Kumar, V.; Grama, A.; Gupta, A.; Karypis, G.. *Introduction to Parallel Computing: Design and Analysis of Algorithms*. The Benjamin/Cummings Publishing Company, Inc.. 0-8053-3170-0.

McJones, P.; Swart, G.. *Evolving the UNIX System Interface to Support Multithreaded Programs*. Proceedings Winter 1989 USENIX Conference, January 1989.

Peacock, J. Kent. *File System Multithreading in System V Release 4 MP*. Proceedings Summer 1992 USENIX Conference, pp. 19-29, June 1992.

Saxena, Sunil; Peacock, J. Kent; Yang, Fred; Verma, Vijaya; Krishnan, Mohan. *Pitfalls in Multithreading SVR4 STREAMS and Other Weightless Processes*. Proceedings Winter 1993 USENIX Conference, pp. 85-96, January 1993.

Schmidtmann, Carl; Tao, Michael; Steven, Watt. *Design and Implementation of a Multi-Threaded Xlib*. Proceedings Winter 1993 USENIX Conference, pp. 193-203, January 1993.

Index

Symbols

`__thread` 213
`_exit()` 65, 182
`_POSIX_C_SOURCE` 37, 38
`_POSIX_SOURCE` 37, 38
`_POSIX_THREAD_ATTR_STACKADDR` 39, 47
`_POSIX_THREAD_ATTR_STACKSIZE` 40, 47
`_POSIX_THREAD_DESTRUCTOR_ITERATIONS` 44
`_POSIX_THREAD_KEYS_MAX` 44
`_POSIX_THREAD_PRIO_INHERIT` 40, 47, 161
`_POSIX_THREAD_PRIO_PROTECT` 40, 47, 161
`_POSIX_THREAD_PRIORITY_SCHEDULING` 40, 47
`_POSIX_THREAD_PROCESS_SHARED` 41, 47
`_POSIX_THREAD_SAFE_FUNCTIONS` 41, 47
`_POSIX_THREAD_THREADS_MAX` 44
`_POSIX_THREADS` 39, 47
`_POSIX_VERSION` 38
`_PTHREAD_CHOWN_RESTRICTED` 36
`_SC_THREAD_ATTR_STACKADDR` 47
`_SC_THREAD_ATTR_STACKSIZE` 47
`_SC_THREAD_DESTRUCTOR_ITERATIONS` 47
`_SC_THREAD_KEYS_MAX` 47
`_SC_THREAD_PRIO_INHERIT` 47
`_SC_THREAD_PRIO_PROTECT` 47
`_SC_THREAD_PRIORITY_SCHEDULING` 47
`_SC_THREAD_PROCESS_SHARED` 47
`_SC_THREAD_SAFE_FUNCTIONS` 47
`_SC_THREAD_STACK_MIN` 47
`_SC_THREAD_THREADS_MAX` 47
`_SC_THREADS` 47

Numerics

1x1 Model 26, 31, 140, 279
    advantages of 27
    disadvantages of 27
    parallel execution 27
    scheduling 26

A

`access()` 182
`acct()` 289
`acl()` 289
`aio_error()` 182
`aio_return()` 182
`aio_suspend()` 182, 193
`alarm()` 182, 283, 291, 329, 341, 355
Amdahl's Law 18
Application 2

LICENSE AGREEMENT AND LIMITED WARRANTY

READ THE FOLLOWING TERMS AND CONDITIONS CAREFULLY BEFORE OPENING THIS CD PACKAGE. THIS LEGAL DOCUMENT IS AN AGREEMENT BETWEEN YOU AND PRENTICE-HALL, INC. (THE "COMPANY"). BY OPENING THIS SEALED CD PACKAGE, YOU ARE AGREEING TO BE BOUND BY THESE TERMS AND CONDITIONS. IF YOU DO NOT AGREE WITH THESE TERMS AND CONDITIONS, DO NOT OPEN THE CD PACKAGE. PROMPTLY RETURN THE UNOPENED CD PACKAGE AND ALL ACCOMPANYING ITEMS TO THE PLACE YOU OBTAINED THEM FOR A FULL REFUND OF ANY SUMS YOU HAVE PAID.

1. **GRANT OF LICENSE:** In consideration of your purchase of this book, and your agreement to abide by the terms and conditions of this Agreement, the Company grants to you a nonexclusive right to use and display the copy of the enclosed software program (hereinafter the "SOFTWARE") on a single computer (i.e., with a single CPU) at a single location so long as you comply with the terms of this Agreement. The Company reserves all rights not expressly granted to you under this Agreement.

2. **OWNERSHIP OF SOFTWARE:** You own only the magnetic or physical media (the enclosed CD) on which the SOFTWARE is recorded or fixed, but the Company and the software developers retain all the rights, title, and ownership to the SOFTWARE recorded on the original CD copy(ies) and all subsequent copies of the SOFTWARE, regardless of the form or media on which the original or other copies may exist. This license is not a sale of the original SOFTWARE or any copy to you.

3. **COPY RESTRICTIONS:** This SOFTWARE and the accompanying printed materials and user manual (the "Documentation") are the subject of copyright. The individual programs on the CD are copyrighted by the authors of each program. Some of the programs on the CD include separate licensing agreements. If you intend to use one of these programs, you must read and follow its accompanying license agreement. If you intend to use the trial version of Internet Chameleon, you must read and agree to the terms of the notice regarding fees on the back cover of this book. You may not copy the Documentation or the SOFTWARE, except that you may make a single copy of the SOFTWARE for backup or archival purposes only. You may be held legally responsible for any copying or copyright infringement which is caused or encouraged by your failure to abide by the terms of this restriction.

4. **USE RESTRICTIONS:** You may not network the SOFTWARE or otherwise use it on more than one computer or computer terminal at the same time. You may physically transfer the SOFTWARE from one computer to another provided that the SOFTWARE is used on only one computer at a time. You may not distribute copies of the SOFTWARE or Documentation to others. You may not reverse engineer, disassemble, decompile, modify, adapt, translate, or create derivative works based on the SOFTWARE or the Documentation without the prior written consent of the Company.

5. **TRANSFER RESTRICTIONS:** The enclosed SOFTWARE is licensed only to you and may not be transferred to any one else without the prior written consent of the Company. Any unauthorized transfer of the SOFTWARE shall result in the immediate termination of this Agreement.

6. **TERMINATION:** This license is effective until terminated. This license will terminate automatically without notice from the Company and become null and void if you fail to comply with any provisions or limitations of this license. Upon termination, you shall destroy the Documentation and all copies of the SOFTWARE. All provisions of this Agreement as to warranties, limitation of liability, remedies or damages, and our ownership rights shall survive termination.

7. **MISCELLANEOUS:** This Agreement shall be construed in accordance with the laws of the United States of America and the State of New York and shall benefit the Company, its affiliates, and assignees.

8. **LIMITED WARRANTY AND DISCLAIMER OF WARRANTY:** The Company warrants that the SOFTWARE, when properly used in accordance with the Documentation, will operate

in substantial conformity with the description of the SOFTWARE set forth in the Documentation. The Company does not warrant that the SOFTWARE will meet your requirements or that the operation of the SOFTWARE will be uninterrupted or error-free. The Company warrants that the media on which the SOFTWARE is delivered shall be free from defects in materials and workmanship under normal use for a period of thirty (30) days from the date of your purchase. Your only remedy and the Company's only obligation under these limited warranties is, at the Company's option, return of the warranted item for a refund of any amounts paid by you or replacement of the item. Any replacement of SOFTWARE or media under the warranties shall not extend the original warranty period. The limited warranty set forth above shall not apply to any SOFTWARE which the Company determines in good faith has been subject to misuse, neglect, improper installation, repair, alteration, or damage by you. EXCEPT FOR THE EXPRESSED WARRANTIES SET FORTH ABOVE, THE COMPANY DISCLAIMS ALL WARRANTIES, EXPRESS OR IMPLIED, INCLUDING WITHOUT LIMITATION, THE IMPLIED WARRANTIES OF MERCHANTABILITY AND FITNESS FOR A PARTICULAR PURPOSE. EXCEPT FOR THE EXPRESS WARRANTY SET FORTH ABOVE, THE COMPANY DOES NOT WARRANT, GUARANTEE, OR MAKE ANY REPRESENTATION REGARDING THE USE OR THE RESULTS OF THE USE OF THE SOFTWARE IN TERMS OF ITS CORRECTNESS, ACCURACY, RELIABILITY, CURRENTNESS, OR OTHERWISE.

IN NO EVENT, SHALL THE COMPANY OR ITS EMPLOYEES, AGENTS, SUPPLIERS, OR CONTRACTORS BE LIABLE FOR ANY INCIDENTAL, INDIRECT, SPECIAL, OR CONSEQUENTIAL DAMAGES ARISING OUT OF OR IN CONNECTION WITH THE LICENSE GRANTED UNDER THIS AGREEMENT, OR FOR LOSS OF USE, LOSS OF DATA, LOSS OF INCOME OR PROFIT, OR OTHER LOSSES, SUSTAINED AS A RESULT OF INJURY TO ANY PERSON, OR LOSS OF OR DAMAGE TO PROPERTY, OR CLAIMS OF THIRD PARTIES, EVEN IF THE COMPANY OR AN AUTHORIZED REPRESENTATIVE OF THE COMPANY HAS BEEN ADVISED OF THE POSSIBILITY OF SUCH DAMAGES. IN NO EVENT SHALL LIABILITY OF THE COMPANY FOR DAMAGES WITH RESPECT TO THE SOFTWARE EXCEED THE AMOUNTS ACTUALLY PAID BY YOU, IF ANY, FOR THE SOFTWARE.

SOME JURISDICTIONS DO NOT ALLOW THE LIMITATION OF IMPLIED WARRANTIES OR LIABILITY FOR INCIDENTAL, INDIRECT, SPECIAL, OR CONSEQUENTIAL DAMAGES, SO THE ABOVE LIMITATIONS MAY NOT ALWAYS APPLY. THE WARRANTIES IN THIS AGREEMENT GIVE YOU SPECIFIC LEGAL RIGHTS AND YOU MAY ALSO HAVE OTHER RIGHTS WHICH VARY IN ACCORDANCE WITH LOCAL LAW.

ACKNOWLEDGMENT

YOU ACKNOWLEDGE THAT YOU HAVE READ THIS AGREEMENT, UNDERSTAND IT, AND AGREE TO BE BOUND BY ITS TERMS AND CONDITIONS. YOU ALSO AGREE THAT THIS AGREEMENT IS THE COMPLETE AND EXCLUSIVE STATEMENT OF THE AGREEMENT BETWEEN YOU AND THE COMPANY AND SUPERSEDES ALL PROPOSALS OR PRIOR AGREEMENTS, ORAL, OR WRITTEN, AND ANY OTHER COMMUNICATIONS BETWEEN YOU AND THE COMPANY OR ANY REPRESENTATIVE OF THE COMPANY RELATING TO THE SUBJECT MATTER OF THIS AGREEMENT.

Should you have any questions concerning this Agreement or if you wish to contact the Company for any reason, please contact in writing at the address below.

Robin Short
Prentice Hall PTR
One Lake Street
Upper Saddle River, New Jersey 07458